The Development of Oral and Written Language in Social Contexts

edited by

ANTHONY D. PELLEGRINI
University of Georgia
Athens, Georgia

and

THOMAS D. YAWKEY
Pennsylvania State University
University Park, Pennsylvania

VOLUME XIII in the Series

ADVANCES IN DISCOURSE PROCESSES

Roy O. Freedle, *editor*

Ⓐ ABLEX Publishing Corporation
Norwood, New Jersey 07648

Copyright © 1984 by Ablex Publishing Corporation

All rights reserved. No part of this book may be reproduced in any form, by photostat, microfilm, retrieval system, or by any other means, without the prior permission of the publisher.

Printed in the United States of America

Library of Congress Cataloging in Publication Data
Main entry under title:

The Development of oral and written language in social contexts.

(Advances in discourse processes ; v. 13)
Bibliography: p.
Includes index.
1. Language acquisition.   2. Sociolinguistics.
I. Pellegrini, Anthony D.   II. Yawkey, Thomas D.
III. Series.
P118.D45   1984   401'.9   84-369
ISBN 0-89391-171-2
ISBN 0-89391-172-0 (pbk.)

ABLEX Publishing Corporation
355 Chestnut Street
Norwood, New Jersey 07648

Dedication

To my parents, Ann and Antonio

— A. P.

Contents

Preface to the Series .... **x**
Preface to Volume XIII.................................. **xii**

PART I LANGUAGE DEVELOPMENT IN A SOCIAL CONTEXT

1 Mother–Infant Interaction: Features and Functions of Parental Speech in English and Spanish
Ben G. Blount 3

Introduction   3
Parental Speech: Some Early Studies   5
English and Spanish Parental Speech   6
Parental Speech: English and Spanish Comparisons   21
Parental Speech Functions   25
Summary and Conclusions   26
References   28

2 Maternal Input Adjustments and Non-Adjustments as Related to Children's Linguistic Advances and to Language Acquisition Theories
Keith E. Nelson, Marilyn M. Denninger, John D. Bonvillian, Barbara J. Kaplan, and Nancy Baker 31

A Clear Case of Maternal Non-Adjustment in MLU   32
Auxiliaries in Input: An Apparent Shift toward Greater Adjustment as Children Advance   32

A Broad-correlational Look at Cross-sectional Samplings: Noncontingent Maternal Syntax as Related to Child Syntax   33
Contingent Maternal Replies as Predicators of Children's Syntactic Growth   36
Discussion   45
Reference Notes   53
References   53

3 The Development of the Functions of Private Speech: A Review of the Piaget–Vygotsky Debate
Anthony D. Pellegrini 57

Abstract   57
Introduction   57
The Social Origins of Private Speech   58
The Cognitive Functions of Private Speech   60
Soviet Views of Language and Thought   60
Empirical Studies on the Cognitive Function of Private Speech   63
References   68

4 Parents as Teachers of their Children: A Distancing Behavior Model
Irving E. Sigel and Ann V. McGillicuddy-Delisi 71

Introduction   71
The Occurrence of Parental Distancing Behaviors   79
Relationship of Parent Distancing Verbalizations and Child Ability Levels   81
Conclusions   87
References   90

PART II   THE CONTEXT OF SOCIAL PLAY

5 The Language of Social Play in Young Children
Thomas D. Yawkey and Thomas J. Miller 95

Introduction   95
Social Play as Context   97
Language Functions   99
Language Adaptations to Environmental Demands   100
Conclusions   101
Reference Notes   102
References   103

6 Narrative Competence: Play, Storytelling, and Story Comprehension
Lee Galda **105**

Dramatic Play and the Development of Narrative Competence 105
The Development of Narrative Competence Through Dramatic
    Play 111
Reference Notes 115
References 115

7 Planning in Pretend Play: Using Language to Coordinate Narrative Development
Jacqueline Sachs, Jane Goldman, and Christine Chaille **119**

Introduction 119
Method 120
Results 120
General Conclusions 125
Reference Notes 127
References 127

8 The Effects of Classroom Ecology on Preschoolers' Functional Uses of Language
Anthony D. Pellegrini **129**

Introduction 129
Method 131
Results 133
Discussion 136
Reference Note 140
References 140

PART III THE CONTEXT OF SCHOOL

9 Classroom Status From a Sociolinguistic Perspective
Louise Cherry Wilkinson **145**

Introduction 145
Assumptions 145
Status From a Sociolinguist View 146
Previous Research 148
Future Research 150
References 152

10 Learning to Communicate in the Classroom
Johanna S. DeStefano 155

Language in School   155
School Language and the Culturally Different   156
Language in Literacy Learning   158
Conclusions   162
Reference Notes   165
References   165

11 Oral Language Competence and the Acquisition of Literacy
Nancy Torrance and David R. Olson 167

Introduction   167
Method   168
Analyses   169
Results   170
References   181

12 Learning Through Writing: A Rationale for Writing Across the Curriculum
Richard Beach and Lilian Bridwell 183

Introduction   183
A Range of Writing Tasks   187
Learning to Consider Context Conventions and Audience   191
Learning to Evaluate Information Critically Through Writing   193
Writing to Learn About Oneself   194
General Implications   195
Reference Notes   196
References   197

PART IV   SOCIAL CONTEXT AND WRITTEN LANGUAGE

13 The Development of Writing Abilities During the School Years
James L. Collins 201

Introduction   201
Cognitive Development and Writing   202
Literacy and Writing   203
Contexts of Writing   204
Reference Notes   208
References   208

14 The Influence of Communicative Context on Stylistic Variations in Writing
Donald L. Rubin 213

Introduction   213
Rhetorical Conception of Style   214
Constituents of Communicative Situations   215
Conclusion   226
Reference Notes   227
References   228

15 Children's Written Dialogues: Intermediary Between Conversation and Written Text?
Suzanne Hidi and Roslyn Klaiman 233

Method   236
Results   237
Discussion   240
Reference Notes   241
References   241

16 The Interaction Between Text and Context: A Study of How Adults and Children Use Spoken and Written Language in Four Contexts
Jane M. Danielewicz 243

The Communication Continuum   243
The Data   244
Data Analysis   245
Unplanned Spoken Discourse   246
Planned Written Language   250
Planned Spoken Language   252
Unplanned Written Discourse   254
Children's Spoken and Written Language   255
Conclusions   258
References   259

Author Index 261

Subject Index 269

Preface to the Series

Roy O. Freedle
Series Editor

This series of volumes provides a forum for the cross-fertilization of ideas from a diverse number of disciplines, all of which share a common interest in discourse—be it prose comprehension and recall, dialogue analysis, text grammar construction, computer simulation of natural language, cross-cultural comparisons of communicative competence, or other related topics. The problems posed by multisentence contexts and the methods required to investigate them, while not always unique to discourse, are still sufficiently distinct as to benefit from the organized mode of scientific interaction made possible by this series.

Scholars working in the discourse area from the perspective of sociolinguistics, psycholinguistics, ethnomethodology and the sociology of language, educational psychology (e.g., teacher-student interaction), the philosophy of language, computational linguistics, and related subareas are invited to submit manuscripts of monograph or book length to the series editor. Edited collections of original papers resulting from conferences will also be considered.

Volumes in the Series

Vol. I. Discourse Production and Comprehension. Roy O. Freedle (Ed.), 1977.
Vol. II. New Directions in Discourse Processing. Roy O. Freedle (Ed.), 1979.
Vol. III. The Pear Stories: Cognitive, Cultural, and Linguistic Aspects of Narrative Production. Wallace L. Chafe (ed.), 1980.
Vol. IV. Text, Discourse, and Process: Toward a Multidisciplinary Science of Tests. Robert de Beaugrande, 1980.
Vol. V. Ethnography and Language in Educational Settings. Judith Green & Cynthia Wallat (Eds.), 1981.

Vol. VI. Latino Language and Communicative Behavior, Richard P. Duran (Ed.), 1981.
Vol. VII. Narrative, Literary and Face in Interethnic Communication, Ron Scollon & Suzanne Scollon, 1981.
Vol. VIII. Linguistics and the Professions. Robert J. DiPietro (Ed.), 1982.
Vol. IX. Spoken and Written Language: Exploring Orality and Literacy, Deborah Tannen (Ed.), 1982.
Vol. X. Developmental Issues in Discourse. Jonathan Fine & Roy O. Freedle (Eds.), 1983.
Vol. XI. Text Production: Toward a Science of Composition. Robert de Beaugrande, 1984.
Vol. XII. Coherence in Spoken and Written Discourse. Deborah Tannen (Ed.), 1984.
Vol. XIII. The Development of Oral and Written Language in Social Contexts. Anthony D. Pellegrini & Thomas D. Yawkey (Eds.), 1984.

Preface to Volume XIII

Anthony D. Pellegrini

The common thread running through the papers in this volume is the interrelations between language and the social context in which it is generated. Though the authors approach the topic of the development of oral and written language from different vantage points (e.g., anthropology, developmental and applied psychology, and education), they all view language and social context as interdependent.

This theoretical orientation of viewing language and context as interdependent might be traced to the work of English (e.g., Firth, 1957; Halliday, 1967; Malinowski, 1960) Czech (e.g., Vachek, 1961), and American (e.g., Chafe, 1970; Hymes, 1967) scholars who believe that language develops out of social context and language users' conveyance of meaning is a social interaction phenomenon. Researchers with this orientation are concerned with how language functions in social contexts and how various functions and contexts, in turn, affect the structure of utterances. Halliday's work on register has formalized the relations between context and text structure. He outlines how specific contextual variables (e.g., subject matter of the discourse; situation type; participants' roles within the discourse; mode of discourse; and medium) map onto texts. For example, discourse on a technical subject, between a teacher and students, should be characterized by text that lexicalizes meaning rather than text that relies on shared assumptions to convey meaning.

Relations between various social contexts and children's development of oral and written language will be discussed in this volume. In the first section, Language Development in a Social Context, the papers suggest that a child's language develops in the context of dialogue with a more mature language user. Blount contrasts the language addressed to infants by Anglo and Hispanic parents. Nelson and his colleagues identify specifically those aspects of mother-child verbal interaction that predict children's oral language development. Pellegrini reivews the literature in Soviet and Western psychology suggesting that children's ability to regulate their own behavior originates in the dialogues between adults and young children. Sigel discusses a project that is examining the ways in which parents talk to and ask questions of children and how specific styles of parental language relate to children's performance on a number of cognitive measures.

The reports in Section II, The Context of Social Play, describe ways in which children use oral language while they are interacting with peers and adults in play contexts. Yawkey and Miller discuss social play in terms of the types of language elicited in spontaneous peer play and adult-directed play. The Galda review paper makes the point that children's narrative competence (i.e., the ability to use narrative structures and conventions) is related to, and probably develops in, fantasy play contexts. Sachs, Goldman, and Chaillé extend Galda's chapter by describing ways in which preschoolers use narrative-like language (i.e., language to plan, frame, and negotiate) during fantasy role episodes. Pellegrini's observational study describes how preschoolers develop the ability to use different functions of oral language within preschool classrooms.

The third section of the volume addresses ways in which teachers and students use, and can use, oral and written language in classrooms. Wilkinson's paper provides a valuable overview of the basic assumptions of a sociolinguistic approach to examining classroom interaction and how children use oral language to convey social status in the classroom. The DeStefano chapter examines further the relations between students' status and the ways in which they interact with their teacher in the context of a reading group. Torrance and Olson document those specific aspects of children's conversational skills that predict early reading achievement. The last chapter in this section, by Beach and Bridwell, reviews the literature that suggests ways in which students and teachers can use writing across school curricula.

The final section of the volume contains papers which examine the relations between social contexts and written language. Collins' review paper makes the case that school-age children's writing abilities are affected by an interaction between their cognitive processes and the cultural contexts in which writing is used. Rubin's chapter outlines how specific aspects of context (i.e., pragmatic meaning) are encoded into written text. The Hidi and Klaiman paper presents data suggesting that children's ability to write dialogues may be a precursor to the ability to write more advanced texts. The Danielewicz paper contrasts the ways adults and children use spoken and written language in different contexts.

The papers in this volume document the interaction among context, language functions and structure. These papers add to the extant descriptive literature on children's language development. In addition, this information has pedagogical value: educators and applied psychologists can use it to structure situations that facilitate the development of oral and written language.

REFERENCES

CHAFE, W. *Meaning and the structure of language*. Chicago: University of Chicago Press, 1970.
FIRTH, J. *Papers in linguistics*. London: Oxford University Press, 1957.
HALLIDAY, M. Notes on transitivity and theme in English, Part 2. *Journal of Linguistics,* 1967, *3,* 199–274.
HYMES, D. Models of interaction of language and social setting. *Journal of Social Issues,* 1967, *23,* 8–28.
MALINOWSKI, B. The problem of meaning in primative languages. In C. Odgen & I. Richards (Eds.) *The meaning of meaning*. London: Routledge & Kegan Paul, 1960.
VACHEK, J. (Ed.). *A Prague school reader in linguistics*. Bloomington: Indiana University Press, 1961.

LANGUAGE DEVELOPMENT IN A SOCIAL CONTEXT

1 Mother-Infant Interaction: Features and Functions of Parental Speech in English and Spanish*

Ben G. Blount
University of Georgia

INTRODUCTION

The past decade has witnessed the development of a relatively new area of inquiry in the social sciences, the study of mother-infant interaction. Related to antecedent issues in child development such as attachment, bonding, cognitive growth, and language acquisition, widespread interest in mother-infant interaction emerged in the 1970s. The growth was due in large part to the recognition that social interaction could not be viewed simply as a mechanism that produced a particular cognitive or emotional state or condition. Social interaction itself was defined as problematic and worthy of study in its own terms. Interaction came to be recognized as a complex set of behaviors requiring a developed research focus and methodology. Indeed, studies during the past decade have revealed that interaction is an interesting and complex social process and that it is an essential part of the socialization of children. Children's acquisition of interactional skills is a fundamental aspect of their development, and early mother-infant interactions serves as a basis for acquisition of language (see Bullowa, 1979; Lewis & Rosenblum, 1977; Schaffer, 1977).

At a general level, mother-infant interaction studies during the past decade

---

*Research on this project was made possible by an Office of Education Grant, OEG–72–3945 and by an institutional National Science Foundation Grant, GU–1598. Due to budgetary constraints, the data collection and reduction had to be accomplished within a specified and limited period. The project included several co-workers, whose contributions and patience were necessary for the success of the project. The individuals were Willett Kempton, Andrea Meditch, Marylou White, and Dorothy Wills.

can be characterized by three features. The first of these is the interest in process. Interaction is a dyadic, temporally organized activity that is patterned by the mutual contributions of the interactants (Kaye & Fogel, 1980; Stern, 1977; Trevarthen, 1979). Virtually any facet of the patterned activity can be subject to interesting research questions, e.g., play (Bruner, 1975; Garvey, 1977), joint visual attention (Butterworth & Cochran, 1980; Stern, 1974), interactive synchrony (Chappell & Sander, 1979; Farran, Hirschbiel & Jay, 1980), cognitive development (Bakeman & Brown, 1980; Lewis & Coates, 1980), and maternal speech (Blount, 1977; Kaye, 1980; Wills, 1977), to name only a few topics.

The fact that mother-infant activity is coordinated leads to a second general feature of recent studies. Infants are not merely passive respondents to maternal initiatives. They contribute in a variety of ways to the ongoing flow of interactions and help to define, sometimes extensively, the patterning of interaction (Gustafson, Green, & West, 1979; Lewis & Rosenblum, 1974; Newsome, 1979). A growing body of evidence also indicates that infants are preadapted in various ways for social interaction and that their social participation is a natural phenomenon (Brazelton 1982; Eilers, 1980; Freedle & Lewis, 1977; Sander, 1977).

The third general feature of mother-infant interaction studies is a concern with methodology. The complexity of the subject matter necessitates this concern. Social interaction is a subtle process, difficult to record, characterize, segment, and analyze. The process of interaction is constituted by a complex stream of behaviors, multifaceted in their interrelationships, and often fleeting in duration. A microlevel approach is thus essential for the description and analysis of the interactive process. Minute details of gesture, gaze, body position, and vocalization must be recorded: otherwise the intricacies of interaction would remain opaque (Collis, 1979; Stern, Beebe, Jaffe, & Bennett, 1977). A research priority has been the development of adequate descriptive and analytic techniques.

A practical problem of research methodology in mother-infant interaction is how to record the behavior. Systematic observations of the stream of interactive behavior are extremely difficult—at times virtually impossible—without an effective way of recording the behavior for repeated observations. Single, "one-time" observations may prove useful in a preliminary or anecdotal way, but they usually cannot capture the complexities of the interactive process. Recordings, audio-visual or audio, that allow multiple, repeated observations are essential for reliable, sound data reduction. Even with recordings, technical and methodological problems remain, such as the angle of camera for filming gaze behavior and, all important, the possible effect of the recording equipment on the behavior of the interactants. The methodological issues are far from resolved, and the only current solution is to identify and acknowledge in specific studies the constraints and limitations that are posed by the recording techniques employed.

The three general features of mother-infant interaction—the patterned dyadic and temporal organization of the interactive process, the social preadaptiveness and the interactive contributions of infants, and the microlevel descriptive and analytic research techniques—all are discussed in the following sections of the paper. They are viewed in the context first of early studies in parental speech and then of a project on parental speech in English and Spanish. The speech characteristics of parents constitute one important facet in the genesis of interaction, and they contribute to the development of infants' interactive skills in specific ways.

PARENTAL SPEECH: SOME EARLY STUDIES

Prior to the 1970s, information on the characteristics of mother-infant vocal interaction was limited. A number of earlier studies had identified characteristics of baby talk (i.e., parental speech) in a few societies, e.g., Comanche (Casagrande, 1948) and Hidatsa (Voegelin & Robinett, 1954). In the early, pre-1970 studies, baby talk was viewed exclusively in terms of the code form, essentially as modification of adult linguistic forms or substitution of special "baby" forms for adult ones. Examples would be *doggie* for *dog* and *choo-choo* for *train*.

An article by Ferguson in 1964, "Baby talk in six languages," summarized much of what was known about characteristics of baby talk as a special code. Ferguson identified several recurrent characteristics. Canonical structure tends to be CVC and CVCV, with basic consonants (stops and nasals) and common vowels; phonological reduplication is common; inflectional affixes are generally absent, except for a special baby talk affix; and the lexical domains (semantic fields) are mostly kin terms, body parts, and animals. Ferguson's descriptive catalogue was of linguistic form and restricted to the segmental code—phonological, grammatical, and lexical units. Suprasegmentals were not investigated, although as will be seen below, they are fundamental parts of the code and of interaction. Interactional questions were addressed, but only in a limited sense. Ferguson suggested that baby talk might be functional in assisting children with language acquisition, although he noted other uses and functions, such as evoking aspects of a nurturant relationship.

Although Ferguson's interest was not in the process of interaction, his work contributed to early interactional studies. Two logical steps could be taken to continue the work: (a) the identification of further characteristics of the code; and (b) descriptions of usage patterns through examination of interaction. An effort in each of these directions was made by the author in an early study of mother-infant interaction among the Luo of Kenya. The results of the study have been published elsewhere (Blount, 1972) and need be only briefly summarized here. The study had two major conclusions. The most distinctive characteristics of maternal speech were suprasegmentals, not segmentals, and the distribution of the features in maternal speech differed according to the ages of the children in the range 6–14 months. The distribution of features was correlated, loosely, with the infant's growing awareness of the social environment and with the ability to respond vocally to maternal input speech. The speech appeared to be adaptive, socializing, and thus important developmentally. The central importance of the speech features seemed to be in their contribution to the development of social interaction.

In an effort to further pursue the identification of features of maternal speech to infants, to search for cross-linguistic differences, and, secondarily, to examine the association of the input speech with emerging social interactional development in infants, a parental speech project was begun in 1972 on English and on Spanish. The study was conducted in Austin, Texas.

ENGLISH AND SPANISH PARENTAL SPEECH

Methodological Background

The project was designed to be exploratory and preliminary and to focus primarily on the code. The sample size, age range of the children, and the data collection, reduction, and analytic techniques were all defined to be consistent with the preliminary, feature-discovery orientation of the project. The original aim was to collect tape-recorded verbal interactions of parents and infants from a small sample size spread over a child age range of approximately 9 to 24 months. Given the constraints of time and personnel on the project and the considerable research-hours necessary to analyze taped interaction, sample size was sacrificed for age span and Spanish-English comparison. The idea was to select four families for each language, and for the children's ages, collectively, to span 15 months of development-age. The span, 9 to 24 months, would cover the period of prelexical development, the onset of the one-word stage, and the transition into the grammatical, or two-word stage, of development.

A sample of four English-speaking and four Spanish-speaking families was selected, more or less consistent with the above guidelines. Data collection was begun on a periodic, weekly basis and continued for approximately 2½ months. The children in the English-speaking sample had a collective age span from 9;2 (9 months; 0 weeks) to 18;2, and the children in the Spanish sample had collective age spans from 8;1 to 13;1 and from 18;1 to 22;2. The ages of the individual children are given in Table 1. Each child was the only child in the family, except for Luis, who had a sibling a few weeks old.

The father of each family was an advanced undergraduate or graduate student at the University of Texas. Their age range was approximately 21 to 32 years. The mothers of three children—Miranda, Rebecca, and Analisa—were also students; the others were housewives. Their age range was approximately 20 to 25 years. Each of the English-speaking individuals was either native to Texas

TABLE 1
Child Sample Population

	Gender	Age Range	No. of Sessions
English			
Miranda	F	9;0–13;0	13
Jeanne-Marie	F	11;0–13;1	10
Rebecca	F	14;0–16;1	11
Adam	M	15;0–18;2	13
Spanish			
Valente	M	8;1–10;4	14
Analisa	F	10;4–13;1	9
Christian	M	18;1–20;1	11
Luis	M	20;0–22;2	12

or a long-term resident of that state. The Spanish-speaking sample was not so homogeneous. One couple was native to Texas, one couple was from Mexico City, one couple was from Chile, and in the remaining family the father was from Peru and the mother was from Argentina. Although a standardized sample of parents would have been preferred, it was not viewed as necessary, given the preliminary, exploratory nature of the project.

The central objective in the collection of parental and child speech samples was to obtain samples of natural vocal interaction. The goal was to tape-record vocal interactions as they would occur normally and naturally in the course of everyday affairs in the household. The parents were asked in a preliminary, explanatory session to record the vocalizations of the children at times and circumstances in which they would regularly interact with them. The parents were told that the goal of the recording was to obtain samples of the children's speech, as the children participated in social interactions with the parents. The investigators emphasized the point that they did not want special, staged productions. Each of the families indicated that they had times during the day when they regularly interacted vocally with the children; i.e., the focus and purpose of the interaction was vocal exchange, not feeding, bathing, etc.

In the preliminary session, each family was taught to record with a Uher 1000–Report–L portable tape recorder. The recording arrangement was to deliver a recorder to the family on a weekly basis, approximately, for a period of 24 or 48 hours and ask the family to tape at least 20–30 minutes of vocal interaction during that period. Each family indicated that they had no difficulty in making the recordings (except in a few instances where a child was sick), and they each expressed in a follow-up interview that naturalness of interaction was not a problem at all.

The decision to tape-record without an observer present undoubtedly facilitated naturalness of interaction. Prior experience had shown that whereas after a few visits young children would lose their reticence to vocalize in the presence of an observer, they would still not interact in a completely natural way with their parents. Parents, also bound by the social constraints of the presence of an observer in the home, would modify their behavior so as to include the observer in interaction. Although a long period of exposure to the presence of an observer might have overcome those difficulties, the decision was made to record without an observer present and thereby to eliminate the bias that such a presence would create.

The decision to tape-record in the absence of an observer represented a considerable loss of contextual information. The most obvious and serious loss was of all indices of interactional data except for vocalizations. Although it was usually possible to discern from the content of the interaction the nature of the activity (e.g., playing with an object, looking at a picture-book, etc.), important interactional information was nevertheless lost. The role of vision and touch in the structuring of interaction was impossible to discern, posing stringent limitations on the interpretation of the vocal data. The loss of contextual information hampered some analyses, although, again, the trade-off was tapes of natural interaction.

Methodological Issues

The tapes were all transcribed, the parents' speech in standard orthography and the children's utterances phonetically. The transcriptions raised immediately a number of practical and theoretical issues. A standardized format for transcribing interactional information, vocal or otherwise, has yet to be developed. In practice, each investigator tends to develop an ad hoc transcription system, motivated, at best, by the goals of the study. As a consequence, the units of transcription, and thus of analysis, may not be equivalent across different studies. To compound the problem, units that are comparable are often given different terms by different investigators, and the use of the same term across studies may refer to quite different phenomena.

A complete review of the transcription-terminology problem is clearly beyond the bounds of the present paper, but a brief discussion will serve to provide examples of the difficulties that all investigations of mother-infant interaction face and to provide a background for the "solutions" employed in the Spanish-English project. Given the fact that conversations and nonverbal interactions are minimally dyadic in structure and involve exchange of information, a central, salient characteristic of the interactions is turn-taking (Ervin-Tripp, 1979). Speakers alternate in more or less regular fashion taking turns at speaking. A technical definition of turn, then, would seem advisable, and in most studies of social interaction investigators provide one. They tend, however, not to provide the same one. In fact, a surprisingly large number of definitions have been provided (see Edelsky, 1981, for a good summary). A turn may be merely the talk that a speaker produces, i.e., what speaker A says to B and what speaker B says, adjacently, to A, and so forth. To expand the definition slightly, a turn may be a segment of speech bounded by either what a coparticipant says or by a significant pause (the latter common in parent-child interaction). To extend the definition still further, a turn may be defined only as the speech of participants that has some transition relevance to the speech of other participants; i.e., the turns must have some natural relationship (e.g., question-answer) and not merely follow one another. To give one last example, a turn may involve, by definition, a speaker's intention, the "message," and thus involve several units of speaking, interspersed with what a coparticipant says.

Similar definitional problems emerge with other units of interaction, such as utterances, rounds, the floor, and side-sequences (Goodwin, 1981). In the present study, the concept of utterance was particularly problematic, especially in relation to the concept of turn. A turn was defined in terms of a participant's right to an interactional slot. This definition seemed to be consistent with parental speech behavior. A parent would speak, wait for the child to vocalize, and then speak again, wait again, and so forth. The parental model, clearly, was one of taking turns, allocating interactive rights to themselves and then to the children to contribute to the ongoing stream of behavior. Since the conversational skills of the children were limited, the ideal model of vocal exchange was often not met. The contributions were frequently one-sided, the parents providing a preponderance of the verbal behavior and being met with silence, disregard, or nonconversational behavior such as crying or banging toys on the floor. Although the parents attempted to maintain a model of interaction defined in terms of equal rights to turns of speech, their operational success was, at best, mixed.

The irregular success at turn-taking structured the nature of the parental turns. A parental turn might contain only a single word, the child's name, or an attentional "look!" or "¡mira!" if the child then responded vocally. The absence of a vocal response, on the other hand, might lead to a lengthy, repetitious series of the child's name, attentionals, descriptions of pictures in books, renditions of animal noises, etc. The series would contain pauses of variable lengths. A practical difficulty, then, in the transcription and analysis was the identification of pauses in parental speech to define turns and smaller units, utterances. Although an element of subjectivity is always involved, three durations of pauses, or silence, could be readily discerned. The shortest was sentence juncture, the pause between sentences, whether of single or multiple words. Sentences tended to be brief, many of them only two or three words. Lengthy pauses, of several seconds duration, were defined as turn-marking, as indicating that an appropriate period of time had been granted for a turn to be assumed or claimed.

Intermediate between the sentence and turn was another kind of pause, one that was defined as separating, or marking, utterances. An utterance was thus defined as a structural unit, different in kind from a sentence and a turn. Functionally, however, it could coincide with either or both. To illustrate these points with an example, take the following form of parental speech. "Miranda, . . . look at this . . . look at this picture . . . see the kitty." Depending on the lengths of the pauses, the stretch of speech could be three or possibly four separate turns, i.e., if a parent waited appropriately for a response after each unit. If that were the case, each unit was also counted as an utterance, or in other words, for the parents a turn had to contain at least one utterance. An utterance, a turn, and a sentence then could all be the same unit. On the other hand, the entire stretch might be one turn, with the pauses between the units of shorter-than-turn duration. Depending on the length of those pauses, the stretch of speech could be one utterance or as many as four. If the structure was "Miranda (brief pause) look at this (slightly longer pause) look at this picture (brief pause) see the kitty," the scoring would be one turn, two utterances.

After each tape was transcribed, one of the project members would identify and number consecutively the utterances in each recording session. Relatively systematic reliability checks were made for the utterance scoring, and they were always high, in excess of 85% agreement and often approaching unanimity. Coders had little difficulty in identifying parental utterances. The utterances, it should be kept in mind, were usually brief and simple.

The next step in the analysis was the identification of utterances as parental speech, i.e., either as baby talk or as nonparental. In effect, the investigators wanted to know the relative proportion of speech in the sample that contained vocal characteristics marking the speech as especially appropriate for addressing children as compared to speech neutral with respect to social or age characteristics of the addressee. The distinction is not always exact, and fine-grained subjective judgments were sometimes necessary. Ideally, a controlled procedure would have been employed whereby each of the utterances would be rated independently of context and by a panel of independent judges. Instead, the ratings were made by members of the project, listening to the taped speech. Since the coders knew that the parents were speaking with the children, the search procedure was to listen for utterances that in context would have a vocal quality or characteristic rendering the utterance (a) acceptable for speech addressed to young children and (b) unacceptable or with a highly restrictive distribution and function in speech addressed to adults. An example of the latter would be lover's talk.

The instructions given to the coders was simply to use an acceptable-nonacceptable distinction in judging the utterances as parental speech or otherwise. Although the procedure is subject to error, it proved to be reliable. Random checks of coders' reliability showed uniformly high levels of agreement, almost always more than 90% and often approaching unanimity. Noting that no parental speech features had as yet been formally identified (i.e., the coders did not have a checklist of features available), two points should be made concerning the high levels of agreement.

One point is that the discovery procedure employed is common in some types of linguistic and anthropological research. Native speaker intuitions about language were tapped for acceptability judgments. Grammatical distinctions are usually the subject matter of native speaker judgments, but in principle, speech register appropriateness should also be suitable for folk judgment. A similar procedure is also a fundamental aspect of anthropological research. The discovery of folk categories and their behavioral correlates are primary objectives of anthropological inquiry. In that regard, covert cultural categories are assumed to underlie the organization of behavior. In the present study, the assumption was made that, as native speakers, the coders, had covert categories of speech appropriateness that they could utilize in their judgments of the parents' speech to the children. In a broader sense, an assumption was also made that parents in each language group also had language-specific categories of appropriateness. The discovery of the speech characteristics utilized by parents to express the appropriateness distinctions was, in a direct way, a major goal of the project. Stated otherwise, previous studies (e.g., Ferguson, 1964) had shown the existence of a baby talk speech register in several languages, including English and Spanish, implying that speakers in each language have culturally real categories that they employ. The coders as native speakers had access to the information and could make judgments as to whether the category had been invoked by parents in their utterances.

The second point concerning the high levels of coder reliability is that the parents without exception invoked the parental speech "category" in virtually all their utterances to their children. As can be seen in Table 2, the percentage of

TABLE 2
Percentages of Utterances with Parental Speech Features

	Number of Utterances			
	Features Present	*Features Absent*	*Total*	*Percent Present*
English				
Miranda	1,564	38	1,602	97.6
Jeanne	2,096	53	2,149	97.5
Rebecca	693	4	697	99.4
Adam	3,051	72	3,123	97.7
Spanish				
Valente	1,058	3	1,061	99.8
Analisa	665	7	672	99.0
Christian	1,010	5	1,015	99.5
Luis	925	8	933	99.2

utterances identified as parental speech is uniformly high, the average across sessions per family being 97.5% or more. The Spanish-speaking families as a group showed a range from 99.0% to 99.5%; and collectively (i.e., summing their scores), they used parental speech 99.4% of the time. The English-speaking parents showed a slightly higher range, 97.5% to 99.4%. Their summed score was 97.8%. In other words, the children were far more likely than not to hear speech with special characteristics. The context of that phenomenon, it should be recalled, is parents attempting to interact verbally with the children. The parents extend efforts, patiently, time after time, to establish a dyadic vocal exchange. Whatever the various functions may be that the parental speech serves, the achievement of a turn-taking dialogue is the fundamental one. It should be emphasized that no claim is made that parents always speak in all contexts to their young offspring with such a high frequency of parental speech.

Table 2 reveals another aspect of the data that requires discussion. The total number of utterances addressed to each child ranges from a low of 672 (Analisa) to a high of 3,123 (Adam). Since the duration of recorded interaction was not controlled or standardized, the amount varied from session to session and across families. Ideally, we wanted and requested of the parents a minimum total of 30 minutes, and in almost all cases, the parents were able to meet the request. The number of utterances in 30 minutes of recording, however, could vary considerably. The procedure adopted was to transcribe and eventually code all the utterances of each session to a total of 250. In the case of some children, e.g., Adam, that number was obtained in most of the sessions. In the case of others, e.g., Rebecca, the total of 250 was never obtained. Her maximum was 131. No reliable claims can be made concerning naturalistic variation across families and children, since the differing amounts of parental speech could simply reflect the diligence with which the recordings were made. It was our impression, however, that considerable diversity did exist across families in the amount and frequency of focused verbal interaction, although we did not have a way to measure the diversity effectively.

Once the utterances had all been coded for presence or absence of parental speech features, a search began for the identification of the features. The procedure was to listen to randomly selected sections of the tapes and to identify and describe in linguistic and social interactional terms the features that characterized an utterance as parental. This discovery procedure was followed until further repeated inspection of taped sections of interaction revealed no new features.

Inventory of Features

The search for parental speech features ultimately yielded a catalogue of 34 distinct features. The richness of the catalogue was one of the major accomplishments of the project. Compared to the previous inventories of baby talk characteristics, as noted earlier in this paper, this inventory of 34 features is considerably larger and more detailed. In addition to expanding the number of identifiable linguistic characteristics of parental speech, several interactional characteristics were also identified. These constituted a new dimension of parental speech studies.

The list of the parental speech features is given in Table 3. The features are also categorized. In the early stages of the coding procedure, the features were listed under a number of categories in the following sequence: prosody, paralinguistics, lexicon, grammar, and interactionals. The distinctions between the categories are, however, not always completely clear. Prosody and paralinguistics are difficult to distinguish, especially if function levels are not strictly defined and maintained (e.g., physiological, linguistic, referential, social). The classification here is revised from previous publications (Blount & Padgug,

TABLE 3
Categories and Features of Parental Speech

I. *Prosody*
   A. Volume: air
      Breathiness
      Breath held
   B. Volume: sound
      Whisper
      Lowered volume
      Raised volume
   C. Pitch/Intonation
      Falsetto
      High pitch
      Low pitch
      Exaggerated intonation
      Singing
   D. Rate of speech
      Slow rate
      Fast rate
   E. Duration
      Lengthened vowel
      Lengthened consonant
      Shortened vowel
      Shortened consonant

II. *Paralinguistics*
   A. Nonsegmental
      Creaky voice
      Tenseness
      Stress
      Nasality
      Rounding
   B. Segmental (phonetic)
      Alteration
      Substitution

III. *Lexical-Grammatical*
   A. Lexical
      Special lexical items
      Nonsense forms
   B. Grammar
      Grammatical deviations

IV. *Interactionals*
   A. Structural
      Attentionals
      Prompters
      Tag questions
      Repetition
   B. Modeling
      Imitation
      Turn substitution
      Personal pronoun substitution
      Interpretation

1977), and an effort was made to be consistent in defining the features in linguistic and social terms. The categories as listed in Table 3 may still have some inconsistencies. If not completely definitive, the categories are, however, illustrative of the types of features the parents used. Table 3 classifies by category, subcategory, and feature.

One of the first characteristics to note about Table 3 is the diversity of mechanisms by which parents modify their speech when addressing young children. They can modify volume of air, loudness, pitch levels, intonation contours, speech rate, duration, articulory properties of segmentals and nonsegmentals, lexical features, grammatical properties, and structural interactional properties. In effect, virtually any aspect of vocal interaction can be altered to accommodate to a parental speech register.

A number of the features are self-explanatory. Others, more obscure, need identification and clarification. Of the prosodic features, lengthened and shortned segments may pose problems. Vowels, nasals, and continuants in those categories were either sustained or clipped in articulation, providing different durational units. In the paralinguistic list, *Creaky voice* refers to articulation with tension, laryngealization, and low-amplitude pitch movement. *Stress* refers to what one commonly means linguistically by the term, but a technical definition involves problems.[1] From a listener's perspective, stress is perceived as a volume (i.e., loudness) phenomenon, whereas from a speaker's perspective, intensity is the dominant characteristic (see Lehiste, 1970). The former perspective was used in the present study. *Rounding* refers to lip-rounding. *Phonetic alteration* includes a variety of paralinguistic phenomena, including excessive ejection, retroflex, and palatalization. *Phonetic substitution* is a broader category, involving the replacement of a segmental unit with another, as in *wabbit* for *rabbit*.

Special lexical items include the standard characteristics, e.g., *choo-choo* for *train,* *doggie* for *dog,* etc. Nonsense forms—meaningless clusters of sounds—were also encountered. These appeared to constitute a form of sound-play or perhaps word-play. Grammatical deviations included all constructions that violated standard grammatical patterns, such as *no like that.*

In a fundamental sense, all of the 34 features are interactional. They occur in that context and function to facilitate interaction. Several characteristics of parental behavior, however, were strictly interactional in nature, constituting integral parts of the flow, sequencing, and turn-taking of behavior. Those features appeared to the observers to be modifications especially for child-oriented

---

[1] In previous publications on the project, stress was identified in broader terms as the feature instructional. *Instructional* was defined pragmatically, in terms of function primarily and of articularly properties secondarily. The definition included stress, and in order to be more consistent with the definitions of the other features, the name of the feature was changed to correspond to the major articulatory property.

interaction. Their usage was not what one would expect in adult-adult interaction. Take, for example, the structural interactional feature attentionals. These were the children's names, and expressions such as "Hey!" and "look!" and the Spanish equivalents "¡oye!" and "¡mira!" These features certainly occur in adult-oriented speech, but usually not several times in rapid succession nor at the beginning of several turns of interaction in a row. Nor are they likely to be said to an adult whose attention wanders in the course of interaction. Prompters also occur in adult-oriented speech, as [nn] or [hn] (orthographically as "Hmm?" or "huh?"). The usage, again is different in speech addressed to the children. The expressions were used almost entirely in instances in which a child failed to give a vocal response. They were, in other words, prompters to participate verbally, not requests for a repeat utterance or a clarification as they are predominantly in adult speech. Repetition, a parent's repeating his or her preceding utterance, serves the same purpose as a prompter, the elicitation of interaction.

Still another feature that reflects the same special usage in adult-child speech is the tag question, a device that repeats the truth content of a declarative sentence in interrogative form, as in "That's rich, isn't it?" or "You don't like him, do you?" Although tag questions may serve a variety of linguistic or sociolinguistic functions in adult speech (e.g., there is some evidence that women use them more than men), in child-orientation speech the tag seems to be exclusively a request for a response. Asking a child for the verification of the truth content of a declarative seems unlikely, and the subtler meanings of tags (e.g., sarcasm, ridicule, etc.) seems equally unlikely.[2]

Several interactional features appear to serve a modelling role, in which a parent provides a unit or characteristic of speech appropriate for the child to vocalize. One of these is parental imitation of a child's preceding utterance. Since children also frequently imitate parental utterances, the strategy here seems to be that imitation of a child's utterance will prompt him or her to imitate, in turn, what he or she has heard. Several interactional turns in succession may consist of mutual imitation. A second modeling device is turn substitution. Children as young as those in this study often fail to respond vocally to their turn slot. When that happens, parents sometimes take the child's turn, i.e., respond for the child in his or her slot. For example, consider the following sequence. A child's mother says "See the picture of the giraffe? (silence on the part of the child); can you say giraffe?" (silence); "giraffe" (silence); "giraffe?" "Oh, I can't say giraffe" (mother speaking for the child). The example also shows another modeling feature, personal-pronoun substitution. In speaking for a child, a parent substitutes, or switches, the person in the pronominal usage, such that in the example above "I" equals "you." That, of course, models the correct usage for a child, contextualizing the model in interactional structure (see Wills, 1977,

---

[2]The interaction facilitation of a tag question might reside in the intonation pattern. The tag is a vehicle for terminal rising intonation patterns, which might be the salient feature of the utterance.

for further examples and discussion). A final feature, interpretation, was the parental attribution of meaning to a child's vocalization even though no apparent characteristics of the vocalization indicated that a meaning was intended. Parents modeled the appropriate meaningful response on the basis of context, as for example a mother saying "thank you" to a child who handed her a toy, saying "ta ta."

Usage Patterns

Once the 34 features were identified and defined, each parental utterance in the sample was scored for each feature. The scoring was on the basis of presence or absence of each feature per utterance, not on an absolute basis. Multiple occurrences of a feature in an utterance thus were not counted. The scoring, when completed, provided usage profiles for the parents across the age range of each child and longitudinally for the two language groups.

Prior to a description of the profiles and an interpretation of the patterns in them, a brief note on coder reliability is needed. Since this aspect of the study has already been discussed in detail elsewhere (Blount & Padgug, 1977), only a summary is provided here. Five individuals were responsible for the coding, all graduate students at the University of Texas. Three of them were native speakers of English and two were native speakers of Spanish. Comparisons of randomly selected samples during the coding procedures revealed no significant differences among the English-speaking coders, and their reliability scores were all 80% or higher. The Spanish coder results were also consistent, with 80% or higher reliability scores on all but four features. One coder's scores showed usage rates on those features significantly out of proportion to those for all parents across all sessions; consequently, her scores were not used in the analyses of those features. The Spanish results were overall more problematic than the English ones, since there were fewer coders and less coder reliability. Except for four features, however, the reliability scores were acceptable.

At the beginning of the project, the researchers had two major expectations concerning the distribution of features in parental speech. The first was that the features known at the time, especially exaggerated intonation contours and special lexical items, would have high rates of occurrence in the speech of all the parents. The assumption here is simply that the most salient features were also likely to be the most frequent ones. The second expectation was that the usage of the features would change as the children advanced in age. Although knowledge of feature usage or function was not sufficient to allow prediction as to which features might change in which direction, the fact that most 2-year-olds are considerably more linguistically advanced than 1-year-olds led us to believe that parental input speech would reflect those differences. Parental accommodation to the language capacity of the children, in other words, should yield a differential rate of feature usage. We lso felt that the accommodation would have an effect on children's interactional skills and thereby on their acquisition of language, although the data were not yet available for direct analyses on that point.

Once coding of the parental speech was complete, sums by feature were totaled for each session, then for each child, and then also aggregated for each language group. The first set of measurements was on the totals across sessions for each child to establish rate profiles and to look for changes in feature rate across the age spread. The rate profiles are given in Tables 4 (English) and 5 (Spanish). The rate scores were multiplied by 100 for ease of reading; the numerals are thus the rate usage per 100 utterances. The features are listed in the same order as in Table 3.

Analyses of Tables 4 and 5 are presented in answer to the following questions: Which features are low rate across three or more families? which features show a rate for only one family significantly higher or lower than for other families? which features show uniform rates across three or more families? and which features appear to correspond to age differences of the children? The answers are given first for the English-speaking families and then for the Spanish-speaking families.

The English-speaking parents had low rates of occurrence for three families, defined as less than a rate of 5, on 16 features: breath held, whisper, raised volume, singing, lengthened consonant, shortened vowel, shortened consonant, nasality, alteration, substitution, grammatical deviation, attentionals, prompters, tag questions, turn substitution, and personal pronoun substitution. These low-rate features are probably of marginal significance in English parental speech, although rate-usage threshold effects can't be ruled out. Another point of interest is that the list includes features that are sometimes considered to be stereotypical of baby talk, specifically whisper, phonetic alteration, phonetic substitution, and grammatical deviation. These may have high perceptual salience for adults but probably not for infants.

The Spanish-speaking parents had low rates of occurrence for 16 features also: breath held, whisper, singing, slow rate, lengthened consonant, shortened vowel, tenseness, nasality, rounding, alteration, substitution, nonsense forms, grammatical deviations, tag questions, and turn substitution. These features—comparable to the English results—are probably of marginal significance in Spanish parental speech.

Some features are probably of limited value in both languages. Six features have low rates in all the families in each language group. Singing is probably best viewed as a form of exaggerated intonation; in fact, singing was sometimes difficult to distinguish from that feature. Shortened vowel would likely have low perceptual salience. Nasality, phonetic substitution, tag questions, and turn substitution all show infrequent usage.

Some features have rates of occurrence for one of the families out of proportion to those for the others, indicating a family perferential use. Among

TABLE 4
Profile Rate Scores, English

Features	Miranda	Jeanne	Rebecca	Adam
Breathiness	23.3	34.4	20.8	35.5
Breath held	0.1	6.7	3.0	1.4
Whisper	2.1	3.0	3.4	3.5
Lowered volume	15.5	14.8	10.8	12.5
Raised volume	4.5	2.7	5.7	3.8
Falsetto	18.4	8.6	11.2	5.0
High pitch	26.0	27.7	23.1	26.7
Low pitch	6.8	13.5	5.0	3.5
Exaggerated intonation	67.2	73.5	77.5	64.7
Singing	0.2	0.0	0.0	0.3
Slow rate	5.0	3.1	7.2	4.6
Fast rate	2.8	5.9	5.0	2.9
Lengthened vowel	26.4	18.4	20.9	23.3
Lengthened consonant	0.6	0.1	7.5	0.1
Shortened vowel	0.9	1.7	1.7	1.4
Shortened consonant	0.4	0.0	7.7	0.3
Creaky voice	9.6	17.2	15.1	14.9
Tenseness	3.7	15.2	15.6	9.7
Stress	16.6	13.3	25.5	7.6
Nasality	0.1	0.3	4.2	0.2
Rounding	7.2	6.8	1.1	1.9
Alteration	2.7	8.4	0.4	1.3
Substitution	0.3	0.0	0.0	0.0
Special lexical items	15.5	7.8	1.9	8.7
Nonsense forms	11.4	6.3	2.3	3.2
Grammatical deviation	0.8	2.0	0.1	1.3
Attentionals	3.2	5.3	3.0	1.9
Prompters	2.9	6.7	4.4	4.6
Tag questions	1.6	1.2	2.6	2.3
Repetition	27.8	35.2	18.8	19.5
Imitation	4.1	6.6	6.2	9.1
Turn substitution	0.2	1.6	0.4	1.3
Personal pronoun substitution	3.5	6.0	0.3	3.7
Interpretation	0.8	3.4	10.8	8.8
Totals	312.2	357.4	323.2	316.8
Average = 327.4				

the English-speaking families, Jeanne's parents rely in that way on breath held, low pitch, and alteration. Rebecca's parents show a comparative preference for lengthened consonant, stress, and nasality and a disinclination to use special lexical items and personal-pronoun substitution. Miranda's parents showed preferences for falsetto, special lexical items, and nonsense forms, avoiding (again, comparatively) creaky voice. Adam's parents showed lower preference for falsetto and stress and higher preference for imitation. In Miranda's and Adam's

TABLE 5
Profile Rate Scores, Spanish

Features	Valente	Analisa	Christian	Luis
Breathiness	12.9	9.2	13.5	12.1
Breath held	0.0	0.0	0.3	0.2
Whisper	2.5	3.1	3.9	1.2
Lowered volume	19.6	18.9	33.5	19.0
Raised volume	22.9	23.7	26.6	17.8
Falsetto	9.1	3.9	15.6	13.7
High pitch	19.3	18.3	57.5	15.4
Low pitch	5.2	4.2	8.0	2.6
Exaggerated intonation	42.0	52.2	59.7	60.0
Singing	2.4	0.7	2.3	0.9
Slow rate	4.0	4.5	15.1	2.0
Fast rate	19.2	18.5	44.2	30.5
Lengthened vowel	13.5	37.2	22.7	16.0
Lengthened consonant	0.7	2.7	4.2	0.3
Shortened vowel	0.9	1.2	3.8	1.4
Shortened consonant	0.2	1.2	1.4	0.5
Creaky voice	8.4	2.5	6.4	14.9
Tenseness	2.5	0.6	3.2	2.4
Stress	27.1	45.0	30.6	33.6
Nasality	0.0	0.0	0.0	0.0
Rounding	2.8	0.7	3.9	2.7
Alteration	2.5	7.3	2.5	3.1
Substitution	0.0	0.3	0.1	0.0
Special lexical items	9.5	2.1	5.6	7.3
Nonsense forms	23.0	2.6	1.2	6.1
Grammatical deviation	0.3	0.6	10.6	1.1
Attentionals	28.5	32.0	23.8	21.3
Prompters	19.2	12.9	28.8	11.6
Tag questions	0.7	0.0	2.7	6.6
Repetition	44.6	67.1	65.3	39.8
Imitation	12.3	1.5	10.2	15.4
Turn substitution	4.0	2.2	1.9	2.4
Personal pronoun substitution	26.0	24.6	4.5	28.8
Interpretation	7.0	1.8	26.2	42.1
Totals	392.8	403.3	539.8	432.8
Average = 442.2				

cases, the different rates could reflect developmental factors, although the sample size precludes making a specific claim to that effect.

In the Spanish-speaking sample, Valente's parents differ from the others in showing a higher rate of nonsense forms, and Luis' parents use comparatively more creaky voice and interpretation but comparatively less repetition. Each of those may reflect developmental factors, although no firm claims can be made. Analisa's parents show a depressed score for falsetto, creaky voice, special lexical item, and interpretation, while giving a considerably higher score for lengthened vowel. Christian's parents diverge the most in their usage, showing a higher preference for lowered volume, high pitch, slow rate, high rate, grammatical deviations, and prompters and a lower preference for personal-pronoun substitution.

The records show clearly that in each language group, each family has preferences in the usage of features. In some cases, a feature is used at a significantly higher rate, and in other cases at a significantly lower rate. Preference may be shown, in other words, for either low-rate or high-rate features.

One of the least anticipated results of the rate scores was the consistency of usage across the parents in each group, regardless of the age of the child. The rates are, in fact, remarkably the same in each language group. In the English-speaking sample, only 1 of the features shows a highly divergent pattern across all families—falsetto—and only 6 of the 34 features show a high rate of divergence across two families—tenseness, stress, rounding, special lexical items, nonsense forms, and interpretation. In only 2 features—breathiness and rounding—does the divergent pattern of two high rates and two low rates occur. In only a total of 8 features, then, does a pattern of variation across two or more families exist. In the remaining 26 features, the parents in the four families used a consistent rate of the features in their speech to the children.

The Spanish-speaking families behaved in a similar fashion. Only 2 features—falsetto and interpretation—show a marked divergence rate among all the families. Five features—fast rate, lengthened vowel, creaky voice, exaggerated intonation, and prompters—show diversity across two families, and 2 features—attentionals and repetition—show two families with high rates and two with low rates. Nine features thus show diverse patterns of rates across two or more families, and 25 features reflect consistent rate patterns.

Two conclusions are drawn concerning similarity and diversity in rate usage. Despite the age range of the children in each group, the rate usages show far more similarity than diversity. Anticipating a comparison between English and Spanish, we note that among the features showing divergent rates across two or more families, only falsetto and interpretation are common to each language group. The two language groups differ considerably, then, in terms of the intra-language diversity they reflect in parental rate usage.

Prior to an English and Spanish comparison, the question of developmental rate usage should be addressed. Do any of the rates increase or decrease systematically with the age range? In English, only rounding, nonsense forms, repetition, and interpretation reflect a possible pattern whereby parents modified their rate of feature selection according to the children's age or language development. Higher rates of rounding, nonsense forms, and repetition were recorded for the two younger children, Miranda and Jeanne, and higher rates of interpretation were recorded for the two older children, Rebecca and Adam. In the latter case, parental attribution of meaning to the children's utterances would be consistent with an expectation that the children had the capacity to produce or to understand the meaning of the parental utterances. The lower rates for nonsense forms and repetition for the older children could also be indicative of an increased language awareness. Rounding could possibly distort utterances to the point of interfering with the children's acoustic perception, although no evidence is available to substantiate that.

In Spanish, the features fast rate and interpretation show increases in rate usage for the two oldest children, Christian and Luis, whereas attentionals show a slight rate decrease in the parental speech addressed to them. Interpretation and attentional rate differences would be expected if the children were more proficient in their language use or if their parents expected them to be more proficient. Fast rate may be related to perceptual salience, although, again, no evidence has been adduced to that effect.

PARENTAL SPEECH: ENGLISH AND SPANISH COMPARISONS

A convenient way to summarize the interpretation of Tables 4 and 5, the profile rate scores, is to compare and contrast the English and Spanish groups. First, each family used a large percentage of the total number of features in the inventory. In the English-speaking sample, the families exhibited the following pattern: all 34 features (Miranda), 33 features (Adam), 32 features (Rebecca), and 31 features (Jeanne). In the Spanish-speaking sample, the pattern is: 32 features (Christian and Luis), and 31 features (Valente and Analisa). Each family thus used an abundant number of different kind of features, the lowest being 31 and the highest being 34.

Although each child was addressed with a wide range of parental speech features, the rates of occurrence varied widely across features. Approximately one-half of the features for each child in each language group were used less than five times per 100 utterances. The low-rate features showed some overlap across language (i.e., singing, shortened vowel, nasality, phonetic substitution, tag questions, and turn substitution), but language-specific patterns also occurred, as listed earlier.

High-rate features also showed consistent patterns. Table 6, derived from Tables 4 and 5, contains a listing of the seven most frequently occurring features. The table lists the features by percentage of rate score, i.e., the rate of each feature divided by the total number of features per child. Note that all but five of the features occur at rates in excess of five times per 100 utterances. Inspection of Table 6 yields several interesting results. In each case, the seven features account for more than 50% of the total rate figures. Furthermore, if only the three most frequently occurring features are considered, approximately 40% of the total is accounted for in English and approximately 34% in Spanish. Although

TABLE 6
Percentages of Parental Rate Scores for High-Rate Features

English

Miranda		Jeanne		Rebecca		Adam	
Feature	%	Feature	%	Feature	%	Feature	%
Ex. inton.	21.5	Ex. inton.	20.6	Ex. inton.	24.0	Ex. inton.	20.4
Repetition	8.9	Repetition	9.8	Stress	7.9	Low vol.	12.5
Leng. vowel	8.5	Breathiness	9.6	High pitch	7.1	Breathiness	11.2
High pitch	8.3	High pitch	7.8	Leng. vowel	6.5	High pitch	8.4
Breathiness	7.5	Leng. vowel	5.1	Breathiness	6.4	Leng. vowel	7.4
Falsetto	5.9	Crky voice	4.8	Repetition	5.8	Repetition	6.2
Stress	5.3	Tenseness	4.3	Tenseness	4.8	Crky voice	4.7
Total	65.9		62.0		62.5		70.8
All other features	34.1		38.0		37.5		29.2
	100.0		100.0		100.0		100.0

Spanish

Valente		Analisa		Christian		Luis	
Feature	%	Feature	%	Feature	%	Feature	%
Repetition	11.4	Repetition	16.6	Repetition	12.1	Ex. inton.	13.9
Ex. inton.	10.7	Ex. inton.	12.9	Ex. inton.	11.1	Interpret.	9.7
Att'nals	7.3	Stress	11.2	High pitch	10.7	Repetition	9.2
Stress	6.9	Leng. vowel	9.2	Fast rate	8.2	Stress	7.8
Pers. pron.	6.6	Att'nals	7.9	Low. vol.	6.2	Fast rate	7.0
Nonsense	5.9	Pers. pron.	6.1	Stress	5.7	Pers. pron.	6.7
Rsd. vol.	5.8	Rsd. vol.	5.9	Prompters	5.3	Att'nals	4.9
Total	54.6		69.8		59.3		59.2
All other features	45.4		30.2		40.7		40.8
	100.0		100.0		100.0		100.0

the parents in each language group use a large number of different features, they use three features for approximately one-third of the total and seven features for more than one-half of the total. Moreover, they are remarkably consistent in their selection of those features and in the frequency with which they are used.

The English-speaking parents all used exaggerated intonation as the most frequent feature and all at a rate of approximately 20 occurrences per 100 utterances. In addition to exaggerated intonation, the features repetition, lengthened vowel, high pitch, and breathiness are among the top 6 features, all of them as fairly constant rates. Note also that only a total of 10 different features are included in the list in Table 6, and the only feature that occurs in only one list is lowered volume.

The Spanish-speaking record as shown in Table 6 also reveals a high degree of similarity across families, but the list of features is different from English. First, the feature showing the highest rate is repetition and the second highest rate is for exaggerated intonation. The fourth family (Luis) shows exaggerated intonation as the top feature, and repetition is third. It is noteworthy that the rates for exaggerated intonation in Spanish are approximately one-half of those in English, whereas the rates for repetition are approximately twice as high as the ones in English. Other than exaggerated intonation and repetition, stress is the only feature to appear in all four lists. Spanish shows more variability than English, with 12 different features as opposed to 10 in English. Four features in Spanish appear in only one list (one for each family)—nonsense forms, lengthened vowel, lowered volume, and interpretation. Although more variability is found in the Spanish record than in English, the point should be stressed that the rates across the families are still overall uniform. The range in frequency for exaggerated intonation, for example, is only from 10.7 to 13.5%; for personal-pronoun substitution, 6.1 to 6.7%; and for repetition, only from 9.2 to 16.6%.

If feature and percentages are compared directly across languages, a number of points emerge. Note has already been made that the one-two order of the top features in English—exaggerated intonation and repetition—is reversed in Spanish and that repetition occurs at twice the frequency in Spanish whereas exaggerated intonation occurs at twice the frequency in English as compared to Spanish. Also, several features are specific to each language in these priority lists (Table 6). Lengthened vowel, high pitch, breathiness, creaky voice, and tenseness all occur in the lists for two or more children in English, whereas only one of those—lengthened vowel—appears at all in the Spanish list. By contrast, attentionals, stress, personal-pronoun substitution, raised volume, and fast rate are found in two or more of the children's list in Spanish. Only one of those, stress, is included in the English sample.

The comparison between English and Spanish can be summed up in the following way. Although English speakers and Spanish speakers used exaggerated intonation and repetition in essentially reverse order and proportion, ratewise, the two features together account for approximately 25 to 30% of the feature usage. An additional 8 to 10 features account for approximately 30 to 40% of the usage, and those features are specific to each language group, with only 2 features showing cross-language overlap. The remaining 30 to 45% of feature usage is made of 20 to 22 low-rate features, reflecting only minor differences across language. The bulk of Spanish-English differences lies in 10 features, and specifically in the rates for the features that show consistent, uniform usages across the families. To further elaborate the differences, we can look at the characteristics of the features.

The English features, again, are lengthened vowel, high pitch, breathiness, creaky voice, and tenseness. The Spanish features are attentionals, stress, personal-pronoun substitution, raised volume, and fast rate. The English-speaking parents relied comparatively more on prosody—pitch, intonation, duration, breath, and tension. In contrast, the Spanish speakers relied more specifically on interactional features and on prosody. Except for exaggerated intonation, however, they relied on different aspects of prosody—stress, volume, and rate. At the risk of overgeneralization, the differences can be collapsed even further. The English prosodic features all involve amplitudes of tension—pitch levels, duration, breath control, and tenseness across segments. The Spanish prosodic features involve volume and tempo. These differences are, again to keep proper perspective, matters of degree, but one of their more interesting aspects is that they are uniform across the families. Quite specific language differences exist. Parental speech has culturally specific patterns in these two languages, and each set of parents adhered rather closely to the patterns.

To return to Table 6 for one more comparison, can any association of rate percentages and ages of the children be made, and if so, do the languages differ? In English, repetition reflects a possible association, occurring at the second most common feature in the speech to the two younger children and dropping to the sixth level for the two older children. In Spanish, raised volume is the seventh most common feature in the speech to the two younger children, but it is not above the 5.0 rate level in the speech to the two older children. They, on the other hand, receive comparatively more fast rate, a feature not above the 5.0 rate level for the younger children. A difference is also seen for attentionals, occurring at a higher percentage for the two younger children than for the two older ones. Differences do, in fact, exist between the two languages in terms of feature and age association. In English, the older children received comparatively less repetition, whereas in Spanish, the older children received less raised volume and attentionals but more fast rate.

Again, as one would now expect, the usage rates and percentages do not overall show more than a possible and slight relationship with age of the children. This means that although parents are taking account of the limited linguistic skills of the children and using a special speech register with them, they do not appear on distributional evidence of the features alone to accommodate to the different linguistic levels of development that the children actually have.[3] Valente, who had no recognizable words as such received speech substantially the same as Luis, who could produce limited two-word constructions. This raises the question of why these diverse specialized features of speech are employed liberally by the parents in each family. At one level, we can simply say that they mark or identify the speech register as appropriate, i.e., that the speech convention

---

[3]The slight distributional evidence for correspondence between parental usage and language development level of the children does not necessarily mean that no developmental functions are served. Analysis of the feature distribution on the basis of co-occurrence restrictions (i.e., which features can occur together and which are mutually exclusive) has indicated that developmental factors may exist (Blount & Kempton, 1976). The development, however, is in terms of the infants' interactive skills, not language skills alone.

requires use of the parental register to young children. Specific questions, however, need to be addressed about the feature usage. What purposes and functions might they be serving?

PARENTAL SPEECH FUNCTIONS

The place to begin seeking an answer to the issue of function is in the arena of interaction. Parental actions in the parent-child activity are designed to involve the children in turn-taking, in a protoconversation, even though what the children could say or vocalize would be highly limited. The parents' concerns were not primarily what the children would, or even could, say but that they vocalize. They wanted a vocal response, even if the response was a long string of babbled syllables. Shaping or guiding the vocal responses toward recognizable language structure was of course also a goal and perhaps even the ultimate one. It was not, however, the prior or immediate one. In utterance after utterance, session after session, the parents would work to initiate a round of vocal interaction with their children, respond to the children's vocalizations, and entice the children to continue the flow of turn-taking. Success was measured in how they managed to initiate and sustain vocal interaction.

The primary function of the parental speech features appears to be interaction-related. They contribute to the initiation and continuation of interaction in a variety of ways. Central to these is the establishment of attention. A practical consideration of a parent in trying to enlist infants as interactive partners is getting the infant's attention to the activity. Once gotten, an infant's attention is not easy to sustain, given the brief attention span of very young children and the ease with which they may be distracted. The abundance of parental speech features, an average of more than three per utterance, is probably a function of the elusiveness of attention and thus sustained interaction. More specifically, the characteristics of the parental speech features can also be related directly to the interactional requirements.

All of the prosodic and most of the paralinguistic features have exaggerated articulation processes in comparison with standard adult usage. The perceptual salience is heightened by the exaggerated vocal characteristics, and the effect is a functional attention-getting device. The exaggerations constitute a vocal way of getting an infant to pay attention to the social activity at hand, and moreover, the acoustic properties of the high-rate prosodic and paralinguistic features are well designed to elicit attention. Essentially from birth, infants have the capacity to distinguish, through physiological response mechanisms, changes in the pitch level of vocalizations (Stratton & Connolly, 1973; Whitaker, 1973), and within a few months of age, infants can distinguish between supragegmental and segmental acoustic cues (Morse, 1972; Spring & Dale, 1977). Infants also are able to exhibit some vocal control of duration and pitch level in their vocalizations at about 16 weeks of age (Stark, 1980). Certainly by the age of 8 to 9 months, variations in pitch levels, duration, volume, rate, and intensity of vocalizations are within an infant's capacity to process, productively and receptively. Those suprasegmental features are aspects of infants' capacity ontogenetically prior to segmentals, even in patterned babbling sequences before the onset of lexical and phonological development (Blount, 1982).

The distribution of the high-rate prosodic and paralinguistic features in parental speech is consistent with the facts of early perceptual and vocal development in infants. Exaggerated intonation, the most prominent feature, includes pitch amplitude and duration aspects. Each of the other high-rate features in each language group involves exaggerated qualities of tension, duration, or rate. In English, the features were lengthened vowel, high pitch, breathiness, and creaky voice; in Spanish, they were stress, raised volume, and fast rate.

The argument that parental speech features primarily serve interactional functions is also consistent with the use of high-rate interactionals. Repetition, the most frequent interactional, is an economical way to manage the attention-getting requirement, especially considering that the majority of parental utterances contain prosodic or paralinguistic features. Attentionals, by definition, are designed to attract an infant's attention, and other interactionals such as prompters also contribute in direct ways to the flow of interaction.

Two additional points are in order concerning the parental speech features and their social interaction functions. None of the features earlier considered diagnostic of baby talk are among the most common features in the speech of any of the families in the English-Spanish project. Special lexical items are the most frequently occurring of the early features, but they are low rate overall in the project; and phonetic and grammatical features, also once considered diagnostic, are of even lower frequency. The second point is that although the parental speech features attract attention and promote social interaction, no experimental work has as yet been carried out to measure the effects of the individual features. At present, no metric of efficiency exists, although one is certainly needed.

SUMMARY AND CONCLUSIONS

The acquisition of social interactional skills in children has increasingly become an important area of investigation in child development. A characteristic of the research during the past decade has been a focus on process, on how social interaction gets accomplished and on the factors that contribute structurally and developmentally to the process. A major facet of the process is the parental contribution, the question of what parents do to structure the exchange of behavior. One dimension of research on the parental contribution is their vocal behavior. The central research question is what parents do vocally to further social interaction with their young children.

The present paper has described the results of a preliminary study designed to give some answers to that question. Investigation of parental speech in English and in Spanish to children in the age range of 9 to 24 months yielded several findings. One was the large number of different features used by the parents. A total of 34 speech features were identified, and each family used 31 or more of the features in their speech to the children. Parents also used an abundance of features, an average of 3.27 features per utterance in English and 4.42 in Spanish. Another finding was that in each language group, family preferences for some features over others were clearly present. Overall, however, the patterns of usage were highly similar across families, indicating clearly the presence of a cultural speech register for addressing children in each language group. The parents used a similar pattern of features regardless of the ages or language skills of the children. Exaggerated intonation and repetition were the most frequent features in each language, the former preferred more in English and the latter in Spanish. Otherwise, the highest-rate features were language-specific, English speakers using prosodic features on intensity and duration dimensions and Spanish speakers using more interactionals and prosodic features on volume and rate dimensions.

Only a minority of features (two to three in each language) showed any correlation between age of child and patterns of parental usage. The predominant function of the speech features thus was not assistance with language acquisition or instruction directly but rather the development of social interaction. The features served as attention-getting devices, providing parents with a mechanism for dealing with their most difficult practical problem in their interaction with their children. The acoustic properties of the parental vocalizations are ideally suited to attract infants' attention through their exaggeration and their match with the ontogenetic development of infants' capacity to process suprasegmentals.

The findings of the English and Spanish project are consistent with and contribute to the three general dimensions of mother-infant interaction research identified in the introduction to this chapter. The parental speech registers form a structural component to the interactive process, they function to initiate and sustain the process through their adaptiveness to the infants' attention-response capabilities, and they were described and analyzed using microlevel techniques. The results should prove useful in several specific ways. The inventory of features is a resource that can be employed in the study of other language and cultural groups, thereby adding to our limited knowledge of the cultural diversity and similarities that may exist in this important area of socialization. Measures of the efficacy of the individual features as attention-getting devices are especially needed. They would provide a base for much more precise statements about the contributions they make to the development of interactional skills. A clearer understanding of the parental contribution to the structure of social interaction with infants would be a major advance in this area of inquiry.

REFERENCES

BAKEMAN, R., & BROWN, J. V. Early interaction: consequences for social and mental development at three years. *Child Development*, 1980, *51*, 437–447.

BLOUNT, B. G. Aspects of Luo socialization. *Language in Society*, 1972, *1*, 236–248.

BLOUNT, B. G. Parental speech to children: cultural patterns. In M. Saville-Troike (Ed.), *Linguistics and anthropology*. Washington, DC: Georgetown University Press, 1977.

BLOUNT, B. G. The ontogeny of emotions and their vocal expression in infants. In S. Kuczaj (Ed.), *Language development* (Vol. 2, *Language, thought, and culture*). Hillsdale, NJ: Erlbaum, 1982.

BLOUNT, B. G., & KEMPTON, W. Child language socialization: Parental speech interaction strategies. *Sign Language Studies*, 1976, *12*, 251–277.

BLOUNT, B. G., & PADGUG, E. Prosodic, paralinguistic, and interactional features in parent-child speech: English and Spanish. *Journal of Child Language*, 1977, *4*, 67–86.

BRAZLETON, T. B. Joint regulation of neonate-parent behavior. In E. Z. Tronick (Ed.), *Social interchange in infancy: Affect, cognition, and communication*. Baltimore, MD: University Park Press, 1982.

BRUNER, J. The ontogenesis of speech acts. *Journal of Child Language*, 1975, *2*, 1–19.

BULLOWA, M. (Ed.). *Before speech: The beginning of interpersonal communication*. Cambridge: Cambridge University Press, 1979.

BUTTERWORTH, G., & COCHRAN, E. Towards a mechanism of joint visual attention. *International Journal of Behavioral Development*, 1980, *3*, 253–272.

CASAGRANDE, J. B. Comanche baby language. *International Journal of American Linguistics*, 1948, *14*, 11–14.

CHAPPELL, P. F., & SANDER, L. W. Mutual regulation of the neonatal-maternal interactive process: Context for the origins of communication. In M. Bullowa (Ed.), *Before speech: The beginning of interpersonal communication*. Cambridge: Cambridge University Press, 1979.

COLLIS, G. M. Describing the structure of social interaction. In M. Bullowa (Ed.), *Before speech: The beginnings of interpersonal communication*. Cambridge: Cambridge University Press, 1979.

EDELSKY, C. Who's got the floor? *Language in Society*, 1981, *10*, 383–421.

EILERS, R. E. Infant speech perception: History and mystery. In G. H. Yeni-Komshian, J. F. Kavanaugh, & C. A. Ferguson (Eds.), *Child phonology* (Vol. 2, *Perception*). New York: Academic, 1980.

ERVIN-TRIPP, S. Children's verbal turn-taking. In E. Ochs & B. B. Schieffelin (Eds.), *Developmental pragmatics*. New York: Academic, 1979.

FARRAN, D. C., HIRSCHBIEL, P., & JAY, S. Toward interactive synchrony: The gaze patterns of mothers and children in three age groups. *International Journal of Behavioral Development*, 1980, *3*, 215–224.

FERGUSON, C. A. Baby talk in six languages. *American Anthropologist*, 1964, *66* (Pt. 2), 103–114.

FREEDLE, R., & LEWIS, M. Prelinguistic conversations. In M. Lewis & L. A. Rosenblum (Eds.), *Interaction, conversation, and the development of language*. New York: Wiley, 1977.

GARVEY, C. *Play*. Glasgow, Scotland: Fontana/Open Books, 1977.

GOODWIN, C. *Conversational organization: Interaction between speakers and hearers*. New York: Academic, 1981.

GUSTAFSON, G. E., GREEN, J. A., & WEST, M. J. The infant's changing role in mother-infant games: The growth of social skills. *Infant Behavior and Development*, 1979, *2*, 301–308.

KAYE, K. Why we don't talk "baby talk" to babies. *Journal of Child Language*, 1980, *7*, 489–507.

KAYE, K., & FOGEL, A. The temporal structure of face-to-face communication between mothers and infants. *Developmental Psychology*, 1980, *16*, 454–464.

LEHISTE, I. *Suprasegmentals*. Cambridge, MA: MIT Press, 1970.

Lewis, M., & Rosenblum, L. A. (Eds.) The *effect of the infant on its caregiver*. New York: Wiley, 1974.
Lewis, M. & Rosenblum, L. A. (Eds.) *Interaction, conversation, and the development of language*. New York: Wiley, 1977.
Morse, P. A. The discrimination and speech and nonspeech stimuli in early infancy. *Journal of Experimental Child Psychology*, 1972, *14*, 477–492.
Newsome, J. An intersubjective approach to the systematic description of mother-infant interaction. In H. R. Schaffer (Ed.), *Studies in mother-infant interaction*. New York: Academic, 1977.
Lewis, M., & Coates, D. L. Mother-infant interaction and cognitive development in twelve-week-old infants. *Infant Behavior and Development*, 1980, *3*, 95–105.
Sander, L. W. The regulation of exchange in the infant-caretaker system and some aspects of the context-content relationship. In M. Lewis & L. A. Rosenblum (Eds.), *Interaction, conversation, and the development of language*. New York: Wiley, 1977.
Schaffer, H. R. (Ed.). *Studies in mother-infant interaction*. New York: Academic, 1977.
Spring, D. R., & Dale, P. S. Discrimination of linguistic stress in early infancy. *Journal of Speech and Hearing Research*, 1977, *20*, 224–231.
Stark, R. E. Stages of speech development in the first year of life. In G. Yeni-Komashian, J. Kavanaugh, & C. Ferguson (Eds.), *Child phonology* (Vol. 1, *Production*). New York: Academic, 1980.
Stern, D. N. Mother and infant at play: The dyadic interaction involving facial, vocal, and gaze behaviors. In M. Lewis & L. A. Rosenblum (Eds.), *The effect of the infant on its caregiver*. New York: Wiley, 1974.
Stern, D. N. *The first relationship: Infant and mother*. Cambridge, MA: Harvard University Press, 1977.
Stern, D. N., Beebe, B., Jaffe, J., & Bennett, S. L. The infant's stimulus world during social interaction: A study of caregiver behaviors with particular reference to repetition and timing. In H. R. Schaffer (Ed.), *Studies in mother-infant interaction*. New York: Academic, 1977.
Stratton, P., & Connolly, K. Discrimination by newborns of the intensity, frequency, and temporal characteristics of auditory stimuli. *British Journal of Psychology*, 1973, *64*, 219–232.
Trevarthen, C. Communication and cooperation in early infancy: A description of primary intersubjectivity. In M. Bullowa (Ed.), *Before speech: The beginning of interpersonal communication*. Cambridge: Cambridge University Press, 1979.
Voegelin, C. F., & Robinett, F. M. "Mother language" in Hidatsa. *International Journal of American Linguistics*, 1954, *20*, 65–70.
Whitaker, H. A. Comments on the innateness of language. In R. Shuy (Ed.), *Some new directions in linguistics*. Washington, DC: Georgetown University Press, 1973.
Wills, D. D. Participant deixis in English and baby talk. In C. Snow & C. Ferguson (Eds.), *Talking to children: Language input and acquisition*. Cambridge: Cambridge University Press, 1977.

2
Maternal Input Adjustments and Non-Adjustments as Related to Children's Linguistic Advances and to Language Acquisition Theories*

Keith E. Nelson
Pennsylvania State University

John D. Bonvillian
University of Virginia

Marilyn S. Denninger
Pennsylvania State University

Barbara J. Kaplan
Mount Holyoke College

Nancy D. Baker
Pennsylvania State University

A debate has raged between advocates of the position that adults provide few useful language adjustments to young language-learners and advocates of the position that adults, and particularly mothers, provide fine-tailored, well-adjusted input that is maximally designed to facilitate the progress in language of young children (e.g., cf. Menyuk, 1971, or Newport, Gleitman, & Gleitman, 1977, or Shatz, 1981, with Gleason & Weintraub, 1978, or Moerk, 1972, 1974, or Snow, 1977).

We shall begin with illustrations of an empirical sort that seem to support *both* positions. This will put us very much in the position of the judge sitting with an apprentice as first a man came to tell his tale of injustice at the hands of a woman, and then the woman came to tell her opposite account. To each the judge said, "Yes, I understand. Your views are entirely correct." The apprentice paused after the second interview, frowned deeply, and burst out: "But they can't both be correct in their views!" And the judge replied, "Yes, yes, you are

---

*Conduct of much of the reported research and preparation of this paper were aided by a Fulbright Commission Research grant and by National Science Foundation Grant BNS–8013767 and National Institutes of Health Grant MH 19826–01 to Keith E. Nelson. Special thanks for many considerations go to Lars Nystedt, David Magnusson, Barbro Svensson, Fredrik Hjortzberg-Nordlund, and Carl Rollenhagen of Stockholms Universitet.

right." Our approach will be to go beyond an illustration of both sides, input adjustment, and input nonadjustment, to suggest a more differentiated framework for analysis.

A CLEAR CASE OF MATERNAL NON-ADJUSTMENT IN MLU

Between 22 and 27 months of age we observed a sample of 25 children in the Fiffin Project. Early reports (e.g., Nelson & Bonvillian, 1978) were centered on semantic concepts—Fiffins, Wangsops, Lobsters, Pulleys, and their relatives— and their acquisition. However, this is an unusually large sample in language acquisition research and there is a wealth of information now coded on syntactic growth and relevant input components. Here we will report on mean length of utterance (MLU) coded in a way that makes the fewest possible assumptions about the child's morphemic system—namely, MLU in numbers of words for both mothers and children.

The mothers in this sample as a group failed to adjust their utterance lengths in any sensitive way to their children's utterance lengths. There were two indications to support this conclusion. First, there was only a trivial and statistically nonsignificant correlation between mothers' and children's MLUs; $r = -.15$ at 22 months, and $r = .18$ at 27 months.

The other major barometer of nonadjustment in MLUs was the pattern across time. At 22 months the children's MLU was 1.48 words, as against 4.00 for their mothers. The gap is reduced by 27 months—but only because the children advance and the mothers remain unchanged! Thus, at 27 months the mothers are still very close to an MLU of 4 (4.02), whereas the children have now reached an MLU of 2.19 words.

An incidental measure backs the conclusion that mothers were *not* adjusting their MLUs in any consistent way to children's MLUs. Mothers varied enormously in how widely their utterance lengths exceeded their children's; the range for mother-child pairs was from $+1.31$ to -3.96 words for 22-month-olds and from $+.43$ to $+3.03$ words for 27-month-olds.

AUXILIARIES IN INPUT: AN APPARENT SHIFT TOWARD GREATER ADJUSTMENT AS CHILDREN ADVANCE

When the children were 22 months of age, they averaged only .024 auxiliaries per verb construction. Mothers used a mean of .218 auxiliaries per verb and their rate of auxiliary use correlated very negligibly with the children's rates; $r = -.02$.

However, as the children raised their auxiliary use, both the maternal mean level and the maternal-child correlation increased. The 27-month-olds' rate of .067 auxiliaries was now met with .246 auxiliaries per verb by their mothers, and the correlation between measures was a positive .53. Overall, this pattern is compatible with a conclusion of maternal adjustment to the child's increased production of auxiliaries. As detailed below, other factors in the maternal input also must be considered. But it is of further interest to note here that the child's level of auxiliary use at 27 months was predictable from the frequency of auxiliary use per verb by the mothers when the children were 22-months old; $r = .62$. This finding raises the possibility that a mother who adjusts *early,* who increases her verb complexity by increasing her rate of auxiliary use relatively early in her child's development, may stimulate auxiliary development by the child. Once again, however, caution is in order until further factors are considered and until experimental work follows up this intriguing observational outcome.

A BROAD-CORRELATIONAL LOOK AT CROSS-SECTIONAL SAMPLINGS: NONCONTINGENT MATERNAL SYNTAX AS RELATED TO CHILD SYNTAX

We move now to a series of analyses concerned with multiple child measures as tied to multiple maternal measures. In following sections, material is presented that bears on how the mother's contingent replies are related to the child's language growth. Such material is of considerable interest theoretically because it bears directly on models that assume the child is an active but limited information processor whose steps forward in language will depend primarily on the *particular contingent replies* to what he or she has just said rather than on the overall use of certain elements in the mother's speech. In this section, however, we must first establish in fact whether *overall* levels in maternal input of certain forms are correlated with the children's concurrent levels of language mastery. This information is important for comparisons with prior correlational projects and also as a lead-in to the data on contingent maternal input components.

Children's Measures

Syntactic complexity measures included global indexes based on utterance length and more specific syntactic indexes concerning questions and verbs. In the case of each measure of the child's language calculated at age 22 months, a corresponding *follow-up* measure was calculated. The follow-up measure employed in each instance was chosen so as to give the least confounding with the corresponding measures at 22 months; i.e., it showed the least correlation, positive or negative, with maternal and child language when the child's age was 22 months. The follow-up was either (a) the child's level on the measure at 27 months or (b) the child's change on the measure between the two periods. All of the follow-up variables thus represent the children's degree of language progress by 27 months, and by choosing the particular variables in this way it proved possible to see how much prediction maternal variables give of language progress when significant confounding was avoided both for child and maternal status at the point of origin (22 months) and for the child's follow-up and initial status. For all child and maternal measures, raters were pretrained until interrater agreements exceeded 89% of total judgments.

1a. 22-Month MLU (C). Mean lengh of utterance in words was calculated using all the child's spontaneous utterances that were intelligible. Excluded as nonspontaneous, for this and all measures of syntax in this chapter, were immediate imitations composed only of words drawn (in the same order) from the immediately prior utterance of the mother.

1b. Follow-up MLU (C). This measure was the change (nearly always an increase) in MLU between 22 and 27 months.

2a. Longest Utterance at 22 Months. This and all subsequent measures used the same definition of spontaneous utterances as that employed in 1a above. Total words in the child's longest utterance was the measure here.

2b. Follow-up Longest Utterance. This was the longest utterance at 27 months.

3a. 22-Months Question Index. After work by Cazden (1965) children's questions were ranked on a scale of development where 1 (intonation questions only) represented the lowest level and 6 (all basic question forms, including tags) topped the scale.

3b. Follow-up Question Index. The same scale applied to questions at 27 months. The children ranged from 1 to 6 in their scores.

4a. Auxiliaries at 22 Months (C). The mean number of auxiliary elements per main verb was computed as one measure of verb complexity. This variable was, of course, .000 for children who employed no auxiliaries at all.

4b. Follow-up Auxiliaries. At 27 months these scores ranged from .000 to .284.

5a. 22-Month Verbs. This was an overall index of verbs beginning with a score of 1 for simple present tense only to a score of 5 for a complex including multiple auxiliaries and present, progressive, past, and future tenses.

5b. Follow-up Verbs. The change in overall verb level between 22 and 27 months was calculated.

Unconfounded Follow-up Measures

Table 1 shows the relationships between each criterion, follow-up measure, and the corresponding 22-month variable for the children. In no instance does the correlation approach significance. Therefore, in the results and discussion that follow we can rule out the possibility that successful predictions of follow-up levels from the mother's language variables (taken when the children were 22-month-olds) could simply rest indirectly on confounding with the children's variables across the two age periods.

Noncontingent and Contingent Maternal Indices

At both 22 and 27 months, for syntax three measures were calculated for the mothers' utterances overall: (a) MLU, as defined above for the children; (b) auxiliaries per verb, again as specified above for the children; and (c) total elements per verb, a wider-ranging variable than the verb measure for the children (on which the mothers were all at or near ceiling; a similar condition also led to the restriction of a Question Index to children only). These measures included all maternal utterances regardless of whether an utterance was immediately contingent to a prior utterance by a child.

Overall "Adjustment" Between Children and Mothers at 22 and 27 Months

Tables 2 and 3 show, respectively, the correlational data when the children are 22 and 27 months of age. In general it is clear there is low "adjustment" in that few correlations reach significance between maternal noncontingent indices and indices of the children's syntax, and none exceed .53 (less than 30% of the

TABLE 1
Low, Nonsignificant Correlations between Follow-up Child Measures and Corresponding Children's Scores at 22 Months

Child Follow-up Measures to 27 Months	22-Month C MLU	22-Month C Longest Utterance	22-Month C Question Index	22-Month C Auxiliaries	22-Month C Verbs
1b. MLU	.05				
2b. Longest utterance		.17			
3b. Questions			.27		
4b. Auxiliaries				.04	
5b. Verbs					−.08

TABLE 2
Single "Adjustment" Variables: Maternal Noncontingent Indices
When Children Were 22 Months

Child Measures at 22 Months	M MLU	M Verbs	M Auxiliaries
MLU	−.15	.20	.44*
Longest utterance	.10	.12	.25
Question index	−.11	.18	.32
Auxiliaries per verb	−.20	−.19	−.02
Verb complexity	−.19	.17	.25

* $p < .05$.

variance). The highest adjustment occurs in the case we have highlighted already—at 27 months maternal auxiliaries are correlated .53 with children's auxiliaries, indicating relatively high complexity in auxiliaries tends to co-occur for mother and child in our dyads.

CONTINGENT MATERNAL REPLIES AS PREDICTORS OF CHILDREN'S SYNTACTIC GROWTH

Here we examine how the child's growth in syntax is related to the quality of contingent reply immediately given by mothers to their children's prior utterances. The follow-up growth measures for the children will be those we examined in Table 1 and found to be unconfounded variables.

Contingent Maternal Reply Variables

Each contingent reply by the mother to the child's immediately preceding utterance was placed in one of the mutually exclusive categories specified below. For theoretical reasons and on the basis of prior studies, Recasts, Continuations, and Topic Changes are of particular interest. In theoretical terms we have argued (e.g., K. E. Nelson, 1977a, b, 1980, 1981; Nelson et al., 1973; Nelson et al., Note 1) that the child advances in large part through successively analyzing sentences more complex than those in the system already, and that in turn conversational partners who use such sentences in direct, topic-continuing replies to the child's utterance may thereby facilitate language acquisition. This leaves the problem of specifying how much "change" in meaning still should leave the maternal sentence overall scored as some kind of topic "continuation" of the child's original gambit. Below we have tried to be explicit about the possible roles of continuations of different sorts across different developmental levels. Here we would note further only that experimental work has backed the

TABLE 3
Single "Adjustment" Variables: Maternal Noncontingent Indices
When Children Were 27 Months

Child Measures at 27 Months	M MLU	M Verbs	M Auxiliaries
MLU	.18	.29	.22
Longest utterance	.46*	.42*	.32
Question index	.04	.16	.19
Auxiliaries per verb	−.04	.42*	.53*
Verb complexity	.24	.20	.24

* $p < .05$.

notion that topic-continuing Recasts can be effective faciliters of syntactic advance (Nelson et al., 1973; Nelson, 1977a, b, 1981, 1982; Nelson & Denninger, Note 2) and that in one form or another a wide set of investigators has commented on the potential importance for the child's language growth of topic continuations that not only incorporate selected elements of what the child has just said but also add, extend, expand, both add and delete, recast, or otherwise depart from the child's precise structure (e.g., Brown & Bellugi, 1964; Gleason & Weintraub, 1978; Moerk, 1972; Snow & Ferguson, 1977).

Simple Recasts

These replies definitely continued reference to the central meanings in the child's preceding utterances but departed structurally by slight or moderate changes. Such change, by definition, was limited to just one major component of the child's sentence—the subject, the verb, or the object. *Expansions* are a subset of simple recasts—in our data maternal expansions involved change in just one major sentence component, and they "expanded" an incomplete sentence by the child without reordering any elements of the child's sentence. When the child says "Broke." the mother may expand by saying "The truck broke." In contrast, a simple recast may be given to either a complete or incomplete sentence. Examples include: C, "The boy built that house." M, "Oh, was that house built by the boy?"; and, C, "She's funny." M, "Yeah, she is pretty funny."

Complex Recasts

If a maternal utterance kept some direct overlap in meaning but structurally changed two or more of the main components (subject, verb, object) of the child's sentence, then it was called a *complex recast*. The changes involved could be supplying entire new subjects, verbs, or objects or could be revisions of what the child expressed. "It fell." (c) followed by "The barrel fell off the wagon and rolled down the hill," (M) gives one illustration.

Imitations

Exact, immediate imitations of a complete (all the words, same order) or partial (some of the words, but these in the child's order) nature were counted together in this category. In terms of topic there is clearly a continuity of topic between child-utterance and mother reply not only for imitations but also for both kinds of recasts. (Imitations add *no* new words or orders.)

Continuations

These replies were comprised by all topic-continuing responses that did *not* satisfy the definitions for recasts or imitations. Continuations, as compared with these other kinds of reply, thus maintained topics without much explicit overlap in the words of the child's and adult's utterances. Structurally they could have any degree of similarity or dissimilarity to the preceding utterance by the child.

Topic Changes

Semantically these adult replies provided a clear change from the topic of the child's utterance, and they could be expressed in any syntactic form.

A Note on Future Differentiation

If we had collected a substantially larger corpus of data, then it would have been appropriate to also analyze separately many subvarieties of each of the above variables, e.g., simple recasts focused on verb changes. In future work it is anticipated that many investigators will get around to detailing when and how certain highly specific kinds of replies are potent influences in particular phases of language growth.

Outcomes for Separate Maternal Predictors

In Table 4 there are two maternal variables that show positive associations with children's language growth—high maternal use of simple recasts and of topic continuations were both positively associated with the children's language growth, and 6 of 10 possible correlations fell in the range between $+.30$ and $+.45$. By contrast, all 10 correlations were skewed without overlap toward the negative scale for complex recasts and topic changes by the mothers—their

TABLE 4
Children's Syntactic Growth as Predicted by Separate Maternal Language Indices

Child Growth Measures to 27 Months	Maternal Reply Categories When Children Were 22 Months of Age				
	Simple Recasts	Complex Recasts	Imitations	Continuations	Topic Changes
MLU	.34*	−.40**	.03	.36*	−.26
Longest utterance	.43**	−.41**	−.15	.28	−.06
Question index	.25	−.26	−.38*	.35*	.11
Auxiliaries per verb	.35*	−.19	−.10	.12	−.06
Verb complexity	.34*	−.45**	−.10	.33	−.09

** $p < .05$.
* $p < .10$.

correlation with child language growth fell between +.11 and −.45. Likewise, high use of maternal imitations generally showed a modest correlation with slow language growth by the child.

In looking over these data and the extant literature on overall language indices (cf. Brown, 1973; Miller, 1981), we saw no strong reasons to treat MLU or any other single variable as a favored major index of children's language growth. Instead we decided to combine our five unconfounded child variables to give one overall index and to then look at how children low and high on this index compared in terms of the input they received. Our analyses are presented in the next section.

Outcomes for Composite Variables: Positive and Negative Predictors of Syntactic Advances

To give a composite syntactic growth score for each child the child's rank on each of the five variables in Table 4 were summed and averaged. This overall syntactic growth score was then used to see if children high (N = 13, top 13 scores) and low (N = 12, lowest 12 scores) received different input when the input was reduced to just 3 scores at 22 months, where each score reflected a possible common operation for the mother: (a) simple recasts plus continuations—keeping the topic by a simple structural change or by an essentially new structure; (b) imitations, presenting no new semantic or syntactic information; and (c) complex recasts plus topic changes, both of which definitely involve substantial semantic change and may also involve considerable structural departure from the child's prior utterance.

Although we recognize that there are other ways of grouping such maternal data, the reduction was accomplished in this fashion for several primary reasons. First, imitations stand alone as completely borrowed from the child's utterance, whereas simple recasts and continuations may reflect a maternal strategy of maintaining semantic continuity that provides 22-month-olds with opportunities to directly analyze new (for them) syntactic forms in the simple recasts and to indirectly have readiness for such needed analysis encouraged by a fairly frequent influx of these recasts mixed with varied continuations. In contrast, if too much semantic change (in topic changes) or too much syntactic change (in complex recasts) is presented to the 2-month-old, it may be difficult for the child to relate the form or meaning of the maternal sentence back to his or her own syntactic system in a way that will encourage new analysis and syntactic growth.

Reducing our data (though still essentially correlational) to these few variables gives us a picture that seems to make sense both for theory and for possible interventions when certain children are deficient in input. Children who are high in syntactic growth received significantly *more* input as *Simple Recasts/ Continuations* and significantly *less* input as *Complex Recasts/Topic Changes* when compared with the low group in terms of syntactic growth, as Table 5 demonstrates. In addition, the high group's mothers provide relatively fewer imitations (though not significantly so) than do the low group's mothers. (Of course, when one group is higher on one of the composites, given that maternal replies will add—except for rounding—to 1.00, then the other composite and/or imitation must show a reverse pattern between groups. The analyses thus are not independent, but each of the t tests still carries information.)

In sum, because we used unconfounded syntactic growth variables, we have confidence that these outcomes hold an important clue about a facilitating pattern of maternal input to 22- to 27-month-olds: most often staying on the topic either with simple recasts (limited structural changes) or with brand new sentences serving as good topic continuations (total here is 57% of opportunities), and conversely, using only a minority of outright topic changes or structurally complex departures on the child's topic (total here is 34%), and, more speculatively, keeping imitations on the low side also (here, 11%).

TABLE 5
Children's Syntactic Growth as Related to Maternal Composite Input to 22-Month-Olds

Maternal Input Variable as Predictors: Proportions of Reply Opportunities	Children High in Syntactic Growth		Children Low in Syntactic Growth		Differences between Groups	
	Mean	SD	Mean	SD	t	p
1. Simple Recasts plus Continuations	.57	.121	.31	.215	5.03	<.001
2. Complex Recasts plus Topic Changes	.34	.082	.51	.254	3.07	<.003
3. Imitations	.11	.121	.18	.214	1.15	Not sig.

In the discussion below we will argue that these few reduced variables give us a specification of *conversational strategies* that parents and teachers will find feasible to monitor and adjust. Here we offer a similar but distinct set of outcomes when the child growth composite variable concerns noun growth: the mean of the child's rank on (a) comprehension performance for noun concepts first introduced to the children in the Fiffin Project (see Nelson & Bonvillian, 1978) plus (b) 27-month noun phrase complexity (elements per noun phrase). Note that mothers were held to the same number of uses of the new nouns but that they, and the children, were free to use the nouns in any kind of sentence and with any kinds of modifiers and suffixes. Table 6 shows again the pattern observed in Table 5 (for child syntax) in terms of direction of effect: children high in language growth—here, on nouns—had mothers who used more continuations and simple recasts, fewer topic changes and complex recasts, and less imitation. The differences are that for noun growth, as opposed to other syntactic growth, imitations were more strongly detrimental and topic changes along with complex recasts were less detrimental. The one facilitative (positively associated) set of conversational replies for both growth areas was frequent maternal use of simple recasts and continuations.

Further Evidence on Varying Maternal Assumptions About Appropriate Adjustments

At 27 months as well as 22 months of age for the children, the mothers in this well-educated, essentially middle-class American sample appeared to make very widely disparate assumptions about how to reply to children. This buttresses observations in other American samples and in other cultures which point toward the view that *few* kinds of replies to children at any particular stage are *necessary*

TABLE 6
Children's Composite Noun Phrase Growth as Related to Maternal Composite Input to 22-Month-Olds

Maternal Input Variable as Predictors: Proportions of Reply Opportunities	Children High in Growth		Children Low in Growth		Differences between Groups	
	Mean	SD	Mean	SD	t	p
1. Simple Recasts plus Continuations	.55	.081	.34	.260	3.74	<.002
2. Complex Recasts plus Topic Changes	.38	.098	.47	.271	1.50	Not sig.
3. Imitations	.08	.091	.21	.211	2.80	<.02

for the child's progress in syntax. In our sample, children's rates of progress between 22 and 27 months and between 27 months and 4½ years could be related, as we have seen, to how mothers typically replied. But even the slow progressers, given few "positive catalysts," still tended to make considerable advances over time and to end up as linguistically well-endowed 4½-year-olds. Table 7 shows the remarkably wide contrasts between maternal reply strategies. The next section provides some concrete examples of reply strategies.

Excerpts Illustrating Frequent Seizing of Opportunities for Simple Recasts and Topic Continuations (Child's Age = 22 Months)

Child No. 4

C	(58):	Mine.
M	(131):	Yours?
C	(71):	I got it.
M	(144):	You got what?
C	(111):	This swim.
M	(313):	Yea, that swims.

Child No. 5

C	(175):	Swim him, ocean, huh?
M	(206):	I don't think he does. (Continuation)
C	(176):	Look at!
M	(209):	Look at that.

Child No. 6

C	(51):	It's pretty.
M	(63):	It is pretty.
C	(231):	I hold.
M	(260):	All right. (Continuation)
C	(267):	This gone.
M	(301):	What is gone?

These examples illustrate *rare events*. Once in awhile an adult has a clear opportunity to give a simple, informative, easy-to-process reply to a child in such a way that it is likely to illustrate new ways of forming even simple sentences. "Mine" changed to the question "Yours?" is a beautifully simple example. Similarly, the contracted auxiliary in "It's pretty" is recast as an uncontracted auxiliary in "It is pretty."

A strong input contrast holds between the dyads with children 4, 5, and 6 and those with children 1, 2, and 3. The value of this comparison is enhanced

TABLE 7
Variation in Maternal Replies (Proportions of Reply Opportunities) When Children Are 22 and 27 Months of Age

	To 22-Month-Olds					To 27-Month-Olds				
	Mean	SD	3 Lowest Scores			3 Highest Scores			Mean	SD	3 Lowest Scores			3 Highest Scores		

	Mean	SD	3 Lowest Scores			3 Highest Scores			Mean	SD	3 Lowest Scores			3 Highest Scores		
1) M Simple Recasts	.104	.103	.000	.000	.000	.250	.267	.333	.087	.067	.000	.000	.000	.200	.200	.222
2) M Continuations	.331	.189	.000	.000	.000	.550	.644	.667	.402	.184	.000	.000	.182	.568	.638	.800
Sum of 1 + 2	.435	.206	.000	.000	.000	.600	.616	.667	.490	.192	.000	.000	.304	.723	.750	.800
3) M Complex Recasts	.256	.165	.000	.000	.000	.500	.667	.667	.264	.133	.000	.000	.100	.426	.455	.500
4) M Topic Changes	.166	.151	.000	.000	.000	.333	.333	.667	.082	.077	.000	.000	.000	.197	.200	.261
Sum of 3 + 4	.422	.202	.000	.200	.217	.667	.834	1.000	.346	.151	.000	.118	.182	.500	.546	.652
5) M Imitations	.144	.171	.000	.000	.000	.400	.400	.500	.152	.214	.000	.000	.000	.333	.500	.999

TABLE 8
With Initial-Level Matches for Excerpted Children, Rate of Syntactic Growth and Maternal Replies Are Related

S#	Rank on Syntactic Growth	MLU 22 Months	Longest Utterance 22 Months	Simple Recasts	Continuations	Complex Recasts	Topic Changes
Low-Growth Subjects							
1	16.5	1.44	3	.053	.368	.368	.158
2	25	1.62	4	.000	.000	.667	.333
3	14	1.57	4	.000	.167	.167	.667
High-Growth Subjects							
4	6	1.64	4	.100	.550	.050	.150
5	8	1.45	4	.150	.450	.250	.100
6	1	1.64	3	.067	.433	.267	.100
Mean for All Subjects	12.5						

because the 6 child-mother pairs are both matched and different. As Table 8 shows, the children at 22-months-old are matched on mean and maximum utterance length. But the mothers nevertheless show a contrast: Maternal responses to children 4, 5, and 6 are weighted much more heavily toward simple recasts and continuations whereas the relative weighting for replies to children 1, 2, and 3 is toward complex recasts and continuations. In line with our discussions and data above, relatively rapid syntactic growth (rankings in top 13 out of 25) between 22 and 27 months is clearly associated with the "stage-appropriate" replies of simple recasts and continuations for 22-month-olds when we match for their language levels. In combination with our other evidence, these results also point toward the conclusion that *some* (but not all) mothers of 22-month-olds successfully combine high use of the "positive catalysts" (simple recasts, continuations) with low use of the "negative catalysts" (complex recasts, topic changes).

DISCUSSION

Drawing upon many other recent projects as well as the data presented above, a series of conclusions and implications are organized according to separate themes.

Theme One: Stage-Appropriate Recasts and Continuations Matter at Least as Positive Catalysts

Language growth for 22- to 27-month-olds was facilitated in our data above by maternal replies that either continued the topic with a fundamentally new sentence or that continued the topic by providing a recast (with expansions as one subtype) with the same core meaning but with simple, limited structural change. Variations on recasts (with diverse labels provided) in other correlational work also have been among a small number of maternal reply categories that are positively associated with syntactic advance by 12- to 33-month-olds (Newport, 1977), 19- to 33-month-olds (Cross, 1977, 1978), and 18- to 42-month-olds (Wells, 1980; Wells et al., 1983). Furthermore, experimental introduction of a "bonus" of adult recasts in conversations with a child has been shown in a series of studies (see Nelson, 1980; Baker, Note 3) to aid in the young child's progress in syntax.

The tendency in most prior work to consider one simple variable at a time may lead us to overlook important strategies that parents and teachers may adopt. Although our suggestions here are tentative, it appears to us that children's syntax facilitation is related to a fairly natural strategy on the part of mothers— *either* to continue the conversational topic with a fundamentally new reply structurally *or* to continue the conversational topic with a simple recast that introduces moderate structural change relative to the child's preceding sentence (cf. Tables 6 and 8). Choices constantly arise in converstion with a language-learning child, and a skillful conversational partner may seize recasting opportunities when they arise and may seize other means of topic continuation when recasts are simply not possible or not appropriate, given the context and the child's prior utterance. Adults who thus present to 22- to 27-months-olds a lot of topic continuations that are *not* recasts when recasts would be inappropriate may thereby enhance the child's persistent attention to adult replies (they are usually relevant, good continuations of some sort) and in turn lead the child to pay close attention to and encode relatively simple recasts when they can be formulated by the adult. The argument, thus, is that *moderate departures structurally (simple recasts) from the child's utterances may enhance syntactic advance for the child if they are embedded in smoothly continuing discourse*. We would like to see much more intensive data on this question, but our point again is that a particular reply such as one particular simple recast has effects that are dependent on other speech acts, other aspects of adult-child discourse. Accordingly, as news from varied projects comes in, it is hoped that both theoretical models and intervention designs may move away from simplistic counts of particular utterances or utterance types or speech acts to models that represent strategies adults can use for dealing with a child at a specified language level. Such strategies would encompass the many choices adults have for appropriate replies across relatively long discourse sequences and thus would be concerned with attention maintenance and the child's discourse skills, not solely with the child's level of syntactic development.

Thinking a bit further about an agenda for future work, the delineation of answers to the following is needed: (a) Are recasts more than mere positive catalysts or "helpers?" (b) What other reply strategies besides recasting-or-continuing have positive roles in language acquisition? (c) How closely "stage-appropriate" do recasts need to be? Here much finer differentiation than "simple recasts" (positive correlations with 22-month-olds' growth) and "complex recasts" (negative correlations with growth) need to be tested out in both naturalistic and experimental research. (d) Particularly since recasts have been reported to decline in frequency as the child's syntactic skills reach higher levels (e.g., Cross, 1977; see also Table 7 above), are there developmental points where their impact ceases? (e) How can useful recasts and other replies be best embedded in long discourse sequences?

Theme Two: Remarkably Wide Individual and Cultural Differences Still Leave Room for Input Effects

If we ask the question "Do all mothers and caretakers in every culture conversationally 'adjust' in the same ways to their children's language levels?" the answer is "Definitely not!" The answer remains unchanged if we stay within a single culture. And it is further clear that even if we bypass a look at "all" children, then among children who have been shown to progress well in syntax there is a very wide range of differences in the input they received (see Nelson, 1980, 1982). Together these observations demand the conclusion that there are *many* components of input for most children that are *not necessary* for their syntactic growth. We shall next examine a few intriguing angles on this problem—in terms of empirical observations and theortical argument. But the preface is needed that even limited quantities of certain important input elements may play sufficient or catalytic roles in acquisition, no matter how strong the evidence that they are not absolutely necessary elements.

The Kaluli

Among the Kaluli of Papua, New Guinea, the cultural assumptions about the social exposure and the language exposure appropriate to offer to 1- to 4-year-olds appear substantially different from those observed in most other cultures studies so far. Schieffelin (1979) showed that Kaluli mothers will hold the child in various social situations so that the child becomes the apparent addressor of another person while the mother supplies the child's part in the dialogue, as when the mother "says" for the child "Is that yours?!" in a sarcastic tone to shame (on the child's part) an older child who has food or other resources belonging to the language acquirer. Moreover, the child is asked to regularly repeat complete or "hard" adult sentences of this sort (rather than simplified "Motherese") through a standard repetion request: For example, "Is that yours? REPEAT." Thus, more competence of the young child to cope with complex linguistic structures and complex social roles is assumed than in American or European cultures. Nevertheless, preliminary observations indicate the Kaluli master language well and on the same sort of timetable observed in other cultures. These data support suggestions made on other grounds that much of what we see in adult input to children in terms of reduced rate of speech and altered structures of sentences, when compared to adult-to-adult conversation, is not necessary for the child's gradual, progressive movement toward adult grammatical structures (De Paulo & Bonvillian, 1974; Nelson, 1980; Nelson et al., 1973; Newport et al., 1978).

Unusual or Disturbed Language

If the child or the parent is seriously deviant in language, then what are the relations between input variations and language growth? This question is not well researched, but a few interesting beginnings deserve mention. Cross, Nienhuys, and Kirkman (1983) have found evidence suggestive of special maternal adjustments (effects yet to be tested) to children who are autistic or dysphasic. From another angle, Schiff (1979) provides some evidence that normal language growth can occur despite substantial deviations in input—a point made easier to understand by a theory stressing the child's capacity to effectively utilize appropriate but infrequent examples (cf. rare events, below) mixed with more numerous, nonstimulating input examples. In addition, the child may seize upon valuable but infrequent input from visitors or family members who are not the primary source of input. Other forms of "adjustment" in input are of course required if the child has specific processing or moter output difficulties (Bonvillian & Nelson, 1982). Finally, it is clear that extreme deprivation of input and conversations in any fluent and processable mode can severely curtail language acquisition (Curtiss, 1977; Sachs & Johnson, 1976).

Daycare and Language Acquisition

Many reports on children in daycare indicate that 1- to 5-year-olds given "high-quality" (as defined by ratio of teacher to children, curriculum, education of teacher, and other resources) daycare make equivalent progress in language acquisition to children from similar backgrounds who stay home with their mothers during weekdays. In a series of varied and informative studies on this topic, Cross and her colleagues (Cross et al., Note 4) find that despite overall fluctuations in input attributable to daycare personnel as opposed to mothers, Australian children in daycare show few deficits in comparison with matched children at home with their mothers. Again, these data are particularly persuasive on the point that *high quantities* of "typical," "Western" maternal replies to children are *not required* for the children's success in code cracking. But they leave open which qualitative aspects of input may be essential and/or helpful to the child's development of language.

Theme Three: Rare Events

The notion of rare events can be put simply: a little of the right kind of evidence for the child's current level is often all that is required to induce an advance to the next level. In the preschool period, this principle seems to hold for many areas beyond syntax, as documented by input-controlled studies in such domains as semantic concept acquisition (Bates et al., 1983; Nelson & Bonvillian, 1973, 1978; Nelson & Nelson, 1978; Oviatt, Note 5), graphic representational skills (Wilson & Wilson, 1982), and object permanence (Nelson, 1971, 1973).

For syntax, one indication that only a little bit of the right evidence will induce change comes from experimental work in which new adult sources supply recasts in the form of sentences with complex-verb, passive, or tag structures and in which children who lacked these forms now begin using them after a few minutes or a few hours of such recasting (Nelson, 1977a, b; 1980, 1981, Note 9).

Similarly, many correlational studies—such as our own data in the immediately preceding section—support the notion that many children who receive very low frequencies of certain structures in input still succeed in analyzing these structures and incorporating them into their own productive systems for both first and early second (or coordinate) languages (cf. Brown & Hanlon, 1976; Gleason & Weintraub, 1978; Aronsson, Note 6; Lindholm, 1980; Nelson, 1980).

A Closer Look at Frequency

At first glance, our discussion of rare events of far might seem to imply that the child's strong abilities—in analyzing rare but highly appropriate examples input when they are encountered—would preclude any substantial effect of the frequency of the to-be-acquired forms in input. But in our view, whether more frequently presented examples in input are more rapidly acquired by the child than less frequent examples in input depends entirely upon *how* those examples are inbedded in the fabric of conversation. That is, we have argued that only a small minority of the examples will actually influence the child's advance in language. This means that some very frequently used examples, some favorite expressions of a mother or a father, may have virtually no impact on the child's progress, because they do not occur in just the right fashion in context nonverbally, in context verbally, and in relation to the child's attention. Conversely, examples that do not occur with low frequency may be very important examples because they are very nicely dropped into conversations so that the child can process them fully. Nevertheless, for the broader picture, as frequency of a form increases in input to the child, it seems likely that acquisition will be aided for many, if not all, forms. This is so because, all other things being equal, more carefully attended to and successfully analyzed examples (rare events) will be found for those semantic forms, phonological forms, pragmatic forms, and syntactic forms that have the highest frequency in input. It is essential to add that frequency effects need not follow a simple, linear, consistent pattern: all other things are *not* always equal and there are all kinds of attentional and contextual constraints that preclude simply doubling or tripling or quadrupling the amount of attention and analysis the child will be able to give to a particular form.

Theme Four: "General" Adjustments Such as Rate, Pitch, and Intonation May Matter Too, But Only as Catalysts

Most adults studied so far in most cultures "adjust down" to language-learning children from adult-to-adult conversational levels, in these senses: young children receive sentences with higher pitch, slower rate, and altered, more contrastive intonation patterns (e.g., Blount, 1972, 1977, 1981; Blount & Padgug, 1977; DePaulo & Bonvillian, 1978; Snow, 1972, 1977; Snow & Ferguson,

1977). Even among the Kaluli, where, as we have seen, the complexity of utterances and discourse to the young child appear not to reflect adjustment to the child's young linguistic age, pitch and other speaking-cue adjustments are made to language learners (Schieffelin, 1979). For a variety of reasons, we are willing to speculate that these adjustments are not necessary to the child's acquisition of a first or second language, the foremost reason being that there is as yet no evidence at all that points toward such a necessary role. In addition, it is clear that one role of these general "baby talk" features may be to make the adult speaker more comfortable (even when alone with the child) and in social situations to signal to other mature listeners that they are not the target of the speech. At the same time, of course, the child may benefit from clear signals that particular utterances are directed to him or her; attention to the speech and the context may be enhanced. Overall, it is likely that some input adjustments in pitch, rate, pausing (cf. Prorok, 1983), and intonation will be *positive catalysts*, through enhanced attention and processing, for the acquisition of syntactic and discourse skills. However, it is possible that some adults may "overdo" such adjustments and may speak slowly enough or with enough exaggeration in voice qualities to make processing and memory more rather than less difficult; in such cases the input adjustments would be *negative* catalysts. A nice experimental demonstration that an optimal rate—neither too slow nor too fast—of adult speech applies when children's sentence imitations are at issue has been provided by Bonvillian, Raeburn, and Horan (1979). Similarly, experimental techniques are revealing for language comprehension, showing that both verbal redundancy and nonverbal contextual support enhance language comprehension (da Costa, Note 7; Schwam, 1982; Shatz & Gelman, 1973; Shipley, Gleitman, & Smith, 1973; Smith, 1970; cf. also Wheldall & Swan, 1976, on intonation).

Theme Five: Beyond Level-of-Acquisition Adjustments, Different Children May Have Different Sensitivities to the Same Input Characteristics

This conclusion is suggested in part by evidence that there are not only important style and strategy differences in how children put language together but also that "mismatches" between maternal style and child style may complicate and at least slow down the child's progress in language acquisition (Bloom et al., 1974; Nelson, 1973, 1981; K. E. Nelson, 1981; Nelson et al., Note 8).

A second line of data that indicate different children may respond to input in different ways comes from work with children who have serious difficulties in language acquisition. Rutter (1978) finds that even when maternal speech input is matched for autistic and normal, nonautistic children, there are profound language-learning deficits; thus, similar input appears to be treated very differently by the autistic child. On the other side of the coin, when switches to sign language or other special input adjustments have been made, certain autistic and other language-deviant children have shown a great sensitivity to and efficient use of the new input in progressing in language levels (e.g., Bonvillian & Nelson, 1982).

The Opening Theme Revisited: Input Both Matters and Doesn't Matter

Given all the data and arguments to this point in this chapter, it seems safe to state that some input is "well-adjusted" and "important" to the child's acquisition of language and other input doesn't matter at all for language progress. Goldin-Meadow (1979, 1983) has in a related manner indicated that different aspects of the child's emerging system may have different requirements—some may be "resistant" and depend on very little necessary input and others may be more "fragile" and subject to many required inputs as well as many helpful but not necessary inputs. These concerns are addressed by Nelson in a fairly differentiated scheme presented in 1980 (Nelson, 1980). There it is argued that for any particular structure at any particular stage in acquisition, an adequate theory would specify which inputs fall into the following categories: irrelevant, negative catalyst, positive catalyst (facilitator), sufficient only, necessary, and necessary and sufficient. Building on this scheme, below we detail the considerations appropriate to an analysis of all potential varieties of "positive" effects of input on a child's progress in syntax acquisition.

So, specification of an input adjustment that will have a positive effect at a catalytic, or sufficient, or necessary, or necessary and sufficient level should be given in the following ways:

1. Adjusted to the child's current *structural level*—above but not too far above that level.
2. Adjusted to the *discourse* situation—placed so that the child has a good chance to attend to, make social sense of, and encode the input example (cf. Sachs, 1983; Wells, 1980; Zukow, Reilly, & Greenfield, 1982).
3. Adjusted to the child's *strategic approach* to learning language—input that works well for one child at a certain stage may be useless or detrimental for another child operating with another strategy (cf. esp. Bloom et al., 1974; Clark, 1982, 1983; Kuczaj, 1982; K. Nelson, 1973, 1975, 1981; K. E. Nelson, 1981, 1982; K. E. Nelson et al., Note 8).
4. Adjusted to the *other* inputs the child receives. When a full set of useful input for the child's current stage is not supplied by the primary interaction partner (whether mother, father, grandmother, sibling, or whoever), then the child may fill *gaps* in the input through interaction with others. Westerman and Havstad (1982) indicate in a case study how this process may proceed. But thorough research that details and

differentiates the actual patterns of input from multiple sources is very badly needed to give us a realistic picture of the child's language-acquisition processes.

Note again that the focus is not on simple "input effects." Instead, the crucial events—the rare events that make for change—are seen as combinations of *readiness* by the child, in terms of prior linguistic structures in place, prior cognitive structures in place, and current, momentary, attention and processing tendencies, together with a flow of conversation which makes available in input those examples which challenge the current level of the child and do so in a way that makes attention and processing easy.

We are searching especially for necessary and sufficient events of this sort, through a series of studies (e.g., Nelson, 1980; Baker, Note 3). We think there is a realistic chance of finding many such examples. In the meantime, it has been possible to definitely show that certain kinds of examples of passives or tag questions or other forms which the child lacks may be triggered within a few hours (or less) of conversation that has been designed to incorporate the target examples in ways we think enhance processing and comparison by the child. The evidence establishes that the intervention in each of the series of studies now completed was *sufficient* for inducing change (Nelson, 1977, 1980; Nelson & Denninger, Note 2). So at the very least we have established that the boost in certain kinds of input that we provided, together with inputs the child was already receiving, is sufficient for change. The detailed examples that we provided in the input during intervention may have been either just positive catalysts which would not have been sufficient without the other pieces of input to induce change, or they may have been sufficient in themselves for inducing the change. This latter interpretation seems particularly promising in the case of forms like passives where our sampling of maternal input included very few or no examples of passives prior to intervention (Nelson, Note 9; Baker, Note 3). This interpretation is further enhanced by the fact that full passives using a wide range of verbs and both reversible and irreversible passives were induced within several hours of intervention in children below 4 years of age. This contrasts sharply with the account of passive acquisition given by nearly all other investigators. Some of them argue, as does Horgan (1978), that productive control of such a wide range of passives may not be achieved until 11 years of age when no special input has been provided to the child.

Closing Theme: Specificity in Theories Allows Specificity in Education and Intervention

In the absence of well-elaborated theories of how the child attends to and analyzes different input components, most intervention attempts for the last 50 years have paid little attention to the input received by the child with language delay or language deviance. Instead, if a child lacked certain structures or skills, the therapists "drilled" the child on these deficits, paying little attention to *how* the forms should be embedded in therapeutic input, and asked the parents to do little. A new approach to intervention becomes possible as we construct a detailed, well-documented theory of how specific input influences acquisition of particular language structures. With such a theory in place, the strategy of choice would be to analyze both the child's language level and any gaps or idiosyncracies in input to the child. Then the interventions can be conducted by parents and therapists and can be directed at filling gaps in input and at tailoring conversations to the specific needs of the child. In consequence, the power of intervention may be greatly enhanced by having multiple input sources redirecting their conversational efforts away from any negatively catalytic or irrelevant replies to the child (at this stage) and toward the necessary and helpful variations on conversation for this child at his or her current level of language mastery.

REFERENCE NOTES

1. NELSON, K. E., DENNINGER, M., KAPLAN, B. J., & BONVILLIAN, J. D. *Varied angles on how children progress in syntax.* Paper presented to the Society for Research in Child Development, San Francisco, March 1979.
2. NELSON, K. E., & DENNINGER, M. *The shadow technique in the investigation of children's acquisition of new syntactic forms.* Manuscript New School for Social Research, 1977.
3. BAKER, N. *The effects of recasting versus modeling: An intensive language input study.* Unpublished Master's Thesis, The Pennsylvania State University, 1982.
4. CROSS, T. G., PARMENTER, J., JUCHNOWSKI, M., & JOHNSON, G. *Effects of day-care experience on the formal and pragmatic development of young children.* Paper presented to the International Association for the Study of Child Language, Vancouver, August 1981.
5. OVIATT, S. L. *The development of language comprehension in infancy.* Unpublished doctoral dissertation. University of Toronto, 1979.
6. ARONSSON, K. *Bilingual acquisition and metalinguistic skills.* Unpublished doctoral dissertation. University of Lund, Sweden, 1980.
7. DACOSTA, A. NICOLACI. *Redundancies and children's language comprehension.* Paper presented to the 1982 Child Language Seminar, University of London, March 1982.
8. NELSON, K. E., BAKER, N., DENNINGER, M., BONVILLIAN, J. D., & KAPLAN, B. J. *Language learning styles that combine semantic, syntactic, and discourse components.* Paper presented to the International Association for the Study of Child Language, Vancouver, August 1981.
9. NELSON, K. E. *Individual differences and rare events in language acquisition.* Guest lecture presented to the 1982 Child Language Seminar, University of London, March 1982. (*First Language,* in press.)

REFERENCES

BATES, E., BRETHERTON, I., SHORE, C., & MCNEW, S. Names, gestures, and objects: Symbolization in infancy and aphasia. In K. E. Nelson (Ed.), *Children's language* (Vol. 4). Hillsdale, N.J.: Erlbaum, 1983.
BLOOM, L., HOOD, L., & LIGHTBOWN, P. Imitation in language development: If, when, and why. *Cognitive Psychology,* 1974, *6,* 380–420.

BLOUNT, B. D. Parental speech and language acquisition: Some Luo and Samoan examples. *Anthropological Linguistics*, 1972, *14*, 119–130.
BLOUNT, B. G. Parental speech to children: Cultural patterns. In M. Saville-Traike (Ed.), *Linguistics and anthropology*. Washington, DC: Georgetown University Press, 1977.
BLOUNT, B. G. Elicitation strategies in parental speech acts. In P. S. Dale & D. Ingram (Eds.), *Child language: An international perspective*. Baltimore, MD: University Park Press, 1981.
BLOUNT, B. D., & PADGUG, E. J. Prosodic, paralinguistic, and interactional features in parent-child speech: English and Spanish. *Journal of Child Language*, 1977, *4*, 67–86.
BONVILLIAN, J. D., & NELSON, K. E. Exceptional cases of language acquisition. In K. E. Nelson (Ed.), *Children's language* (Vol. 3). Hillsdale, N.J.: Erlbaum, 1982.
BONVILLIAN, J. D., RAEBURN, V. P., & HORAN, E. A. Talking to children: The effects of rate, intonation, and length on children's sentence imitation. *Journal of Child Language*, 1979, *6*, 459–467.
BROWN, R. *A first language: The early stages*. Cambridge, MA: Harvard University Press, 1973.
BROWN, R., & BELLUGI, U. Three process in the child's acquisition of syntax. *Harvard Educational Review*, 1964, *34*, 133–151.
BROWN, R., & HANLON, C. Derivational complexity and order of acquisition in child speech. In J. R. Hayes (Ed.), *Cognition and the development of language*. New York: Wiley, 1970.
CAZDEN, C. Environmental assistance to the child's acquisition of grammar. Unpublished doctoral dissertation. Harvard, 1965.
CLARK, R. Theory and method in child-language research: Are we assuming too much? In S. A. Kuczaj (Ed.), *Language development: Syntax and semantics*. Hillsdale, NJ: Erlbaum, 1982.
CLARK, R. How do children learn to talk? In K. Wheldall & R. Riding (Eds.), *Psychological aspects of learning and teaching*. London: Croom Helm Ltd., 1983.
CROSS, T. G. Mother's speech adjustments: The contribution of selected child listener variables. In C. E. Snow & C. A. Ferguson (Eds.), *Talking to children*. Cambridge: Cambridge University Press, 1977.
CROSS, T. G. Mothers' speech and its association with rate of linguistic development in young children. In N. Waterson & C. Snow (Eds.), *The development of communication*. New York: Wiley, 1978.
CROSS, T. G., NIENHUYS, T. G., & KIRKMAN, M. Parent-child interaction with receptively disabled children: Some determinant of maternal speech style. In K. E. Nelson (Ed.), *Children's language* (Vol. 5) New York: Gardner Press, 1983.
CURTISS, S. *Genie: A psychological study of a modern-day "wild child"*. New York: Academic, 1977.
DEPAULO, B. M., & BONVILLIAN, J. D. The effect on language development of the special characteristics of speech addressed to children. *Journal of Psycholinguistic Research*, 1978, *7*, 189–211.
FERGUSON, C. A. Baby talk in six languages. *American Anthrolopogist*, 1964, *66*, 103–114.
GLEASON, J. B., & WEINTRAUB, S. Input language and the acquisition of communicative competence. In K. E. Nelson (Ed.), *Children's language* (Vol. 1). New York: Gardner Press, 1978.
GOLDIN-MEADOW, S. Structure in a manual communication system developed without a conventional language model: Language without a helping hand. In H. Whitaker & H. A. Whitaker (Eds.), *Studies in neurolinguistics* (Vol. 4). New York: Academic, 1979.
GOLDIN-MEADOW, S. Language development under atypical conditions: Implications of a study of deaf children of hearing parents. In K. E. Nelson (Ed.), *Children's language* (Vol. 5). Hillsdale, N.J.: Erlbaum, 1983.
HORGAN, D. The development of the full passive. *Journal of Child Language*, 1978, *5*, 65–80.
KUCZAJ, S. A. On the nature of syntactic development. In S. A. Kuczaj (Ed.), *Language development: Syntax and semantics*. Hillsdale, NJ: Erlbaum, 1982.
LINDHOLM, K. J. Bilingual children: Some interpretations of cognitive and linguistic development. In K. E. Nelson (Ed.), *Children's language* (Vol. 2). New York: Gardner Press, 1980.

MENYUK, P. *The acquisition and development of language.* Englewood Cliffs, NJ: Prentice-Hall, 1971.
MILLER, J. F. *Assessing language production in children.* Baltimore, MD: University Park Press, 1981.
MOERK, E. Principles of interaction in language learning. *Merrill-Palmer Quarterly,* 1972, *18,* 229-257.
MOERK, E. Changes in verbal child-mother interactions with increasing language skills of the child. *Journal of Psycholinguistic Research,* 1974, *3,* 101-116.
NELSON, K. Structures and strategies in learning to talk. *Monographs of the Society for Research in Child Development,* 1973, 149, *38* (1-2).
NELSON, K. Individual differences in early semantic and syntactic development. *Annals of the New York Academy of Sciences,* 1975, *263,* 132-139.
NELSON, K. Individual differences in language development. *Developmental Psychology,* 1981, *17,* 170-187.
NELSON, K. E. Facilitating children's syntax acquisition. *Developmental Psychology,* 1977, *13,* 101-107. (a)
NELSON, K. E. Aspects of language acquisition and use from age two to age twenty. *Journal of the American Academy of Child Psychiatry,* 1977, *16,* 584-607. Also appears in *Annual Progress in Child Psychiatry and Child Development (volume 11),* S. Chess and A. Thomas (Eds.) (b)
NELSON, K. E. Theories of the child's acquisition of syntax: A look at rare events and at necessary, catalytic, and irrelevant components of mother-child conversation. *Annals of the New York Academy of Sciences, 345,* 1980.
NELSON, K. E. Toward a rare event cognitive comparison theory of syntax acquisition. In P. S. Dale & D. Ingran (Eds.), *Child language: An international perspective.* Baltimore, MD: University Park Press, 1981.
NELSON, K. E. Experimental gambits in the service of language acquisition theory: From the Fiffin Project to Operation Input Swap. In S. A. Kuczaj (Ed.), *Language development: Syntax and semantics.* Hillsdale, NJ: Erlbaum, 1982.
NELSON, K. E., & BONVILLIAN, J. D. Early language development: Conceptual growth and related processes between 2 and 4½ years of age. In K. E. Nelson (Ed.), *Children's language* (Vol. 1). New York: Gardner Press, 1978.
NELSON, K. E., CARSKADDON, G., & BONVILLIAN, J. D. Syntax acquisition: Impact of experimental variation in adult verbal interaction with the child. *Child Development,* 1973, *44,* 497-504.
NEWPORT, E. Motherese: The speech of mothers to young children. In N. Castellan, D. Pisoni, & G. Potts (Eds.), *Cognitive theory* (Vol. 2). Hillsdale, NJ: Lawrence Erlbaum Associates, 1977.
NEWPORT, E. L., GLEITMAN, H., & GLEITMAN, L. R. Mother, I'd rather do it myself: Some effects and non-effects of maternal speech style. In C. E. Snow & C. A. Ferguson (Eds.), *Talking to children.* Cambridge: Cambridge University Press, 1977.
PROROK, E. M. S. Language development in the natural environment: A functional analysis of mother-child speech. In K. E. Nelson (Ed.), *Children's language* (Vol. 4). Hillsdale, N.J.: Erlbaum, 1983.
RUTTER, M. Language disorder and infantile autism. In M. Rutter & E. Schopler, *Autism: A reappraisal of concepts and treatment.* New York: Plenum, 1978.
SACHS, J. Talking about the there and then: The emergence of displaced reference in parent-child discourse. In K. E. Nelson (Ed.), *Children's language* (Vol. 4). Hillsdale, N.J.: Erlbaum, 1983.
SACHS, J., & JOHNSON, M. L. Language development in a hearing child of deaf parents. In W. von Raffler-Engel & Y. Lebrun (Eds.), *Baby talk and infant speech.* Lisse, Netherlands: Swets & Zeitlinger, 1976.

SCHIEFFELIN, B. B. Getting it together: An ethnographic approach to the study of the development of communicative competence. In E. Ochs & B. Schieffelin (Eds.), *Developmental pragmatics*. New York: Academic, 1979.

SCHIFF, N. The influence of deviant maternal input on the development of language during the preschool years. *Journal of Speech and Hearing Research,* 1979, *22,* 581–603.

SCHWAM, F. Signs and strategies: The interactive processes of sign language learning. In K. E. Nelson (Ed.), *Children's language* (Vol. 3). Hillsdale, N.J.: Erlbaum, 1982.

SHATZ, M. On mechanisms of language acquisition: Can features of the communicative environment account for language acquisition? In L. Gleitman & E. Wanner (Eds.), *Language acquisition: The state of the art*. New York: Cambridge University Press, 1981.

SHATZ, M., & GELMAN, R. The development of communication skills: Modifications in the speech of young children as a function of listener. *Monographs of the Society for Research in Child Development,* 1973, *38* (5), 152.

SHIPLEY, E. S., SMITH, C. S., & GLEITMAN, L. R. A study in the acquisition of language: Free responses to commands. *Language,* 1969, *45,* 322–342.

SMITH, C. S. An experimental approach to children's linguistic competence. In J. R. Hayes (Ed.), *Cognition and the development of language*. New York: Wiley, 1970.

SNOW, C. E. Mothers' speech to children learning language. *Child Development,* 1972, *43,* 549–565.

SNOW, C. E. Mothers' speech research: From input to interaction. In C. E. Snow & C. A. Ferguson (Eds.), *Talking to children*. London: Cambridge University Press, 1977.

SNOW, C. E., & FERGUSON, C. A. (EDS.), *Talking to children*. London: Cambridge University Press, 1977.

WELLS, G. Apprenticeship in meaning. In K. E. Nelson (Ed.), *Children's language* (Vol. 2). New York: Gardner Press, 1980.

WELLS, G., BARNES, S., GUTFREUND, M., & SATFERLY, D. Characteristics of adult speech which predict children's language development. *Journal of Child Language,* 1983, in press.

WESTERMAN, M. A., & HAVSTAD, L. F. A pattern-oriented model of caretaker-child interaction, psychopathology, and control. In K. E. Nelson (Ed.), *Children's language* (Vol. 3). Hillsdale, N.J.: Erlbaum, 1982.

WHELDALL, K., & SWANN, W. The effect of intonational emphasis on sentence comprehension in severely subnormal and normal children. *Language and Speech,* 1976, *19,* 87–99.

WILSON, B., & WILSON, M. *Teaching children to draw*. Englewood Cliffs, N.J.: Prentice-Hall, 1982.

ZUKOW, P. G., REILLY, J., & GREENFIELD, P. M. Making the absent present: Facilitating the transition from sensorimotor to linguistic communication. In K. E. Nelson (Ed.), *Children's language* (Vol. 3). Hillsdale, N.J.: Erlbaum, 1982.

3
The Development of the Functions of Private Speech: A Review of the Piaget–Vygotsky Debate

Anthony D. Pellegrini
University of Georgia

ABSTRACT

The paper reviews the seminal theories of Piaget and Vygotsky on origins and functions of private speech. The theories of both Piaget and Vygotsky are outlined regarding the social origins of private speech and the cognitive functions of private speech. First, empirical research relating to the social sensitivity of young children's language will be reviewed: infant-mother interaction studies and the effect of different contexts on the generation of preschoolers' private speech. Second, studies investigating the development of the self-regulating functions of private speech will be reviewed, i.e., verbal mediation studies, Soviet studies, naturalistic studies of spontaneously generated private speech.

INTRODUCTION

In this chapter the literature on the development of functions preschoolers' private speech will be reviewed. Private speech is defined here as language to self. The seminal work on private speech was done by Piaget (1926) and Vygotsky (1962, 1978). In this chapter each of these theories and research relevant to them will be reviewed. The review will be limited to a discussion of these two positions because of space limitations; Fuson's extensive review (1979) should also be referred to by students of private speech. This chapter on private speech is organized in the following manner. First, the debate over the social origins of private speech will be discussed. Next, the cognitive functions of private speech will be reviewed. Within this section Piaget's views on language and cognition

57

will be contrasted with the traditional Soviet stand on the subject. Last, empirical studies relating to the cognitive functions of private speech will be discussed and evaluated.

THE SOCIAL ORIGINS OF PRIVATE SPEECH

Piaget (1926) characterized preschoolers' private speech as egocentric. He divided egocentric speech into three categories: repetition, where the children merely repeat sounds; monologue, where children alone speak to themselves as if they were thinking aloud; and collective monologue, where children use monologue in social settings but do not take listeners' viewpoints into consideration. Piaget believed that preschoolers' egocentric speech is a result of their inability to keep their thoughts to themselves. They are characterized as being incapable of differentiating their own perspective of events from the perspective of others: "one of the most basic cognitive inadequacies of the young child" (Kohlberg, Yaeger, and Hjertholm, 1968, p. 692). Because of this cognitive inadequacy, the lack of will to share coexists with the inability to distinguish those attitudes that can be shared from those that cannot be shared. As children develop cognitively and become more adept in communicative skills, their egocentric speech diminishes in favor of more socially oriented speech. But as preschoolers they possess neither the will nor the ability to take listeners' roles into consideration; this disposition results in egocentric speech.

Vygotsky's (1962, 1978) position is very different from the Piagetian stand. Vygotsky stated that private speech originated in the social dialogue between children and adults. Young children are said to respond to and initiate dialogue with adults as they engage in joint activities such as peekaboo play and joint referring to objects in the environment. Adults' utterances in these contexts typically guide children's attention and actions. As children develop, they internalize these same adult dialogue strategies to regulate their behavior. That is, children come to use adult dialogue forms as overt private speech. These private speech forms have their origin in social dialogues between adult and child. With development, children internalize these dialogue strategies in the forms of covert private speech, or inner speech (Vygotsky, 1962). The ontogeny of private speech—whereby children are initially guided by adult utterances, then use the utterances overtly as private speech, and finally internalize the utterances as private speech to guide behavior—moves from an interpsychological (between people) to an intrapsychological (within one person) plane. That is, private speech originates in social dialogue. With development, it is internalized by children, first as overt private speech then as covert inner speech.

Recent research by Jerome Bruner (1974, 1975) and Blount (this volume) further support the Vygotskian notion that young children learn language by interacting with adults in dialogue. Bruner suggested that children's acquisition of syntax may originate in dialogue. He found that in adult-infant dyads, adults often focus infants' attention on one object or event. Infants or adults subsequently vocalize after they have both focused on the event or object. The events or objects focused on by the dyad are "known information" between them, i.e., topics. The vocalizations add "new information" to, or comment on, the event/object. Such a notion of new/old information is the basis of the subject/predicate or topic/comment syntactic structure. That is, in oral discourse, information shared between interlocutors is typically encoded into the syntactic subject. Vocalizations about the focused event/object are comments on the known information because they add new information to the event/object. Bruner hypothesizes that children acquire the basic topic/comment structure by engaging in dialogue. Thus, syntax may have a social interaction origin.

Research conducted by Pellegrini (1981b) and Rubin (1979) supports Vygotsky's position that private speech becomes more covert, and probably internalized, during the preschool period. Both researchers, following Piaget (1926), used the coefficient of egocentricism (i.e., the ratio of private speech to total speech) as a metric to determine the extent to which private speech becomes covert with age. Pellegrini (1981b) found that older preschoolers, i.e., 5-year-olds, generate proportionally less overt private speech than do 3- and 4-year-olds. Rubin (1979) examined children in grades 1, 3, and 5 and found no effect for age on coefficients of egocentricism. That is, children's proportions of private to social speech was not significantly different in grade 5 than it was in grade 1. These two studies together indicate that private speech is internalized by the end of the preschool period.

Given the evidence on the social interaction origins of many aspects of language, one may question Piaget's (1926) notion that preschoolers' language is egocentric. Recall, Piaget (1926) stated that preschoolers were both unwilling and unable to take listeners' needs into consideration. In order for the Piagetian hypothesis to be supported, it would have to be shown that the quantity of children's language does not change as a function of social context. Vygotsky (1962) tested this hypothesis by placing preschoolers in contexts that varied according to the responsiveness of interlocutors. He found that children generated more private speech in contexts that were supportive of discourse than when they were in a noisy room or with a deaf child. Preschoolers generated private speech when there was good likelihood of receiving a response.

Pellegrini (1981a) further examined this question by analyzing the amount of private speech generated by preschoolers in different social contexts. He examined preschoolers' private speech in two different contexts. One context was supportive of oral discourse, i.e., a peer group in the housekeeping corner; and the other context was not supportive of discourse, i.e., doing a puzzle next to a nonresponsive adult. Children generated significantly more private speech in the more social context than in the less social context. The Vygotsky (1962) and Pellegrini (1981a) studies both seem to indicate that preschoolers generate private speech when there is a likelihood of eliciting a response. This is probably a result of the social dialogue origins of private speech.

The research cited on the social origins of private speech suggests that children's language develops in a dialogic context. Such social interactions probably sensitize children to the contingencies of oral discourse. Through repeated and varied dialogues children become more adept at analyzing interlocutors' needs and generating context-appropriate language. Granted, preschoolers are still developing these skills, but they seem willing and somewhat able to use context-appropriate language.

THE COGNITIVE FUNCTIONS OF PRIVATE SPEECH

The second major area of disagreement between Piaget and Vygotsky is on the cognitive functions of private speech during the preschool period. Vygotsky believed that private speech serves a cognitive, self-guiding function for children by the end of the preschool period. Piaget (1926) stated that cognitive development is the result of young children's acting on objects. As a result of these actions, children formed representations, or symbols, that serve as bases of subsequent cognitive growth. Language, according to Piaget, is a symbol system developing out of these sensorimotor representations. For the preschooler, according to Piaget, private speech, *per se,* can have no cognitive function because it, along with other forms of language, is dependent upon action-based cognitive structures. Preschoolers are still forming concepts by acting upon objects. Only formal operational children can use language to direct thought.

Vygotsky (1962) also believed that language and thought had separate origins. Vygotsky (1967) stated that children's symbolic thought originates in their fantasy play with objects. However, he noted that language-to-self could be used to regulate behavior by the end of the preschool period. As was stated above, Vygotsky (1962) believed that language and thought become one, in inner speech, when children internalize adult dialogue strategies. Covert private speech and thought were believed to merge by the end of the preschool period. In order to fully understand Vygotsky's concept of language and thought, it is necessary to put his ideas in the larger context of Soviet psychology.

SOVIET VIEWS OF LANGUAGE AND THOUGHT

The importance assigned to language by Soviet psychologists may be the result of an ideological legacy left by Marx, Engels, and Lenin. They believed that "ideas do not exist apart from language" (Sokolov, 1961, p. 669). This being the case, people can use language to free themselves from their immediate environmental constraints (Slobin, 1966). That is, behavioral patterns can be changed through verbal interaction. This notion was presented earlier in the theory that social verbal interaction shapes children's behavior. An external agent's language first guides the child's behavior. The child later internalizes these dialogue strategies to guide his/her own behavior. Vygotsky's hypothesis that the ability to regulate one's actions is the result of internalized social speech is congruent with the Marxist notion that intellect is the product of the individual's immediate and past environments (Luria, 1979). Language is the medium by which ideas are transmitted, historically and socially.

Luria (1979), in his autobiography, stated that Soviet psychologists generally, and Vygotsky and he specifically, were attempting to build a psychology based on Marxist tenets. As part of this effort they wanted to establish a material basis of mind. They used Pavlov's psychophysiological research as a starting point.

Pavlov (Slobin, 1966) attempted to explain the effect of language on thought in both neurological and behavioral terms. According to Pavlov, humans receive two types of stimuli, first and second signals (Slobin, 1966). First signals, also perceived by lower animals, are the physical stimuli provided by the environment. Second signals, unique to humans, are words, with the primary function of abstraction and generalization of stimuli. Second signals, in turn, effect the functioning of the first signal system (Sokolov, 1961). Pavlov (Wilder, 1975-6) stated that the second signal system provides kinesthetic stimulation, originating in the speech organs and traveling into the cortex of the brain; speech signals act as feedback impulses. Pavlov included auditory stimulation as a component of kinesthetic feedback.

First and second signals are transferred from stimuli perceived in the environment into the cortex. An association in the cortex between stimuli is formed when the "two nervous centers are connected, [and] the nervous processes move from one direction to the other" (Zankov, 1957, p. 153). These connections remain in the cortex even after the stimulus has subsided. Objects and their properties can be impressed in the cortex only if they are separated from their surroundings by means of the second signal system, or language, as the analyzer mechanism. When an object is perceived, excitation is conducted along those nerves that make up the nerve center. This is where the trace of excitation is formed and retained. The second signal system functions as an analyzer mechanism because verbally encoding the name of an object separates the object from its context. The second signal system is an effective analyzer mechanism as a direct result of kinesthetic and aural stimulation (Zankov, 1957).

Chuprikova (1972) stated that the formation of conditioned neural connections is closely related to excitability at the cortical points to which the stimuli are addressed; that is, the brain areas associated with a reinforcing stimulus are especially susceptible to excitability. As a response becomes more conditioned, the stimulus threshold is lowered. In animal experiments, a rise in excitation at the participating cortical points does not occur immediately. In human experiments involving verbal instructions, on the other hand, excitation is recorded immediately after verbal instructions are given. Thus, the effectiveness of verbal instructions, as evidenced by increased excitation at cortical points addressed by a neutral stimulus; verbal stimulation results in immediate irradiation of excitation in the areas involved.

Luria (1957) argued that if a conditioned stimulus (CS) is replaced by a word, the verbal stimulus will be more effective and the subject will react to the stimulus with more intensity. A system of connections conditioned with the aid of language does not fade until it is cancelled by another verbally conditioned connection. Thus, when language is used as a stimulus, neural networks are more effectively formed. These neural networks are the bases of concepts to the extent that concepts are formed when related neural networks are interconnected. Language is seen as serving this connective role.

According to Liublinskaya (1957), children's ability to use verbal stimuli is built upon the relation between the first and second signal systems. By making simple connections between physical stimuli and the words used to describe the stimuli, children are gradually able to master words as signals, "which generalize a whole group of similar stimuli by abstracting the essential common features" (p. 198). The more experience children accrue, the more efficiently they will be able to make use of the second signal system to isolate and differentiate features of stimuli. Vygotsky (in Luria & Yudovich, 1971) also noted this phenomenon. He stated that "perception and memory acquire new features" (p. 27) under the influence of the word. In this way perceived stimuli become more intelligible. That is, by verbally encoding the name of an object the object is put into a verbal category. As a result of this categorization the specific object now shares features of other objects in that category. The concept of that object, then, is enriched because it now contains more features than the one specific object.

The Soviet position states that oral language serves a cognitive function in early childhood. Vygotsky used Pavlov's theories of excitory and inhibitory processes to describe the effect of language on thought. Young children's language and action were said to be fused. Language is capable of initiating actions due to the excitory, or motoric, aspect of utterances. With development, children use the semantic content of words, not the excitory properties, to analyze stimuli and, subsequently, to regulate behavior. Vygotsky (1962) stated that preschoolers' ability to use private speech to regulate their behavior was a gradual process. At first children's private speech does not serve a self-guiding function: they speak after they have completed an action. Language at this point does not direct actions because of an immature neurological system. With development, speech serves a self-guiding function: children speak while they are acting and then speak before acting. In the lower forms of self-regulating private speech, children's language accompanies their actions. It serves to separate stimuli from their immediate context. The higher form of self-regulation has children generating utterances before action initiation. These actions are often guided by the semantic, not the motoric, aspect of the utterances. That is, the meaning of the utterance provides a guide for children's future actions. Private speech with illocutionary force of directives (directing an action) and commissives (committing a speaker to a future action) are characteristic of semantically self-guiding speech. Vygotsky hypothesized that by the end of the preschool period children would use private speech to regulate their behavior. The remainder of this chapter will review research related to this hypothesis.

EMPIRICAL STUDIES ON THE COGNITIVE FUNCTIONS OF PRIVATE SPEECH

Luria (1961) conducted a series of experiments to test Vygotsky's theory of the ontogeny of the self-regulating function of private speech, i.e., that self-regulation originates in adult-child dialogue and the progression from motoric to semantic self-regulation. Based on these experiments, Luria outlined age-specific characteristics of self-regulating speech. In Luria's (1961) first stage of development, approximately 1½ to 3 years, certain directed movements were elicited from children by an adult's verbal commands (e.g., clap hands). However, at this stage, adult commands were ineffective in inhibiting an action already in progress. In the imitation-inhibition paradigm (Wozniak, 1972), adult instructions given to inhibit children's ongoing activity only resulted in Stage 1 children intensifying their actions. In another experiment, Stage 1 children were instructed to squeeze a ball when they saw a light flash; they squeezed when they heard "when you see a light." They often squeezed continuously, even after the light had gone out. Inhibition of an ongoing process was attained only when a movement was subordinated to a nonverbal inhibition task: "When you see the light, squeeze the ball and then touch your knee." The second instruction inhibited more squeezing because a new movement was initiated. Also in Stage 1, children were told to "press the balloon at the flash and thereby put out the light" (Wozniak, 1972). In this case, any inhibition that resulted was caused by stimulus feedback, i.e., the exteroceptive signal provided by the light going out. Thus, at Stage 1, children's actions are initiated by the motoric aspect of adults' language. They cannot inhibit ongoing action.

Luria's (1961) second stage, approximately 3 to 4½ years was marked by children's own external speech acting as the initiating and inhibiting agent. Children were capable of using adult instructions before a task began because they did not respond immediately to the stimulus provided by the verbal instructions. They waited for the signal before responding, but they still could not inhibit ongoing responses. When children were told to say "go" when a light flashed and then squeeze, all excitory squeezing was successfully inhibited. The inhibitory effect of children's speech in this case resulted from the utterances' motor component, not their semantic component.

In Luria's (1961) double-discrete-vocalization paradigm (Wozniak, 1972) children successfully squeezed the balloon twice when instructed to say "go," but did not respond correctly when told to say "I shall press twice." The semantic aspect of the utterance did not guide action. In the discrimination-vocalization paradigm, children were instructed to say "press" and press to a positive signal and to say "don't press" and refrain from pressing to a negative signal. Stage 2 children responded verbally correctly to both types of stimuli, but the discriminative motor responses broke down. "Press" lead to a concentration of stimulation and produced distinct motor reactions coordinated with the signal. "Don't press" led to the disinhibition of the motor response which was stimulated by the verbal impulse. When children were told not to respond verbally to the negative signal and refrain from pressing, only 42% of the responses were impulsive, compared to 70% when children verbalized "don't press." The motoric, not semantic, component of State 2 children's speech to self was dominant.

The success in the press condition can be explained by the excitation provided by the verbal stimulus' motor component, which irradiated to a motor response. The don't-press condition was not successful for the same reason: the children were responding to the motoric aspect of the utterance. Wozniak (1972) speculated that the failure of the don't-press condition may lie in Pavlov's inhibition-of-inhibition phenomenon; if one has a conditioned response (the idea don't press) and if another agent (the utterance "don't press") is added, the latter will inhibit the former.

Stage 3 was characterized by Luria as a "transfer of the regulation function of speech from the impulsive side . . . to the analytical system of elective connections which are produced by speech [and by the simultaneous shift] from the external to the internal speech of the child" (Wozniak, 1972, p. 15). That is, the semantic content of the utterances guided and inhibited actions. Children also internalized adult strategies into inner speech.

There have been a number of Western efforts to replicate Luria's results (e.g., Joynt & Cambourne, 1968; Miller, Shelton, & Flavell, 1970). Only Joynt and Cambourne (1968) successfully replicated Luria's results. Possible explanations for the general failure to replicate might be that the experimenters did not follow Luria's (1961) procedures closely or that Luria's (1961) results are simply not replicable. Wozniak (1972) argued that the former proposition is the more likely. He noted that Western psychologists, including Joynt and Cambourne, misunderstood the Soviet notion of self-regulation. Western psychologists typically see self-regulating language in terms of a verbal-mediation paradigm wherein language only initiates immediate actions, i.e., $S \ldots rv \ldots sv \ldots R$. Such an assumption led Miller et al. (1970) to instruct children to "speak, then act." The Miller et al. (1970) study indicated that children did not speak before acting. Soviets stress both the initiating and inhibiting functions of language.

Wozniak's criticism of Miller et al. (1970) may be valid in terms of the study's being a specific attempt to replicate Luria (1961). However, the verbal-mediation paradigm can be used to test one aspect of Vygotsky's hypothesis, i.e., the extent to which preschoolers' language precedes action. In the remainder of this section, empirical studies relating to the general question of children using private speech to regulate their behavior will be examined. Two types of studies will be reviewed: studies of verbal-mediation training and studies of children's use of spontaneous private speech in different contexts.

Jensen (1969) stated that verbal mediation is crucial in any learning that involves the covert manipulation of symbols. In this paradigm, young children respond more or less directly to stimuli, S——R. More mature children respond with the aid of a verbal mediator, S . . . V . . . R. The verbal component in this paradigm is labeled a secondary reinforcer. Jensen (1967) stated: "it appears that beyond a certain age the child's own verbal behavior may become the most important source of immediate reinforcement" (p. 125).

Kendler (1967) studied the development of children's mediation skills by examining their ability to mediate their responses in two-dimensional discrimination problems. Children were first trained to criterion to discriminate on one dimension between two stimuli; they verbally encoded the relevant dimensions before they were asked to discriminate. Next, children were presented with the same stimuli but they had to discriminate between stimuli differing on brightness (black vs. white) and size (large vs. small). Initially, the child was rewarded for responding to black, independent of size. Learning to respond to white would be a reversal shift, whereas responding to small would be a nonreversal shift. These were the two possible responses in this problem-solving situation, reversal and nonreversal shift responses. The former required the subject to respond in an opposite way to the previously relevant dimension; the latter required the subject to respond to the previously irrelevant dimension. In experiments with only two choices for each dimension, subjects can usually switch responses easily in the reversible shift condition because the initially relevant dimension continues to be relevant. The child can use the previously conditioned verbal mediator in the new condition because relevant dimension does not change. In the situation requiring a nonreversible shift, the previously relevant dimension becomes irrelevant, thus making this task more difficult than the former condition. In this condition the previously conditioned mediator is irrelevant. Thus, in order to solve the problem, the child must generate a new mediator for the new dimension. The results of Kendler's, and others', experiments (Kendler & Wells, 1960) corroborate mediation-theory expectations: most young children choose the nonmediating reversible shift strategy. These results indicate that young children do not spontaneously use verbal strategies to mediate their actions in a discrimination task. Kendler (1967) stated that less than 50% of her subjects between 3 and 4 years of age mediated under experimental conditions, rising to just above 50% for subjects between 5 and 7 years.

Kendler (1967) found that nonmediating children could verbally describe the stimuli as well as the mediating children, but they were incapable of using these descriptions as mediators, a mediation deficiency. A production deficiency is when a child is not capable of producing the response necessary to mediate the experimental task. In this case the child would not have been able to produce a description. Kendler (1967) saw the reversal choice as the highest stage where covert responses can occur but fail to mediate.

Flavell (1970) conducted a number of studies related to the various types of deficiencies in the verbal mediation paradigm. In one study he found that subjects showing a production deficiency, i.e., children who do not spontaneously produce a mediator, could be induced to use verbal mediation through rehearsal, thereby making them indistinguishable from their mediating age-mates. However, they soon lapsed back to their nonproducing habits when they were not constantly reminded to mediate. Some members of his youngest group, kindergarteners and first graders, were found to be deficient in production only. Older subjects mediated more spontaneously, whereas most of the younger subjects had to be induced to mediate. In a recall task reported by Flavell (1970), older elementary students did as well under conditions of induced verbalization as they did under conditions of free observation, suggesting that they were mediating spontaneously. The younger elementary children, however, did better under the induced-verbalization conditions.

To summarize, the verbal-mediation literature indicates that preschoolers and young elementary students do not spontaneously generate verbal mediators, but they can be trained to use language as an intermediary between stimuli and responses. Training young children to use mediators does seem to temporarily improve their performance on memory and discrimination tasks. However, the sustaining and transfer effects of these treatments is suspect. That is, children were able to use mediators immediately after they were trained. They did not use the mediators after an elapsed time. These data seem to indicate that young children do not spontaneously use private speech to mediate their actions.

A few studies have been conducted to examine preschoolers' spontaneous use of private speech to regulate their behavior. In this section, studies conducted by Pellegrini (Pellegrini, 1980, 1981b; Pellegrini & DeStefano, 1979) and Rubin (1979) will be discussed.

Pellegrini and DeStefano (1979) examined the extent to which preschoolers (3 to 5 years old) regulated their behavior with private speech by analyzing their generation of overt private speech *before* or *after* action initiation in two contexts: doing jigsaw puzzles and in free play. In both contexts preschoolers generated significantly more private speech after action initiation than before action initiation. In a follow-up study, Pellegrini (1980) reexamined the data from the puzzle context only. In this study, self-guiding private speech was defined on two dimensions: motoric (utterances preceding actions) and semantic self-regulation (commissives and directives) [Searle, 1976]). Self-regulating private speech in this study was the sum of all utterances preceding actions and all commissive (i.e., utterances containing a future-tense verb) and directives (i.e., imperatives). Again, children generated a significant number of *non*regulating private speech utterances while doing puzzles.

In both Peilegrini studies (1980; Pellegrini & DeStefano, 1979), the development of self-regulation within the preschool period was not examined. In a subsequent study by Pellegrini (1981b), age effects were examined for children 3 to 5 years of age. Following the hypotheses put forward by Vygotsky (1962) and Luria (1961), Pellegrini (1981b) hypothesized that the ability to regulate behavior would develop during the preschool period. Self-regulating private speech was defined on a motoric level (i.e., utterances *accompanying* or *preceding* actions) and on a semantic level (i.e., utterances indicating a planning or an analytic function). The Vygotskian model of the development of self-regulating private speech stated that children would use private speech initially following actions, then accompanying actions, and finally preceding actions. Children's ability to use semantically self-regulating utterances was hypothesized to develop by the end of the preschool period. Data from the Pellegrini (1981b) study indicated that preschoolers, despite age, generated private speech accompanying actions. These data are similar to Rubin's (1979) findings on preschoolers' self-regulating private speech. Data from both of these studies indicate that children across the preschool period use the lower form of self-regulation private speech, speech accompanying action. The developmental theory put forward by Vygotsky (1962) and Luria (1961), stating that preschoolers' private speech first follows, then accompanies, and eventually precedes action initiation, was not supported by Pellegrini's (1981) and Rubin's (1979) research. Preschoolers use private speech to verbally encode their on-going actions.

Pellegrini's (1981b) analyses of preschoolers' semantic self-regulation did not follow the developmental trend outlined by Vygotsky (1962, 1978) and Luria (1961). That is, older preschoolers did not seem to use more private speech to analyze situations and plan future actions than younger preschoolers. The only semantic self-regulation category found to differ significantly across the preschool period was questions-to-self. The age effects, however, were not in the hypothesized direction: 3-year-olds posed significantly more questions to self than either 4- or 5-year-olds. The extent to which all children used other forms of semantic self-regulation, i.e., plans and commands, did not vary significantly with age. The final analysis in the Pellegrini (1981b) study examined the effect of age on all types of self-regulation, i.e., utterance preceding and accompanying actions plus all semantic self-regulation; no age effects were observed. Preschoolers, despite age, used private speech to encode ongoing actions.

To summarize the studies on the self-regulating function of spontaneous private speech, the developmental hypotheses put forth by the Soviets were not supported. The data from Pellegrini (1981b) and Rubin (1979) suggest that preschoolers use private speech to verbally encode ongoing actions.

Wertsch (1981) stated that young children's private speech accompanying actions serves a mediating role between actions and the objects being acted upon. This form of private speech is used to verbally encode aspects of a situation which the speaker views as most relvant to the solution of the problem at hand. It has been argued (Levina, 1981; Pellegrini, 1982; Pellegrini & Greene, 1980; Sigel, 1979) that verbally encoding perceptually present objects and actions is related to a child's being able to mentally represent those aspects of a situation. That is, verbally encoding perceptually present aspects of a task helps children accumulate mental images of effective ways in which objects were used to solve problems. This collection of mental images should enable children to use problem-solving strategies that are not based on perceptually present objects. It is argued that private speech accompanying actions helps children build a repertoire of problem-solving strategies. Verbally encoding actions and objects helps children remember the most effective strategies. To this extent, preschoolers' private speech serves a cognitive function.

REFERENCES

BRUNER, J. S. The ontogenesis of speech acts. *Journal of Child Language,* 1974, *2,* 1–19.
BRUNER, J. S. From communication to language: A psychological perspective. *Cognition,* 1975, *3,* 255–87.
CHUPRIKOVA, N. The completion of temporary connections speech. *Soviet Psychology,* 1972, *10,* 271–308.
FLAVELL, J. H. Developmental studies of mediated memory. In H. W. Reese & L. P. Lipsett (Eds.), *Advances in child development and behavior* (Vol. 5). New York: Academic, 1970.
FUSON, K. C. The development of self-regulating aspects of speech: A review. In G. Zivin (Ed.), *The development of self-regulation through private speech.* New York: Wiley, 1979.
JENSEN, A. R. Social class and verbal learning. In M. Deutsch (Ed.), *Social class, race and psychological development.* New York: Holt, 1967.
JENSEN, A. R. Conceptions and misconceptions about verbal mediation. *Claremont Reading Conference Yearbook,* 1969, *30,* 134–41.
JOYNT, D., & CAMBOURNE, B. Psycholinguistic development and the control of behavior. *British Journal of Educational Psychology,* 1968, *38,* 249–260.
KENDLER, H., KENDLER, T. S., & LEARNERD, B. Mediated responses of size and brightness as a function of age. *American Journal of Psychology,* 1962, *75,* 71–82.
KENDLER, H., & WELLS, D. Reversal and nonreversal shifts in nursery school children. *Journal of Comparative and Physiological Psychology,* 1960, *53,* 83–88.
KENDLER, T. Development of mediating responses in children. In J. S. DeCecco (Ed.), *The psychology of language, thought, and instruction.* New York: Holt, 1967.
KOHLBERG, L., YAEGER, J., & HJERTHOLM, E. Private Speech: Four studies and a review of theories. *Child Development,* 1968, *39,* 690–736.
LEVINA, R. Vygotsky's ideas about the planning function of speech in children. In J. Wertsch (Ed.), *The concept of activity in Soviet psychology.* Armonk, NY: Sharpe, 1981.
LIUBLINSKAYA, A. A. The development of children's thought and speech. In B. Simon (Ed.), *Psychology in the Soviet Union.* Stanford, CA: Stanford University Press, 1957.
LURIA, A. The role of language in the formation of temporary connections. In B. Simon (Ed.), *Psychology in the Soviet Union.* Stanford, CA: Stanford University Press, 1957.

LURIA, A. Experimental analysis of the development of voluntary action in children. In *The central nervous system and behavior*, Translations from the Russian Medical Literature. Sponsored by the Josiah Macy, Jr. Foundation. Washington, D.C.: U.S. Department of HEW, 1960.
LURIA, A. *The making of mind*. Cambridge, MA: Harvard University Press, 1979.
LURIA, A. & YUDOVICH, F. *Speech and the development of mental processes in the child*. Harmondsworth: Penguin Books, Ltd., 1971.
MILLER, S., SHELTON, J., & FLAVELL, J. A test of Luria's hypotheses concerning the development of a verb self-regulation. *Child Development*, 1970, *41*, 651–665.
PELLEGRINI, A. D. The semantic structure of private speech. *International Journal of Psycholinguistics*, 1980, *5*, 278–292.
PELLEGRINI, A. D. The social orientation of private speech. *Child Study Journal*, 1981a, *11*, 25–33.
PELLEGRINI, A. D. The development of preschoolers' private speech. *Journal of Pragmatics*, 1981b, *5*, 278–292.
PELLEGRINI, A. D. Learning through verbal interaction. The effects of three conceptual conflict strategies on preschoolers' associative fluency. *Journal of Applied Developmental Psychology*, 1982, *3*, 39–46.
PELLEGRINI, A. D., & DESTEFANO, J. Functions of private speech in preschoolers. *International Journal of Psycholinguistics*, 1979, *15*, 27–42.
PELLEGRINI, A. D., & GREENE, H. The use of a sequenced questioning paradigm to facilitate associative fluency in preschoolers. *Journal of Applied Developmental Psychology*, 1980, *1*, 189–200.
PIAGET, J. *The language and thought of the child*. London: Routledge and Kegan Paul, 1926.
RUBIN, K. The impact of the natural setting on private speech. In G. Zivin (Ed.), *The development of self-regulation through private speech*. New York: Wiley, 1979.
SEARLE, J. R. A classification of illocutionary acts. *Language and Society*, 1975, *5*, 1–23.
SIGEL, I. On becoming a thinker: A psycho-educational model. *Educational Psychologist*, 1974, *14*, 70–78.
SLOBIN, D. I. Soviet psycholinguistics. In N. O'Conner (Ed.), *Present day Soviet psychology*. New York: Pergamon, 1966.
SOKOLOV, A. N. Studies on the problems of the speech mechanisms of thinking. In *Psychological science in the USSR* (Vol. I). Washington, D.C.: Joint Publications Research Services, 1961.
TIKHOMIROV, I. K. The formation of voluntary movements in children of preschool age. *Soviet Psychology*, 1975–6, *14*, 48–135.
VYGOTSKY, L. S. *Thought and language*. Cambridge, MA: MIT Press, 1962.
VYGOTSKY, L. S. Play and its role in the mental development of the child. *Soviet Psychology*, 1967, *5*, 6–8.
VYGOTSKY, L. S. *Mind in society*. Cambridge, MA: Harvard University Press, 1978.
WERTSCH, J. Introduction to the concept of activity in Soviet psychology, in J. Wertsch (Ed.), *The concept of activity in Soviet psychology*. Armonk, NY: Sharpe, 1981.
WILDER, L. The verbal control of behavior. *Soviet Psychology*, 1975, *14*, 3–12.
WOZNIAK, R. H. Verbal regulation of motor behavior . . . Soviet research and non-Soviet replications: A review and explication. *Human Development*, 1972, *15*, 13–57.
ZANKOV, L. V. The theory of memory. In B. Simon (Ed.), *Psychology in the Soviet Union*. Stanford, CA: Stanford University Press, 1957.

4 Parents as Teachers of Their Children: A Distancing Behavior Model*

Irving E. Sigel
Educational Testing Service

Ann V. McGillicuddy-Delisi
William Paterson College

INTRODUCTION

Numerous studies have indicated that parents' speech is a critical factor influencing children's language acquisition and that children's level of language ability, in turn, appears to affect the way parents talk to their children. Indeed, psycholinguistic research was one of the first areas in which the recognition of mutual influences between parent and child was actively translated into interpretation of empirical studies, despite the fact that investigators of parent-child relationships and family processes have been pointing to the need for such a perspective for years (e.g., Bell, 1968). For example, Brown (1973) has indicated that a parent's expansions of his/her child's utterances seems to help the child learn syntactical rules, and phenomena known as prompting, echoing, or recasting help the child recognize variations in deep structure. Moerk (1974), on the other hand, has shown that mothers are very sensitive to the language skills of their preschool-age children, and both the syntax and content of mothers' speech become more complex as the child becomes more skilled in language ability.

Unfortunately, researchers who have focused on children's intellectual development, and specifically upon representational abilities that are not included under the rubric of language, have taken a somewhat different approach

---

*Part of the research reported in this chapter was supported by the National Institute of Child Health and Human Development Grant No. R01–HD10686 to Educational Testing Service, National Institute of Mental Health Grant No. R01–MH32301 to Educational Testing Service, and Bureau of Education of the Handicapped Grant No. G007902000 to Educational Testing Service.

to the study of effects of the family environment. A basic thesis of this chapter is that conversations between parent and child are a major vehicle through which the parent acts as teacher to the child, affecting many aspects of the child's intellectual functioning in addition to linguistic aspects such as syntactic and semantic understanding. We propose that the relationship between parents' conversations with children and cognitive outcomes for the child has not been adequately represented in the literature because current psychological research has utilized macroanalytic analyses of environmental factors influencing cognitive growth. A review of current research reveals that the family environment is often conceptualized in global terms such as social status or family size, or else measurements focus on the way the home environment is set up, types of activities parents encourage, etc. (Marjoribanks, 1979; Zajonc & Markus, 1975). Very few studies have assessed verbal exchanges between parent and child as they relate to the child's *cognitive development* (Masur & Gleeson, 1980). We shall present a conceptualization of an environmental model that focuses on ways parents' verbalizations are hypothesized to influence children's intellectual functioning. It should be noted that we do recognize that many nonverbal behaviors of parents may have potent impact on children, in terms of nonverbal methods of communication and teaching (e.g., modeling, demonstration, gestures, facial expressions) and methods of organizing the home (e.g., providing appropriate play things, physical or perceptual stimulation, etc.). At this point, however, our focus is upon aspects of parents' verbal communication that facilitate or enhance children's intellectual functioning. The results of three research projects will be presented which demonstrate how parental conversations in teaching context contain important elements that provide the child with significant experiences for cognitive development. But first we must clarify our views of environment to place our research in a proper context.

Views of Environment

There have been a number of different attempts to define the construct "environment." Lewin's (1936) field theory, Barker's (1968) interest in behavior settings and Bronfenbrenner's (1979) "ecological validity" represent some of the efforts to conceptualize the environment. Among the inclusive constructs proposed as heuristically appropriate analytic concepts are those proposed by Eckland (1975) in his study of the relationship between deprivation and mental ability. The three classes of environmental variables he proposes have general applicability to all populations. They are described as follows: "One group of variables is *physical* or *biological* in nature, such as prenatal care, nutrition and birth order" (p. 67). "A second set of correlates of social class that sometimes contribute to the variance in mental ability is *cultural*" (p. 67). The third general group of environmental variables that may contribute to cognitive growth "is *social struc-*

tural, usually defined as differential access to the institutionalized means for achieving culturally prescribed goals'' (p. 67).

The variables Eckland identifies are macrogenic. Hence, they do not provide the details needed for explanations of how and what factors of the environment affect cognitive development. To be sure, there have been some studies that demonstrate the significance of family or home environment variables in relation to children's intellectual abilities (e.g. Bradley, Caldwell & Elardo, 1979; Marjoribanks, 1979). Although such studies have made a significant contribution by going beyond general descriptive characteristics such as social class and family constellation, they remain tied to parental reports of how the home environment is organized rather than focusing on how parents talk to their children.

Our argument is that to fully understand and evaluate the environment as a factor influencing intellectual growth, it is necessary to approach the definition of the environment from a psychological-behavioral perspective. While parents' encouragement of particular activities, provision of appropriate playthings, press for achievement, etc., are no doubt important influences on children, it is the quality and frequency of parental behaviors which communicate information, parental wishes, values, and aspirations stimulating many cognitive processes in the thinking child. That is, these behaviors serve as stimuli that explicitly influence the parent-child interaction (Sigel, 1982).

Organism-Environment Interaction

It is likely that psycholinguistic researchers have focused on the study of relationship between parents' language to children and the development of children's language abilities as a result of their recognition of the necessity of interaction between organism and environment. Few language-acquisition theorists, including Chomsky, deny that the speech children hear affects their language development. At the same time, the role of the child's cognitive development in the development of various language abilities has been recognized and studied. Despite a general agreement among cognitive-developmental psychologists regarding the significance of interaction between organism and environment, current theories and research have had great difficulty in explaining the role of each factor and the nature of the interaction effect. Although current work has attempted to include both organism and environment, it has effectively emphasized one or the other side, neglecting the concept of interaction beyond a simple acknowledgment of its existence or importance (Fischer, 1980).

For example, Bijou (1971), representing a "traditional" behaviorist theory, writes, "instead of asking how much an individual is influenced by his environment, we should ask which stimuli have influenced an individual's behavior in the past and which stimuli are influencing his behavior now'' (p. 228). While Bijou denies that the environment is simply something out there, and proposes that interactions of the organism with the environment alter the environment as well as the behavior of the individual, the emphasis is clearly upon the manner in which environmental stimuli affect the organism. On the other hand, Piaget provides virtually no conception of the environment, nor does he attend to the details of social interaction (Sigel, 1981). He has preferred to focus on the developmental processes performed by the organism, although he does maintain that experience (environmental engagement) is one of the three critical factors that must be taken into account to understand cognitive growth.

Of course some conceptualizations of organism-environment relationships have been proposed, e.g. Sameroff and Chandler's (1975) transactional analysis. However, such perspectives have not focused clearly either on the level of interaction that incorporates the specific stimulus events that Bijou argues for or on the organism's capacity to assimilate and accommodate to the experience. Simply put, classes of environmental factors that theoretically influence the quality and direction of the child's cognitive growth must be investigated with the child's present level of ability included as a starting point.

This chapter is not intended to develop a grand or comprehensive theory of environments; rather, it will focus on one class of environmental interactions embedded in the family milieu, i.e., verbal interactions between parent and child. These interactions comprise a large part of the child's representational experiences, and as we shall see, representational abilities of the child apart from language are likely to be affected.

Verbal Interactions Between Parent and Child

Parent-child interactions involve a host of definable encounters in a variety of contexts, each of which provides the opportunity for the parent to orient the child to individuals, objects, and events. It is through the course of such interactions that most parents fulfill their role as teacher and socializer of the young child. Most interactions between parent and child involve verbal exchanges, but such conversations involve instruction, information giving and getting, with little discourse in the sense of sharing ideas (Ervin-Tripp & Miller, 1977). Rather than viewing such verbal interactions as deficient in this regard, conversations between parent and child can be viewed as a major vehicle through which parents can influence their children's use of representational or cognitive skills across a variety of areas as discussion of the topic of conversation is guided by the parent.

Although it may seem obvious that parents engage in conversations with their children and such occurrences are likely to affect cognitive outcomes in children, few studies have examined relationships between parental conversational styles and children's cognitive abilities. Yet it is obvious that parents with different types of linguistic structures and verbal styles provide the child, in the early years at least, with different environmental experiences (cf. Hess & Shipman, 1967). Does it not seem reasonable to expect that these experiences will influence the quality of children's reasoning and patterns of thinking, as well as their language development? Current reviews of the literature do describe mother-child language interactions but do not report the relationship between different types of verbal exchanges and the child's general level of cognitive functioning or representational abilities (Hoff-Ginsberg & Shatz, 1982). This may be due in part to the lack of a model or theory that links the verbal interactions between parent and child directly to cognitive outcomes in the child. In fact, hypotheses proposed over the past 10 years do systematically relate verbal behaviors of adults to children's development in specific domains, although this framework, known as Distancing theory (Sigel, 1971), has only recently been applied to parent-child interactions.

Verbal Distancing Behaviors as an Environmental Feature

"Parental distancing behaviors are verbal, social, interactive events that "demand" the child to separate him/herself mentally (via representation) in space or time from the ongoing observable field" (Sigel, 1981). In reality, most verbal behaviors probably carry some small degree of distancing, and it is easiest to conceptualize distancing behaviors as existing on a continuum that varies in the degree to which the child must separate him/herself from the concrete observable present circumstances or event.

Distancing behaviors occur in the context of adult-child interactions. The parent does not necessarily use such strategies deliberately, but as s/he is engaged in conversation with the child, his/her verbalizations will vary in the degree to which they encourage the child to use mental representation to transcend the observable present. As we define distancing behaviors more fully, the reader will note that it is not the syntactic aspect of the verbalizations that determines the degree of the demand quality of distancing behaviors, but the content of the message, i.e., the representational content that different parental verbalizations potentially activate in the child.

The basic hypothesis underlying distancing behaviors is that certain verbal strategies influence the child's development and use of representational abilities. In this context, representational abilities are broadly defined to include the ability to anticipate outcomes; recall objects, people, and events; and attend to transformations of objects or phenomena. The common theme uniting these three aspects is that some mental process, without a necessary concordant physical manipulation, is involved. It is assumed that all children have an inherent capability to represent experience, although this capability develops over time, and that the demand quality of various distancing behaviors stimulates particular cognitive processes involved in representation.

The degree to which parent verbalizations encourage representation varies with the content of the message. In the case of a preschool-age child, verbalizations that require simple associations do not stimulate or demand that the child use complex representational skills. Therefore, demands to observe ("see the boat"), describe ("it's big and has a sail") or label ("it's called a ship") are low in distancing potential for the preschool child. Note that for a 2-year-old child, these might, in fact, be high-level distancing demands, for such verbalizations would, in fact, encourage a preverbal, pre-classifactory-ability child to engage in representation that is high level given his/her present cognitive level. Since we have worked mainly with preschool and young school-age children, we shall, however, restrict our description of parent distancing behavior to the ability level of children 4 to 7 years old.

Parental verbalizations that focus on getting the child to propose alternatives, to evaluate consequences, to infer cause-effect, to plan, etc. (e.g. "I wonder what it would look like if you folded it"; "When I cover the candle, the light goes out") are higher-level distancing strategies for a preschool child because they encourage greater psychological distance from the present concrete situation, as well as demand greater representational ability on the part of the child. A complete description of parent verbalizations that can be categorized as low-, intermediate- or high-level distancing is included in the *Parent-Child Interaction Manual,* which is available from the authors.[1] (See Table 1 for types of distancing strategies.)

The linguistic forms distancing strategies take may vary, i.e., telling, imperative, or inquiry. The distinction between telling and inquiry has been important in this context. Telling is the presentation of ideas to the child where the demand quality is to attend and to assimilate the information. Little mental activity is demanded of the child. Whatever the content, the interaction can be diagrammed as Ⓐ→Ⓒ→Ⓐ→Ⓒ . . . The child in this case is a relatively passive recipient of the adult's message. Inquiries, on the other hand, require a verbal response and may in fact encourage the child to engage actively in representational thinking as part of the process of responding. The same informational content can be presented in different forms, but with the same content or level of distancing demand. The following example illustrates this issue. The content of the utterance may focus the child's attention on details, e.g., "Look at the red colors on the flower" or on inquiry, "What colors do you see on the flower?" or on causal relations, "When I cover the lighted candle, the flame goes out" or an inquiry, "What happens when I cover the flaming candle?" In every case the child construes the meaning of the utterance. In the telling condition, however, there is no way to ascertain what the child's interpretation is and the child does

---

[1]The Parent-Child Interaction Manual is available from Irving Sigel, Educational Testing Service, Princeton, New Jersey 08541. It involves, in addition to distancing strategies, management strategies, emotional support systems, form of utterances, etc. Complete project reports are also available from Irving Sigel.

TABLE 1
Mental Operational Demands (MOD) on the Child through Parent Distancing Strategies

High-Level Distancing	Medium-Level Distancing	Low-Level Distancing
evaluate consequence	sequence	label
evaluate competence	reproduce[a]	produce information
evaluate affect	describe similarities	describe, define
evaluate effort and/or performance	describe differences	describe—interpretation
evaluate necessary and/or sufficient	infer similarities	demonstrate
infer cause-effect	infer differences	observe
infer affect	symmetrical classifying	
infer effect	estimating	
generalize	asymmetrical classifying	
transform	enumerating	
plan	synthesizing within classifying	
confirmation of a plan		
conclude		
propose alternatives		
resolve conflict		

Note. Three main groupings will be used based upon the level of the distancing demand upon the child.

[a] Reproduce/_____ (another MOD)—These will be grouped according to the MOD, ignoring the reproduction aspect. Example: reproduce/lab—Low MOD; reproduce/plan—High MOD.

not have to anticipate possible consequences. In the inquiry condition, the child's response provides a clue regarding the child's understanding, as well as encourages the child to engage in anticipation. The parent, in response to the child's utterance, is in a position to clarify, if there is doubt as to conjoint meaning, or to accept, thus reassuring the child that there is concordance between each participant in the conversation.

Distancing strategies, as indicated, vary in form (telling or asking) and in level of demand. The research question, then, is, What is the relationship between variation in distancing strategy and the development of representational competence? To answer this question we embarked on a comprehensive research program investigating, among other issues, the question posed above, but defined with greater specificity at least as far as the dependent intellectual variables. In our research we focused on three aspects of representational thinking: *anticipation*—i.e., planning and predicting—essentially ideational activity focusing on the future; *hindsight*—i.e., memory reconstruction, associative memory—essentially recall of past events; and *the transcending of the ongoing present*—essentially focusing on the nonobservable transformations in the contemporaneous present. In addition, we did use standard intelligence test measures in several instances in order to determine relationships between distancing verbalizations of parents and children's general intellectual status.

Our hypothesis was that children's competence to represent past, present or planned experiences will vary with frequency of high- and low-level distancing strategies the child's parents used during interactions on two tasks. Although we assume that the competence to remember, to plan, and to transcend the ongoing present is inherent in the child's biological repertoire, the capability of the child to utilize these representations and the levels usually employed by the child are functions of his/her previous experience in representing. Distancing strategies by parents encourage and provide such experiences, in our view. For example, children whose parents tend to engage them in planning activities, in anticipating, or in games of prediction (high-level distancing) would more likely have better developed schema for anticipation, thereby performing better on anticipatory tasks than children whose parents use lower level distancing strategies, e.g., labeling, observing, and the like.

The data to be reported are part of three separate projects, each of which shared a common procedure for identifying parental communication strategies. A total of 360 families were involved in the different studies. Study I involved 120 families with three family-constellation patterns and two socioeconomic levels (middle- and working-class). The target child was approximately 4 years of age, and children exhibited no known pathologies. Study II also involved 120 families, 60 with a communication-handicapped child and 60 with nonhandicapped children. The target child also averaged 4 years of age. The socioeconomic status of this group was generally middle-class. The 120 families who participated in study III resembled those of study II, except that the target child was 5 to 7 years old. In the latter two studies, families in the handicapped and nonhandicapped groups were matched for socioeconomic status, family size and sex, birth order, and children's age.

The data to be reported will focus on the relationship between the parental distancing behaviors observed while the parents taught their child two tasks and the child's performance on cognitive tasks assessing the three components of representational competence, i.e., memory, anticipation, and transcending the ongoing present, as well as on mental ability tests.

Assessment of Parental Distancing Behaviors and Children's Ability Levels

Mothers and fathers performed two teaching tasks with their child, a story-telling task and an origami (paper-folding) task. Two different stories and two different paper tasks were used so each father and mother would use a different story or paper task with his/her child, but the story tasks were equated for length and theme and the paper tasks for number of horizontal and vertical versus diagonal folds. Each parent-child interaction was videotaped through a one-way mirror for later coding. The dialogues between parent and child were coded separately for each task using the parent-child interaction schedule. In this report we shall describe only the occurrence of distancing strategies. Estimates of reliability between coders of the observations for 20% of the videotapes ranged from 72% to 99%, with an average agreement of 86.5%.

THE OCCURRENCE OF PARENTAL DISTANCING BEHAVIORS

Task Differences

There were some consistencies in the frequencies of high and low distancing demands, number of questions, and number of statements evidenced by parents across the two tasks (correlations ranged from .16–.51 across tasks for the three samples). However, the differences in amount of distancing behaviors that occurred when parents were telling a story versus constructing a paper object were more salient and interesting than patterns of similarity.

A similar pattern of differences arose in each of the three studies and were characteristic of parents of both normally developing and communication-handicapped children. Specifically, parents' conversations with their children included more high-level distancing demands during paper-folding than during story-telling (e.g., means = 18.14 and 13.19 for study III). Parents in study III also asked more questions during the paper-folding task (means = 22.16 and 18.20 for the paper and story task respectively). As a result of such findings, we must conclude that the particular context in which the interaction between parent and child occurs influences the degree to which parents will place representational demands on the child. We were, in fact, surprised to find that the parents exhibited more inquiries during the paper task as this task seemed to us to be more conducive to directive, authoritative communications than to more open, inquiry-based teaching styles. Nonetheless, the structured, product-oriented task appears to be a more conducive context for stimulating representational skills through high-level distancing verbalizations than the more open-ended story-telling context.

The fact that differences in parents' conversations occur with the nature of the task is probably a positive aspect of parental teaching styles. It indicates that parents are flexible in the content of their communication strategies. It is possible, for example, that parents viewed the paper-folding task strictly as an opportunity to teach the child, and therefore increased the frequency of cognitive demands on the child. The story-telling task, on the other hand, may serve a different purpose in the parent's mind, perhaps as an occasion to relax and enjoy each other's presence as they share a story together. As a result, the parent's attempts to stimulate representational thinking in the child occur less frequently, and other important aspects of the interaction, such as feelings and sharing the information in the story, outweigh the parent's role as teacher or source of stimulation/information.

Mothers' versus Fathers' Use of Distancing Strategies

We had hypothesized, based on previous studies and general knowledge of the higher verbal ability attributed to females, that mothers would ask more questions than fathers during interactions with their children. This was confirmed in only the first of the three studies (Sigel, McGillicuddy-Delisi & Johnson, 1980). An interesting finding concerning the sex of the child also arose in this study, with respect to the high- and low-level distancing demands. Mothers of sons evidenced more high-level distancing strategies than mothers of daughters. Fathers of daughters, on the other hand, tended to use high-level demands as a communication strategy more often than fathers of sons. For this sample of families, at least, there appeared to be a cross-sex effect, with parents using verbalizations that encourage representational thinking most often during interactions with children who are of the opposite sex. It is possible that these findings did not occur in the remaining two studies because there were relatively few female target children. For the most part, children in studies II and III were boys, whereas half the children in study I were females. (The incidence of communication handicaps is higher in males than in females, which is why the samples in studies II and III consisted predominantly of male target children.)

Comparison of Parents' Use of Distancing Strategies With Normally Developing versus Communication Handicapped Children

As you will recall, studies II and III focused on families with a communication-handicapped (CH) child, and in each study a contrast group with a nonhandicapped child was included. In each case the families of nonhandicapped children were matched to one of the families in the CH group on the basis of parents' level of education and age, sex, and birth order of the target child. All children in the CH group had been diagnosed by a professional external to Educational Testing Service, usually a child study team or a speech and hearing center at one of the hospitals or universities in the community. In most cases, the child had a language production problem.

Parents' use of high- and low-level distancing strategies and of questions and statements were compared across the two groups (CH versus non-CH child) in each study. Parents of CH children tended to use significantly more low-level distancing demands with their children than parents of non-CH children, and parents of CH children aged 5 to 7 years also asked more questions than other parents (based on four MANCOVAs; results of these analyses are available upon request from the authors).

At first glance, these results might be interpreted as indicating that parents are failing to stimulate their CH children's representational abilities through the frequent use of low-level distancing strategies, perhaps exacerbating the child's problems with various forms of representation. However, parents of CH children did *not* differ from other parents in the frequency of use of high-level distancing strategies. Rather, in both studies, the total number of parent verbalizations was greater when the child involved in the interaction was communication handicapped. Perhaps this occurred because the CH children did less talking, or perhaps because parents of CH children feel there is greater need to stimulate the child verbally. Regardless of the cause, the outcome is that the CH child is exposed to high-level distancing demands at about the same frequency as other children, but s/he also experiences a greater number of low-level distancing demands than a non-CH child. This, taken in combination with the relatively high frequency of questions by parents of CH children (about 22 in a 5-minute period), suggests that parents of CH children *do* use distancing behaviors to encourage representational thinking, and they stimultaneously attempt to encourage verbalization on the child's part through inquiry techniques.

To summarize thus far, parents do engage in various levels of distancing behaviors during verbal interactions with their children. The particular task in which the parent and child are engaged does seem to have an effect in the extent to which the parent will attempt to encourage the child to engage in representational thinking. Higher-level cognitive demands were expressed more often in parents' verbalizations during the structured teaching task of paper folding. On the other hand, the parents of CH children did evidence more low-level distancing demands in the content of their verbalizations regardless of the task in which parent and child engaged. This finding suggests that the verbal or productive speech ability level of the child has an impact on the nature of parents' conversations with children.

The relationship between distancing demands of parents and children's ability levels was investigated in terms of children's performance with anticipation and recall tasks as well as with standard tests of intelligence. These results are presented in the next section.

RELATIONSHIP OF PARENT DISTANCING VERBALIZATIONS AND CHILD ABILITY LEVELS

Standard Tests of Intellectual Ability

The WPPSI was administered to the 120 preschool-age children who participated in study II. Since half the sample was identified as communication handicapped, verbal and performance scores were analyzed separately. The scores of CH and non-CH children differed significantly on both subtests, although the discrepancy between groups was greater for the verbal subtest; means and (S.D.) =

95.60 (22.27) and 116.42 (13.96) for the CH and non-CH group respectively on the verbal subtest and 98.47 (24.82) and 116.25 (15.28) on the performance subtest; Univariate test following MANCOVA $F(1,111)$'s = 39.43 verbal and 21.83 performance; p's < .01.

Correlations computed on frequencies of parents' use of levels of distancing strategies and children's verbal and performance IQ scores are included in Table 2. As the correlations indicate, there are few significant relationships between parental distancing strategies during either task and children's WPPSI scores in the non-CH sample. Only three significant relationships were obtained: (a) children of mothers who used greater numbers of low-level distancing behaviors during the paper-folding task scored lower on the verbal subtest; (b) children of fathers who used a high number of statements during the paper task scored lower on the performance subtest; and (c) children of mothers who used more questions during the paper task performed at higher levels on the performance subtests. Although the direction of the significant relationships was consistent with the assumptions underlying distancing theory, these results can hardly be taken as providing powerful support for the notion that parent verbalizations that vary in the level of distancing are related to the cognitive development of children.

However, inspection of the relationships between parent and child variables obtained for the CH sample reveal a different pattern. Frequent use of high-level distancing strategies was positively related to children's WPPSI scores, with the exception of fathers' behaviors during the paper task. Furthermore, a consistent negative relationship, which was particularly strong for behaviors observed during the story task, was obtained between low-level distancing by parents and children's verbal and performance abilities. With the exception of positive correlations between fathers' use of statements during the paper task and children's IQ scores, results with the CH sample are consistent with predictions that variability in the types of demands parents verbally place on their child influence the development of children's intellectual ability.

Table 2 also presents the scores of children of study III on a different set of standard intelligence tests in relation to parent behaviors. Those relationships provide interest when compared to those for the study II sample, since the target children in study III were older. Replication of a similar pattern of results with a different sample and instruments would help to establish the reliability of these findings. Results were similar to those obtained in study II. For non-CH children, the only significant relationship between mothers' behaviors and children's intellectual scores was a negative relationship between low-level distancing behaviors during the story task and children's scores on the Raven's test. For fathers, the more they evidenced low level distancing demands during story telling, the lower their child scored on tests of verbal ability (PPVT and Crichton). Fathers' use of high-level distancing demands during paper-folding was positively related to children's Raven's performance. As was the case with

TABLE 2
Correlations between Frequencies of Parental Distancing Strategies and Children's Scores on Tests of Intelligence[a,b] Group and Task

	CH Children					Non-CH Children				
	Verbal WPPSI	Performance WPPSI	PPVT Raw	Raven's Total	Crichton Total	Verbal WPPSI	Performance WPPSI	PPVT Raw	Raven's Total	Crichton Total
Story task behaviors[c]										
High Level										
M	.29*	.28*	−.05	−.08	−.02	−.07	.07	.01	−.09	.05
F	.35*	.36*	.06	.08	.09	−.01	.00	−.17	−.02	−.09
Low Level										
M	−.51*	−.52*	−.53*	−.53*	−.46*	−.24	−.16	.21	−.25*	−.01
F	−.48*	−.43*	−.64*	−.54*	−.48*	−.33*	−.24	−.29*	−.09	−.29*
Questions										
M	.08	.11	−.40*	−.42*	−.39*	−.19	−.15	.06	−.16	.05
F	−.13	−.10	−.28*	−.36*	−.33*	−.07	−.09	−.26*	.03	−.24
Statements										
M	−.12	−.17	−.23	−.34*	−.20	−.10	−.09	.05	−.15	−.11
F	.04	−.00	−.47*	−.27*	−.22	−.17	−.17	−.24	−.14	−.22
Paper task behaviors										
High Level										
M	.26*	.24	.13	.03	−.00	−.04	.01	.08	−.04	−.01
F	.23	.16	−.05	−.02	−.15	−.02	−.00	−.03	.30*	.10
Low Level										
M	−.36*	−.38*	−.19	−.29*	−.19	−.09	−.18	−.05	−.05	−.08
F	−.25*	−.24	−.15	−.13	−.13	−.10	−.13	.05	−.11	.03
Questions										
M	.17	.14	−.08	−.11	−.22	.04	.01	.02	−.10	−.06
F	.10	.11	−.18	−.18	−.35*	−.04	−.10	−.25*	−.01	−.14
Statements										
M	−.06	−.16	.10	−.16	.03	−.07	−.26*	−.01	−.11	−.05
F	.30*	.25*	.08	.22	.25*	−.14	−.18	.20	.09	.15

* $p < .05$.
[a] WWPSI from study II, PPVT, Raven's and Crichton from Study III.
[b] M = Mothers; F = Fathers.

non-handicapped children's scores on the WPPSI, these relationships are in the predicted direction.

Results with the CH sample were a little disappointing when parental distancing behaviors during the paper task were considered. Significant negative relationships between use of low-level distancing demands occurred between mothers' behaviors and children's Raven's scores. Parent behaviors during the story telling tasks were very promising, however. Both mothers' and fathers' use of low level distancing strategies was negatively related to each child measure. In addition, parents' use of statements was negatively related to children's Raven's scores, and fathers who showed high frequencies of statements had children who also performed more poorly than other children on the PPVT.

Relationships between parents' use of distancing and children's cognitive abilities as assessed by standard measures of intellectual development were generally in directions that support the notion that distancing by parents affects intellectual development. The fact that a greater number and stronger relationships were obtained in samples of CH children is probably due to the greater variability or range of performance on the child assessments reported above. This is not to deny that the relationships exist, however. The pattern is quite consistent—parents' use of communication strategies that place low representational level demands on the child are strongly related to low levels of performance on intellectual measures by their children (in some cases, the correlation coefficient is in the .50–.65 range). While these results are encouraging as a test of the hypothesis that parents who stimulate their children through high-level distancing demands are enhancing their children's cognitive growth, several problems remain to be addressed.

First, the pattern of results is most impressive when viewed from a negative standpoint. That is, correlations for standard intelligence performance indicate that use of low-level demands by parents is related to lower performance scores of children. There were relatively few indications, however, that parents' use of high-level distancing strategies was associated with enhanced performance of their children on such tests. At this point, then, we can only advise parents of types of cognitive or representational demands that they should *avoid* if they are interested in advancing their child's intellectual growth. Perhaps the case is that parents have little impact in promoting skills tapped by intelligence tests, although they have the potential to hinder or block the growth of skills by focusing on mental processes that provide minimal representational challenges.

Second, the finding that relationships were stronger for CH children than for non-CH children leads us to consider the very real possibility that the parent is not stimulating the growth of ability in the child as much as s/he is reacting to the existing ability level, or at least his/her perception of the child's ability. That is, the association between low-level distancing by parents and children's intellectual performance may be due to the fact that parents correctly perceive their child's ability level and when it is low, their conversations with children contain more low-level demands as they attempt to "match" quality of stimulation to the child's capabilities. This possibility will be returned to in a later discussion. At this point, it is necessary to investigate relationships between parental distancing and children's performance on tasks designed specifically to assess representational thinking. Since distancing theory is focused directly on this aspect of cognitive development, results might help clarify the two points above.

Assessment of Children's Representational Abilities

Relationships between parents' use of distancing and children's performance on the conservation, anticipatory imagery, reproductive memory, and object classification tasks used in study I have been reported elsewhere (Sigel, 1982). To briefly summarize the findings, mothers' use of high-level distancing was related to children's anticipatory imagery and object classification performance, whereas fathers' distancing strategies were related to children's memory performance. These relationships were significant even after social class and family-constellation factors were taken into account.

Correlations between frequencies of parent distancing strategies and children's performance on representational tasks used in study III are reported separately for CH and non-CH children in Table 3. With respect to non-CH children's performance, mothers' and fathers' levels of distancing during the paper task were related to anticipatory imagery in directions proposed by distancing theory. In addition, mothers who used statements frequently had children who were less successful on this task. Low-level distancing by both parents during the storytelling task was negatively related to non-CH children's performance on the memory and sequencing task and memory for sentences task. As Table 3 indicates, children whose parents frequently used low distancing demands tended to score lower on most of the representational ability tasks.

A similar pattern was observed in the sample of CH children, although the magnitude of the relationships is slightly higher for the CH children than for the non-CH children. In addition, both fathers' and mothers' use of high-level distancing behaviors during the story interaction was associated with higher levels of performance of CH children on anticipatory imagery and seriation problems. The children of mothers who used high-level distancing strategies during the paper task achieved higher anticipatory imagery and memory for sentences scores.

The relationships between verbal teaching strategies that vary along a distancing dimension and children's performance on these tasks provide support for our hypothesis that higher-level distancing strategies stimulate children to engage in representational thinking. These findings suggest that parents match the level of their cognitive demands to the capabilities of the child, but also support the idea that the parent's use of higher levels of distancing relate to the

TABLE 3
Correlations between Frequencies of Parental Distancing Strategies and Children's Scores on Representational Task[a] Group and Task

	CH Children							Non-CH Children					
	Anticipation	Memory Sequencing (Familiar)	Memory Sequencing (Geometric)	Seriation	Memory for Sentences	Simon	Anticipation	Memory Sequencing (Familiar)	Memory Sequencing (Geometric)	Seriation	Memory for Sentences	Simon
Story task behaviors													
High Level													
M	.30*	−.01	−.01	.26*	.11	.12	.06	.08	.06	−.06	−.01	−.19
F	.37*	.19	.03	.39*	.16	.24	.10	.13	.18	−.04	.05	−.03
Low Level													
M	−.51*	−.54*	−.44*	−.44*	−.43*	−.41*	.11	−.36*	−.30*	−.27*	−.43*	−.22
F	−.34*	−.40*	−.29*	−.20	−.39*	−.41*	−.02	−.30*	−.24	−.21	−.30*	−.23
Questions													
M	.15	−.04	−.04	.02	−.01	.04	.03	−.13	−.16	−.23	−.10	−.25*
F	.04	−.03	−.11	.11	−.11	−.09	.07	−.06	.05	−.16	−.17	−.13
Statements													
M	−.27*	−.35*	−.24	−.12	−.23	−.18	.08	−.21	−.11	−.10	−.38*	−.10
F	−.11	−.21	−.14	.07	−.08	−.09	.06	−.28*	−.24	−.08	−.09	−.14
Paper task behaviors													
High Level													
M	.30*	.01	.01	.24	.27*	.18	.01	−.08	−.05	−.20	−.08	−.11
F	.17	.08	.05	.15	.00	.11	.32*	.18	.18	.18	−.01	−.21
Low Level													
M	−.31*	−.35*	−.30*	−.34*	−.34*	−.35*	−.27*	−.08	−.16	−.24	−.15	−.21
F	−.09	−.25*	−.20	−.01	−.30*	−.27*	−.05	−.12	−.07	.04	.04	−.30*
Questions													
M	.20	−.05	−.07	.03	.12	−.03	.16	−.10	−.12	−.20	−.10	−.18
F	.16	.00	−.02	.08	−.13	.06	.26*	−.07	−.08	.03	−.12	−.28*
Statements													
M	−.03	−.24	−.21	.01	−.02	−.02	−.39*	−.20	−.15	−.14	−.30*	−.17
F	.22	.10	.10	.24	.15	.11	.03	−.11	−.00	.14	−.08	−.12

* $p < .05$.
[a] M = Mothers; F = Fathers.

children's ability to demonstrate high anticipatory and memory skills. Parents' behaviors have an impact in promoting such skills. At this point, however, the question of causality cannot be answered, i.e., parent affecting child or reacting to the child. It is worth noting the *association* between high-level demands of parents and high levels of representational ability in the child and between low-level demands of parents and lower performance levels on such tasks by children. We suspect that, in fact, the direction of influence is mutual, with parent affecting child and child affecting parent. It is of considerable import for our understanding of children's cognitive development that an association between the content of their verbalizations and children's ability levels has been found. This suggests that indeed parents do not operate in isolation from feedback from the child; and a match has occurred, for whatever reason, with increased demands for representation when the child is at higher developmental levels and thereby likely to benefit from such challenges.

With respect to the particular challenges of the CH child, parents seem quite capable of adopting strategies to meet the challenge. The parents continue to use verbalizations that contain high-level demands, although they simultaneously use more low-level strategies than parents of non-CH children. The strength and direction of the relationships between high- and low-level distancing by parents and children's performance on the representational tasks suggest, at the least, that the distancing content of parents verbalizations is an important factor in the CH child's development.

CONCLUSIONS

After reviewing this complex set of results, it becomes apparent that determining the significance of parental teaching strategies vis à vis children's cognitive performance is no simple matter. Relationships were bound to vary with task and pathogenic status of the child. Nevertheless, each of the factors comprises the ingredients inherent in the human condition we are working with. At issue, of course, is how to determine the hierarchy of significant factors. The results of these three studies yield generalizations that have potential explanatory power for our coming to understand the role of parental teaching strategies and children's cognitive growth.

To set the stage for that discussion, it is important to clarify an important revision we had to make in categorizing our data. It will be recalled that in the introductory comments, much emphasis was paid to *inquiry* as a teaching strategy. Although we still contend that inquiry as described in those opening comments performs the functions described, it seems that a too heavy reliance on the *form* of the communication as the most significant factor may place too heavy a burden on the form of the message while minimizing the role of content. The high-level distancing demands, while initially planned to be classified on the basis of form as well as content, eventually were separated on the basis of content level, i.e., the cognitive message to the child. The child has to process the message irrespective of form; and as the results indicate, outcomes in the child seem to be based on the content more than the form of the communication from the parent (Pellegrini, 1982).

A related concern has to do with the sequence in which inquiry was used. At this stage we did not do a sequential analysis, i.e., a determination of when the inquiry was introduced or how it was followed up. There is some indication that follow-up questions have a positive effect on children's performance on problem-solving tasks (Rosner, 1978). Our interpretation of higher-level distancing strategies must be construed in terms of content of cognitive demand at this time, however.

Returning now to our results, of major significance is the consistency of the obtained correlations between distancing strategies and cognitive performance in each of the three studies, for all samples studied. The evidence is overwhelming in its consistency that those verbal teaching strategies which contain low-level distancing demands relate negatively to children's representational abilities and, to some degree, to intellectual skills assessed by IQ tests. Even though the magnitude of these correlations varies with a number of factors, the frequency and consistent directionality indicate that types of verbal teaching strategies are related to the development of representational competence.

We ask why is this the case? Our contention is that low-level distancing strategies do not provide opportunities for the child to be an active thinker. To solve many of the representational problems given to the children in these studies requires that they actively engage in constructing plans and reconstructing present events. In each of these types of cognitive activities, the child has to be active—engage in mental processes that involve representation. When children are accustomed to receiving input from adults that does not stimulate or encourage such mental activities, they are at a disadvantage as compared to other children who have a history of experience in using and developing such processes because their parents have encouraged them through the use of high-level distancing communications. Thus, statements and low-level distancing strategies tell the child what to do and require less active thinking. With little experience or encouragement to assume responsibility for "thinking," there is little opportunity to develop thinking skills. For these reasons, we are concerned that children experiencing low-level demands during parent-child interactions are less competent in tasks requiring representational thinking.

Turning now to distancing strategies and child outcomes, we found relatively consistent significant positive relationships between high-level distancing strategies and child outcomes for preschool-age CH children. Within the distancing framework, these results are taken to indicate that children who have problems in one area of representation, i.e., oral speech or language, can indeed develop high levels of representational ability in areas such as anticipation and memory when parents' verbal communications contain messages that focus on these abilities. While we would certainly encourage parents of CH children to focus their communication strategies on developing oral skills, it is equally important that they include high-level distancing demands in their communications to their children. It may well be that children of this age with this handicap need more opportunities to become actively involved in representation in general. CH children who are exposed to high-level cognitive demands were able to respond and their ability levels were related to parents' use of such demands to a greater degree than their non-CH peers. This finding suggests that in spite of CH children's difficulty to respond verbally, verbal teaching strategies play an important role in their representational development.

With respect to the question of direction of causality posed in previous discussions of results, let us return to the psycholinguistic literature for the moment. Studies of parent-child interaction during the years of language acquisition generally show that communications by parents both affect and are affected by their children's level of language ability. That is, parents appear to "teach" their children about nearly every aspect of language through their verbal communications (Bloom, Rocissano & Hood, 1976; Moerk, 1976). At the same time, parents seem to be sensitive to the particular abilities their child has developed and adapt their verbal communications in accordance with this ability (Moerk, 1974). There is no reason to suppose that the same bidirectional influence is not operating in the cognitive demand quality of parents' verbal communications to children. That is, the parent strives to "teach" the child representational skills through high-level distancing demands, stimulating anticipation and memory, focusing on transformations rather than stages as they engage in verbal communication with the child. Simultaneously, both the degree (frequency) and the quality (low versus high level) of these demands is dependent on the representational ability level of their own child.

Such a perspective is salient in interpretation of results obtained with the CH child. Countless parents of CH children have told us that professionals working with the child "made them feel" that they, the parents, were responsible for the child's problem, at least in part. While much of this may be due to the parents' own constructions, as opposed to any real communication of responsibility by practitioners, results of the studies reported here indicate that parents of CH children do place high-level demands on their children, at the same time that they increase the frequency of low-level demands. It is to parents' credit that they adapt their communications to the child's ability level, searching for a "match" between demands placed on the child and the ability levels the child has developed.

Task demand differences also play an important role since the two tasks involved in these studies allowed for, and perhaps even required, different teaching strategies. The story-telling task enables the parent to use a large variety of strategies by just reading in a lively voice, engaging the child with questions.

The paper-folding task on the other hand, has a defined outcome, a specific set of necessary steps, to achieve the objective. Thus, the parent's teaching responsibility is to get the child to participate, and in a sense, to solve the problem of how to make the boat, the fish, or whatever the goal is (Sigel, 1982).

These results highlight the complexities involved in trying to unravel the knotty problem of identifying the critical familial factors influencing the child's cognitive growth. In spite of the complexities, the fact that the significance of some of the relationships obtained in this study transcended different tasks, ages, and child verbal ability among other variables, supports the idea that some generalizations are possible.

The fact that such other factors as task, for example, have a unique influence challenges us to revise both our conceptualization and methods to deal with issues that arise as a function of these differences. It may well be that new research strategies and different expectations regarding outcomes are needed.

If in fact it is the case that different tasks elicit different strategies from adults, and if these various strategies contribute in their totality to the outcomes for the child, then it behooves researchers to determine what kinds of experiences children have with their mentors, be they parents or teachers. The tasks should be analyzed in terms of the cognitive demand they require so that a broader sample of parental teaching strategies can be obtained.

Finally, the results of these studies point to the relevance of parent-child interaction in teaching contexts for the development of representational competence. The interaction must be examined in a context that includes participants and task. Microanalytic strategies applied to the context provide important data relative to the role of the environment. In spite of the vast array of details accumulated by such an approach, this fine-tuning allows for greater understanding of this complex problem.

> It is important to emphasize that the relationship [between adult and child discourse] is never a static one but, rather, shifts and varies according to the experience of the individual child and his developing linguistic and cognitive capacities. (Bloom, 1974, p. 308)

Embedding Bloom's conclusion in a social context and social content essentially sums up the perspective we have been striving to present.

REFERENCES

BARKER, R. G. *Ecological psychology*. Stanford, CA: Stanford University Press, 1968.
BELL, Q. A reinterpretation of the direction of effects in studies of socialization. *Psychological Review*, 1968, 75, 81–95.
BIJOU, S. W. Environment and intelligence: A behavioral analysis. In R. Cancro (Ed.), *Intelligence: Genetic and environmental influences*. New York: Grune & Stratton, 1971.

BLOOM, L. Talking, understanding, and thinking. In R. L. Schiefelbusch & L. L. Lloyd (Eds.), *Language perspectives—Acquisition, retardation, and intervention*. Baltimore, MD: University Park Press, 1974.
BLOOM, L., ROCISSANO, L., & HOOD, L. Adult-child discourse: Developmental interaction between information processing and linguistic knowledge. *Cognitive Psychology*, 1976, *8*, 521–552.
BRADLEY, R. H., CALDWELL, B. M., & ELARDO, R. Home environment and cognitive development in the first two years: A cross-lagged panel analysis. *Developmental Psychology*, 1979, *15*, 246–250.
BRONFENBRENNER, U. *The ecology of human development: Experiments by nature and design*. Cambridge, MA: Harvard University Press, 1979.
BROWN, R. *A first language*. Cambridge, MA: Harvard University Press, 1973.
ECKLAND, B. K. Social class structure and the genetic basis of intelligence. In R. Cancro (Ed.), *Intelligence: Genetic and environmental influences*. New York: Grune & Stratton, 1971.
ERVIN-TRIPP, S., & MILLER, W. Early discourse: Some questions about questions. In M. Lewis & L. A. Rosenblum (Eds.), *The origins of behavior* (Vol. 5): *Interaction, conversation, and the development of language*. New York: Wiley, 1977.
FISHER, K. W. A theory of cognitive development: The control and construction of hierarchies of skills. *Psychological Review*, 1980, *87*, 477–531.
HESS, R. D., & SHIPMAN, V. C. Cognitive elements in maternal behavior. In J. P. Hill (Ed.), *Minnesota Symposia on Child Psychology* (Vol. 1). Minneapolis: University of Minnesota Press, 1967.
HOFF-GINSBERG, E., & SHATZ, M. Linguistic input and the child's acquisition of language. *Psychological Bulletin*, 1982, *92*, 3–26.
LEWIN, K. *Principles of topological psychology*. New York: McGraw-Hill, 1936.
MAJORIBANKS, K. *Families and their learning environments: An empirical analysis*. London: Routledge & Kegan Paul, 1979.
MASUR, E. F., & GLEASON, J. B. Parent-child interaction and the acquisition of lexical information during play. *Developmental Psychology*, 1980, *16*, 404–409.
MOERK, E. Changes in verbal child-mother interactions with increasing language skills by the child. *Journal of Psycholinguistic Research*, 1974, *3*, 101–116.
MOERK, E. Processes of language teaching and training in the interactions of mother-child dyad. *Child Development*, 1976, *47*, 1064–1078.
PELLEGRINI, A. D. Learning through verbal interaction: The effects of three conceptual conflict strategies on preschoolers' associative fluency. *Journal of Applied Developmental Psychology*, 1982, *3*, 67–81.
ROSNER, F. C. An ecological study of teacher distancing behaviors as a function of program, context and time. (Doctoral dissertation, Temple University, 1978). *Dissertation Abstracts International*, 1978, *39*, 760A. (University Microfilms No. 7812235).
SAMEROFF, A. J., & CHANDLER, M. J. Reproductive risk and the continuum of caretaking casualty. In F. D. Horowitz (Ed.), *Review of child development research* (Vol. 4). Chicago, IL: The University of Chicago Press, 1975.
SIGEL, I. E. Social experience in the development of representational thought: Distancing theory. In I. E. Sigel, D. M. Brodzinsky, & R. M. Golinkoff (Eds.), *New directions in Piagetian theory and practice*. Hillsdale, NJ: Erlbaum, 1981.
SIGEL, I. E. The relationship between parents' distancing strategies and child's cognitive behavior. In L. M. Laosa & I. E. Sigel (Eds.), *Families—Research and practice* (Vol. 1): *Families as learning environments for children*. New York: Plenum, 1982.
SIGEL, I. E., MCGILLICUDDY-DELISI, A. V., & JOHNSON, J. E. *Parental distancing, beliefs and children's representational competence within the family context*. (ETS RR 80-21) Princeton, NJ: Educational Testing Service, 1980.

SIGEL, I. E., & OLMSTED, P. The development of classification and representational competence. In R. J. Gordon (Ed.), *Readings in research in developmental psychology*. Glenview, IL: Scott, Foresman, 1971.

ZAJONC, R. B., & MARKUS, G. B. Birth order and intellectual development. *Psychological Review*, 1975, *82*, 74–88.

II THE CONTEXT OF SOCIAL PLAY

5

The Language of Social Play in Young Children*

Thomas D. Yawkey and Thomas J. Miller
Pennsylvania State University

INTRODUCTION

This chapter focuses on the relation between children's use of language and social play. More specifically, it examines selected ways in which language and play are related and defines aspects crucial to that relationship within social-environment contexts.

Previously—and from behavioral perspectives, characteristic of the 1950s—explanations of language use rested on the children's appropriate modeling of adults' language and successive approximations of their responses (Skinner, 1959). In the 1960s, the nativist perspective emphasized the innateness of language and the basic "language inventiveness" of the child (Chomsky, 1965). Excellent reviews of both positions are found elsewhere (McNeil, 1966; Skinner, 1959). The behavioral perspective of the 1950s and the nativist position largely of the 1960s gave little or no mention or attention to the role that environments play in using (or acquiring) language.

---

*The senior author's research and writing on constructivist play, cognition, and communication are supported in part by grants from the United States Department of Education; the Margaret M. Patton Foundation, Kittanning, Pennsylvania; and Penn State's Division of Curriculum and Instruction, Professor Fred Wood, Chair. The views expressed in this and other documents are the authors', not the funding agencies', divisions' or institutions'.

In addition, the senior researcher wishes to thank the teachers, parents, paraprofessionals, children, and research staff of Project P.I.A.G.E.T., experimental and federally funded preschool and family programs for which he serves as Penn State's Director and Principal Investigator, for providing opportunities to operationalize the psychological principles underlying the language of social play.

However, the most recent perspective stresses that language use develops and can best be studied in social-interaction environments. This most current perspective can best be termed "constructivist" or "developmental interactionist" (Fein, 1981). It stresses the experiential history of the child and intentional and interactive variables. The supportive environment defines the social context in which the language is used and studied. Language use, then, is a function of both the child and the social environment. As such, the child is capable of exerting moderating influences on it and in turn is influenced by it (Peters, Neisworth, & Yawkey, in press).

From a constructivist perspective, one of the richest settings for studying children's use of language is natural, ongoing, social play. The relationship between children's use of language and social play is reinforced by current developmental theory. First, pretend play and language could well reflect parallel development of symbolic activity in young children (Nicolich, 1981). Correspondence can be seen in the representational nature of speech in regard to objects and events in the real world and similar qualities observed in the gestural and play themes of children. Both involve the sharing of information with others and performing symbolic transformations in the process of testing hypotheses and mastering their environment.

Second, youngsters who exhibit high levels of pretend play also show more complex language use (Rosenblatt, 1977). Evidence also exists for the co-occurrence of first words and pretend play behaviors (Bates, Camaioni, & Volterra, 1975; Volterra, Bates, Benigni, Bretherton, & Camaioni, 1979; Werner & Kaplan, 1963). Later, developing combinations become socially negotiated, rule-based, and less tied to contextual restraints (Werner & Kaplan, 1963). In sum, standardizations of language form permit generalization, organization, and appropriate utilization of symbolic behavior and pretend play more effectively and in accord with the prevailing coding system (McCall, Eichorn, & Hogarty, 1977).

Beyond the level of a rather general relationship, association, or parallel between children's use of language and social play, research studies from constructivist perspectives have identified specific ways, or aspects, in which they are related and defined variables crucial to that relationship within social contexts. Using results of selected research studies, the remainder of the chapter provides specific evidence for, and describes and defines variables crucial to, this relationship within social contexts.

For purposes of discussion, the remainder of the chapter is organized around these research studies, which are grouped into categories based on similarity of aspect or variable crucial to the relationship between language use and social play. Explanations of these categories in each of the sections follow: (a) social play as context; (b) language and function; and (c) language adaptations to environmental demands (Garvey, 1974; Shantz, 1975).

SOCIAL PLAY AS CONTEXT

The research studies categorized as social play as context pinpoint variables operating between various forms of play and language use. Further, these variables define the relation between play and language use within social contexts. Three studies that explore and provide further knowledge of this relationship in social contexts were conducted by Garvey (1974); Ratner and Bruner (1978); and Sachs, Goldman, and Chaille (1982).

Garvey (1974) describes the structure of spontaneous dyadic play episodes and suggests basic competencies that underlie play activity within social contexts. She distinguishes four possible states that may exist when two children are together in a play setting: social nonplay (e.g., both youngsters may collaborate to repair a broken toy); nonsocial nonplay (e.g., one or both may independently explore an object); nonsocial play (e.g., one or both may engage in an independent imaginative activity); and social play (e.g., one's behavior becomes modified by another's nonliteral and sequential behaviors, which occur in sequences and revolve around a theme). In operationalizing these states, the observer must carefully and accurately distinguish play (or nonliteral) from nonplay (or literal) acts. Playful exaggeration of gestures and the existence of laughter, giggles, and smiles are used in making such distinctions in studies by Bateson (1956) and Lieberman (1977).

In Garvey's study, children were accompanied by their nursery school teacher to a laboratory play setting. They formed three age-groups of 12 dyads each: younger (i.e., 3½ to 4½ years); middle (i.e., 4½ to 5 years); and older (i.e., 5 to 5½ years). A total of 36 play sessions were videotaped, and the results showed that focused interaction or mutual engagement occurred an average of 66% in each session. Speech occurred at the rate of one utterance every 4 seconds. Garvey's results demonstrate that the youngster and his/her partner recognized when a play state existed and developed mutually binding rules for interaction. Second, content of the play themes was subject to modification by both individuals in the dyad. These modifications were based on reciprocity and taking turns. Third, the children in the dyads showed greater person-centered, rather than object-centered, concerns. Person-centering is necessary for the flexible and rapid development of play themes. Fourth, observation revealed that the play participants often checked or made active efforts in evaluating the play status by announcing the intent to pretend or by designating explicit role assignments. These play behaviors relate specifically to language development. For example, in both social play and language children use socially agreed-upon, rule-governed symbol systems to convey meaning. Furthermore, both conversation and social play involve children learning reciprocity and turn taking.

Ratner and Bruner (1978) conducted a longitudinal study on the social nature of play and language that involved two children whose play and language behaviors were observed in social-exchange games such as peekaboo with their mothers. The first child was observed over a period of 5 months; the second was monitored for 9 months. This study also showed the interrelated effects of mother-child social play and development of potential communication skills in very young children. The results of the study show that early games and play between mother and child can assist the youngster's mastery of forms of native language. First, the social context of play with parent provides an accepting and supportive setting whereby the child is free to initiate variations without erring. This implies that play and language both have a restricted activity framework or "semantic" domain. Play provides the framework for the child's syntactic development. Examples include adult-child games like peekaboo, in which children learn to "comment" upon the "topic" of mothers' actions.

Second, the results indicate that social play permits the development of reversible role relationships between mother and child. These role reversals mean that actions between mother and child are reciprocal and fluid. This reversible role relationship also reinforces the verbal and/or motoric actions of both mother and child. Third, the results demonstrated that mother-and-child social-exchange play and games provide predictable, recognizable, and functional social- and language-task structures. This result suggests that the ordering of events in communication and play has a clearly marked beginning, middle, and end used for prediction of the children's actions.

Sachs, Goldman and Chaille (1982) focused on nature of social play and explored the use of narrative language during social pretend play. The 36 children were videotaped in same-gender and same-age dyads in spontaneous pretend play having the theme of doctor. The first 16 minutes of videotape from each play session across dyads were analyzed for speech changes in planning, framing, and negotiating during these pretend episodes. For the four 2-year-old dyads, the results show that no real reciprocal role play occurred between the children of same age and gender. No actual plots were observed, but the dyads did show joint uses of objects in these pretend transpositions. For the six 3½-year-old dyads, the results indicate that real reciprocal role play occurred between dyads at this age. No actual plots or coherent narrative lines were observed between individuals in the dyads, but simple joint uses of play objects were noted. For the eight 5-year-old dyads, the results indicate that real reciprocal role play and coherent narrative lines did occur. However, Sachs et al. note that the narrative lines observed in the 5-year-old dyads were limited by their lack of shared or mutual experiences and understandings and their relating and subsuming plot to object vis à vis object to plot.

In sum, results of these selected studies of social play as context further define the relation between use of language and play. First, the results of Garvey, Ratner and Bruner, and Sachs et al. all show that play states and their subsequent actions and activities are recognizable by the individuals. Each of these individuals possessed the minimal cognitive competencies to create and develop the play and the language skills to communicate and exchange their thoughts. Second, the result of the studies show the necessity for reciprocal role reversals that ultimately define the nature of social play. Child and adult exchange roles in social play. These reciprocal role exchanges between individuals can be motoric (e.g., using and shaking a rattle) and/or verbal (e.g., uttering and expanding on similar words or phrases in the play interaction).

LANGUAGE FUNCTIONS

The discussion of language functions reviews studies that focus on language used as a tool by the child in interacting and responding within his/her social play experiences (Nelson, 1974). Children attend to dynamic events that are functional for them in their social worlds, from which evolve speech forms and concepts commensurate with these interactive stimulus events. The studies of Mueller (1972) and Bruner (1975) show clear relationships between the use of language as a tool and play within social contexts.

First, Mueller(1972) noted historically that, in regard to the child's social speech, the focus was on language form rather than function. Further, the focus on form implies that children talk primarily to themselves and that verbal messages are poorly adapted to the listener's perspective. Mueller proposed to examine the maintenance of verbal exchanges between 24 pairs of children 3½ to 5½ years of age. These same-gender pairs were introduced to each other outside a playroom equipped with a variety of toys and games, and they were told to do whatever they liked with the tangibles. These dyadic play sessions were recorded on videotape and analyzed by a coder. Mueller's results show that utterances occurred at the rate of one every 9 seconds, that 62% of these utterances received a definite response, and that 23% attracted the listener's attention. Mueller pointed out that these results did not support previous findings of high degrees of communicative failure in the spontaneous speech of 4-year-old children. Such discrepancies reflect the manner in which children respond in unstructured, naturalistic settings. Previous work (e.g., Glucksberg & Krauss, 1967) focused on a structured environment and specified precise communication tasks for the children to complete. Mueller's results show that processes found to be important in the maintenance of verbal exchanges may emerge at younger ages than previously thought. Indeed, these discourse skills seem to develop in peer play contexts.

Second, Bruner (1975) hypothesized that "joint attention" and "joint activity" are the processes by which the child uses language to sustain social interaction and to learn, among other things, syntax. Bruner's concern focuses on the relation between functional aspects of language and syntactic structure. In

Bruner's scheme, joint attention refers to the attending of both parties (e.g., adult and child) to the same object or topic. Joint action refers to the listener's understanding of the speaker's meaning and the resultant perception of language by the child as being useful in attainment of goals and pleasurable experiences.

In sum, the study of language function identified several variables that further define the nature of the child's use of language in social play contexts. First, the function of communicative exchanges and their subsequent exploration assumes (a) an interactive setting between individuals and (b) communicative messages that are adaptive to another's perspective. Second, the processes of joint activity and joint attention are significant elements in the maintenance of verbal exchanges between individuals in play settings.

LANGUAGE ADAPTATIONS TO ENVIRONMENTAL DEMANDS

The third category of studies, language adaptations to the demands of an environment, focuses on modifications of verbal and nonverbal communication strategies in group settings. Such studies reviewed in this section include Garvey and Hogan (1976) and Sachs and Devin (1976).

Garvey and Hogan (1976) videotaped 18 child dyads, 3½ to 5 years old, in 15-minute play sessions. Behavior was coded in respect to the time spent in mutually focused interaction (i.e., the state in which activities of members of a dyad are interdependent). In the study, social speech, defined as speech strictly adapted to the verbal or nonverbal behavior of the partner, was coded according to its consequence. Five categories of consequences were (a) no apparent consequence, (b) unrelated speech, (c) attending behavior, (d) appropriate nonspeech behavior, and (e) appropriate speech. The results of the study indicate that the overall rate of appropriate speech was twice that reported by Mueller (1972). This result might be explained by the fact that these children were acquainted with one another for a longer period of time than Mueller's youngsters. First, the dyads were considered to be "in focus," or mutually engaged an average of 66% in each session. Periods judged "out of focus" were brief, with only one exceeding 2 minutes. Second, the time spent engaged in focused social speech among the older children ranged from 48% to 77% of the utterances coded and 21% to 64% for the younger children. Older dyads tended to produce longer verbal exchanges (i.e., 11 out of 12 of the older dyads produced sequence of six exchanges, whereas only 3 out of 6 of the younger dyads did so). Third, the results indicate that the children spend considerable time in social interaction that is mutually satisfying to both partners and that much of the interaction consisted of social speech. Fourth, results show that genuine social behavior does occur between children in the age range of 3½ to 5 years. The four results taken together reflect the emergence of social understanding beyond that suggested by

Piaget (1926). Language, then, may serve to coordinate and facilitate mutual engagement in play settings. It was also suggested that play activity becomes less important in promoting these mutual relationships as verbal facility increases.

Sachs and Devin (1976) found that children's language play-settings reflected their sensitivity to listeners' status. Four children 3.9 to 5.5 years old were recorded talking to different listeners (i.e., adult, peer, baby, and baby doll) and, in role-playing, a baby just learning to talk. The results show that the speech of children differed on such measures as (a) pre-verb length (i.e., mean number of words before the main verb); (b) names (i.e., use of listener's name for attention getting); and (c) imperatives (i.e., commands, rules, and orders). Second, the children observed did not talk to young listeners in the same manner as they did to their mothers or peers. Third, speech to the baby doll was different from speech to the mother and peers. Fourth, the results show that speech used in role-playing (a baby learning to talk) reflected that all the children were aware of phonological and prosodic characteristics associated with babies' speech.

Based on these four results, Sachs and Devin suggest that speech cannot be viewed simply from a grammatical point of view and that the characteristics of the person perceiving the communicative event contribute strongly to the nature of speech output in young children. Second, in play contexts, children use language that is sensitive to listeners' different roles. Thier speech is sociocentric, not egocentric.

In sum, examining selected studies focusing on the language adaptation to environmental demands show several interesting results. First, language may be adapted in quantity of utterances in order to coordinate and facilitate mutual engagement in play settings. The length of time children are acquainted with one another may also be an environmental factor in adapting language. Third, communication may be adapted depending on whether the listener is an adult, a similar-age peer, or a different-age peer. Language modifications also occur when mothers are communicating to their children. Speech used with a baby doll as a play object was different in quality and quantity from speech to mother or peer. Relative to adaptation of language to environmental demands, it appears that the essence of social play resides in the way it is done rather than what is done and that behavioral-affective systems evolve, at least partly, out of the quality of interactional social play.

CONCLUSIONS

The constructivist perspective of children's language and play in social settings stresses the relationship between language and its use in supportive interactional environments. In addition, the notions of parallel development between pretend play and language (Nicolich, 1981) and positive relationships between exhibiting high levels of pretend play and using complex language (Rosenblatt, 1977) sketch these relations and, at most, provide a descriptive base for further research.

From an examination of selected research studies, rather specific ways are described in which language use and social play are related, and particular variables are identified within the existing relationships. For purposes of discussion, research studies stressing the relation between language use and social play were identified and then grouped into categories based on similarity of result. These categories are (a) social play as context; (b) language and function; and (c) language adaptations to environmental demands.

Within the category of social play as context, an examination of the results of several studies pinpointed variables existing between the children's use of language and social play. First, the players can recognize when the states of play exist and can develop rules for communicative interaction. Second, players recognize sequential events in play: beginning, middle, and ending points. Third, play relates to the individual's use of the language in terms of syntactic and pragmatic development.

The studies concerning language and function illuminated the use of language as a tool by children in social play contexts. First, verbal exchanges in such contexts were purposeful, meaningful, and relative to interactive stimulus events. On a related note, these verbal exchanges not only were adapted to the listener's perspective but also were maintained for some duration and at an earlier age than previously thought possible. Second, the variables joint activity and joint attention evolve from group interaction in social play contexts. They are crucial in maintaining verbal communication between individuals in social play.

Language adaptations to environmental demands, the third category, focused on modifications of verbal and nonverbal communication strategies required by the demands of the environment. First, language is adapted in social play contexts depending on the age of the listener. Second, players also adapt their use of language depending on whether they are talking to play tangibles or to a parent or peer.

In the constructivist tradition, the relations between the children's use of language and their social play provide rich, viable, and rapidly expanding areas for investigation. Further identifying the ways in which they relate and defining the variables fundamental to this relationship will result in increasing amounts of research knowledge regarding language use and social play and related factors contributing to the quantity and quality of communicative interaction within social play contexts.

REFERENCE NOTES

1. SACHS, J., GOLDMAN, J., & CHAILLE, C. Planning in pretend play: Using language co-coordinate narrative development. Paper read at the American Educational Research Association, New York, April, 1982.

REFERENCES

Bates, E., Camaioni, L., & Valterra, V. The acquisition of performatives prior to speech. *Merrill-Palmer Quarterly*, 1975, *21*, 205–266.

Bateson, G. The message "This is play." In B. Schaffner (Ed.), *Group processes*. New York: Macy Foundation, 1956.

Bruner, J. The ontogenesis of speech acts. *Journal of Child Language*, 1975, *2*, 1–19.

Chomsky, N. *Aspects of the theory of syntax*. Cambridge, MA: MIT Press, 1965.

Fein, G. G. The physical environment: Stimulation or evocation. In R. Lerner & M. Busch-Rossnogel (Eds.), *Individuals as producers of their development*. New York: Academic, 1981.

Garvey, C. Some properties of social play. *Merrill-Palmer Quarterly*, 1974, *20*, 163–180.

Garvey, C., & Hogan, R. Social speech and social interaction: Egocentrism revisited. *Child Development*, 1973, *44*, 562–568.

Glucksberg, S., & Krauss, R. M. What do people say after they have learned to talk? Studies of the development of referential communication. *Merrill-Palmer Quarterly*, 1967, *13*, 309–316.

Lieberman, M. J. *Playfulness: Its relationship to imagination and creativity*. New York: Academic, 1977.

McCall, R. B., Eichorn, D. H., & Hogarty, P. S. *Transitions in early mental developmental*. Society for Research in Child Development, 1977, Monograph No. 171.

McNeil, D. Developmental psycholinguistics. In F. Smith & G. Miller (Eds.), *The gensis of language*. Cambridge, MA: MIT Press, 1966.

Mueller, E. The maintenance of verbal exchanges between young children. *Child Development*, 1972, *43*, 930–938.

Nelson, K. Concept, word, and sentence: Interrelations in acquisition and development. *Psychological Review*, 1974, *81*, 267–285.

Nelson, K. Individual differences in language development: Implications for development and language. *Developmental Psychology*, 1981, *17*, 170–187.

Nicolich, L. Early pretend games and potential parallels with language. *Child Development*, 1981, *52*, 785–797.

Peters, D., Neisworth, J. T., & Yawkey, T. D. *Child development and early education: From theory to practice*. Monterrey, CA: Brooks Cole, in press.

Piaget, J. *The language and thought of the child*. New York: Harcourt Brace, 1926.

Ratner, M., & Bruner, J. S. Games, social exchange, and the acquisition of language. *Journal of Child Language*, 1978, *5*, 391–402.

Rosenblatt, D. Developmental trends in infant play. In B. Tizard & D. Harvey (Eds.), *Biology of play*. London: Heineman, 1977.

Sachs, J., & Devin, J. Young children's use of appropriate speech styles in social interaction and role playing. *Journal of Child Language*, 1976, *3*, 81–98.

Shantz, C. U. The development of social cognition. In E. M. Hetherington (Ed.), *Review of Child Development Research* (Vol. 5). Chicago: Society for Research in Child Development, 1973.

Skinner, B. F. *Verbal behavior*. New York: Appleton-Century-Croft, 1957.

Volterra, V., Bates, E., Benigni, L., Bretherton, S., & Camaioni, L. First words in language and action: A qualitative look. In E. Bates (Ed.), *The emergence of symbols: Cognition and communication in infancy*. New York: Academic, 1979.

Werner, H., & Kaplan, B. *Symbolic formation*. New York: Wiley, 1963.

6 Narrative Competence: Play, Storytelling, and Story Comprehension

Lee Galda
University of Georgia

The use of dramatic play to increase children's appreciation for and understanding of literature has been suggested by a number of educators and psychologists. Very rarely, however, do these same educators attempt to articulate the reasons underlying the effectiveness of dramatic play as a pedagogical strategy. It is here proposed that this effectiveness has its roots in the free play of young children. Some observers of child development contend that "the path from play to internal processes in school age—endophasia, association, logical memory, abstract thinking—is the main path of development; one who understands this connection understands the main element in the transition from preschool to school age" (Vygotsky, in El'Konin, 1971, p. 230). First, this chapter will discuss how children's play in a narrative mode (dramatic play) may be related to their development of narrative competence. Basic narrative competence includes the ability to construct a story that combines an appropriate setting with characters who react to a central problem through a sequence of events that move to a logical conclusion. Next, studies that have used play to facilitate narrative competence will be reviewed. Following this review, possible factors within play that relate to the development of narrative competence will be discussed.

DRAMATIC PLAY AND THE DEVELOPMENT OF NARRATIVE COMPETENCE

Where does narrative competence begin? The impetus for developing narrative competence seems to lie in our human predisposition to make sense of our experiences and to tell others about ourselves through story (Britton, 1970). All of us tell stories. Children hear stories constantly, not only through books, television, and movies, but also in their parents' answers to "How was your day, dear?" and their siblings' excited descriptions of what happened on the way home from school; sources of story are endless. As children's linguistic competence grows, so does their ability to tell stories. One way to observe this process of children acquiring narrative competence is to watch them play.

An inclusive definition of play holds that it is "intrinsically motivated, spontaneously emitted, pleasurable, and self-generated" (Rubin, 1980, p. 70). Play is also "nonserious" and differs from exploration in its "nonliteral" or "pretense" character (Rubin, 1980). The presence of pretense differentiates symbolic play from exploration, functional play, and constructive play (Fein, 1979; Smilansky, 1968). Further, as symbolic play is not governed by externally imposed rules, it is also differentiated from games with rules. Two kinds of advanced symbolic play related to the development of narrative competence have been identified: sociodramatic play and thematic fantasy play. Smilansky (1968) defines sociodramatic play as play that involves imitating an aspect of the player's experience through actions and verbalizations. It includes pretending about objects, actions, and situations while verbally communicating within a play frame with at least one other player. A typical sociodramatic play episode would be playing house or school or doctor. Thematic fantasy play was distinguished from sociodramatic play by Saltz and his colleagues (Saltz, Dixon, & Johnson, 1977; Saltz & Johnson, 1974). Thematic fantasy play involves all of the elements cited by Smilansky except that players do not imitate an aspect of their experience. Rather, thematic fantasy play is concerned with roles, events, and themes that players have not experienced in real life. Sources of such play themes are literature and film. Typical thematic-fantasy play episodes would be playing *Star Wars* or *The Three Bears* or "Mork and Mindy." In this paper both kinds of dramatic play will be discussed, referring to dramatic play when both are of concern and to their specific labels when that distinction is pertinent.

Both kinds of dramatic play are symbolic in that they involve substituting signifiers (words and gestures) for the signified objects. For example, "I'll be the nurse" has the word *nurse* changing the real role of the child into the signified role of nurse. According to Piaget (1962), it is through play and imitation that a child learns to separate signifiers from the signified, and attach meanings to symbols. Piaget called this process the semiotic function, defining it as "the ability to represent an object which is absent or an event which is not perceived by means of symbols or signs" (1970, p. 17). Symbols are signifiers that are differentiated from, but reflective of, the signified. For example, a crayon can signify a cigarette; a wedge of clay can replace a piece of pie. The use of signifiers makes play symbolic. Play also uses language, the signifier par excellence. Language is a sign system with a priori, socially agreed-upon referents for the signifiers (words). In play, children use language to transform roles, objects, and situations from their real, to a pretense, function. Thus, symbolic actions and language use are interrelated; they are both used in play and share in the semiotic function. It is, therefore, both logical and widely held that there is a basic relation between the abilities to use language and to play (McCune-Nicolich, 1981; Sachs, 1980).

Just as there are different kinds of play, there are also different ways of using language in play. A wide variety of studies have investigated the relations between play and accompanying uses of language (Pellegrini, this volume; Rubin, Fein, & Vandenberg, 1983). Sachs (1980), investigating the use of narrative language in play, described how toddlers interact with adults and peers with simple actions and goals in mind. As they mature their play becomes more complex. Roles, that reflect the real world, such as "daddy" or "teacher," are chosen, and play actions reflect the childplayer's view of what behaviors those roles involve. Players also begin to relate more to other players' actions. Through this interaction in role playing, simple plots emerge. Children may not explicitly plan the sequence of actions because they share expectations about appropriate behaviors for these familiar actions (Sachs, 1980). Such criteria typify dramatic play, with themes usually drawn from life experiences. From these simple plots in play episodes emerges a richer and more complex form of dramatic play in which many elements of story structure are present; play now involves characters dealing with a problem that leads to lengthy interaction revolving around one theme (Sachs, 1980). Children explicitly encode verbally role (or character) assignments, specify settings, and state problems (Pellegrini, 1982; Sachs, 1980).

The developmental trend from disconnected play actions (for example, a toddler putting a doll in a cradle) to more complex dramatic play episodes evident in 4 and 5-year-old children can be facilitated. Adults help guide, or scaffold (Snow, Shonkoff, Lee, & Levin, Note 1) children into a narrative mode by providing a "narrative thread" for early, disconnected play actions. They can suggest reasons for the child's actions, such as, "Did you bathe baby because she was dirty?" They can also suggest ideas to extend observed actions, for example, "Why don't you dry her and dress her?" (Sachs, 1980). Further, the stories children hear both read and told serve as sources of information about narrative structure as well as providing the raw material for thematic fantasy play. Indeed, children often spontaneously play about stories they have heard, not meticulously following the story's plot, but assuming roles of the characters and often explicitly planning their own plot (Sachs, 1980). Anyone who has eavesdropped on a preschool group playing *Star Wars* will attest to this planning process. Adult guidance and literary input are clearly two sources of stimulation for the child's developing narrative competence.

Gardner (1980) also noted the patterns of narrative structure in children's dramatic play. He found that narrator and character voices begin to be differentiated by 4 years of age. That is, children alter their voices when speaking in a character role, "Help!," rather than in a role as play instigator or sustainer,

"Next, my car will crash." By 4 years, play generally includes a central problem that is worked out in a logical sequence of events. For example, driving in the car results in a crash that brings the doctor and nurse and is resolved with bandages and shots. Further, Gardner and his colleagues (Shotwell, Wolf, & Gardner, 1979; Wolf & Gardner, 1978) have posited the development of two distinct modes of symbolization. On the one hand are the *patterners*, whose predominant mode of symbolization is configurational. On the other are the *dramatists*, whose predominant mode is narrational; these children gravitate toward dramatic play and story-telling. As early as age 2 children tell recognizable stories (Applebee, 1978). Following Vygotsky's (1962) notion of concept development, Applebee (1978) found that the structure of young children's stories evolves from unrelated "heaps" of actions, to unfocused sequences of actions, to focused sequences of actions, to focused and sequential narratives. In another study of the development of story-telling which used pictures as prompts with 4- to 7-year-old children, John, Horner, and Berney (1970) found that children's stories developed with age from sequential picture labeling, to a "skeleton story," to an "embroidered story," to an accurate and concise retelling. Further, by age 5, children are peopling their stories with characters drawn from their real-life experiences and their experiences with story, just as they do in play. As in play, they have developed expectations about appropriate behaviors for characters. The complexity and structure of children's stories seem to develop in a manner parallel to the development of their dramatic play. Thus, exposing children to narrative in many forms, through telling personal stories, reading stories, telling literary stories, and asking them to talk and play about them should facilitate children's developing narrative competence.

A parallel between story-telling and dramatic play further illustrates this point. Both have conventional markers that distinguish them from reality. Stories are often announced by "once upon a time," both in books and in young children's oral stories. Other story markers include use of formal closings, ranging from "and they all lived happily ever after" to a simple "the end," use of the past tense, use of a special story voice, as well as the use of fictional and stock characters and events. Use of these basic conventions evolves into well-developed strategies for gaining and holding an audience (Labov, 1972). Even 2-year-old children include some story conventions in the majority of their stories. Applebee (1978) analyzed Pitcher and Prelinger's (1963) corpus of stories told by 2- to 5-year-old children for presence of formal beginnings, formal endings, and consistent past tense. He found that use of all three conventions rose steadily and significantly with age. All but two of the 5-year-olds' stories contained at least one convention, with almost half containing all three. Young children (2-year-olds) can and do use markers to indicate *This is a story!* and the use of such markers, or conventions, increases with age.

In a similar fashion, children use markers to indicate *This is play!* Garvey (1974) has proposed that the ability to distinguish play from nonplay underlies social play. "In order to play one must have a grasp of what is not play—of what is and is not 'for real' " (p. 170). In play, children not only announce their play roles but may also signal a play episode by modifying their voices and/or acting in a manner different from their normal manner (Garvey, 1977). Children also smile or giggle to signal *Let's pretend!* (Bateson, 1956) and can move from pretend to reality and back to pretend with seeming ease (Rubin et al., 1983). Another parallel, then, between storytelling and symbolic play is that there are conventions—quite similar conventions—operating in both. Children can and do learn to use these conventions with facility.

Although children do use conventions to mark story and play, they seem better able to distinguish between play and nonplay than between fantasy and reality in story. Whereas preschool children are readily able to distinguish play from nonplay, children as old as age 6 are uncertain of the reality of story characters and events (Applebee, 1978). When asked where Cinderella lives, many 6-year-olds give a specific, though often inaccessible, place for an answer. They recognize the storyness of the tale of Cinderella but are not certain if she is make-believe or real outside the story world. Thus, whereas the act of playing is differentiated from not-playing early on, and story differentiated from not-story, the distinction between fantasy and reality remains problematic well into the school years (Applebee, 1978).

The paths of spontaneous dramatic play and story-telling seem to diverge once school begins. Just as the post-kindergarten school environment encourages story-telling, it discourages spontaneous dramatic play. Play, at least in school, generally becomes game playing (Rubin et al., 1983), whereas narrative language in speaking, reading, and writing increases in importance. In school, teachers foster the development of a specific "literary" (Scollon & Scollon, 1980) kind of narrative competence in a variety of situations.

Just as adults scaffold children's development of a "narrative thread" in their dramatic play (Sachs, 1980), the interactions between children and teachers help children develop narrative structure in their story-telling. McNamee (1979) observed ways in which a kindergarten teacher supported her students' story constructions. This particular teacher encouraged the children to dramatize the stories they had heard (thematic-fantasy play, although not spontaneous). She also asked her children to retell these stories. As she did so, she asked questions such as "What happened then?" and "How did it end?" Through the use of these questions she was helping children comprehend the specific story and at the same time teaching them basic principles of how to tell a story. Thus, both McNamee (1979) and Sachs (1980) see the origins of the development of narrative competence in the social interaction between a child and an adult around a story.

Michaels and Cook-Gumperz (Note 2) also studied a teacher's interaction with her students and the resulting effect on the students' development of narrative competence. The researchers recorded the sharing time in a first-grade classroom. They detailed the teacher's interventions to help children construct well-formed narratives. They also recorded how the same teacher could intervene in a child's discourse to change a potential narrative into a description. For example, a child might begin to tell about an object with the purpose of telling a story about how s/he found it. The teacher, not knowing the child's purpose, might intervene with questions that elicit a description rather than a story. The fact that the teacher's ideas about well-formed narratives and descriptions had a "literate" bias directly affected her responses to her children's sharing. The teacher concentrated on her literate model of sharing, which demanded decontextualized and fully explicated details as well as explicit temporal and causal sequencing of events. This focus put many of the children, especially the black children, at a disadvantage, as they had not internalized the "literate" narrative frame. Their stories were generally composed of events linked by "and." The teacher, assuming that they knew how to tell a focused, literate story, did not ask them the kinds of questions that would allow them to build on what they knew and develop their narrative competence. This study clearly indicated how the interaction between teacher and child can hinder, as well as promote, the child's developing narrative competence, depending on the assumptions shared or not shared between teacher and child.

Another study has examined how children's stories develop this literate quality during the school years. Ives, Silverman, Kelly and Gardner (1981) elicited both spontaneous and retold stories from 15 kindergarten, 15 first-, and 15 third-grade children each year for 3 years. These researchers sought to obtain some measure of the literary quality of the stories. Accordingly, they rated the stories on competence, which involved dimensions such as clarity of characters, connectedness, and number of episodes; flavor, which involved dimensions such as figurative language, descriptive phrases, and elaboration of setting; and uniqueness, which involved dimensions such as unusual subject, unusual words, and unusual imagery. The results from the first year of data indicated that, in general, story-telling competence increased significantly between each grade level, as did flavor. Uniqueness also increased, although not significantly. The longitudinal results of the spontaneous story task indicated that story-telling competence steadily increased between kindergarten and fourth grade but dropped slightly by fifth grade as children begin to enter the formal operations stage. This decline in story-telling competence was also noted by Gardner and Gardner (1971).

Most children enter school with a relatively sound story schema (Applebee, 1978; Mandler & Johnson, 1977; Stein & Glenn, 1978), and the literary quality of children's stories markedly increases during the school years (Ives et al., 1981). Some of this development is fostered by the social interaction between teacher and student (McNamee, 1979; Michaels & Cook-Gumperz, Note 2). Another way of fostering this developing narrative competence is to use dramatic play, in which we have alreacy found the roots of narrative, as a method of teaching about story. The remainder of this chapter will review studies that have attempted to explicate the effect of dramatic play on the story comprehension of preschool and school-age children.

THE DEVELOPMENT OF NARRATIVE COMPETENCE THROUGH DRAMATIC PLAY

A number of studies have attempted to demonstrate the positive effect of training in dramatic play on a variety of cognitive constructs. These include perspective-taking skills (Rosen, 1974); creativity (Dansky & Silverman, 1973; Feitelson & Ross, 1973; Pellegrini, 1981; Pellegrini & Greene, 1980); problem solving (Hartshorn & Brantley, 1973; Sutton-Smith, 1968); IQ (Saltz, Dixon, & Johnson, 1977); imaginativeness (Dansky, 1980); and cohesive oral language (Pellegrini, 1982, in press). However, as Rubin et al. (1983) point out, it is difficult to make general claims for the scope and power of the efficacy of dramatic play due to a wide variety in constructs measured, kinds of measures used, variation in amount and quality of training time, and variation in age, socioeconomic status, and general cognitive development of the subjects. Additional studies (Dansky, 1980; Pellegrini & Galda, 1982; Saltz, Dixon, & Johnson, 1977; Saltz & Johnson, 1974) examined the effect of dramatic play on the comprehension and production of sequential narrative.

Saltz et al. (1977) attempted to replicate results obtained in an earlier study (Saltz & Johnson, 1974), which indicated that thematic fantasy play improved story recall and story-telling abilities in young children. They tested the effect of thematic fantasy play training, sociodramatic play, fantasy discussion, and control conditions on the story interpretation, fantasy judgment, and sequential memory of lower socioeconomic status (SES) preschoolers. They found no significant effect for the separate play conditions on story interpretation, although a significant interaction between play conditions and IQ was indicated. They found no significant effect for condition on sequential memory. Thematic fantasy play did significantly increase fantasy judgment. In an effort to support their contention that it is the fantasy element in thematic fantasy play which contributes to cognitive growth, the authors seemed to ignore their results. That is, fantasy was only significantly related to the reality-fantasy distinction measure. Further, the results obtained were confounded by adult tuition in the fantasy play condition as compared to adult presence without tuition in the social-dramatic play condition (Rubin, 1980). That is, adults helped structure thematic fantasy play episodes but not sociodramatic play episodes. Therefore, there was social interaction between adults and children in the thematic fantasy play condition, a factor that could promote the development of narrative competence regardless of condition. Thus the causal factors in thematic-fantasy play responsible for improved narrative competence remained unclear.

Generally, the lack of significant effects for play conditions on story interpretation and sequential memory may be due to the subjects used—very young and lower SES preschoolers. Other studies have indicated that SES may be a factor in the results of studies of the effects of play. Some research has indicated that higher SES children engage in more pretense play at an earlier age than do lower SES children (Eifermann, 1971; Smilansky, 1968). However, McLoyd (1980) examined the play of low-income black preschoolers and found that between one-third and one-half of their utterances represented fantasy transformations. These findings were similar to those of Matthews (1977), who studied the play of white middle-income children. Therefore, the effect of SES on the Saltz (Saltz & Johnson, 1974; Saltz et al., 1977) findings remains unclear.

Age might also have influenced the results of the Saltz et al. (1977) study. There is evidence that the frequency and complexity of dramatic play increases with age from 3 to 6 years (Rubin et al., 1978; Smilansky, 1968). Dansky's (1980) sample was composed of older preschoolers from a middle-class environment, differing from Saltz's sample on both age and SES dimensions. Not making the distinction between thematic fantasy and sociodramatic play, Dansky looked at the effects of dramatic play, free play, and exploration on a variety of measures. While the Saltz et al. (1977) findings indicated positive but not significant effects for play conditions, Dansky's findings revealed significant effects for the play condition on measures of sequential memory, story recall, and organization and sequential quality of verbal production. Thus, play training may be more effective with older preschoolers than with younger preschoolers. SES differences may also influence play training effectiveness.

The causal factors within dramatic play itself still remain elusive. Other researchers have suggested that linguistic transformation of roles and props (Sachs, 1980), as well as peer interaction (Rubin, 1980), are the elements of play that enable children to sequentially recall stories. Linguistically transforming roles and props ("I'll be the bad guy and this stick is my gun.") and accommodating to other players' concepts of story require children to consider multiple aspects of objects, persons, and situations. Being able to do so involves a number of cognitive skills. Specifically, to be involved in successful dramatic play a child must differentiate literal and play roles and activities and be able to consider various roles simultaneously within a play frame (Rubin et al., 1983). These abilities should facilitate narrative competence because the distinction between literal and nonliteral is also important in narrative construction and comprehension, as is narrative sequence.

Pellegrini and Galda (1982) also concluded that verbal reconstruction through peer interaction in thematic fantasy play resulted in improved story comprehension. Their study involved training lower SES kindergarten, first-, and second-grade children in one of three conditions: dramatic play, discussion, or drawing. Dramatic play required verbal reconstruction, fantasy, and peer interaction; discussion required verbal reconstruction with minimal peer interaction; drawing was neither verbal nor interactive. Children were trained in their respective conditions for two sessions before the criterion phase of the study. In the criterion phase, each group of four children in each condition was read a fantasy story (*Little Red Cap*). They were then exposed to their conditions for approximately 15 minutes. An adult was present in each condition, as a player in dramatic play, discussion leader, or dispenser of crayons and paper in the drawing condition. Next, each participant was given a criterion-referenced multiple-choice comprehension test and then asked to retell the story. These procedures differed from those followed in Saltz et al., (1977) and Dansky (1980) in that the subjects were older and they were tested on the story heard and then reconstructed through play, discussion, or drawing.

A significant grade by condition interaction was observed on a criterion-referenced test of story comprehension. Kindergarten and first-grade children in the play condition scored significantly higher than those in the discussion condition, who in turn did significantly better than those in the drawing condition. No effect for condition was observed in the second grade. Retellings were scored for number and sequence of events recalled. Players recalled significantly more events, and in a more accurate sequence, than the children in discussion or drawing conditions. Second graders recalled significantly more events in a more accurate sequence than did kindergarteners or first graders. No other conditions or interactions were significant. A trend toward a significant effect for specific roles played on total recall at the kindergarten level was present. That is, those children who had the most active roles, Red Cap and the wolf, remembered more of the story than did children with less active roles, hunter and grandmother, although all players recalled more than nonplayers. Thus, the degree of active involvement in play—in verbal reconstruction and peer interaction within a story frame—leads to increased comprehension of the story being played about.

The observed positive effects of dramatic play in the Pellegrini and Galda (1982) study were, however, not significant at the second-grade level. Second-grade players did not score significantly higher than nonplayers when comprehension was measured by a criterion-referenced test or number and sequence of events recalled. These measures, however, are fairly gross. For example, there was no provision made for differences in unelaborated and elaborated retellings. In addition, sequence and recall were confounded. Therefore, a study that combines oral retell (to measure events recalled and elaborations) and ordering pictures (to measure sequence) is needed.

The narrative skills used in playing about the story and the verbal interaction that accompanied them helped the kindergarten and first-grade children to retell the story. These children were still in the process of developing narrative competence (Applebee, 1978; Brown, 1975). According to measures of number and sequence of events recalled in the Pellegrini and Galda (1982) study, the second graders' narrative competence was not facilitated by play. This corroborates Brown's (1975) findings that by second grade, children have acquired basic narrative skills that enable them to adequately retell the story. However, we know that children continue to develop narrative competence as they progress in school (Applebee, 1978; Gardner & Gardner, 1971; Ives et al., 1981). Thus, it seemed that a closer analysis of the second graders' recalls might reveal differences between the players and the nonplayers. Consequently, an analysis of the retells using Labov and Waletsky's (1967) system for analyzing narratives was performed. This system was particularly useful since it takes into account elaborations in narrative. Since the second graders retold the basic narrative across condition, differences, if any, would occur in amount and kind of elaboration.

Preliminary results indicate that second graders who played about the story retold qualitatively richer stories than did children who did not play about the story. They were also more apt to include motivations than were nonplayers. These findings are not surprising. When children assume a story role and interact with other players in their roles, they must think of more than a simple sequence of events. The child-wolf must understand some of the trickery involved in sending Red Cap off to pick flowers while he rushes off to eat Grandma. The child-Red Cap must have pleasant tingles of fear as she engages the disguised wolf in the traditional dialogue, knowing that he is going to eat her up. Playing about a story seems to result in a greater understanding of cause and effect and the motivations and emotional responses of characters. It seems to aid the shift from focus on the physical events in a story to a more psychological, character-oriented focus (Galda, 1982; Gardner, 1980).

The question of how narrative competence develops and what facilitates this development is still being explored. Presently we have descriptions of the development of structural complexity (Botvin & Sutton-Smith, 1977), literary conventions (Applebee, 1978) and literary quality (Ives et al., 1981) in children's oral narratives. We have also seen that the kind and quality of social interaction between parent and child (Sachs, 1980) and teacher and child (McNamee, 1979; Michaels & Cook-Gumperz, Note 2) influences the development of narrative competence. Finally, we have evidence that dramatic play influences the narrative abilities of constructing and recalling stories during preschool through the early elementary school period. The strength of this evidence, however, has been challenged by Brainerd (1982). He questions whether the effects we see are "performance" effects rather than "competence" effects. That is, are children learning through play more about how to reconstruct stories than about the stories themselves? Further, even if observed effects are really competence effects, the magnitude of the effects is disappointingly small (Brainerd, 1982). Rubin et al. (1983) also note that variations in sample size and characteristics (age and SES), amount and kind of training, and measures make generalizations about the effectiveness of dramatic play difficult.

Although these studies showing the effectiveness of dramatic play for facilitating narrative competence are flawed to the extent that no causal variables have been clearly identified, dramatic play does seem to be an effective facilitator of narrative competence. Further study is needed to explicate those factors in dramatic play responsible for improved narrative competence.

REFERENCE NOTES

1. SNOW, C., SHONKOFF, F., LEE, K., & LEVIN, H. Learning to play doctor: The acquisition of knowledge about roles. Unpublished paper, Harvard University, 1983.
2. MICHAELS, S., & COOK-GUMPERZ, J. A study of sharing time with first grade students: Discourse narratives in the classroom. Unpublished paper, University of California at Berkeley, 1979.

REFERENCES

APPLEBEE, A. N. *The child's concept of story.* Chicago: University of Chicago Press, 1978.
BATESON, G. The message "This is play." In B. Schaffner (Ed.), *Group processes.* New York: Macy Foundation, 1956.
BOTVIN, G. J., & SUTTON-SMITH, B. The development of structural complexity in children's fantasy narratives. *Developmental Psychology,* 1977, *13,* 377–388.
BRAINERD, C. J. Effects of group and individualized dramatic play training on cognitive development. In D. Pepler & K. Rubin (Eds.), *The play of children: Current theory and research.* Basel, Switzerland: Karger, 1982.
BRITTON, J. B. *Language and learning.* London: Allen Lane The Penguin Press, 1970.
BROWN, A. L. Recognition, reconstruction, and recall of narrative sequences by preoperational children. *Child Development,* 1975, *46,* 156–166.
DANSKY, J. L. Cognitive consequences of sociodramatic play and exploration training for economically disadvantaged preschoolers. *Journal of Child Psychology and Psychiatry,* 1980, *20,* 47–58.
DANSKY, J. L., & SILVERMAN, I. W. Effects of play on associative fluency in preschool-aged children. *Developmental Psychology,* 1973, *9,* 38–43.
EIFERMANN, R. R. Social play in childhood. In R. E. Herron & B. Sutton-Smith (Eds.), *Child's play.* New York: Wiley, 1971.
EL'KONIN, D. Symbolics and its functions in the play of children. In R. E. Herron & B. Sutton-Smith (Eds.), *Child's play.* New York: Wiley, 1971. Source: *Soviet Education,* 1966, *8*(7), 35–41.
FEIN, G. S. Play and the acquisition of symbols. In L. Katz (Ed.), *Current topics in early childhood education.* Norwood, NJ: Ablex, 1979.
FEITELSON, D., & ROSS, G. The neglected factor—play. *Human Development,* 1973, *16,* 202–223.
GALDA, L. Assuming the spectator stance. *Research in the Teaching of English,* 1982, *16,* 1–20.
GARDNER, H. E. Children's literary development: The realms of metaphors and stories. In P. McGhee & A. Chapman (Eds.), *Children's humor.* New York: Wiley, 1980.
GARDNER, H. E., & GARDNER, J. Children's literary skills. *The Journal of Experimental Education,* 1971, *39* (4), 42–46.
GARVEY, C. Some properties of social play. *Merrill-Palmer Quarterly,* 1974, *20,* 163–180.
GARVEY, C. *Play.* Cambridge, MA: Harvard University Press, 1977.
HARTSHORN, E., & BRANTLEY, J. C. Effects of dramatic play on classroom problem-solving ability. *The Journal of Educational Research,* 1973, *66,* 243–246.

IVES, W., SILVERMAN, J., KELLY, H., & GARDNER, H. Artistic development in the early school years: A cross-media study of storytelling, drawing, and clay modelling. *Journal of Research and Development in Education,* 1981, *14* (3), 91–105.

JOHN, V. P., HORNER, V. M., & BERNEY, T. D. Story retelling: A study of sequential speech in young children. In H. Levin & J. P. Williams (Eds.), *Basic studies on reading.* New York: Basic Books, 1970.

LABOV, W., (ED.). *Language in the inner city: Studies in the black English vernacular.* Philadelphia: University of Pennsylvania Press, 1972.

LABOV, W., & WALETZKY, J. Narrative analysis: Oral versions of personal experience. In J. Helms (Ed.), *Essays on verbal and visual arts.* Seattle: University of Washington Press, 1967.

MANDLER, J. M., & JOHNSON, N. S. Remembrance of things parsed: Story structure and recall. *Cognitive Psychology,* 1977, *9,* 111–151.

MATTHEWS, W. S. Modes of transformation in the initiation of fantasy play. *Developmental Psychology,* 1977, *13,* 212–216.

MCCUNE-NICOLICH, L. Towards symbolic functioning: Structure in early pretend games and parallels with language. *Child Development,* 1981, *52,* 785–797.

MCLOYD, V. C. Verbally expressed modes of transformation in the fantasy play of black preschool children. *Child Development,* 1980, *51,* 1133–1139.

MCNAMEE, G. D. The social interaction origins of narrative skills. *The Quarterly Newsletter of the Laboratory of Comparative Human Cognition,* 1979, *1* (4), 63–68.

PELLEGRINI, A. D. A sequenced questioning paradigm as a general facilitator of preschoolers' associative fluency. *Perceptual and Motor Skills,* 1981, *52,* 649–650.

PELLEGRINI, A. D. The construction of cohesive text by preschoolers in two play contexts. *Discourse Processes,* 1982, *5,* 101–107.

Pellegrini, A. D. The effect of social dramatic play on children's generation of cohesive text. *Discourse Processes,* in press.

PELLEGRINI, A. D. The effects of classroom ecology on preschoolers' functional uses of language. In A. D. Pellegrini & T. Yawkey (Eds.), *The development of oral and written language in social contexts.* Norwood, NJ: Ablex, in press.

PELLEGRINI, A. D., & GALDA, L. The effects of thematic fantasy play training on the development of children's story comprehension. *American Educational Research Journal,* 1982, *19,* 443–452.

PELLEGRINI, A. D., & GREENE, H. The use of a sequenced questioning paradigm to facilitate associative fluency in preschoolers. *Journal of Applied Developmental Psychology,* 1980, *1,* 189–200.

PIAGET, J. *Play, dreams, and imitation in childhood.* New York: Norton, 1962.

PIAGET, J. Piaget's theory. In P. H. Mussen (Ed.), *Carmichael's manual of child psychology.* New York: Wiley, 1970.

PITCHER, E. G., & PRELINGER, E. *Children tell stories: An analysis of fantasy.* New York: International Universities Press, 1963.

ROSEN, C. E. The effects of sociodramatic play on problem-solving behavior among culturally disadvantaged children. *Child Development,* 1974, *45,* 920–927.

RUBIN, K. H. Fantasy play: Its role in the development of social skills and social cognition. In K. H. Rubin (Ed.), *Children's play (New directions for child development, No. 9).* San Francisco: Jossey-Bass, 1980.

RUBIN, K. H., FEIN, G. G., & VANDENBERG, B. Play. In E. M. Hetherington (Ed.), *Carmichael's manual of child psychology: Social development.* New York: Wiley, 1983.

RUBIN, K. H., WATSON, K., & JAMBOR, T. Free play behaviors in preschool and kindergarten children. *Child Development,* 1978, *49,* 534–536.

RUBIN, S., & WOLF, D. The development of maybe: The evolution of social roles into narrative roles. In E. Winner & H. Gardner (Eds.), *Fact, fiction, and fantasy in childhood (New directors of child development, No. 6).* San Francisco: Jossey-Bass, 1979.

SACHS, J. The role of adult-child play in language development. In K. H. Rubin (Ed.), *Children's play (New directions for child development, No. 9)*. San Francisco: Jossey-Bass, 1980.

SALTZ, E., DIXON, D., & JOHNSON, J. Training disadvantaged preschoolers on various fantasy activities: Effects on cognitive functioning and impulse control. *Child Development*, 1977, *48*, 367–380.

SALTZ, E., & JOHNSON, J. Training for thematic-fantasy play in culturally disadvantaged children. *Journal of Educational Psychology*, 1974, *66*, 623–630.

SCOLLON, R., & SCOLLON, S. B. K. Literacy as focused interaction. *The Quarterly Newsletter of the laboratory of comparative human cognition*, 1980, *2* (2), 26–29.

SHOTWELL, J. M., WOLF, D., & GARDNER, H. Exploring early symbolization: Styles of achievement. In B. Sutton-Smith (Ed.), *Play and learning*. New York: Gardner Press, 1979.

SMILANSKY, S. *The effects of sociodramatic play on disadvantaged preschool children*. New York: Wiley, 1968.

STEIN, N. L., & GLENN, C. G. An analysis of story comprehension in elementary school children. In R. O. Freedle (Ed.), *Advances in discourse processes: New directions, (Vol. 2)*. Norwood, NJ: Ablex, 1978.

SUTTON-SMITH, B. Novel responses to toys. *Merrill-Palmer Quarterly*, 1968, *14*, 151–158.

VYGOTSKY, L. S. *Thought and language*. Cambridge, MA: Massachusetts Institute of Technology Press, 1962.

WOLF, D., & GARDNER, H. Style and sequence in early symbolic play. In M. Franklin & M. Smith (Eds.), *Early Symbolization*. Hillsdale, NJ: Erlbaum, 1978.

7
Planning in Pretend Play: Using Language to Coordinate Narrative Development*

Jacqueline Sachs
University of Connecticut

Jane Goldman
University of Connecticut

Christine Chaille
University of Oregon

INTRODUCTION

In recent years, researchers in the area of language acquisition have become increasingly interested in the development of the use of language. We use language both in social situations and internally in our own thinking processes. In social situations, we use language to share our feelings, to provide information, to influence others' behavior. We use language in our own internal processing to regulate our behavior, to solve problems, to reflect upon the past, to plan the future, to categorize perceptions. Researchers interested in the area of language use are attempting to understand what is entailed in the use of language in both realms. What kinds of rules, strategies, and knowledge enable us to be effective users of language? How does the child acquire this system?

Children are quite different from adults in terms of their use of language, and we would like to better characterize the differences both in the social and cognitive realms. In this project, we are studying language use in preschool children in a dyadic pretend play situation. We chose to look at play rather than other conversational settings because play is much affected by an important

*We wish to acknowledge the assistance of the University of Connecticut Child Development Laboratories, Richard Seewald, Deborah Pierson, James Donnelly, Elaine Dickinson, Deborah Gabriele, Bianca Lauro, and Judy Spencer.

cognitive change: decontextualization. That is, one pervasive theme in development is the child's increasing independence from the limitations of current stimuli and increasing control of his/her own behavior by means of internal processes. In language, this development is reflected by the fact that children start out talking about objects and events in the current context and only gradually make a transition to talking about topics that are not in the here and now. Pretend play is one of the earliest realms in which children advance from dealing exclusively with their perceptions to displaying internal mental constructions. Young children begin pretending with isolated pretend transformations that depend heavily on the properties of objects at hand. They gradually move toward sustained pretense that is relatively free from the current situation (see Rubin, Fein, & Vandenberg, 1983; Sachs, 1980).

Language appears to be crucial to this developmental change, especially in social pretense. Sociodramatic play among peers requires that children communicate and negotiate to jointly create a fictional world, as shown by Garvey and Berndt (1977), Gearhart (1979), Pellegrini (1982), Rubin (1980), and others.

In this paper, we will focus on preschoolers' use of language in planning their social dramatic play, and we will show some of the ways in which their play becomes more structured, sustained, and context-free as they develop.

METHOD

Eighteen boys and 18 girls (24 to 64 months) were observed in same-age, same-gender dyads. There were four 2-year-old dyads, six 3½-year-old dyads, and eight 5-year-old dyads. All children were enrolled in a university preschool program. To insure familiarity, members of each dyad were drawn from the same preschool class and had been classmates for the greater part of the school year. Furthermore, the members of a dyad were screened by their teacher for incompatibility.

The pairs were brought into a small playroom, told that they had a long time to play, and were left alone together. The playroom contained many objects suggesting a doctor theme, as well as some objects not specific to that theme such as pieces of fabric, pieces of styrofoam, wooden blocks, and hats. The play sessions lasted up to ½ hour and were videotaped through a one-way mirror from the next room. The data discussed here are based on the first 16 minutes from each session.

RESULTS

First, let us imagine two people in a room with many toys relevant to a doctor-patient play theme. The people might first decide whether to play with the toys or do something else. If they used the toys, they might at an early point decide who was going to take which role, reflecting thier knowledge of the situation the toys represented: a patient visiting a doctor. When they began to play, objects would be used as needed, but sometimes if an object was not available, the players might assign its function to a different object or even use an imaginary object. The sequence of events or enactments also would reflect their knowledge. For example, a visit to the doctor sometimes occurs because of a symptom (though not always, as in the case of check-ups). The patient would call or go to the doctor. After some preparation (e.g., lying down), the doctor might use instruments in diagnosing the problem and then treating it. The treatment might or might not result in a cure, and there might be instructions (as in ''get lots of rest''). In short, pretend play involves (a) assuming or negotiating the pretend mode; (b) talking about roles, objects, and actions; and (c) constructing a story with a problem, a logical sequence of actions, and an outcome.

Now let's see what the children did in this situation. Did they engage in pretend play? To answer this question, after transcription the children's utterances were coded as: (a) non-play utterances, (b) utterances that were part of play but not involving pretend, (c) utterances that were part of pretend play sequences. The reliability of this coding was .87. The percentage of utterances classified as pretend was 26% for the 2-year-old dyads, 56% for the 3½-year-old dyads, and 63% for the 5-year-old dyads.

Utterances in pretend play sequences were then classified as enactment, where the child was talking in role, or planning. In planning, the child was speaking as him/herself in planning, negotiating, organizing, and managing the play. Such planning is not confined to the beginning of the play session but appears throughout the session. It is these planning utterances that contain most of the speech creating the narrative line of the play. (A similar distinction has been made by Schwartzman, 1976, Sutton-Smith, 1979, and Wolf, 1981, who used the term *context* to refer to planning utterances.) The mean number of planning utterances per dyad was 22.75 for 2-year-olds, 71.50 for 3½-year-olds, and 111.85 for 5-year-olds. For each age, planning utterances made up over 50% of the pretend utterances, with no differences in the percentage of planning by age.

We coded the planning utterances with respect to content as follows:

Role	*I'll be the doctor; You be the doctor.*
Role Characteristic	*I have a fever; Pretend you have a broken leg.*
Object Description	*That's a shot thing.*
Object Transformation	*This is the waiting room; Let's use this for a microphone* [holding up block]
Action	*I put it on; You put it on; Let's put it on.*

The reliability of this coding was .88. With this analysis, we asked: When a child was speaking as self in a pretend sequence, what was the content of that speech? We will next give a brief sketch of some of the characteristics of the play in each of the age groups.

2-year-olds

The 2-year-olds did little pretending. When they did pretend, the most striking difference between the 2-year-olds and older children was that the 2-year-olds never talked about roles. This result is consistent with an observation by Musatti (1980) that 2-year-old subjects playing with peers did not take reciprocal roles.[1]

Object descriptions made up 16% of the 2-year-olds' planning utterances and object transformations 13%. The object transformations were all very conventional transformations: e.g., calling the doll "baby" or calling an empty bottle "medicine."

The majority of the 2-year-olds' utterances were in the action category (71%). These utterances were devoted to describing their own actions and telling the other child how to act. These activities often involved taking turns. For example:

> Bobbie: I'm bringing doggie for a ride with me [puts on beret and takes dog].
> Lydia: I'm gonna bring my doll—dolly for ride with me. Dolly for a ride. Dolly.
> Bobbie: My doll's going for—my—my—my dolly goin' for a ride with me.
> Lydia: Ride um—and my dolly's goes ride for me [picks up doll].

In short, the 2 year olds talked mainly about their actions while engaging in use of objects in a pretend mode.

3½-year-olds

In the 3½-year-olds' play, there were some long sequences of pretend interactions. Eighteen percent of their planning utterances were about roles—a higher percentage than in the 2-year-olds or 5-year-olds. The reason for this focus on roles appears to be that often both children wanted to have the role of doctor and could not resolve their disagreement. Unresolved arguments about roles often even prevented further development of the play. In two dyads, the children solved the problem concerning roles by eventually ignoring the doctor-objects and moving to different themes, in both cases themes that did not involve reciprocal roles. One girl dyad started with the doctor theme but soon modified it to a "mommy-baby" theme, in which each girl played "mommy" using a doll as "baby." The children coordinated their play by saying what they were doing, but without reciprocal roles. A boy dyad used a fantasy theme (Saltz & Johnson, 1974), playing at killing alligators and monsters, with no reciprocal roles and no planning of the actions. The two boys simply enacted a presumably familiar theme with cries like "Pow-pow," "Get it," "It's dead."

---

[1]Wolf (1981) did find some speech about roles in a 2-year-old child she studied. He was playing with an adult rather than a peer.

Object descriptions made up 5% of the planning utterances and object transformations 15%. The object transformations were quite conventional, as was the case for 2-year-olds, such as identifying the empty bottles as "medicine" (except in the case of the two boys who created the imaginary beasts). A more detailed description of the object use in these play dyads is in Chaille, Goldman, and Sachs, 1983.

Action utterances made up 50% of the planning in the 3½-year-olds. Within these action utterances there was little depth of plot: they most often consisted of talking about using the various objects on the other child who was (unwillingly) being "patient." There was little differentiation of various potential plot elements, such as symptoms, diagnosis, treatment, and results.

5-year-olds

Looking at the content of the speech devoted to planning and organization, we see several developments that contributed to better narrative development in some of these dyads.

There was a smaller percentage of role assignments by the 5-year-olds (8%) than by the 3½s. They decided on roles early on, with little disagreement, and were more polite about it. For example, half of the 5-year-olds' role utterances were questions, whereas less than a quarter of the 3½-year-olds' role utterances were questions. One 5-year-old girl could not decide how to best phrase her request for a role, saying "wan' me to—I think I need—who wants to—you could—could I be the little girl?" Also, older girls were more likely to use joint role statements, such as "I'll be the nurse and you be the doctor" or "Then we'll both be doctors, okay?" again suggesting that these children were considering the other child in making plans.

When there were disagreements, the children seemed more able to reach a compromise, calling on notions of turn-taking and fairness, as in: "Your turn to be doctor maybe," and "And then next time you're the doctor for each of the babies, right?"

Role characteristics were heavily used by the two 5-year-old dyads (one male, one female) that showed the most advanced play. They said things like "I have a sore throat," "Are you sick?" and "I steal things, right?" These utterances enriched the play by providing motivation for further action. They can be substituted for explicit directives. If the child says "Put a thermometer in my mouth," s/he is explicitly directing the next action in the play, but if s/he says "I have a fever," perhaps the other child will give him/her the thermometer, reflecting knowledge about behavior appropriate to the role of the doctor. In the second instance, there is more room for inferences and creativity in the play.

Object descriptions made up 13% of the planning utterances and object transformations 17%. Though the percentage of object transformations is not higher than in the 3½-year-olds, there was a qualitative difference. The object transformations were less conventional, with, for example, the fabric used as a rug or nightgown, the medicine bottle used as poison, and the couch used as a train. Some of the older girls used transformations that had to do with locations, conditions, and time, like "Pretend it's cold outside," "Pretend it's the next day," or "Pretend it's tomorrow morning." Such utterances are an indication of an emerging appreciation of the role of time, environmental conditions, and so forth, in determining the activities to follow.

Action utterances made up 49% of the planning. Like the younger dyads, the 5-year-olds used many utterances that described their own actions or directed the other child's actions, as when one eager boy said "Then take your medicine and put on some of these—then do everything!" However, sometimes the 5-year-olds used explicit "pretend" action utterances, which were not found in the younger children, as in "I'm pretending I was just putting the socket in" or "Pretend you put two blankets on me, right?" Another characteristic that appeared in the 5-year-old dyads that did not occur at all earlier was the use of past tense. Some 5-year-olds referred to imaginary past actions, as in "Pretend I was driving in a car and I had an accident, okay?" and "You slept on the floor." They also used other complex descriptions of the temporal ordering of events, as in "After I been at the doctors you come at the doctors."

The plots in the 5-year-olds' play were somewhat more involved than those of the younger children. Where 3½-year-olds used one object after another on the patient, the 5-year-olds had more plot elements: they talked about symptoms, diagnoses, treatments, and follow-ups.

There were still problems that limited narrative development. Sometimes the children's knowledge about the situation was insufficient for development of the play. For example, John used the object to "take blood pressure" on Seth; Seth asked "What—how much is it?" John replied "I don't know, but I took your blood pressure and that's the end of that." John's lack of an appropriate response halted the plot development, and at that point both boys simply looked at the various toys for a while before returning to pretend play. (For further discussion of the role of knowledge in doctor play, see Andersen, 1977, and Snow, Shonkoff, Lee, & Levin, 1982).

A more serious problem in the 5-year-olds' play, however, was that there typically was no overarching narrative organization, so that the elements of a plot, though present, were not ordered correctly. Instead, as a child finished with one object and took up another, a treatment or diagnosis or symptom simply was invented to accompany the ensuing activity. Many times that utterance was not related to past utterances or actions. For example:

       [Karen puts cotton on Sheila's knee]
    Karen: Pretend you had a bad cut, real bad.
       [Karen puts blanket on Sheila]
    Karen: I hafta cover you up. Pretend you had a chill.

Sheila: You put two blankets on me, right? One for my knee.
Karen: What?
Sheila: (irrelevant response)

In this episode, when Karen put cotton on Sheila's knee, she justified her action by referring to an imaginary cut. Next she covered Sheila with a blanket and said "I hafta cover you up." This could be part of the treatment for the cut but instead was justified by reference to "a chill." Sheila tried to integrate the two symptoms in her reply: "You put two blankets on me, right? One for my knee." That utterance confused Karen, who asked for a clarification. Sheila did not respond, and again, development of a plot was stopped.

Going beyond the content categories of action, role, and object, there were several types of framing utterances in the 5-year-old doctor narratives that had not occurred at all in the younger children's play:

Five year olds were much more likely to talk explicitly about the theme: e.g., "Let's play doctor" or "I don't want to play that, I want to play something else instead." They tried to come to an agreement about what they were going to do in the situation, rather than simply be guided by the objects that happened to be available.

Another characteristic contributing to good play found mostly in the older children was the statement checking the reality of the situation, as in:

Jacob: Will it hurt really bad?
Chuck: It will hurt kinda like—uh—we're just playing', right?
Jacob: Right.

The children were constantly moving in and out of pretend in these interactions and it is important to know whether the partner is pretending or not.

These attributes of play just described—the explicit pretend statements, thematic utterances, and reality checks—all help to frame the play. This framing provides enrichment in the plot and allows the children to make inferences about the kinds of activities that could be jointly carried out from there on.

GENERAL CONCLUSIONS

For the most successful sociodramatic play, each child in the interaction has to have a number of abilities:

1. Pretending. We found pretending in all age groups. However, only two of the four 2-year-old dyads engaged in pretending, and in those only a quarter of the total utterances were utterances in a pretend mode. The percentage of pretending was similar for 3½- and 5-year-olds, though there were qualitative differences in the type of pretending.

2. Role-taking. The 2-year-olds in this study did not spontaneously take roles when playing with a peer. All the older children took roles in their play, though not always the reciprocal roles that are typically found in sociodramatic play.
3. Knowledge about the theme of the play. Since we provided many toys suggesting a doctor theme, most dyads attempted to use that theme in their play. However, we found even in the oldest dyads that the children's lack of knowledge about the doctor theme could inhibit their play. We might expect the most successful sociodramatic play to involve themes that are most familiar to young children.
4. Carrying out actions consistent with the theme. Given sufficient knowledge, children typically carry out various pretend actions in play. However, there is considerable variation in how related the actions are to one another. In the younger children, actions were only loosely related in that most derived from the theme of the play. The 5-year-olds often carried out more structured sequences of actions. However, even in the oldest children, there was not an overall narrative line relating the various actions to a "plot." The change in continuity of actions from the youngest to the best 5-year-olds dyads was striking, and we plan further analyses of this developmental change.
5. Communicating ideas. As well as the ability to pretend and create play elements, each child must have the ability to communicate his/her ideas to the other child. Good pretend play requires linguistic communication. Even the youngest children who pretended did not depend solely on observing the other child to coordinate their activities, but talked about their actions. The 3½- and 5-year-olds all talked about roles, objects (including object transformations), and actions. One source of variability in the quality of play may be how effectively the children can communicate. One child might have an excellent idea but be unable to express it so that the other child understands. The child who misunderstands, in turn, may not communicate the misunderstanding. When communication failures occurred, the children in this study were likely to break out of pretending and play individually for a time before reestablishing communication.
6. Resolving conflict. For good play, the children must also agree on what to do. We saw in the 3½-year-olds that many of their utterances focused on role assignments. Often the children could not agree on roles and therefore could not progress further in their pretending. Of course, it is possible for disagreements to be resolved, and this is what we saw in the 5-year-olds. Without adult supervision, the children were quite successful in negotiating and compromising so that a disagreement could be settled.

To conclude, we can summarize our findings for the three age groups. Some of the 2-year-olds did pretend, but they did not engage in sociodramatic play. There were no roles and no real plots, but simply joint use of objects in a pretend mode, with the pretend actions frequently coordinated by language. The 3½-year-olds did take reciprocal roles in sociodramatic play, but this play consisted largely of using one object after another, with no coherent narrative line. Role assignments presented a special problem for these children when they used the doctor theme.

The 5-year-olds' play was supported by devices that provided a richer framework for the pretending, such as the use of explicit pretend utterances and the creation of imaginary past actions. The plots in their play had a greater variety of plot elements than did the younger children's. However, the development of a coherent narrative was still limited by (a) the children's lack of shared knowledge and (b) their tendency to subsume plot to objects rather than to use objects in relationship to an established plot. In the most advanced pretend play, children would have an overall narrative structure in mind and integrate each action into that structure. Although there were episodes in the 5-year-olds' play that showed an integrated sequence of actions, there was never an overall narrative framework that structured the entire play period.

REFERENCE NOTES

ANDERSEN, E. S. Learning to speak with style: A study of the sociolinguistic skills of children. Unpublished doctoral dissertation. Stanford University, 1977.
CHAILLE, C., GOLDMAN, J., & SACHS, J. Representational object use in the symbolic play of preschool children. Paper presented at a meeting of the Society for Research in Child Development, 1983.
GEARHART, M. Social planning: Role play in a novel situation. Paper presented at a meeting of the Society for Research in Child Development, 1979.
MUSATTI, T. Social interaction among toddlers during pretend play. Unpublished manuscript, 1980.
SNOW, C., SHONKOFF, F., LEE, K., & LEVIN, H. Learning to play doctor: The acquisition of knowledge about roles. Paper presented at a meeting of the American Educational Research Association, 1982.
WOLF, D. Playing along: Shared meaning in pretense play. Paper presented at a meeting of the Society for Research in Child Development, 1981.

REFERENCES

GARVEY, C., & BERNDT, R. The organization of pretend play. *Catalog of Selected Documents in Psychology.* American Psychological Association, 7, Ms. #1589, 1977.
PELLEGRINI, A. D. The construction of cohesive text by preschoolers in two play contexts. *Discourse Processes,* 1982, 5, 101–107.

Rubin, K. H. Fantasy play: Its role in the development of social skills and social cognition. In K. H. Rubin (Ed.), *Children's play*. San Francisco: Jossey Bass, 1980.

Rubin, K. H., Fein, G. G., & Vandenberg, B. Play. In E. M. Hetherington (Ed.), *Carmichael's Manual of Child Psychology: Social Development*. New York: Wiley, 1983.

Sachs, J. The role of adult-child play in language development. In K. H. Rubin (Ed.), *Children's play*. San Francisco: Jossey Bass, 1980.

Saltz, E., & Johnson, J. Training for thematic-fantasy play in culturally disadvantaged children. *Journal of Educational Psychology*, 1974, 66, 623-630.

Schwartzman, H. B. The anthropological study of children's play. *Annual Review of Anthropology*, 1976, 5, 289-328.

Sutton-Smith, B. The play of girls. In C. B. Kopp & M. Kirkpatrick (Eds.), *Becoming female: Perspectives on development*. New York: Plenum, 1979.

8

The Effects of Classroom Ecology on Preschoolers' Functional Uses of Language*

Anthony D. Pellegrini
University of Georgia

INTRODUCTION

Many childcare and early childhood educators advocate the use of various types of learning centers as a means of teaching young children (e.g., Montessori, 1971). For example, a classroom might have a tumbling mats center where children go to engage in self- or teacher-directed activity. One instructional goal of such a center might be that children's large motor skills would be developed further. In many childcare/early education programs advocating the learning center approach, teachers typically choose and arrange materials so that the materials themselves elicit specific behaviors from children. Such an approach often involves children interacting with both materials and their peers, with minimal teacher directions. It is incumbent on educators advocating such an approach to articulate the specific ways they expect children to benefit from interacting in each learning center. The intent of the present study was to examine the effects of learning centers commonly used in childcare settings on children's functional use of oral language.

A number of researchers have provided valuable insight into the effects of specific learning centers on children's motor, social, and cognitive behaviors (for a review see Phyfe-Perkins, 1980). Quiltich and Risley (1973) have documented the kinds of social play elicited by props commonly found in early education settings. It was found that when children interacted with crayons and puzzles, their social interactions with peers was minimal. Rubin and Seibel's (Note 1)

---

*I would like to acknowledge Arlyne Hawley for her help with the data collection and Bill Owens, Director of the Institute for Behavioral Research, for his support.

research extended the work of Quiltich and Risley to the extent that they documented how learning centers affected children's cognitive levels of play and social interaction. They utilized the cognitive play hierarchy of Smilansky (1968) and Parten's (1933) social participation continuum to construct a matrix whereby children's play in a specific learning center could be categorized cognitively and socially. For example, the play of two children building separate block structures would be categorized as constructive (cognitive) and parallel (social).

Further research, however, needs to be done on the effects of classroom ecology on a very important aspect of children's behavior: their oral language production. It is indeed surprising that psychological and educational researchers have neglected the effects of specific aspects of classroom ecology on this important outcome variable. As is well known, most childcare and early education programs attempt to stimulate children's oral language skills (see Bartlett, 1972). The research to date that has examined the effects of ecological variables on children's oral language in early education settings has been global. For example, researchers compared children's oral language production in open and traditional classrooms (Borman, 1979; Pinnell, 1975); and compared language uses at home with language uses in nursery school settings (Cook-Gumperz & Corsaro, 1976). This research is global in that we do not know the effects on children's oral language of specific learning centers *within* each of these global settings. For example, what types of language are elicited in a block center? In the present study, the effects of specific learning centers on children's functional uses of language (Halliday, 1969–70, 1971, 1973) will be examined.

Children's command of a large repertoire of functional uses of language is directly related to their ability to communicate effectively in a number of different contexts and with a number of different kinds of people. This skill has been labeled communicative competence by Hymes (1970). Children who have limited or restricted experience using different functions of language have difficulty communicating with people from backgrounds different from theirs (Bernstein, 1970). This competence, although important for all children, is particularly relevant for culturally different children who may not share many common experiences with mainstream-culture children or adults. As a result, culturally different children often encounter difficulty when they try to convey a body of nonshared information to mainstream-culture members. Such miscommunications occur in educational settings where culturally different children and mainstream culture teachers have different points of reference (e.g., Philips, 1972). Experience in using different functions of language in different contexts helps reduce these instances of miscommunication.

The functions of language, as outlined by Halliday (1969–70), include: instrumental, regulatory, interactional, personal, heuristic, imaginative, and representational. The instrumental function, the simplest function, is used to satisfy one's needs; for example, "I want the car." The successful use of the instrumental function in no way depends on how well formed an utterance is. A yell can have successful instrumental function. The regulatory function of language is related to the instrumental function. The former is used to regulate the behaviors of others. Children can regulate others' behaviors by appealing to reason, e.g., "Get me that water because I'm thirsty"; or to positional status, e.g., "Get the water because I'm the leader," "Gimme." If children in formal settings use regulatories that appeal to reason, they are more likely to have their appeals granted in that persons of both higher and lower positional status would be willing to comply.

The interactional function has language being used to define and consolidate a group; for example, "Let's be friends," "Hi." Like regulatory language, the interactional function mediates social relationships. The personal function of language has a person directly expressing his/her feelings and/or attitudes; for example, "I like school." With the personal function, children not only express their feelings and attitudes, they shape their identity through verbal interaction; making public one's identity reinforces that identity. By using the personal function adroitly, children come to see themselves as having the discretion to speak or not to speak. As a result, they feel free to ask questions or volunteer information.

The personal function is closely related to the heuristic function, or using language to explore the environment. By asking questions about one's environment (the heuristic function), one realizes that such questions help shape one's own personal identity and one's concepts of the world; for example, "Why does wood float?" "How come?" The imaginative function of language also enables children to relate to their environment (Halliday, 1969–70). With imaginative language, children are using language to create a fantasy environment; for example, "Let's pretend you're the mommy and I'm the daddy," "Baby come here." They must use explicit language to change real world roles to fantasy roles. The last function described by Halliday (1969–70) is the representational function. This function is used to convey information, or to transmit knowledge; for example, "The car is red," "It's cold out." This function is typically elicited in school settings. The intent of the present study was to describe the extent to which aspects of classroom ecology, i.e., specific learning centers commonly used in early education settings and the number of adults and peers in those centers, elicit these different functions.

METHOD

Subjects

The 30 children involved in this study all attended a university preschool. A sample of 10 children, 5 boys and 5 girls, was drawn from each of three classrooms. The group of 10 2-year-old children comprised the total enrollment of that classroom; they ranged in age from 25 to 34 months ($\bar{X} = 27.1$). Children in each of the 3- and 4-year-old classrooms were randomly chosen from each of their classes. The 3-year-olds ranged in age from 38 to 79 months ($\bar{X} = 73$). The 4-year-olds ranged in age from 49 to 60 months ($\bar{X} = 54.6$).

Procedure

Data were collected according to a time-sampling procedure. Each child was observed for five randomly sampled 1-minute periods during each of his/her free play periods at each of three observation sessions. Children were observed on Mondays and Tuesdays during the fifth, seventh, and ninth weeks of the fall, 1981 academic quarter. Thus, each child was observed in three separate sessions. Each child was observed by the author and a graduate student. All observations were made from behind a one-way viewing screen. The first utterance generated during the 1-minute observation time was the only one recorded. In addition to coding language functions and transcribing the coded utterance at each observation, the specific activity center at which each child was present while s/he was being observed was noted. The number of adults and other children also present at the center was recorded. Children's individual utterances were coded on a coding sheet according to Halliday's (1969–70) functions of language as heuristic, interactional, instrumental, regulatory, personal, representational, or imaginative. Each utterance was scored as serving one or more than one function.

The operational definitions for the language functions were taken from Halliday (1969–70). Reliability for the coding of language functions was established by comparing the simultaneous observations of the two observers on one-third of the total observations. The interrater reliability for the language functions was 89.7%. Each utterance was also coded as responding to or initiating discourse. It was also noted, for each utterance, whether the utterance was addressed to adults, to other children, or to self.

Language Scoring Procedure

Each child was observed five times during each of three observation sessions, for a total of 15 observations. Within each observation each child's first observed utterance was scored as serving one or more than one function. If the child did not generate an utterance in the 1 minute of observation, s/he was given a zero score for each function. For each of the three sessions, each child had five separate scores for each of the language functions. Each child's language function score for a whole session was the mean number of individual functions across the five observations for that session. For example, suppose in the five observations for one session a child generated five utterances, three of which were unifunctional (being only interactional) and two of which were multifunctional (being both interactional and heuristic). The child's interactional function score for that session would be 1 because s/he generated 5 interactionals in 5 observations (5:5 = 1). The heuristic function would be .4 because s/he generated 2 heuristics in 5 observations (2:5 = .4). S/he would be given 0 scores for the other functions in that observation because they were not observed. For each session, each child had a mean score for each function as well as a total function score. The total language functions score was the mean number of different individual language functions per utterance. The total language function score for the above noted example would be .4 because in five observations two different functions were observed (2:5 = .4).

Design and Data Analysis Procedures

The study was a repeated-measure design. The three separate observation sessions were the repeated factors. Gender, activity centers, and age were grouping variables. The dependent variables were individual and total language function scores. Due to the small sample size, the three grouping variables could not be incorporated into one factorial design. Therefore, three separate repeated-measures analyses were calculated to determine the separate effects of age, gender, and activity centers on individual and total language functions. Multiple comparisons on significant main effects were calculated, at the .05 level, using the Student's Newman Keul procedure. Significant interactions were examined, post hoc, according to the simple effects analyses (Winer, 1962) at the .05 level.

In addition to the repeated measures analyses, a correlation matrix was constructed for predictor (gender, individual activity center, number of adults present, and number of other students present) and criterion (individual and total language function scores) variables.

RESULTS

The first series of repeated-measures analyses examined the effect of gender, repeated on sessions, on individual and total language functions. There was a significant effect for gender on the imaginative function, $F(1, 2) = 20.21$, $p < .001$; R-square = .25. Boys ($\bar{X} = .427$) used significantly more imaginative language than girls ($\bar{X} = .133$). There was a significant effect for gender on the total functions $F(1, 2) = 4.29, p < .04; R$-square = .09. Boys ($\bar{X} = 1.743$) used significantly more total functions than girls ($\bar{X} = 1.341$). For the heuristic function there was a significant effect for sex, $F(1, 2) = 3.81, p < .05; R$-square = .13, with girls ($\bar{X} = .09$) using significantly more heuristic language than boys ($\bar{X} = .04$). There was also a significant, but disordinal, gender × session interaction, $F(1, 2) = 3.90, p < .02$. Simple effects for gender at each session were calculated. There was a significant difference for gender only during the third session, where girls ($\bar{X} = .150$) used more heuristic language than boys ($\bar{X} = .000$). There were no effects for gender on any of the other language functions.

The effects of individual activity centers on individual and total language functions, repeated on sessions, were analyzed. For instrumental language, there was a significant effect for center, $F(3, 6) = 3.11$, $p < .03$, and a significant difference between sessions, $F(2, 6) = 5.77$, $p < .004$; R-square $= .22$. The housekeeping ($\bar{X} = .049$) center elicited significantly more instrumental language than both the water-sand ($\bar{X} = .0$) and the block ($\bar{x} = .01$) centers. Significantly more instrumental language was observed in the third session ($\bar{X} = .063$) than in second session ($\bar{X} = .0068$). No other between group differences were significant.

There was a significant effect for center on interactional language, $F(3, 2) = 4.68$, $p < .004$; R-square $= .22$. The housekeeping ($\bar{X} = .927$) elicited significantly more interactional language than both the art ($\bar{X} = .595$) and water-sand ($\bar{X} = .528$) centers. No other between group differences were significant.

There was a significant effect for center on the imaginative function, $F(3, 2) = 20.25$, $p < .0001$; R-square $= .47$. The housekeeping center ($\bar{X} = .696$) elicited significantly more imaginative language than the art ($\bar{X} = .135$), water-sand ($\bar{X} = .095$), and blocks ($\bar{X} = .460$) centers. The blocks center elicited significantly more imaginative language than both art and water-sand centers. No other between group differences were significant.

Last, there was a significant effect for center on total language functions, $F(3, 2) = 6.74$, $p < .0005$; R-square $= .25$. The housekeeping center ($\bar{X} = 2.33$) elicited significantly greater total function scores than art ($\bar{X} = 1.275$), water-sand ($\bar{X} = 1.22$), and blocks ($\bar{X} = 1.84$) centers. Blocks elicited significantly larger total language function scores than both art and water-sand centers. There was no effect for session or center on the remaining functions of language.

The effects of age on individual and total language functions was analyzed next. For the instrumental function, there was a significant effect for age, $F(2, 2) = 3.19$, $p < .04$; R-square $= .26$. Both 3- ($\bar{X} = .05$) and 4- ($\bar{X} = .05$) year-olds generated significantly more instrumental language than 2-year-olds ($\bar{X} = .0$). The disordinal age × session interaction was analyzed by examining the simple effects for age at each session. At session 1, 3-year-olds ($\bar{X} = .11$) generated significantly more instrumentals than both 2- ($\bar{X} = .0$) and 4- ($\bar{X} = .0$) year-olds. At session 3, 4-year-olds ($\bar{X} = .145$) generated significantly more instrumentals than 2-year-olds. No other between group differences were significant.

There was a significant effect for age on interactional utterances, $F(2, 2) = 7.78$, $p < .0008$; R-square $= .22$. Three-year-olds ($\bar{X} = .779$) generated significantly more interactional language than 2-year-olds ($\bar{X} = -.46$). No other between group differences were significant. For imaginative language, there was a significant effect for age $F(1, 1) = 3.23$, $p < .04$; R-square $= .12$. However, there were no reliable differences among the age groups.

For the representational function of language, there was a significant effect for age, $F(2, 2) = 7.46, p < .001$; R-square $= .19$. The 4-year-olds ($\bar{X} = .15$) used significantly more than the 2-year-olds ($\bar{X} = .15$). No other between-group differences were significant. For total functions, there was a significant effect for age $F(2, 2) = 10.67, p < .0001$; R-square $= .25$. Four-year-olds' ($\bar{X} = 1.95$) utterances contained significantly more total functions than did the utterances of 2-year-olds ($\bar{X} = .98$). No other between-group differences were significant. Age did not have a significant effect on the other language functions.

Pearson product moment correlation coefficients were calculated at each age level to determine the relations between predictor and criterion variables. Only statistically significant correlations will be reported in the text. The remaining correlations are reported in Table 1.

For 2-year-olds, sessions correlated significantly and positively with per-

TABLE 1
Correlation Coefficients for Predictors on Language Function by Age

	Instrum.	Regul.	Person.	Interact.	Imag.	Heur.	Rep.	Total
2-year-olds								
Session	.02	−.08	.49**	.30	−.44*	.25	.13	.49
Gender	.01	.17	−.20	.05	−.33	.28	−.07	−.08
Adults	.01	−.04	.18	.50**	−.08	.29	.33	.49*
Students	.00	.01	−.11	−.01	.01	−.05	−.11	−.09
Art	.00	−.15	.02	.04	.25	−.05	−.29	−.05
Water-Sand	.00	.04	.04	−.14	−.34	−.02	.21	−.08
Housekeeping	.00	.16	−.17	.05	−.04	−.09	.15	.05
Blocks	.00	.13	−.08	.10	.08	.09	.09	.15
3-year-olds								
Session	−.27	−.08	.05	−.05	−.08	.11	.25	−.09
Gender	.08	.19	.24	.02	.52**	.27	.15	−.00
Adults	−.11	.04	.00	.30	−.47**	.07	.56**	.13
Students	.04	.10	.24	.28	.22	−.11	−.14	.22
Art	.27	.12	.20	−.01	−.50**	.09	.21	−.01
Water-Sand	.28	.12	.24	.05	.21	.11	.21	.05
Housekeeping	−.12	.04	.01	.18	.48**	.00	.12	.21
Blocks	−.21	−.10	−.27	−.19	.10	−.12	−.13	−.22
4-year-olds								
Session	.46**	−.23	.12	−.03	−.21	−.29	.04	−.07
Gender	.09	.39*	.39*	.52**	.49**	.05	.16	.58**
Adults	−.15	−.38*	−.43*	−.27	−.43*	−.38*	.06	−.27
Students	−.12	.26	.24	.30	.26	.12	.12	.34
Art	.02	−.28	−.10	−.72**	−.64**	−.35*	−.29	−.70**
Water-Sand	−.19	−.22	.09	.02	−.32	.29	.18	−.07
Housekeeping	.29	.34	.06	.32	.56**	.11	−.16	.41*
Blocks	−.08	.22	.00	.48*	.50**	.04	.27	.47**

* $p < .05$.
** $p < .01$.

sonal language, .49, and negatively with imaginative language, −.44. The number of adults present correlated significantly with total functions, .49.

For the 3-year-olds, gender correlated significantly, .52, with imaginative language. The number of adults present had a significant negative relation with imaginative language, −.47, as did art activities, −.50. Housekeeping activities were, however, positively and significantly correlated with imaginative language, .48.

For the 4-year-olds, session was significantly correlated with instrumental language, .46. Gender was correlated significantly with regulative, .39, personal, .39, interaction, .52, imaginative, .49, and total language, .58. The number of adults present was a significant negative correlate of regulative, −.38, personal, −.43, imaginative, −.43, and heuristic, −.38, language functions. Art activities correlated negatively and significantly with interactional, −.72, imaginative, −.64, heuristic, −.35, and total, −.70, language functions. Housekeeping was related significantly to imaginative language, .56, and total language functions, .41. Play with blocks correlated significantly with interactional, .46, imaginative, .50, and total, .47, language functions.

DISCUSSION

The intent of this study was to examine the effects of early education activity centers on children's generation of individual and total functions of language and how these varied according to gender and age. In addition, the number of adults and children present in each center were used as predictors of individual and total language functions. These additional predictor variables were incorporated into the analyses because research has shown that children's verbal and social behavior is related to the presence of adults and other children (e.g., Vygotsky, 1962; Fuson, 1979). Two points of caution, however, will be noted about some of the conclusions made in this study. The first relates to the correlation analyses. The conclusions based on these data should be tempered by their correlational nature. Second, as Rubin, Fein, and Vandenberg (1983) stated, caution should be taken when interpreting the effects of activities and/or learning centers on children's behaviors in a free-play setting. In free-play settings, such as the present study's contexts, children are free to choose the center with which they interact. In this respect, the effects of the centers and individual preference for those centers are confounded. That is, children's behavior in a specific center may reflect not only the effect of that center but also the children's individual differences that caused them to choose that center. To identify the causal nature of each of these centers, a controlled experiment, where exposure to activities is systematically manipulated, is needed.

The analyses for the effects of gender on individual and total language functions indicated that boys used more imaginative language than girls. Boys' individual utterances contained more functions than girls' utterances; e.g., "Hi, Mommy" in fantasy play serves interactional and imaginative functions. Results of the correlation analyses provided insight into these gender differences. Gender was a significant predictor of imaginative language for both 3- and 4-year-olds, not for 2-year-olds. Thus, the gender difference for imaginative language existed only for the older groups.

The significant correlation between gender and presence in housekeeping centers for 3-year-olds further explains this gender difference. More 3-year-old boys than girls tended to play in the housekeeping center. Presence in this center, in turn, was a good predictor of imaginative language. Thus, boys' propensity to play in the housekeeping center may have been responsible for the gender difference for imaginative language. Boys' presence in housekeeping centers may also have been responsible for their generation of more multifunctional utterances than girls. As our data indicate, 4-year-olds' presence in housekeeping centers was a good predictor of multifunctional language, such as "Stop hitting the baby," which serves imaginative and regulatory functions.

That the boys generated more multifunctional utterances indicates that their functional language was more mature than that of the girls. However, both boys and girls generated more multifunctional utterances with age. Halliday (1969–70) noted that as children become adept at using language, their individual utterances tend to serve more than one function. Using total language function score as a marker of functional language maturity (Halliday, 1969–70) seems to be supported by data in the present study to the extent that the 4-year-olds had significantly larger total language function scores than the 2-year-olds.

Housekeeping centers elicited more imaginative language than other centers, e.g., "Good night dear." The block center elicited more imaginative language than both art and water-sand activities. The use of imaginative language in housekeeping centers is certainly not a surprising finding. Rubin and Seibel (Note 1) found that preschoolers tend to engage in dramatic play in housekeeping centers. They also found that blocks elicited dramatic or fantasy play from preschoolers. In their study, fantasy play with blocks resulted when groups of children played with the blocks; constructive play resulted when children played with blocks alone, rather than in a group. This explanation also fits the present study. Children tended to play with blocks in groups. That is, 71% of the times children played with blocks they did so in the presence of at least one other child. However, group block play was significantly related to imaginative language only for 4-year-olds. These analyses indicate that children tend to play with blocks in groups. Blocks and the social groups tended to predict the use of imaginative language only for 4-year-olds. Younger children, even though they are in groups, may use the blocks constructively, rather than in imaginative ways. This may be the reason for their not generating imaginative language in the blocks center.

Presence in housekeeping centers resulted in children's generating more social interactional and multifunctional language. These two measures reflect the extent to which children use language to define social relations (interactional) and the functional complexity of their utterances (total functions). Pellegrini (1982), in a recent analysis of children's language in a housekeeping center, found that this type of activity center elicited language that defined players' roles and transformed props. Players must interact socially and verbally define the transformation of their roles if other players are to understand their transformations. For example, by stating "I'll be the daddy," a child is using an explicit verbal definition to convey to other players the role transformation from child to daddy. Using language to transform roles from reality to fantasy is an excellent example of a multifunctional utterance, serving both interactional and imaginative functions.

Those centers that elicited imaginative language (i.e., housekeeping and blocks, for 4-year-olds) also tended to elicit multifunctional utterances. The reason for this phenomenon may be that interaction in fantasy themes is dependent upon both social interaction and the use of explicit language for sustenance (Pellegrini, 1982; Pellegrini & Galda, 1982). If role and prop transformations are not defined explicitly by individual players, other players will not be able to sustain the play episode. Without explicit verbal transformations, ambiguity results because players do not know what props are supposed to represent in the play episode. Imaginary play, then, elicits multifunctional language because it is dependent on social interaction and the explicit use of language for sustenance.

The imaginative language of housekeeping centers, because it involves social interaction and is dependent upon explicit language, is easily contrasted with the language of art and water-sand centers. The latter activities tended to be individually executed constructive activities. Water-sand and art centers tended to be negatively related to children's use of interactional and multifunctional utterances. Children in these centers do not tend to interact socially with co-present children or adults (Rubin & Seibel, Note 1). The parallel and solitary play characteristic of these centers (Rubin & Seibel, Note 1) is not dependent upon social interaction for sustenance. Children in these centers are typically involved in individual, not group, constructive or functional activities.

The last two ecological factors to be discussed are time elapsed between observation sessions and number of adults present in individual centers. Children were observed every 2 weeks on three separate occasions; a 4-week period elapsed between the first and third session. The relatively few effects due to session is consistent with the literature on children's social behavior in daycare-early education settings. McGrew (1974) found that when children first entered a nursery setting, they were less social than the other children. After 2 months of attendance, the social behavior of these relative newcomers was indistinguishable from the social behavior of their classmates. Rubin and Siebel (Note 1) found similar consistency; preschoolers' social interactions and cognitive forms of play did not vary across a 3-month period.

The relation between adult presence in activity settings and children's functional uses of language was examined through correlation analyses. Generally, adult presence in centers related negatively to the oldest children's use of a number of individual language functions. The inverse relations between adult presence and use of instrumental and regulatory language can be explained in terms of the positional roles of adults and children. Positional role assignment holds that children are subordinate in power to adults (Bernstein, 1970). Children tend not to give orders to others in the presence of adults. That right is typically reserved for the higher status adult (Bernstein, 1970).

It is bothersome, from an instructional perspective, that adult presence is negatively related to 4-year-olds' use of heuristic and personal language. Adults are typically put in daycare-early education settings to stimulate, not inhibit, children's learning. A good student-to-teacher ratio should result in children's receiving more individual attention. Traditionally, it is thought that students benefit intellectually and socially from such individual attention. The data on the 4-year-olds suggest that this may not be the case; children tended not to ask questions or use language to define their individual identities when adults were present. These negative relations were not due to a greater number of adults present in the 4-year-olds' activities centers ($\bar{X} = .5$, $SD = .6$), compared with adult presence in each center for 3- ($\bar{X} = .7$, $SD = .5$) and 2-year-olds ($\bar{X} = .63$, $SD = .44$). The results may be explained, following Rubin, Fein, and Vandenberg (1983), in terms of older preschoolers' ability to sustain group play among themselves. Rubin et al. (1983) suggested that older preschoolers may have the "wherewithal to encourage exploration and higher level play from their playmates" (p. 91). They do not need adults to sustain their activities; they can do it themselves. Indded, adult presence is negatively related to children's social interactions and explorations of their environments.

In line with the proposition that older preschoolers are less dependent on adults for help in sustaining social interactions, 2-year-olds' use of interactional and multifunctional language was positively related to adults' presence. That is, 2-year-olds' interactional language increased in proportion to the number of adults present in each activity setting. Adults may have helped 2-year-olds maintain verbal interaction with other children and adults. However, 2-year-olds' language in the presence of adults was not predominantly addressed to adults; 52% of their utterances were directed to adults and 48% were directed to other children. Adult presence, then, seemed to stimulate equally child-child and child-adult verbal interaction among 2-year-olds. For 3-year-olds the number of adults present was positively related to representational language. Three-year-olds' representational utterances were typically in response to an adult (33/43, or 76%). Adults seemed to help 3-year-olds sustain the use of representational language by eliciting information from the children. Thus, adults tended to support, or "scaffold" (Wood, Bruner, & Ross, 1976), younger children's verbal interaction.

In summary, the data from this study suggested that fantasy-dominated centers (housekeeping and blocks) tended to elicit from preschoolers the most individual and total functions of language. Younger preschoolers are dependent upon present adults to help them initiate and sustain discourse. Four-year-olds seem to be able to help each other initiate and sustain discourse. From a pedagogical perspective, the data suggest that housekeeping settings elicit varied forms of child language. Teachers or other adults present in this center may help elicit different functions from younger preschoolers. For older preschoolers, teachers should encourage groups of children independent of adults to interact in either block or housekeeping centers.

REFERENCE NOTE

1. RUBIN, K., & SEIBEL, C. The effects of ecological setting on the cognitive and social play of preschoolers. Paper presented at the American Educational Research Association, San Francisco, 1979.

REFERENCES

BARTLETT, E. Selecting preschool language programs. In C. Cazden (Ed.), *Language in early childhood education*. Washington, DC: NAEYC, 1972.

BERNSTEIN, B. A critique of the concept "compensatory education". In S. Williams (Ed.), *Language and poverty*. Madison: University of Wisconsin Press, 1970.

BORMAN, K. Children's situational competence. In O. Garnica & M. King (Eds.), *Language, children, and society*. New York: Pergamon, 1979.

COOK-GUMPERZ, J., & CORSARO, W. Social-ecological constraints on children's communicative strategies. *Sociology*, 1977, *11*, 411–434.

FUSON, K. The development of self-regulating aspect of speech: A review. In G. Zivin (Ed.) *The development of self-regulation through private speech*. New York: Wiley, 1979.

HALLIDAY, M. Relevent models of language. *Educational Review*, 1969–1970, *22*, 26–37.

HALLIDAY, M. Language in a social perspective. *Educational Review*, 1971, *23*, 165–188.

HALLIDAY, M. The functional basis of language. In B. Bernstein (Ed.), *Class, codes, and control* (Vol. 2). London: Routledge & Kegan Paul, 1973.

HYMES, D. Competence and performance in linguistic theory. In R. Huxley & E. Ingram (Eds.), *Language acquisition: Models and methods*. New York: Academic, 1970.

MCGREW, W. Aspects of social development in nursery school children, with emphasis on introduction to the group. In N. B. Jones (Ed.), *Ethological studies in child behavior*. New York: Cambridge University Press, 1974.

MONTESSORI, M. *The Montessori method*. New York: Schocken, 1971.

PARTEN, M. Social play among preschool children. *Journal of Abnormal and Social Psychology*, 1933, *28*, 136–147.

PELLEGRINI, A., & GALDA, L. The effects of thematic-fantasy play training on the development of children's story comprehension, *American Educational Research Journal*, 1982, *19*, 443–452.

PHILIPS, S. Participant structures and communicative competence: Warm Springs children in community and classroom. In C. Cazden, V. John, & D. Hymes (Eds.) *Functions of language in the classroom.* New York: Teachers College Press, 1972.
PHYFE-PERKINS, E. Children's behavior in preschool settings. In L. Katz (Ed.) *Current topics in early childhood education, Vol. 3.* Norwood, NJ: Ablex 1980.
PINNELL, G. Language in primary classrooms. *Theory into Practice,* 1975, *14,* 318–327.
QUILTICH, H., & RISLEY, T. The effects of play materials on social play. *Journal of Applied Behavioral Analysis,* 1973, *6,* 573–578.
RUBIN, K., FEIN, G., & VANDENBERG, B. Play. In E. W. Hetherington (Ed.) *Carmichael's manual of child psychology: Social development.* New York: Wiley, 1983.
SMILANSKY, S. *The effects of sociodramatic play on disadvantaged preschool children.* New York: Wiley, 1968.
VYGOTSKY, L. *Thought and language.* Cambridge, MA: MIT Press, 1962.
WINER, B. *Statistical principles in experimental design.* New York: McGraw-Hill, 1962.
WOOD, D., BRUNER, J., & ROSS, G. The role of tutoring in problem solving. *Journal of Child Psychology and Psychiatry,* 1976, *17,* 89–100.

THE CONTEXT OF SCHOOL

9 Classroom Status From a Sociolinguistic Perspective

Louise Cherry Wilkinson
University of Wisconsin-Madison

INTRODUCTION

Sociolinguists are concerned with status, as a *social* variable. A speaker's choice of a particular form can reflect the status of the listener relative to society at large, as well as the particular relationship of the listener to the speaker. Thus, sociolinguists examine the relationship between social relations and language use. Within the last decade, a new tradition of research has developed for the study of social interaction in the classroom: the sociolinguistic approach. This approach is concerned with learning to use language effectively and appropriately in the classroom to achieve communicative goals. These goals may include, for example, requesting information, providing evaluation, managing behavior.

In this chapter, I will review the basic assumptions of a sociolinguistic approach to classroom interaction. Second, I will discuss the concept of social status from a sociolinguistic point of view. Third, I will review some recent relevant research on the development of children's use of language to convey social status. Finally, I will suggest new directions for research in this area.

ASSUMPTIONS

Several assumptions underlie a sociolinguistic approach to the use of language in the classroom (Wilkinson, 1982). First, classroom interaction requires competence in both the structural and functional aspects of language. This has been referred to as *communicative* or *interactional competence*. Classroom competence is an end in itself, as well as a means of achieving other educational objectives. It can serve both academic-cognitive, as well as social-interpersonal, goals. In order to participate effectively in classrooms, children must know how to use language. As Mehan (1979) has stated it:

> they must know with whom, when, and where they can speak and act, and they must provide the speech and behavior that are appropriate to a given classroom situation. Students must also be able to relate behavior, both academic and social, to varying classroom situations by interpreting implicit classroom rules. (p. 133)

In short, when a student speaks in a classroom, s/he is conveying social information; the act of the speech itself conveys how well that child understands the social situation, and correspondingly, how effective that speech will be for that child in securing the communicative goal.

A second assumption underlying sociolinguistic research is that the classroom is a unique communicative context. The kind of competence that is required in this context is very specific, although it may share some general characteristics with others, such as in the home. For example, many communicative interchanges between teachers and students in classrooms are structured to facilitate students' acquisition of academic information. Thus, the content of these exchanges may be more restricted, and the students' contributions may be evaluated more frequently in this context compared to others.

A third assumption is that students may differ in their communicative competence, particularly in aspects that are vital to the classroom. We know that the special aspects of communicative competence are not necessarily taught by teachers or learned by students. Certainly, some students come to classrooms already knowing something about how to use language, and they may have certain expectations about adapting to the new context. However, the special characteristics of the classroom may not be recognized by all students, and they may experience a discontinuity; they may not have within their repertoire the capability of communicating effectively and appropriately in particular classrooms.

The discontinuity between a particular classroom context and others may present problems for some students, interfering with their language development and overall adjustment. Thus, the effects of students' not knowing the standard ways of communicating in the classroom are not limited to the obvious problems that these students face in their unsuccessful interactions with students and teachers in the classroom. In addition, if some children do not understand the social situation and its communicative demands, then they may learn little from the classroom experiences in which they participate (Wilkinson, 1982).

STATUS FROM A SOCIOLINGUIST VIEW

Sociolinguists are concerned with the relationship between language and social variables, such as status. *Status* refers to a person's social position and is reflected by the judgment of that person by a designated social group. In this sense, status can be considered to be an index of social influence. Therefore, sociolinguistics addresses the corresponding relationships between differences in social status and differences in linguistic expression. One aspect of the relationship between language and social status is that the speaker's choice of an utterance can reflect the status of the listener relative to society at large. The other aspect of the relationship between language and social status is the relative status of the speaker to the listener: namely, a speaker's choice of an utterance reflects how that speaker and listener perceive each other in a social sense relative to one another. Sociolinguists believe that the *social context* is a powerful determinant of linguistic expression. Status is seen as a *negotiated* and dynamic aspect of interaction.

Goffman (1967) has contributed the most general theoretical principle regarding the relationship between social status and linguistic behavior: the principle of symmetric relations between status equals and asymmetric relations between unequals. This principle holds that those who have a similar social position are likely to use language in a similar way, such as voice quality, pitch, interruption, and formal aspects, among others. Correspondingly, people who have a different social status from one another will use language differently. For example, in one of the best-known studies of the relationship between language and social status, Brown and Gilman (1960) examined the relationship between terms of address in social status. They found that the status difference between adults was marked by nonreciprocal language usage: lower-status adult speakers used terms of respect such as titles and formal pronouns, whereas higher-status speakers addressed the lower ones more informally, as, for example, by using the first name or by familiar pronouns.

Languages differ with regard to how much and which societal distinctions in status are marked with language. Some cultures make quite marked distinctions, for example in the area of men's and women's language in Japanese (Lakoff, 1973), and virtually all languages studied have some special language reserved for talking to children (Ferguson, 1977). The first aspect discussed between language and social status concerns the general register of language relative to fundamental societal distinctions such as age, gender, and occupation. Language choice can also mark the relative relationship between particular speaker and listener on a variety of dimensions that derive from relative status, such as expertise (teacher vs. student) and familiarity (familiar vs. unfamiliar). Part of learning language is learning to use it effectively, and children have to learn when and how to mark both absolute distinctions and relative ones. In the case of absolute distinctions, children must learn what particular characteristics the society of which they are members views as important; whereas in the case of relative status, children must be able to include a comparison between the self and the other with regard to social status and mark that distinction accordingly with linguistic expression (Shatz, in press).

PREVIOUS RESEARCH

A basic research question from a sociolinguistic perspective is: What kinds of status relationships are children at different ages able to discriminate and express in language? We begin our consideration of the research literature with children younger than school age, since knowledge of social status and linguistic marking appears to develop quite early and differentiate throughout the school-age years.

One of the best documented facts in the developmental sociolinguistic literature is that children as young as 4 years talk differently to children of different status. In a seminal study, Shatz and Gelman (1973) showed that 4-year-olds produce shorter and generally less gramatically complex sentences to 2-year-olds than they do either to same-age peers or to adults. Children as young as 3 show adjustments for younger listeners and even role-play such behavior to dolls (Sachs & Devin, 1976), and even 2-year-olds in nursery school settings seem to be sensitive to listener status differences since they talk more to adults and adjust their adult-directed messages more to take account of listener needs than they do with peers (Wellman & Lempers, 1977). Other researchers have found that preschoolers are more likely to answer questions (Martlew, Connolly, & McCleod, 1978) and more informing (Cooper, 1979) with adults than they are with peers.

Research on young children's linguistic adjustments suggests that an internal representation of the social status of the listener guides speech adjustments. Children aged 2½ to 5 years choose request forms on the basis of age and status characteristics of listeners. Corsaro (1979) found that preschoolers produced more imperatives when acting as a superior addressing a subordinate than vice versa, and Andersen (1978) found that children aged 4 to 7 years revealed knowledge of social status relationships within the family as well as other culturally defined status roles, such as doctors, teachers, and nurses. Andersen asked children to use puppets to role-play these different characters; she found that as "teachers," the children regularly produced imperatives addressed to the lower-status students, but not vice versa. In using a different paradigm, Edelsky (1977) found that children's conceptions of social status and their ability to mark them with language is not completely developed with respect to expressing differences between male and female speech. She found that first graders were inconsistent in judging expressions like "oh dear" or "I'll be damned" as primarily either male or female speech; but by the sixth grade, students' judgments were very much like adults, who do gender-type responses. In contrast, James (1978), using a similar "puppet" paradigm, found that children aged 4 and 5 years were more likely to use direct forms of requests, such as imperatives, with dolls representing younger children than with dolls representing adults or peers. Jacobs (1973) asked 5-year-olds to judge the appropriateness of specific request forms and to select the probable listeners of these different forms. Her data show the children differentiated the listeners according to age status (adult vs. child) and familiarity (familiar vs. unfamiliar).

Genishi and DiPaolo (1982) examined arguments among 3- to 5-year-olds in a preschool classroom. Children's participation in the arguments reflected their social knowledge about how to behave in school as well as how to behave in and out of school roles, such as family member, doctor, or patient, as the children attempted to regulate each other's behavior and assert their own importance. Genishi and DiPaolo believe that children argue for the purpose of social negotiation about the status instead of arriving at a fair resolution of the argument for its own sake. They believe that very early, children's motivation is to manipulate others' actions in order to enhance their own status. Thus, the extensive negotiation for the roles in dramatic play that have been observed may be done more to establish who is higher status than to ensure a "well-cast play."

Research on school-age children on the topic of language marking social status is sparse. Cooper, Marquis, and Ayers-Lopez (1982) examined peer exchanges among kindergarten and second-grade students. They identify seven types of episodes that occur during interaction, such as asking for help, giving information, etc. Their data show that second graders seem more finely attuned to social-status differences among their peers than do kindergarten children. Their analysis brings us closer to understanding how children are affected in attempting to achieve their interpersonal and informational goals with other students. Merritt's (1982) research provides an analysis of students' attempts to signal and obtain information from one another. Her results on school-age children from kindergarten through third grade show that there is a vast differentiation in the ways that students attempt to gain attention and the corresponding success they have in obtaining it. In her studies, high social status can be attributed to those students who are successful in obtaining their teacher's attention, whereas less successful students do not have as much status.

Mitchell-Kernan and Kernan (1977) used a role-playing task involving puppets to elicit request for action object with a group of black American children aged 7 to 12 years. They found that requests and responses to them were used by the children to define, reaffirm, challenge, manipulate, and redefine relative status and rank. Sometimes the requests actually served the specific functions of requests—that is, attempting to get goods and services—while also serving, because of their frequency of occurrence and the particular form they took, as a test of the listener's view of the statuses involved. In other instances, however, speakers produced requests even though they did not expect to obtain what they wanted. Mitchell-Kernan and Kernan inferred that in these cases the intent of the speaker was only to test or manipulate the status relationship. Sometimes, requests were used to establish a relationship of dominance-submission between the speaker and the listener, as exemplified by the child playing the parent role to emphasize the prerogatives of that role. In other instances, requests were used to establish a child in a subservient position. Occasionally, requests were used in a role-playing situation to establish the relative rank of one child versus another and to test this status relationship and the obligations that correspond to that role. A common example was the use of a request in the form of an imperative by a "parent"-playing child to one of the adult researchers. Typically, the children did use imperatives, which is a strong form of request that is only to be used by those in a higher status position, but they softened the hardness of the request through tone of the voice or gestures. Read and Cherry (1978) report similar findings among young children who tend to use gestures and tone of voice to mitigate the harshness of direct requests when speaking to a listener of a higher status.

Ervin-Tripp (1982) reports research on the production and comprehension of social-control acts by children aged 2 to 8 years. The data for her study consisted of videotaped, unstructured, natural interaction in families; comprehension experiments involving responses to picture stories; and structured elicitations. Social-control acts are used by children to control the actions of others. Ervin-Tripp argues that when children use social-control acts, they may want to manipulate others' actions at the same time that they enhance their own status. Asserting one's status may matter as much to the speaker as the actual behavior change. Ervin-Tripp's data show that compliance with social-control acts seem to be related more to the power relationship between the speaker and the listener than to the particular linguistic form used by the speaker. Polite requests seemed the *least* successful in obtaining compliance, and there was no increment in the probability of compliance for the same tasks when more polite requests were used. Ervin-Tripp argues that social meanings and relative status are conveyed by the frequency and type of linguistic expression chosen to convey a social-control act.

The data from preschool through school age suggest that expression of differences to mark social status with language is a skill that continues to develop during the school-age years. It seems likely that there are two sources for this gradual differentiation: a greater knowledge of the social distinctions that are relevant to the child and a greater knowledge of the linguistic expressions that can mark these differences.

FUTURE RESEARCH

Further sociolinguistic research on classroom status should explore two areas: (a) what constitutes the social world of the child—the social variables that structure it, for both *absolute* distinctions and *relative* status; and (b) the use of differences in linguistic expression as markers of social status.

A study that concerns children's awareness of the rules for using language in the classroom is an example of one direction for future research (Wilkinson, Spinelli, Wilkinson & Chiang, 1983). We examined school-age children's *metapragmatic knowledge* of the request function of language in three tasks: reflection, production, and judgment. One of the goals of this study is to explore children's awareness of the social dimensions of the classroom, including the status roles of teacher and student. The reflection task consists of an interview in which children talk about their understanding of the use of requests in classroom activities. The production task consists of a role-playing situation with dolls, where requests for information are elicited in imaginary classrooms with two different kinds of listeners, teachers and students. The judgment task consists of elicitation of judgments of the appropriateness and effectiveness of requests for information in imaginary classroom situations involving teachers and students.

The data from the interview will be briefly summarized. Two questions referred to the form of requests directed to teacher-listeners versus student-listeners. All of the younger children indicated that the form would *not* differ, while about half of the older children said that it depended on the nature of the interactions.

Two questions concerned politeness, and "good" versus "bad" speakers. Half of the younger children's descriptions consisted of evaluative terms such as "nice," "cool," and "mean," while the older children seldom used terms such as these to differentiate between good and bad speakers. Another difference is that younger children included friendliness as a characteristic of good speakers (e.g., "a good talker would be somebody's friend"). Older children's descriptions of good speakers resembled Grice's notions of informativeness and cooperatives. Some examples include the following: "A good talker says it so people can understand it and it makes sense (Be clear)." "Don't say none of your business and get out of here (Be cooperative)." "A person who is not a good talker talks a lot (Be brief)." "A good talker talks if he knows a lot of work (Be informative)." Some of the older children referred to grammaticality, as in the following: "A good talker doesn't say ain't." Two additional responses from older children included references to the use of "thank you" and the use of a pleasant voice. One older child mentioned not using "bad" words. All of the children emphasized politeness rather than informativeness in response to question one, and they included evaluative references such as, "Being some people's friends and like them and being nice to them" as well as the use of "please" with the modal verb.

Two questions referred to the differential effectiveness of types of requests in eliciting help or materials. Almost all of the children agreed with this proposition; however the tendency was more pronounced for the older children (100% versus 85%). Children were asked to provide examples of "good" and "bad" requests. Older children emphasized the use of "please," however. Both younger and older children emphasized the use of indirect forms when requesting materials. For example, some of the younger children used "please" often either with qualifiers such as in the following: "Could I please borrow the book just for a second?" Several younger children suggested that "Just taking it" was a "bad" way to request an object, while several older children mentioned that saying "I got it first" qualified as a "bad" way. Both groups mentioned direct requests as impolite.

In sum, the data from the interview provide ample evidence that young school-age children possess metapragmatic awareness, including awareness of the social status dimensions of language in the classroom, and that this ability emerges and differentiates during the early school years. Older children indicated that different forms of requests should be used for teachers, versus students, depending on the nature of the interaction. In contrast, young children indicated that the former should not differ. Thus, older children seem to be more likely to state their awareness of the status dimensions of teacher versus student. Younger children emphasize affiliation in their view of "good" speakers, while older children conform more to adult (Gricean) notions of cooperativeness and informativeness. All of the children seem to be aware of some fundamental rules governing classroom language usage. They know that there are times to talk and not to talk at school and that different kinds of talking may be differentially effective.

Our research on metapragmatic awareness contributes to our understanding of children's sociolinguistic development during the school years. A more comprehensive understanding of the social world of children and how they use language to communicate that understanding will help us design experiences that maximize opportunities for children's learning in classrooms.

REFERENCES

ANDERSEN, E. Will you don't snore please? Directives in young children's role-play speech. *Papers and reports in child language development*, 1978, *15*, 140–150.

BROWN, R., & GILMAN, A. The pronouns of power and solidarity. In T. A. Sebeok (Ed.), *Style in language*, Cambridge, MA: MIT Press, 1960.

COOPER, M. Verbal interaction in nursery schools. *British Journal of Educational Psychology*, 1979, *49*, 214–225.

COOPER, C., MARQUIS, A., & AYERS-LOPEZ, S. Peer learning in the classrooms: Tracing developmental patterns and consequences of children's spontaneous interactions. In L. Cherry Wilkinson (Ed.), *Communicating in the classroom*, New York: Academic, 1982.

CORSARO, W. Children's conception of status and role. *Sociology of Education*, 1979, *52*, 46–59.

EDELSKY, C. Acquisition of an aspect of communicative competence: Learning what it means to talk like a lady. In S. Ervin-Tripp & C. Mitchell-Kernan (Eds.), *Child discourse*, New York: Academic, 1977.

ERVIN-TRIPP, S. Wait for me roller-skate. In S. Ervin-Tripp & C. Mitchell-Kernan (Eds.), *Child discourse*, New York: Academic, 1977.

ERVIN-TRIPP, S. Structures of control. In L. Cherry Wilkinson (Ed.), *Communicating in the classroom*, New York: Academic, 1982.

FERGUSON, C. Baby talk as a simplified register. In C. Snow & C. Ferguson (Eds.), *Talking to children*. Cambridge: Cambridge University Press, 1977.

GENISHI, C., & DIPAOLO, M. Learning through argument in a preschool. In L. Cherry Wilkinson (Ed.), *Communicating in the classroom*, New York: Academic, 1982.

GOFFMAN, E. *Interaction ritual*. New York: Doubleday, 1967.

JACOBS, D. Request form alternatives of five-year-old children. Unpublished term paper, Department of Psychology, University of California, Berkeley, Berkeley, CA. 1973.

JAMES, S. Effect of listener age and situation on the politeness of children's directives. *Journal of Psycholinguistic Research,* 1978, *7,* 307–317.
LAKOFF, R. Language and woman's place. *Language in Society,* 1973, *2,* 45–80.
MARTLEW, M., CONNOLLY, K., & MCCLEOD, C. Language use, role, and context in a 5-year old. *Journal of Child Language,* 1978, *5,* 81–99.
MEHAN, H. *Learning lessons.* Cambridge, MA: Harvard University Press, 1979.
MERRITT, M. Distributing and directing attention in primary classrooms. In L. Cherry Wilkinson (Ed.), *Communicating in the classroom,* New York: Academic, 1982.
MITCHELL-KERNAN, C., & KERNAN, K. Pragmatics of directive choice among children. In C. Mitchell-Kernan & S. Ervin-Tripp (Eds.), *Child discourse,* New York: Academic, 1977.
READ, B., & CHERRY, L. Preschool children's production of directive forms. *Discourse Processes,* 1978, *1,* 233–245.
SACHS, J., & DEVIN, J. Young children's use of age-appropriate speech styles in social interaction and role-playing. *Journal of Child Language,* 1976, *3,* 81–98.
SHATZ, M. Communication. In J. Flavell & E. Markman (Eds.), Cognitive development. In P. Mussen (Gen. Ed.), *Carmichael's Manual of Child Psychology,* (4th ed.). New York: Wiley, in press.
SHATZ, M., & GELMAN, R. The development of communication skills: Modifications in the speech of young children as a function of listener. *Monographs of the Society for Research in Child Development,* 1973, *38* (5, 152).
WELLMAN, H., & LEMPERS, J. The naturalistic communicative abilities of two-year olds. *Child Development,* 1977, *48,* 1052–1057.
WILKINSON, L. CHERRY. A sociolinguistic approach to communicating in the classroom. In L. Cherry Wilkinson (Ed.), *Communicating in the classroom,* New York: Academic, 1982.
WILKINSON, L. CHERRY, SPINELLI, F., WILKINSON, A., & CHIANG, C. *Metapragmatic knowledge of school-age children.* Unpublished manuscript, 1983, Department of Educational Psychology, University of Wisconsin, Madison.

10 Learning to Communicate in the Classroom*

Johanna S. DeStefano
Ohio State University

LANGUAGE IN SCHOOL

Language use in school is possibly the most powerful tool for both teaching and learning; for through the use of language, teachers communicate much of what is to be learned and students express what they have learned. And it goes further than that, as a major portion of instructional time centers on learning "educated" or more formal language—including the major task of becoming literate. In fact, one of the primary roles of school is the transmission of the ability to control a set of formal registers, both spoken and written. This constitutes an expanding communicative competence in the educational domain—an ability to use language in ways generally not learned elsewhere in our society.

To help accomplish this, the curriculum includes instruction designed to increase ability to communicate orally and in writing (speaking and writing) and to help students comprehend other's speech and writing (listening and reading) (DeStefano, 1978). This intentional part of language education is specifically taught and has official time in the school day. Thus, communicative competence (DeStefano, 1978; Hymes, 1972) means competence in both oral and written modes of expression. As Mehan, Cazden, Coles, Fisher, and Maroules (1976) put it, "Competent membership in the classroom community obviously involves academic skills and abilities. To be successful in the classroom, students must

---

*Research on which this paper is based is supported in part by Grant No. G-79-0032 from the National Institute of Education and by the Mershon Center for Research and Education in Leadership and Public Policy and is under the auspices of the Mershon Center's Program on Language and Policy.

indeed master academic subject matter. They must learn to read, write and compute" (p. 161). Put another way, students are expected to learn a new set of registers, both in the oral and written modes, including appropriate syntax and lexicon.

A second major role language plays in schooling is the language used in educating, or language in education. It is not as intentional as the first role for language but, in some cases, can be more important for students to be able to do well than the first. It is also part of the powerful "hidden curriculum" that exists in schooling. Mehan et al. (1976) describe this curriculum cogently, noting that it is full of "tacit rules" about *form* and that students must master it as well as the overt curriculum containing the content. Success in school, then, involves a student's ability to master both academic and interactional skills. Appropriate information must be conveyed via the appropriate use of language.

Another major research question concerns *who* is involved in language use in the educational domain. Traditionally, education admits to two major participants—the teacher and the student. Obviously both can be learners, but it's clear that the institution of education invests the teacher with more power than the students (DeStefano, Pepinsky, & Sanders, Note 2). Along with this power go certain perogatives for and, hopefully, abilities of language use. And along with being a student go expectations for specific kinds of language learning.

SCHOOL LANGUAGE AND THE CULTURALLY DIFFERENT

In our research (DeStefano, Pepinsky, & Sanders, 1982; Pepinsky & DeStefano, 1983), my colleagues and I centered on research questions dealing with students' expanding communicative competence in the classroom, both in the intentional segment of language education, e.g., learning to become literate, and in learning the tacit rules of discourse, i.e., the "interactional skills" Mehan (1979) has written about. In discussing these questions, I hope to shed more light on *who* learns *what* and *how,* a time-honored question of great relevance to education.

But first, further framework for this research needs to be developed, as it took a problem-centered approach revolving around the widely remarked upon failure of many children from cultures other than North American mainstream culture to learn to become literate, to succeed in school, and even to learn "demanded" oral interaction routines such as those for expressing disagreement (Labov, 1973; Labov & Robins, 1973). Is there something in language education and the language used in education, especially interactional in nature, which could shed light on this enormous and perplexing problem faced in so many desegregated schools in the United States? What happens to the expansion of communicative competence for these children? So we asked, Do culturally different children in first grade learn the discourse rules of literacy instruction?

Why these specific aspects of communicative competence, of learning to communicate in the classroom? It's difficult to underestimate, in schools, the importance attached to literacy. In fact, it plays a major academic and social role in the formal school systems of North America. Thus, learning to read and write is perceived to be a major task for the student and a notable feature of acculturation into mainstream culture. People generally assume that one must possess these skills if one is to become a functioning member of a technological society. Circourel, Jennings, Jennings, Leiter, MacKay, Mehan, and Roth (1974) note that "the child's ability to read and write becomes more of a necessity as he/she enters the second and third grades" (p. 1) if that child is to be considered successful in his/her schooling. In fact, learning to read and write in the first grade or year of formal schooling is synonymous with success in that grade. In practice, though not necessarily in theory, this belief is so prevalent that the entire school day in the first grade may be devoted to that task.

Can this business go on as usual in a desegregated classroom where at least two, if not more, cultures may come in contact? As intimated above, it cannot, as we are witnessing widespread failure to become literate among culturally different children. And who are these children? First of all, they are learning and have learned crucial forms and interactional skills within their own culture. These forms and their skilled use are part of these children's social semiotic environment (Halliday & Hasan, 1980).

The fact that situational expectations and structures for interaction may be different in the home setting than in the school could quite possibly interfere with the acquisition of competence as it applies to literacy learning.

> We do hypothesize that over time children develop particular discourse styles of reasoning, explaining and accounting that form a basis for their social understanding. We are aware that children even at four or five are unlikely to confuse the actual *context* of home and school, but their experience in the home of styles of discourse and reasoning provide an enduring set for the interpretation and understanding of *other* novel, discourse occasions. (Cook-Gumperz, Gumperz, & Simons, Note 1)

The subjects in this research project were three boys in a desegregated first-grade classroom in a large midwestern city. It was the first year of desegregation in the system, which brought together a white, mainstream-culture teacher with 6 years of teaching experience, and children from mainstream culture, both black and white, from black inner-city culture, and from Appalachian culture. We selected a child who was a member, and whose parents were, of each culture through procedures reported elsewhere (DeStefano et al., 1982).

Since we have also detailed at length (DeStefano, in press; DeStefano et al., 1982) characteristics of the three cultures in contact, suffice it to say that both black inner-city culture and Appalachian culture are primarily oral rather than literate in tradition. The first is apparently a northern inner-city phenomenon, albeit with southern rural origins, whereas the latter is currently rural in nature, a product of life in the mountains of states such as Kentucky, Tennessee, and West Virginia.

Mainstream culture is the one that predominates in schooling values throughout the United States, is the culture of the majority of teachers, and is also the dominant one in North American society. Its communicative system also differs from black inner-city culture and Appalachian culture, especially in crucial areas such as adult-child verbal and nonverbal interaction, as well as child-child interaction (see DeStefano, in press; DeStefano et al., 1982)

Within mainstream culture and in the process of schooling—thus, in classrooms—we may expect to find mechanisms by which a desired acculturation or socialization of pupils such as our subjects is to be effected. This implies the existence of tacit or explicit social policies about what is to be learned and how that is to be done. We have called attention (DeStefano et al., Note 2) to two such policies that seem to be guiding instructional procedures within U.S. public schools: (a) pupils are to behave with appropriate orderliness and (b) literacy is to be learned. We may assume that the teacher is able to implement these policies through a use of social power.

Officially, two major classes of persons exist in that classroom. One is the teacher; the other is the set of pupils enrolled in his/her classroom. For the teacher as the one expected to teach, as we have noted (Pepinsky & DeStefano, (1983), a major requirement exists: reduction of the discrepancy between pupils' current status and their desired status. That discrepancy we may identify as an *exigency* that exists for the teacher. What the teacher does in response to what s/he perceives to be the discrepancy we can call *teaching,* or treatment.

The social policies informing the teacher's classroom behavior apparently dealt with the perceived needs for orderly behavior and literacy-learning mentioned above and discussed in greater detail in Pepinsky and DeStefano (1983). How well the children performed in these areas seemed to form much of the basis on which the teacher assessed their relative competence as members of the classroom community.

LANGUAGE IN LITERACY LEARNING

The data base for forming these tentative conclusions was collected in the following manner. The teacher and her pupils were observed over three occasions during the first year of desegregation: 3 weeks after the beginning of school; 6 weeks later; and 3 months after that, at the outset of the second semester. Both video- and audiotaped records of activity in the classroom were obtained, as well as independent direct observations.

Transcripts were made of the taped discourse of the three boys and the teacher during literacy instruction frames and subjected to detailed language analyses of several types. Discourse analytic modes used were those of Sinclair and Coulthard (1975), Mehan (1979) and Halliday and Hasan (1976). However, only the results from the Halliday and Hasan analysis will be reported here. A computer-assisted language analysis system (CALAS), devised by Pepinsky and colleagues for analysis at the clausal level, was also used. (See DeStefano et al., 1982, for a detailed presentation of these analytic modes, and see Pepinsky, 1974, and Pepinsky, Baker, Matalon, May, and Stabus, Note 3, for a detailed description of CALAS.)

Halliday and Hasan's (1976) cohesion analysis was revealing of the boys' learning of discourse rules "required" in the literacy-instruction frames. From cohesion analysis, one might hope to be able to determine something of the nature of how the teacher's discourse cohered with the students', or vice versa, as we know from studies of psychological therapy (Patton & Meara, in press), for example, that the client's talk tends to converge with the therapist's over time as the course of treatment continues. Implicit in this is often the assumption that the patient is therefore learning to be "better," to progress toward "being well." Might not a teacher assume that if a student's discourse more closely matched his/hers, the student would be progressing and learning more satisfactorily than one whose discourse did not converge or cohere as much? In our data, this would be difficult to determine due to the fact that the majority of the discourse was produced by the teacher. However, we can look at degree of convergence in what the students did produce as well as make other initial determinations about the nature of discourse in that classroom as revealed by cohesion analysis.

Cohesive ties were analyzed on the basis that they might yield information about the implicit discourse rules operating in the literacy-learning frames. A tie, according to Halliday and Hasan (1976), is "best interpreted as a *relation*" (p. 329) between two elements, one being the supposed item and the other being the presupposed element. Thus, ties could be viewed perhaps as an indication of the degree of relatedness of the talk among teacher and students, of co-referentiality and building toward a shared meaning and a context within which to learn literacy.

Density of cohesion was first established by determining the mean number of ties per utterance, which turned out to be 1, the range being a high of 1.5 ties per utterance to a low of .5 ties per utterance. It is my feeling that this mean of 1 is not indicative of particularly great density in cohesion and that there could have been more anaphoric reference to presupposed items already introduced into the discourse either by the students or teacher. Thus, the threads of discourse do not seem to be as tightly woven as they could be, which may be partly a function of the teacher's manual accompanying the commercial reading series used in the school system and which the teacher, in turn, followed almost exclusively during the reading lessons.

The discourse demands made by the manual could also perhaps help account for the finding that the teacher tied more with her own discourse than she did with any of the students'. To determine the direction of domination of the ties, e.g., teacher dominated or student dominated, I made four separate determinations: teacher ties with self (with her own discourse); teacher ties with student; student ties with teacher; and student ties with self (with his own discourse). I found that about 42% of all the ties present in the discourse analyzed were made by the teacher back to items she had already introduced.

Of all the ties in the discourse analyzed, 28.5% were made by the students to items in the teacher's speech. Thus, 70% of the total ties produced were dominated by the teacher, either by her tying with her own speech or with the students' tying to her speech.

Student-dominated ties were ties either produced by the teacher to a presupposed item appearing first in the students' speech or a student's tie with his own speech. There were no student ties with other students' discourse, as we analyzed only teacher-student interaction and also as there was virtually no among-student discourse in the reading groups other than reading aloud, which is obviously not "free" production.

In this category of student-dominated ties, by far the most infrequent were student's ties with self, accounting for less than 5% of the total ties produced in the discourse analyzed. This would appear to substantiate the finding that the teacher controlled the discourse. In fact, she asked questions that the students answered, so tying with self generally came about when they were asked to repeat something. The rest of the student-dominated ties were found in the teacher's discourse as she connected with some item introduced by one of the subjects, usually in the form of a request for help on a word when reading silently.

The data are too sparse to be very suggestive of differences in cohesive ties among the three boys, even though each was perceived to be doing very differently in learning to read. The apparent lack of differences could be partly due, however, to the teacher's virtually exclusive use of the manual, which gave her questions to ask for each reading level in the series, thus precluding much task-related interchange aside from what had been created by the series authors for national use.

Predominating types of cohesion produced by the teacher and by Tom, Dick, and Harry were also determined, partially in an attempt to see if convergence in discourse did appear over time in the language produced in the literacy learning frames, and if other discourse rules and level of learning them could be determined through cohesion analysis.

According to Halliday and Hasan's (1976) model, there are three major kinds of textual cohesion: (a) relatedness of form exemplified by cohesion achieved through substitution, ellipsis, and lexical collocation; (b) relatedness of reference exemplified by reference and lexical reiteration; and (c) semantic connection achieved through cohesion by conjunction. Thus, there are five major types of cohesion: reference, substitution, ellipsis, conjunction, and lexical. Each type of cohesive device, such as lexical or ellipsis, is further divided into a variety of subtypes, along with their functions, yielding at least 20 of these subtype categories of analysis. (See Halliday & Hasan 1976, pp. 333-339, for a summary.)

Our data revealed no use of cohesion to achieve semantic connection through conjunction, either by the teacher or by the students. In fact, conjunction as a cohesive device did not appear in the discourse analyzed, e.g., no "He came yesterday. *Yet* he hoped to go today too." This absence could contribute quite a bit to the lack of density and relatedness in the talk as well as to the apparent "simplicity," or at least lack of variation, in the discourse, as conjunction is one of the more proliferated and semantically complex types of cohesion.

We also found virtually no use of substitution as a cohesive device to achieve relatedness of form or to achieve implicitness in language use. The notion of explicitness or implicitness in language could be an important one in education, in particular when different cultures with different presuppositions are in contact. This was the classroom of Tom, Dick, and Harry, and we found the teacher, in that she used virtually no substitution in her language, was explicit in that manner. This also held for the students; their language used in literacy-learning frames did not utilize substitution either.

In this case, I am using *explictness* and *implicitness* to refer to endophoric cohesive devices utilized in discourse. Generally, implicitness tends to refer to exophora, which means reference to the text alone cannot clarify one of the items in the tie. Explicitness thus refers to cohesion achieved within the text itself via endophoric ties. However, in this case, where shared presuppositions between teacher and student would supposedly render less necessary specific, explicit, within-text reference, cohesion through substitution to imply the shared information might be found. Such was not the case within the endophoric devices utilized in our text.

The three major types of cohesive devices found in the data were lexical, ellipsis, and reference. However, within these categories, only a few cohesive possibilities were utilized by the interactants, again demonstrating little of the cohesive variety possible in English. Also, differential patterns of cohesion use were found in the teacher's speech and in that of Tom, Dick, and Harry. The majority of the teacher's cohesion achieved relatedness of reference rather than either form or a semantic connection. She used almost exclusively certain types of reference and lexical reiteration to achieve what cohesion there was in her discourse. In fact, the majority of lexical cohesion she achieved was through the repetition of items, so that cohesion was achieved through use of the same item with an identical reference, only one of the ways to achieve lexical cohesion. Her discourse was replete with:

Is that *Bill?*
Yes, it does look like *Bill.*
Where does it look like *Bill's* going?

She could have used pronominal reference as a cohesive device to achieve something like "Is that Bill? Yes, it looks like *him*. Where does it look like *he*'s going?" However, one could judge her speech to be highly explicit in the sense that the repetition probably served to make unambiguous the character she was referring to.

Her use of reference cohesion was achieved through the use of pronominals, *he, she, it, they,* and through the demonstrative *that,* but not through comparatives at all, for example. Cohesion through reference accounted for less than 30% of the cohesion she achieved in her discourse during the literacy-learning frames that were subjected to cohesion analysis, with the vast majority of the rest being cohesion through "same item" lexical use. So while cohesion through reference could be considered more implicit than repetition of the same word such as *Bill—Bill—Bill,* as in the example above, the explicitness of this last device was the one predominating in the teacher's speech.

CONCLUSIONS

All in all, I would conclude, on the basis of analysis of cohesive devices utilized by the teacher, that her speech was relatively explicit, not varied as to devices employed, not particularly complex, and not very densely cohesive. This possibly helps "explain" the feeling that much of the coherence felt in the reading lessons was exophoric rather than endophoric, that it was not achieved through the creation of text either by the teacher or by her language interaction with Tom, Dick, and Harry, but by the context instead. "Reading Lesson" became, in a sense, the cohering principle for that time slot, and discourse or language behavior rules were subordinated to behavioral rules such as physical presence at the table where formal literacy instruction took place, eyes on teacher or down on the page indicating attention to the appropriate task, or proper turn-taking in the reading-aloud segment of the lesson where textual cohesion was imposed by the materials and not created by the participants.

However, the students' cohesive devices have yet to be considered. When analyzed, it was clear that many of the cohesive devices employed by Tom, Dick, and Harry in the literacy-learning frames were different from the teacher's, some were the same, and yet all converged, in a sense, toward the formal demands of her discourse. Finally, each of the boys showed no major differences among themselves in the types of cohesive devices employed in their speech.

During the first literacy lesson we taped in the first weeks of school, the major cohesive device employed by the three boys, both collectively and individually, was lexical cohesion of the same type as the teacher: repetition of identical items. This relatedness of reference device accounted for almost 63% of the cohesive ties produced by the boys in that first lesson. However, though the type of lexical cohesion employed did not change after the middle of the school year, its use dropped to 24% of the total cohesive ties produced by the boys during their reading lessons subjected to analysis. The teacher's use of lexical cohesion of the identical reference variety remained high over the literacy frames sampled, accounting for 73% of her cohesive ties during the last session we sampled.

But we cannot conclude that the boys' lessened use of lexical cohesion indicated an increased divergence rather than convergence with the discourse of the teacher over the school year, as the use of ellipsis as a cohesive device increased in their discourse. In fact, we might argue that the lessened use of repetition of lexical item is demonstrative of both greater complexity of cohesion and convergence of discourse by the boys as they learned to "fit" the form of their discourse more closely to the teacher's and were able to become more implicit in their expression of understanding. Repetition of the same word is about as explicit as one can get in talk. Using ellipsis, in which most of the proposition expressed prior to its use is eliminated (called *propositional ellipsis* by Halliday & Hasan, 1976) is more implicit in that the material in identity is presupposed, with what is not in identity being made explicit, e.g.:

Teacher: Where is Bob going?
Dick: To the library.

"Bob is going to the library" as a response would contain much that is redundant, as it is assumed we are dealing with the same Bob. Old information is that Bob is going, but the new information is where he is going, so the proposition is eliminated.

By the final session we analyzed, all three of the boys employed ellipsis to achieve an answer to a *wh-* question or a *yes-no* question, and did so as their predominating cohesive device. Ellipsis represented only 18% of the ties in the first reading session analyzed but 64% by the final lessons. So they matched their choice of cohesive devices to the demands of the teacher's discourse, which was replete with *wh-* and *yes-no* questions. In so doing, one could say they achieved a greater implicitness in their discourse, perhaps a greater complexity, but still not much variation. Yet, not much variation in cohesive types seemed called for by the teacher. In fact, Tom, Dick, and Harry matched their selection of cohesive devices quite well with the teacher's discourse. And that appears to be a discourse rule associated with literacy-learning frames—the matching of one's talk with that of the teacher's, the one in social control.

Furthermore, all the boys were able to do that, so that Dick's use of ellipsis virtually matched that of Harry, the mainstream-culture child. Consequently, even though these data were not replete with many and varied cohesive ties, on the basis of cohesion analysis we could conclude that the rules revealed by such analysis were learned and utilized by the boys. Yet each was perceived differently as to his success in learning to read.

In returning to the concept of communicative competence expanding during schooling to include the tacit interactional language skills "required" for classroom membership, it could be concluded that Tom, Dick, and Harry, though members of different cultures, did learn these skills, or at least some of the tactic rules for literacy frame discourse. By mid-year, each boy was responding to the frequent teacher questions with cohesive ellipses. However, there were differences among the boys. For example, as noted above, Dick, the black inner-city-culture child, did not request the teacher's aid in decoding words during silent reading in the group, whereas the other two boys did.

In the case of Tom and Dick, it is clear that their initial experiences with literacy in the first years of schooling were judged by the teacher to be less successful than those of Harry, the mainstream-culture boy. And it is also quite possible they did not read as well as Harry. Furthermore, it is also possible that Tom's and Dick's understanding of literacy was different from Harry's, for there were cultural differences among the boys, with Harry being the one member of a literate culture, the other two from predominately oral cultures with different rules for adult-child interaction as well. Based on the longitudinal study of children's language and literacy development he and others are conducting in Bristol, England (Wells, 1981a), Wells (1981b) suggests that children, to be successful in schools as they currently are, need to come to the first grade with some understanding of what literacy is, and in a broader sense than the conventions of print à la Clay (1972) that we tested for. As he put it (1981b), they need to have some exposure to "the power of literacy in everyday life." And, in fact, the three boys all expressed the opinion that a child would do better in first grade if s/he already know how to read when s/he came to school, perhaps their way of verbalizing something of what Wells is articulating.

When asking questions about children learning to communicate in classrooms in North America, learning language use in education, especially with a problem orientation such as tying it in with culturally different children's widespread failure to become literate, to do well in intentional segments of language education as referred to in the first part of this chapter, one cannot fail to be impressed with the difficulty of interpreting the results. What does come clear is that there seem to be no particularly clear-cut connections between learning to use and interpret many of the tacit, language-in-use rules for literacy-learning frames and actually being successful in learning to read. Perhaps the language used in these lessons we analyzed does not particularly illuminate the process of learning to read, coming as it often does from a teacher's manual. Such a conclusion would match Wells' (1981b) conclusions noted above. Or perhaps the connections are there but have yet to be found. At any rate, much more research in other classrooms and using cohesion analysis is indicated if we are to be able to do more than look through a glass darkly and be tantalized by mere glimpses of mechanisms of effective language-learning taking place.

REFERENCE NOTES

1. COOK-GUMPERZ, J., GUMPERZ, J., & SIMONS, H. *Language at school and home: Theory, methods and preliminary findings.* Unpublished manuscript, University of California, Berkeley, 1979.
2. DESTEFANO, J., PEPINSKY, H., & SANDERS, T. *Making policy: The language of cultures in contact in the educational domain.* Paper presented at the International Language and Power Conference, Bellagio, Italy, April 4–8, 1980.
3. PEPINSKY, H., BAKER, W., MATALON, R., MAY, G., & STABUS, A. *A user's manual for the Computer-Assisted Language Analysis System.* Columbus: Group for Research and Development in Language and Social Policy, Mershon Center, Ohio State University, November 1977.

REFERENCES

CICOUREL, A., JENNINGS, K., JENNINGS, S., LEITER, K., MACKAY, R., MEHAN, H., & ROTH, D. *Language use and school performance.* New York: Academic, 1974.

CLAY, M. M. *A diagnostic survey and concepts about print test, sand.* Aukland, N.Z.: Heinemann Educational Books, 1972.

DESTEFANO, J. S. *Language, the learner and the school.* New York: Wiley, 1978.

DESTEFANO, J. S. LITERACY LEARNING & CULTURAL CONFLICT: THE CASE OF TOM, DICK & HARRY. In R. HASAN (ED.), *Five to nine: Children's language from home to school,* in press.

DESTEFANO, J., PEPINSKY, H., & SANDERS, T. Discourse rules for literacy learning in a classroom. In Louise Cherry Wilkinson (Ed.), *Communicating in the classroom.* New York: Academic, 1982.

HALLIDAY, M. A. K., & HASAN, R. *Cohesion in English.* London: Longman, 1976.

HALLIDAY, M. A. K., & HASAN, R. Text and context, *Sophia Linguistica, 6,* 1980, 1–107.

HYMES, D. Introduction. In C. Cazden, V. John, & D. Hymes (Eds.), *Functions of language in the classroom.* New York: Teachers College Press, 1972.

LABOV, W. Modes of mitigation and politeness. In J. S. DeStefano (Ed.), *Language, society and education: A profile of Black English.* Worthington, OH: Charles A. Jones Publishing Co., 1973.

LABOV, W., & ROBINS, C. A note of the relation of reading failure to peer-group status in urban ghettos. In J. S. DeStefano (Ed.), *Language, society and education: A profile of Black English.* Worthington, OH: Charles A. Jones Publishing Co., 1973.

MEHAN, H. *Learning lessons: Social organization in the classroom.* Cambridge, MA: Harvard University Press, 1979.

MEHAN, H., CAZDEN, C., COLES, L., FISHER, S., & MAROULES, N. *The social organization of classroom lessons.* CHIP Report 67, December 1976.

PATTON, M. J., & MEARA, N. M. The analysis of natural language in psychological treatment. In R. J. Russell (Ed.), *Spoken interaction in psychotherapy.* New York: Irvington Publishers, in press.

PEPINSKY, H. B. A metalanguage for systematic research on human communication via natural language. *Journal of the American Society for Information Science, 1974, 25,* 59–69.

PEPINSKY, H., &DESTEFANO, J. Interactive discourse in the classroom as organizational behavior. In Barbara Hutson (Ed.), *Advances in reading/language research.* Greenwich: JAI Press, 1983.

SINCLAIR, J. McH., & COULTHARD, R. M. *Towards an analysis of discourse: The English used by teachers and pupils.* London: Oxford University Press, 1975.

WELLS, G. *Learning through interaction.* Cambridge: Cambridge University Press, 1981. (a)

WELLS, G. Lecture presented at Ohio State University, May 5, 1981. (b)

11 Oral Language Competence and the Acquisition of Literacy*

Nancy Torrance and David R. Olson
Ontario Institute for Studies in Education

INTRODUCTION

A central problem for educational theory is the differential effects of schooling on children—why some children are better able to master the forms of competence taught in the schools than others. The preferred explanation, and the one examined here, is the relationship that holds between the child's competence with the "mother tongue"—the ordinary oral language of the home—and the more formal, decontextualized, and explicit language that makes up a large part of the language of school.

Two descriptions of the relation between the language of the home and the language of the school have been advanced. Bernstein (1971) attempted to explain school failure by "code" differences between social classes. Because the language of the school was essentially identical to "middle-class" language, middle-class children have less difficulty in school than do lower-class children. A second explanation is that the relation between the language of the home is essentially continuous with the language of the school, and children who are more sophisticated in their uses of that language are better prepared to deal with the language of the school. Wells (1981), for example, has found sizable and reliable relations between oral language competence and progress in learning to read.

Our concerns in this project fall between these alternatives. We have attempted to determine children's competence with a variety of aspects of languages, including both clausal and discourse properties, in an attempt to determine which aspects of oral competence are relevant to the acquisition of the literate skills of reading and writing. Hence, we have attempted to identify the

---

*This research was supported by grants from The Spencer Foundation and the Social Sciences and Humanities Research Council of Canada.

major dimensions of oral language use, to construct scales for measuring these dimensions, and then to relate these dimensions to the children's progress in learning to read and write. We have examined these issues by sampling children's language during the first three years of schooling, as the child is prepared for and eased into early reading (kindergarten to second grade). By examining the relationship between measures of oral performance in these years and some other measures of cognitive, linguistic, and finally reading performance, we intend to uncover the ways in which oral language competence or skill with "the mother tongue" are related to the development of literacy skills.

METHOD

We have collected 2 years of data from our sample of 29 English-speaking children drawn from two Toronto schools, one in a primarily working-class neighborhood, the other in a primarily professional neighborhood. The battery of tasks include:

1. Taped WPPSI vocabulary subtest (Year 1) and WISC vocabulary subtest (Year 2)
2. WPPSI block design subtest (Year 1) and WISC block design subtest (Year 2)
3. Durrell Analysis of Reading Difficulty
4. A block description task in which subjects were asked to describe the location of a star relative to a series of blocks in such a way that their ability to formulate propositionally complex statements could be sampled. The complexity of the minimally adequate descriptive statement depended on the alternatives presented along with the target block.
5. Free speech: Children were paired and left alone in a room for 5 minutes prior to the beginning of the Lego task, ostensibly while waiting for materials to be brought to the test room. They were encouraged by the experimenter to talk to each other. Sessions were tape-recorded, videotaped, and later transcribed.
6. Lego task: Children were paired and asked to build a toy together out of Lego blocks. They were instructed that they were free to discuss what they would build and encouraged by the experimenter to talk. Sessions lasting about 15 minutes were tape-recorded, videotaped, transcribed, and analyzed.
7. Story-retelling task: Subjects were told stories in such a way that they could put a series of pictures in the appropriate order. They were then asked to retell the story—first to the experimenter (to assure that the children understood the story) and then to another child who, on the

basis of the story, was to arrange the same pictures in the appropriate order.
8. Samples of writing have also been collected in the final 2 years of the data collection phase.

Reading, block design, and vocabulary tasks were scored for each child. Language samples were transcribed and analyzed. Several of these analyses are still underway.

ANALYSES

In our analyses of speech samples, we have attempted to find indices of the quality of various aspects of the language and also indications of the ways in which oral language may be specialized to serve the logical and social demands of conversations. Several different analytic devices have been developed for use with speech samples. First, analyses were performed on the structure of the utterances themselves; second, analyses were made in terms of the conversational functions of the successive utterances that make up the discourse.

Structural features included the semantic and syntactic properties of clauses that make up an utterance following methods employed by Wells (1979) and Quirk, Greenbaum, Leech and Svartik (1972). Transcriptions of children's language obtained from the vocabulary, block description, and Lego tasks were analyzed for grammatical well-formedness, clause embedding, length and complexity, use of modifiers and qualifiers, verb inflection and complexity, the management of pronouns, the source of grammatical errors, propositional complexity, and lexical choices in some semantic domains, particularly psychological verbs.

The pronominal analysis has been devised to examine how the effective use of pronouns depends on such variables as the task engaged in, the presence or absence of available referents, and the linguistic competence of the speaker.

The propositional analysis of language attempts to capture the underlying meaning of sentences through the application of predicate calculus to our subjects' utterances. Rules and procedures for propositional analysis, such as rules for transforming a linguistic surface structure into a propositional representation and vice versa, vary between investigators. Although generally accepted and invariant rules have not yet been established in the field, important steps have been made by Kintsch (1974) and Miller and Johnson-Laird (1976). Our procedures draw on their analyses, and it is our contention that a propositional analysis gives a better indication of the semantic complexity of children's utterances than the simple count of MLU (mean length of utterance). Preliminary analyses of the data gathered so far support this view.

Discourse features included various aspects of conversational skill, such as how utterances contribute to the building and maintenance of topics throughout the discourse and to turn-taking in the discourse; we have also looked at some of the devices used in the maintenance of topics and devices used in turn-taking. To obtain some validity for these measures as aspects of conversational skill, we have also obtained independent judgments from raters on the conversational skill of our subjects in the free speech and Lego-building tasks in our sample.

Some analyses have been completed and will be described in detail as our preliminary findings are presented.

RESULTS

To date, we have carried out extensive structural and discourse analyses of the speech samples of the 29 children for two of the oral language tasks from the second-year data. These two samples are free speech with a peer and cooperative play with a peer. Structural and discourse measures have so far been combined across the two tasks, yielding one sample of conversation for each pair. We have related these structural and discourse measures to the children's Vocabulary and Block Design scores and to the results of the standarized reading test (Durrell) administered in March of the second year of the project.

The statistical analyses to date have been mainly correlational. Results of the analyses are subject to more complex statistical procedures, since handling the data we have obtained requires taking into account the lack of independence between partners in our conversational samples. We are currently exploring ways to avoid this problem. Correlational analyses are thus considered exploratory on data of this kind and are therefore reported as preliminary.

Structural analyses

Each utterance that each child in the sample generated while participating in the conversational and cooperative play session was analyzed. To date, we have counted several structural features of those utterances, including the MLU of independent clauses; the ratio of dependent to independent clauses; the number of modifiers and qualifiers in independent and dependent clauses; the number of errors in verbs and verb phrases and in the use of auxiliary verbs; and the use of psychological verbs (*think, know, decide, say, care,* etc.), subordinating and coordinating conjunctions, modal verbs such as *might, could,* and *should,* and complex verbs that take an infinitive complement. Relative to the reliabilities of these scales and to the remarkable diversity and variability of the children's utterances in a free-play situation, several interesting patterns have emerged. The relations between these structural features and particularly their relationships to reading scores are shown in the upper left quadrant of Table 1. A preliminary analysis of the data for 18 subjects revealed that the number of psychological

TABLE 1
The Correlations among Vocabulary, Block Design, Reading, Structural Complexity, and Conversational Skill for 29 6-Year Old Children ($p < .05$)

					Structural Complexity									Conversational			
	VOCAB	BLDES	READ	MLU	MQRAT	DCRAT	SUBTY	CCJ/C	PTYPE	RTYPE	RCOMP	CONV	TURNS	PRO-T	N-TOP	T-OP	RTO
STRUCTURAL																	
BLDES	.53																
READ	.33	.57															
MLU			.33														
MQRAT			(.30)	−.35													
DCRAT			(.30)		.50												
SUBTY					.36	.46											
CCJ/C					.42	.43											
PTYPE				−.42		.44	.33										
RTYPE	.31	.42	.54			.44	.33		.68								
RCOMP			.53			.60	.51		.58	.65							
CONVERSATIONAL																	
CONV	.40			.41													
TURNS												.33					
PRO-T		−.31										.41	.48				
N-TOP												.35					
T-OP							.32	.58	.31		.39	.43	.33	.41			
RTO							.41		.49		.42	.43			.65	.42	
CLD/T	.33				.41		.58	.58	.42		.35	.53	.50	.46			.37

Variable Codes
- VOCAB   Vocabulary score (WISC-R subtest)
- BLDES   Block Design score (WISC-R subtest)
- READ   Reading Score on Durrell
- MLU   Mean length of independent clause
- MQRAT   Ratio of modifiers and clauses in independent clause
- DCRAT   Ratio of dependent clauses per independent clause
- SUBTY   Range of subordinate conjunctions
- CCJ/C   Coordinate conjunctions within turns/clause
- PTYPE   Range of psychological verbs
- RTYPE   Range of restricted cognitive verbs
- RCOMP   Restricted cognitive verbs with complex endings
- CONV   Conversational rating
- TURNS   Number of turns
- PRO-T   Proportion of turnabout turns
- N-TOP   Number of topics initiated
- T-OP   Number of turnabout openings
- RTO   Remote or abstract topics opened
- CLD/T   Coordinate conjunction linking devices per turn

verbs used by the child was the factor most closely related to children's reading ability. These are verbs such as *know, think, say, mean, decide, care, like,* etc. The best readers used many of these and the poorest readers very few of them.

Because these psychological verbs were so promising and because our experimental studies had also found that many were acquired in the first years of schooling, we have carried out further analyses on the use of psychological verbs by the 29 children in our sample. Their psychological verbs fall roughly into four categories; linguistic (*say, talk, call,* etc.); affective (*care, love, hate,* etc.); cognitive (*know, think, mean, understand,* etc.); and perceptual (*see, look, listen,* etc.). One of these categories, cognitive verbs, relates to reading skills in several ways. First, the strongest overall correlation with reading appeared with the number of different cognitive verbs used by the child ($r = .45$) and the number of instances where the verb is completed by a complex infinitive, gerund, or clause structure ($r = .33$). Further, because two of these verbs, *know* and *think,* are used by virtually every child in a variety of structural contexts, we eliminated instances of these from our sample and further analyzed the remaining set. The obtained correlations for reading with number of different cognitive verbs (RTYPE) and with complex completions (RCOMP) increased substantially. However, there is a high relationship between the number of verb types children used and the number of cases in which that verb was followed by a complex clause. That is, the more of these verbs children used, the more opportunities they had for making different complex structural endings. For this reason, multiple regressions were run to predict reading. For 29 children, the number of different cognitive verbs (excepting *know* and *think*) that appeared in their utterances predicts 29% of the variance in reading scores (F (1,27) due to regression = 10.90, $p < .01$). Adding in the second-highest correlate, the factor of complex endings did not significantly increase the prediction.

Interestingly, the correlation previously obtained between reading scores and types of psychological verbs did not replicate over the entire sample. The explanation is relatively straightforward. In choosing the subsample of 18 subjects for pilot analyses, we chose the best and the worst readers in our sample. The best readers used a greater variety of psychological verbs, but most of these come from the subcategory of cognitive verbs. The poorest readers used fewer psychological verbs in any of the four categories. When we enlarged the sample to include those children who are moderate readers, we added children who use as many psychological verbs as our good readers, but now the verbs used tend to come from the remaining three categories, affective, linguistic and perceptual verbs. Hence the pattern of correlation changes so that although the overall relationship between psychological verbs and reading is no longer significant, the relationship between cognitive verbs and reading is highly significant.

The third factor to significantly correlate with reading scores was, as expected, the mean length of utterance for independent clauses. The mean length of independent clauses was longer for good readers. Adding this factor to types of cognitive verbs in the regression equation predicting reading scores did significantly increase prediction (F (1,26) due to regression = 9.67, $p < .01$). These two factors together account for 43% of the variance in our reading scores.

Although the number of modifiers and qualifiers used by the good readers was not different from the number used by poor readers, the poorer readers tended to put more of their modifiers and qualifiers into *dependent* clauses, and good readers tended to put them into *independent* clauses. The ratio of modifiers and qualifiers in independent clauses was the fourth correlate of reading skill. The greater number of modifiers and qualifiers found in independent clauses must, in part, account for the greater MLU of those clauses.

The final significant correlate of reading performance was the ratio of dependent clauses to independent clauses in the children's utterances. Good readers used more dependent clauses, but these clauses tended to carry fewer modifiers and qualifiers than their independent clauses. To simplify, good readers packed more modifiers and qualifiers in the main clause of their sentences, and good readers had a higher ratio of dependent to independent clauses. Indeed, the two poorest readers used only two dependent clauses in their entire 15-minute conversation. Adding in those factors, ratio of modifiers and qualifiers in independent clauses and ratio of dependent to independent clauses, however, did not increase prediction in the regression equation predicting reading skill.

These are some indications that a child's oral language competence relates to his/her learning to read. As mentioned, the child's use of cognitive verbs, those verbs that indicate how the propositional content of the sentence is to be taken, is the highest correlate of reading scores. We analyzed them primarily because we were interested in the possibility that literacy—that is, learning to read and write—encouraged the differentiation of *form* from *meaning*, and hence accentuated the difference between what was *said* and what was *meant*. We will attempt to analyze how children might use these verbs differentially to mark literal from intended meaning. We have known for instance that children from homes in which the distinction between *said* and *meant* is lexically marked tend to differentiate between production errors and comprehension errors; that is, as listeners they know when the speaker did not say what s/he meant (Olson, 1977; Robinson, Goelman, & Olson, 1983). But we are surprised that their use is more closely related to reading than is any other measure of structural complexity.

These relations among reading, cognitive verbs, and complex linguistic structures are interesting, but it remains unclear just why the relations occur. The early reading tests that discriminate better from poorer readers tend to be simple paragraphs—these paragraphs do not contain any complex verbs, they contain no complex clause complements, and yet the children who handle these devices orally tend to be the better readers. We can offer three hypotheses for this relationship, hypotheses that we are in the process of examining empirically.

The first is that good readers use more cognitive verbs because these verbs can occur in complex syntactic environments and it is complex syntax, as a general indication of a high level of structural competence, that predicts reading. It may be recalled as well that good readers tend overall to use more subordinate constructions than do poor readers. These cognitive verbs, then, may play directly into those subordinate constructions to permit the expression of complex ideas. Hence, a child with this complex syntax and these cognitive verbs could express his/her stance to a proposition (John expects that x, John wonders if x, John decided that x, and so on) or interrogate his/her listener's stance towards propositions and, further, can do so in a single utterance. The poor readers in our study were less likely to do so—and perhaps were less able to do so. Instead of saying "Did you know that x?" the poor reader typically says "You know what? X." For example, consider the following utterances. Two children discuss with their partners the task they are involved in:

> Good reader: What game do you think we're gonna play.
> Poor reader: What are we gonna do?

Similarly, two children interrogate their listener's memories in different ways:

> Good reader: Remember when we brang things to the teacher and I fell down.
> Poor reader: We done this last year too in the same time. Didn't we? Remember?

Although these are important differences in oral language competence, they do not directly explain why children who use these devices can read simple paragraphs better than children who do not.

A second possible explanation for the high correlation between reading and the use of these cognitive verbs is that cognitive verbs reflect the child's knowledge of vocabulary in general. It is well known that vocabulary development is highly correlated with reading skill. In fact, our cognitive verbs, including *decide, remember, doubt,* and *expect,* tend to be used by our good readers but not our poor readers. Again, although these are important differences in oral language competence, they do not directly explain why children who use such verbs can read simple paragraphs better than children who do not.

The third hypothesis, and the one we favor, is that these cognitive verbs are part of a system of concepts for decontextualizing language and thought. Basic to this system are the verbs that mark an understanding of the relation between speaker's meaning and sentence meaning (Olson, 1977), that is, between what a word or sentence means rather than what the speaker means by it. It is this differentiation, we believe, that a child must master in learning that not only do people "mean" things by what they say but that the words and sentences, per se, mean something. This is a basic move in coming to recognize "words" as constituents of utterances, and it is a move that may be prerequisite to "reading" any words at all.

Why the other cognitive verbs also relate to reading is not so clear, but it is possible that it is only when a speaker can clearly recognize that what was said was not equivalent to what was meant, and that some sayings are better representations of what was meant than others, that s/he is in a position to choose correctly between the psychological commitment to what is said in terms of such verbs as *know, think, believe, guess, doubt,* and so on. Indeed, Vendler (1970) and Searle (1979) have argued there is an intimate relation between the verbs of saying and the verbs of meaning; for each speech act verb (such as asserting or promising), there is a corresponding psychological verb (such as believing or intending). Hence, the metalinguistic verbs of saying and the metacognitive verbs of meaning may be closely related in acquisition as well as in structure.

We have designed a series of tasks to help us choose among the hypotheses as to why these cognitive verbs should relate to the acquisition of literacy. These tasks are currently being administered as part of the third-year battery. Pilot testing of these tasks confirm that they will serve to differentiate our good from our poor readers. Hence, these tests will not only permit us to make a thorough assessment of children's comprehension and use of these verbs but also, as mentioned, help to determine just why they are relevant.

In regard to the relations within structural variables, the data in the upper left quadrant of Table 1 reveal that many of these structural variables, as expected, are strongly correlated. Specifically, the range of psychological and cognitive verbs are highly interrelated and correlate positively with the interrelated measures of subordination. Children who use more psychological and cognitive verbs, then, also use more subordination. Indeed, many utterances combine the two. For example:

(1) I wonder what Haley did
(2) I told you there's the Lego bag

On the other hand, the ratio of modifiers and qualifiers found in independent clauses correlates negatively with the ratio of subordinate clauses and the use of psychological verbs. The explanation is relatively straightforward. Psychological verbs often take the more complex structure of a clause complement and the psychological stance is simply stated, that is, without modification or qualification. For example:

(3) do you think we will go to bed at school
(4) look what it says
(5) I told ya I had it right

Further, the number of coordinate conjunctions (per independent clause) used to link clauses within a turn is positively related to the number of dependent clauses (per independent clause) and to the range of subordinate conjunctions used. That is, children who use subordination to link clauses within a turn also use coordination to link clauses within a turn.

In summary then, these very preliminary data indicate that at least some aspects of grammatical and lexical structure in a child's oral language are important to his/her learning to read. To at least some extent then, reading capitalizes on the child's knowledge of the structure of his/her oral language; hence, the positive relationships shown in the upper left quadrant of Table 1. Furthermore, we expect that our current studies will disentangle just why these oral competencies relate to reading. But not all this oral competence is relevant to the acquisition of literacy skills; conversational discourse properties of oral language appear to be quite independent of these structural properties. This is shown in the second form of analysis.

Discourse analyses

Each utterance of the corpus for each child was subjected to a second type of analysis, concerned this time not with the grammatical and semantic properties of children's utterances but with their conversational properties, their pragmatic functions, and their illocutionary force. The speech-act analysis was based not on the calculation of the ratio of various speech acts in various contexts (Dore, 1977), but rather on the cohesive ties between adjacent turns in the discourse. We have not yet completed the analysis of the use of cohesive devices *within* a turn. The ones analyzed thus far are between turns. The primary consideration in this analysis was the extent to which utterances (a) picked up the expectancies established by the preceding turn and (b) added expectancies that were to be met by the succeeding speaker. The analysis was based largely on Kaye and Charney's (1980) and on Brown's (1980) analysis of mother-child conversational interaction. Both Kaye and Charney and Brown point out that a primary difference between the conversational contributions of a young child and those of the parent is that the latter both pick up the thread of the previous speaker *and* advance the topic by setting up related expectancies in turn. We find that by the age of 6 children are beginning to use these adult-like discourse structures. Here is an example:

> (1) Experimenter: You will help each other build one thing
> Child: Right, if we have enough Lego after we build the thing could we build something else?

This child's conversational turn looks both backward and forward and is called a *turnabout*. Turnabouts contrast with less discourse-cohesive devices such as simple acknowledgments or responses (that do not set up new expectancies for the listener) and simple comments and directives, which, while they set up expectancies or requirements for the listener, make no acknowledgment of the preceding turn. Here are some examples:

(2) E: What are you going to build?
    J: We'll decide in private. (Response)
(3) A: There's another man
    I: Oh we might as well put shutters here. (Directive)

In addition, we counted the number of topics each speaker introduced, the number of topics that were introduced by turnabouts, the number of remote or abstract topics a speaker introduced, the number of conjunctions that a child used to tie his/her contributions to those of his/her conversational partner, and the number of turns taken by each child. To establish at least some tentative validity for these particular measures, we asked two independent judges to make an overall judgment of each child's conversational skill on the basis of a single viewing of the videotapes. As can be seen from the correlations shown in the lower right quadrant of Table 1, these measures of discourse cohesion tend to be intercorrelated, and they tend as well to correlate with the global judgment of conversational competence.

The conversational rating reported in Table 1 was carried out by having raters view videotapes of the free-speech and Lego interactions. The correlation between ratings for the two independent raters is .76. As Table 1 shows, all our measures of conversational skill are significantly correlated with rater's rankings. The strongest correlate of global skill for these raters is the use of coordinate conjunctions to link a speaker's utterance with the preceding turn. The order of correlation for the remaining variables is the number of topics opened by turns that are turnabouts (that is, both responding to the listener and making demands on the listener); the number of remote topics opened; the proportion of turns that are turnabouts; the number of topics raised by each speaker, and the number of turns each speaker contributes. Given the high expected intercorrelations among these conversational measures, a multiple regression was carried out to determine the best predictors of conversational ratings. Results of this analysis yielded two predictors of conversational skill: coordinate conjunction links to previous turns and the number of turns each speaker contributes (F (2,26) due to regression $= 8.55, p < .01$). These two factors accounted for 40% of the variance in conversational ratings, and no further factor contributed significantly to the prediction. We conclude, then, that our measures of conversational skill do tap at least some of the ways in which good conversationalists manage discourse. Further, this pair of conversational raters appears on the basis of videotape viewing to judge conversational skill in terms of the smoothness of turn-taking and the productive fluency of the speakers.

A second pair of conversational raters, however, rated a subsample of our children in slightly different ways. In judging the skills of 18 of the 29 children, these raters did not view videotapes but rather read through transcripts of the conversational samples. Their ratings were correlated .70. Interestingly, the conversational measures that correlated most strongly with their ratings were the proportion of utterances that were turnabouts, the number of turnabouts used to open topics, and the number of remote topics opened. Again, because of the high expected intercorrelations, a multiple regression analysis was performed. For this set of ratings, the best predictors of conversational skill were the proportion of utterances that were turnabouts and the number of remote topics raised ($F(1,16)$ due to regression = 5.03, $p < .05$). Whereas the previous raters' judgments appear to be based on smoothness and fluency, these raters appear to be judging more on the basis of the maintenance of topics and the quality of topics raised. The reason for this difference may be the different procedures used in obtaining the ratings. In viewing a videotape, the conversation passes rapidly by the viewer; the substance of particular topic sequences may not be easily remembered. In reading through a transcript, however, it may be more difficult to judge the smoothness of turn-taking, and so more attention may be paid to the quality of the discourse topics. Also, in reading transcripts the rater has recourse to rereading passages and verifying his/her hypotheses about speakers' contribution. The reader may be biased in this case to judge the quality of each speaker's utterances rather than the overall flow of conversation.

Gordon Wells (personal communication) has recently made a suggestion to us about the nature of conversational skill that bears interestingly on this point. He suggests that conversational skill may in fact have two dimensions, the one more interpersonal and the other more logical or ideational. In judging fluency and smoothness of turn-taking transfer, we believe our first raters were more concerned with the interpersonal aspect of conversational skill; whereas in judging maintenance and quality of topic, our second raters were more concerned with the logical or ideational aspect. We plan to examine this hypothesis more carefully in future analyses in which we will attempt to shape which aspects of conversation skill our raters were judging, to see if, in fact, we can obtain distinct ratings along these two dimensions. Furthermore, we find a slight tendency for our first set of raters—those who viewed videotapes—to judge members of each pair as more alike than did the raters who read transcripts. This suggests to us that smoothness and fluency of a speaker in conversation—the interpersonal aspect—may be more dependent on conversational partner than are the abilities to build and maintain a sophisticated topic. We shall be able to examine this hypothesis after we have analyzed this year's conversational interactions, for we have designed our conversational tasks this year so that each child in the sample is paired both with a child of similar conversational skill and with a child of dissimilar skill, according to last year's ratings. We will thus be able to compare the child's skill at the more interpersonal aspects of conversation and the more ideational or logical aspects across conversational partners to see which, if any, skills are more variable.

If our hypothesis regarding the interpersonal and logical aspects of conversational skill is correct, we could expect to see some reflection of this in the interrelationships between the structural features of oral language and the conversational features. Specifically, we could expect that the raising of remote topics and the proportion of turnabouts in the maintenance of topics would interrelate with those structural features that in part predict reading skill. The lower left quadrant of Table 1 reveals that this is the case. We find that the raising of remote topics is significantly related to the measures of subordination, particularly the range of subordinate conjunctions and to some extent the ratio of subordinate clauses to independent clauses. Our good conversationalists, then, not only tend to raise more remote topics, they also tend to use more subordinate clause structures and to use a greater variety of subordinate conjunctions. Unlike the good readers, though, they tend to pack more modifiers and qualifiers into those subordinate constructions, hence the negative correlation with MQ ratio per independent clause. Further, with regard to the interrelationships between structural and conversational measures, the good conversationalists tend to use a greater variety of psychological verbs, and the tendency to do so is correlated with most of our conversational measures, most strongly with the proportion of turnabouts, conjunctions as links to previous speakers' utterances, and the raising of remote topics. The use of psychological verbs, then, relates not only to our structural measures of language complexity but also to the raising of remote topics and to the maintence of topics, hypothetically, the more logical aspects of conversational skill. These relationships do not hold, however, for the restricted set of cognitive verbs we looked at. So although the good conversationalists include more linguistic, affective, and perceptual expressions in their utterances than do poor conversationalists, they do not include more cognitive expressions. Good readers, on the other hand, use more cognitive expressions but not more linguistic, affective, and perceptual expressions. Finally, these linguistic, affective, and perceptual expressions appear to be useful for discussion of remote topics and the maintenance of topics through turnabout utterances.

Interestingly, the one correlation of a conversational measure with reading is a negative one between the number of topics introduced by the speaker and reading skill. Our good readers do not generally exercise conversational control by introducing topics but tend merely to contribute to the topics established by their conversational partner.

Finally, with respect to coordinate conjunction links to previous speakers' turns, we see that this conversational device is related to two of our structural measures, the use of coordinate conjunctions within turns and the range of psychological verbs used. We note from our samples that only our best conversationalists use these conjunctions both as turn links and as clause links in a single turn. Here are examples from our best three conversationalists:

> P: *But* we need people in it *or* else it will look ugly.
> J: *But* imagine if you said that *and* she switched the microphone on so it can tape us *and* she said "Who did this?" *and then* you said "Me." I said 'Hello folks.'"
> S: *And* we're not going to put granny . . . like that's one house *but* no granny.

The point to notice is that these conjunctions play both a structural role and a conversational role; they are used both for relating a speaker's clauses to each other and for relating a speaker's clauses to those of the previous speaker. The number of coordinate conjunctions within a turn is positively related to coordinate conjunctions between turns and to the same set of conversational measures as the coordinate conjunctions between turns. These include global rating of conversational skill, the proportion of utterances that are turnabouts, and the number of turnabouts used to raise topics. Hence, the pattern of relationships with conversational variables is the same whether one considers the use of coordinate conjunctions within turns (that is, between clauses) or between turns. Good conversationalists, then, not only link their turns to previous speaker's turns with coordinate conjunctions, they also use more coordinate conjunctions within turns. The structural device of using coordinate conjunctions is thus important not only for stating the logical relationships between clauses in a turn but also for stating the logical relationship between clauses across turns.

To summarize, the interrelationships between the structural and conversational variables we have measured suggest that the more sophisticated maintenance of a topic and the tendency to initiate a topic that is remote or abstract may be related to facility with the more complex structures of language, namely, subordination and coordination, and to the occurrence of a range of psychological verbs.

To conclude, the data suggest some interesting relationships between oral language skill and early reading. Specifically, conversational skill may have at least two aspects: the interpersonal, dealing with production, fluency, and coordination of utterances across turns; and the logical, dealing with the quality of topics raised and the quality of topic maintenance. Whereas the interpersonal aspects tend not to be related to the structural complexity of language, the features that differentiate good and poor readers, the logical do tend to relate to some structural features. Generally, these structural features do not predict reading skill but are nevertheless correlated with the structural features that do. Our good readers, then, do not in fact raise more remote topics or maintain topics with more sophisticated turnabout utterances, whereas our good conversationalists do. Our good conversationalists, however, use some structural devices typical of complex linguistic forms in maintaining and initiating conversations, particularly those conversations dealing with remote or abstract topics.

We have found, then, that although one side of oral competence—that relating to the complexity of linguistic structure—appears to be related to the acquisition of reading skills, a second side of oral competence—that pertaining to the initiation and maintenance of discourse topics in conversation—is not related to reading skill. Finally, we see a relationship between the former and the latter when looking at the quality of topics introduced and the quality of topic maintenance.

However, these findings are based on the data of a small sample of children on a narrow range of oral tasks. Before these findings are of general theoretical value or any practical use in making educational decisions, they must be both deepened and generalized. Over the next year and a half, we will continue to explore the ways in which oral language competence is related to the acquisition of those skills associated with the literate enterprise.

REFERENCES

BERNSTEIN, B. *Class, codes and control,* (Vol. 1). London: Routledge & Kegan Paul, 1971.
BROWN, R. The maintenance of conversation. In D. R. Olson (Ed.), *The social foundations of language: Essays in honor of Jerome S. Bruner.* New York: Norton, 1980.
DORE, J. Children's illocutionary acts. In R. O. Freedle (Ed.), *Discourse production and comprehension* (Vol. 1). Norwood, N.J.: Ablex, 1977.
KAYE, K. AND CHARNEY, R. How mothers maintain "dialogue" with two-year-olds. In D. R. Olson (Ed.), *The social foundations of language: Essays in honor of Jerome S. Bruner.* New York: Norton, 1980.
KINTSCH, W. *The representation of meaning in memory.* Hillsdale, N.J.: Erlbaum, 1974.
MILLER, G. A., & JOHNSON-LAIRD, P. *Language and perception.* Cambridge, Ma: Harvard University Press, 1976.
OLSON, D. R. From utterance to text: The bias of language in speech and writing. *Harvard Educational Review,* 1977, *47,* 257–281.
QUIRK, R., GREENBAUM, S., LEECH, G., & SVARTIK, J. *A grammar of contemporary English.* London: Longman, 1972.
ROBINSON, E., GOELMAN, H., & OLSON, D. R. Children's understanding of the relation between expressions (what was said) and intentions (what was meant). *British Journal of Developmental Psychology,* 1983, *1,* 75–86.
SEARLE, J. Intentionality and the use of language. In A. Margalit (Ed.), *Meaning and use.* Boston: Reidel, 1979.
VENDLER, Z. Say what you think. In J. L. Cowan (Ed.), *Studies in thought and language.* Tucson: University of Arizona Press, 1970.
WELLS, G. Influences of the home on language development. *Bristol Working Papers on Language, 1.* Bristol: University of Bristol, 1979.
WELLS, G. Some antecedents of early education attainment. *British Journal of Sociology of Education,* 1981, *2,* 181–200.

12 Learning Through Writing: A Rationale for Writing Across the Curriculum

Richard Beach
The University of Minnesota

Lillian Bridwell
The University of Minnesota

INTRODUCTION

Along with other writers on the function of writing in schools (Emig, 1977; Herrington, 1981), we believe that writing should have a central place in students' learning experiences. While we do not doubt that the need to express oneself in writing is reason enough for the recent emphasis on writing instruction in schools, we also believe that it is a powerful resource that is often left untapped as a means of learning new information and solving problems, no matter what the discipline. We agree with Herrington (1981) that the responsibility for writing should extend into classrooms beyond the English teacher's domain where it can serve larger curricular goals; to achieve this, however, we believe we must present a strong, positive rationale for the benefits of writing. Along with a review of recent research supporting these benefits, we will discuss some assumptions that will serve as a basis for this positive rationale:

1. That writing, beyond reading or oral language, has some special advantages for learning.
2. That writing can enable students to learn new information in subject area classes.
3. That writing facilitates students' problem-solving strategies for organizing both old and new information.
4. That writing can teach students pragmatic conventions and audience awareness, developmental processes crucial to the ability to communicate successfully.

5. That writing can teach students to evaluate critically the information they are learning.
6. That writing can teach students how they perceive or analyze their own personal experiences.

Based on a series of studies of students identified by teachers as effective versus less effective learners, Bransford (1982) found that when faced with certain problem-solving tasks, effective learners employ heuristic strategies that allow them to approach tasks systematically whereas less effective learners flounder about, lacking any consistent cognitive strategies that would help them solve novel problems. We will argue that writing helps students learn these heuristic strategies. Given the need to "learn how to learn," a central argument of this chapter justifying the significance of writing in all subject matter areas is that in composing, students learn how to generate, define, and apply their own *schemata*, i.e., their own rules for what they know.

Writing versus Reading

Writing differs from reading in that it may require the writer to define and apply his/her own schema. Successful readers, on the other hand, are those who are able to deal with the schema that exists in or is prompted by an author's text (Meyer, 1977). Pickert and Anderson (1976) also define successful reader comprehension as the degree to which s/he recreates the author's schema. Depending on the nature of the writing task, the writer may have no such *a priori* framing device for composing and may well be forced into a more active mode of learning when asked to compose. In addition, writing cannot only demand more cognitive processing, it can also reinforce effective reading processes. For example, Atwell (1980) found that in a "blind writing task," superior readers produce more coherent prose than inferior readers because even if they cannot reread their writing, they have acquired schemata that allow them to sustain their arguments in a coherent manner.

Writing versus Oral Language

Despite a general lack of empirical evidence for the special benefits of writing, we know that it requires an ability to sustain one's thinking in a consistent, systematic way over a stretch of discourse (Olson, 1977). In certain modes of oral discourse, participants do not always have to sustain a line of argument or provide complete cues to the audience for the information they proffer. They have access to an audience that can let them know when they have not made themselves clear, when they should restate an idea, when they should add missing information, and when they should let the listener speak. The writer must anticipate and attempt to control the reader's response through the flow of the text. Of course, as oral language moves from less formal communication to more formal communication, it becomes more like written language. It begins to share another of writing's advantages, the relative stability of the language for reexamination and reformulation.

We acknowledge that all the language skills go hand in hand and that development in one medium drives development in another. We know that students learn pragmatic skills from oral language as they respond to listeners and talk to find out what they know, for example. We also know that the basis for learning what writing should "look like," i.e., what the characteristics of written text structures are, comes from reading widely. Wide reading also increases the student's knowledge, not just of information, but of how that information fits into larger contexts beyond her/his own personal experiences. However, we do believe that writing, as a tool for learning, demands more serious attention in schools than it has been given.

Studies of Writing Across the Curriculum

In making our claims for the value of writing, we have to admit quickly that much of the writing students do in schools will not achieve these ends. One of the first large-scale studies of writing in different subject matter areas was Britton's analysis of writing in British secondary schools (Britton, Burgess, Martin, McLeod, & Rosen, 1975). Based on an examination of 2,000 pieces of writing, Britton et al. argued that writing, like oral language, varies according to its function and audience. Differences in function, according to Britton, fall between two poles, "transactional" and "poetic." Transactional writing uses language to accomplish the more pragmatic, everyday business of the world, often consisting of exchanging information or performing various speech acts: requesting, inviting, ordering, etc. On the other hand, poetic writing involves a more subjective interpretation of experience. Poetic writing places more emphasis on the form in language itself, whereas transactional writing focuses on the pragmatic purposes of the interaction between writer and reader that lead to a concrete response. Under these major categories, Britton developed a number of subcategories ranging from simple reports to tautological arguments to more abstract levels of formalized reasoning. He also developed categories to analyze the writer's relationship to an audience, e.g., "child to self," "pupil to examiner," "writer to unknown reader."

His team's analyses indicated that "transactional classification" dominated school writing and that the audience for most of this writing was the teacher in the examiner role. As they studied children at older ages, they found that students wrote within a narrower range of "function" categories. This finding, according to Britton, showed that as students developed, they were more and more inhibited in their development of more expressive or poetic forms of writing, a situation somewhat similar to what may happen to oral language in schools. He also argued that the predominance of classificatory writing does little to encourage thinking skills. Simply parroting back language formulated by teacher or textbook does not encourage students to make either the language itself or the ideas embodied in the language their own.

Surveys of writing in American schools reaffirm Britton's findings. Students are not challenged often enough to use higher levels of abstraction or independent thinking as they write. Donlan (1980) found, for example, that science and math teachers used writing primarily for reporting information, rather than for any arguments or analyses, types of writing that might have enabled these teachers to teach problem-solving skills. In a survey of the writing practices of 133 high-school science and social studies teachers, Clemmons (1980) found that the most frequently assigned tasks involved answering study questions, taking tests, and reporting information—tasks that generally required nothing more than restating information. Even when the task was more complex, teachers often made assignments without instructing the students in strategies required for successful completion of them.

In a study similar in scope to Britton's, Applebee (1981) analyzed the frequency and nature of student writing based on 259 randomly selected observations of ninth- and eleventh-grade students in two schools. He also conducted a survey of teachers' attitudes, writing practices, and related instructional activities from a stratified national sample of secondary schools. In his report, 44% of the time students spent writing was devoted to mechanical transcribing, short-answer, and fill-in-the-blank tasks; 17% to note-taking; and only 3% to writing of paragraph length or beyond. The results of the teacher surveys indicated that 85% of the writing was used primarily for reporting information. Longer pieces of writing or more imaginative uses of writing were primarily limited to English or social studies classes. The teacher as examiner was the primary audience for student writing in this country as well, according to Applebee. Only 10% of the teachers reported that student writing was read even by other students.

The nature of the writing assigned varied according to the teachers' attitudes toward the use of writing to foster learning. On one dimension, 70% of the teachers believed that writing should be used primarily to foster learning information, whereas 16% were concerned with using writing to allow students to explore personal experiences. On another dimension, 44% used writing primarily for the application of concepts, whereas 24% stressed development of particular writing skills. English teachers more often stressed writing about personal experiences, whereas math and science teachers were more often concerned about acquiring information and applying concepts.

Again, these teaching practices are related to teachers' attitudes about language and learning. Gere, Schuessler, and Abbott (1983) found that English teachers tend to fall into two camps. On the one hand were teachers primarily concerned about students' language development through extensive writing and discussion. These teachers evaluated writing primarily in terms of the ideas or content. On the other hand, the teachers who placed higher priority on learning "correct usage" or "grammar" directed more attention toward the remediation of errors. Maimon and Nodine (1978) found that only 51% of teachers in fields other than English responded to the content in student essays.

These surveys indicate that despite some variation according to subject matter areas, writing is not being used extensively to foster reflective, critical thinking. And, of equal importance, teachers' attitudes about the uses of writing may be constrained by their own prior experiences and attitudes about language learning. Although it is often assumed that certain subject areas (e.g., math, history, science) focus more on "transactional classification" processes, current curriculum theory in these fields stresses the need for higher-level thinking, with an emphasis on developing a broad range of cognitive skills rather than just acquiring information. The commitment of teachers to fostering thinking skills affects their willingness to use writing for purposes other than transcribing and regurgitating information.

Thus, although a range of writing modes or functions exists in schools, not all of them are equally powerful in requiring students to develop their own heuristic strategies for learning or solving problems. Furthermore, those that can be used for these purposes are not used often enough. At this point, we will explore a range of writing tasks in relation to the cognitive or rhetorical demands they place on students and discuss how these kinds of writing are related to the benefits we have outlined for writing—problem-solving, audience awareness, reformulation of ideas, and self-reflection. We will also discuss various implications for teaching specific uses of writing in different subject matter areas, including the teacher's use of writing to derive diagnostic information about students' learning processes.

A RANGE OF WRITING TASKS

We are not questioning the values of the assumption that writing can help students learn "facts." This is the way writing is most widely used, as the surveys above show. However, we do believe that writing can be used for more complex thinking *about* information than is commonly the case. To do this, teachers must examine the relationship that exists between the student and the information that student must learn. We are proposing three different types of relationships: *restating, recasting,* and *inventing.* In restating information, a student is simply recalling information in a text or lecture according to the schemata within the text or lecture. In recasting, a student reshapes existing information, using schemata distinct from those implied in the text or lecture. In inventing, a student formulates new information using his/her own schemata.

These relationships appear to us to be hierarchical, increasing in the cognitive demands they make upon the writer. When restating, a writer can rely on the existing text structure to organize his/her writing. To recast, writers must define and apply their own text-structure schemata to existing information. In inventing, students must both generate and organize information, a task that requires processing at different levels. Without adequate instruction or experiences, students often "downslide" to lower-level processes such as spelling or handwriting (Collins & Gentner, 1980).

Restating

The somewhat limited research on note-taking (see a review by Anderson, 1980) poses some questions about the value of simply restating ideas in writing. Using a variety of outcome measures, the research showed no consistent, strong support for restating as an aid to learning. Students often have difficulty selecting appropriate information, failing to process information according to their own schemata (Hidi & Klaiman, 1982). In their comparison of high-school students with "expert" graduate students, Hidi and Klaiman (1982) found that whereas the experts were able to integrate information into their own structures by selecting, prereading, paraphrasing, and defining their goals for reading, the high-school students often reproduced the information without altering the text's schema.

Note-taking guided by adjunct questions calling the students' attention to certain parts of the text or requiring them to reflect on the material does appear to enhance the learning process (Anderson, 1980). The obvious implication here is that students should be asked to reshape material or add new, implied material if they are to actively integrate the information they are learning into their own frames of reference.

Recasting

By our definition, recasting does not necessarily require a student to develop a new schema; a teacher will often assign a paper with an implied schema that differs from the organization of the existing material from which the student works, as in reshaping narrative material according to a problem/solution structure. The difficulty in recasting lies in abandoning the original schema and reshaping according to a new one. Teachers could assist students by making explicit the heuristics necessary for completing an assignment (Herrington, 1981; Odell, 1980).

For example, "summarizing" requires some fairly complex thinking, the ability to discern the most pertinent information by hierarchically sorting out information. Students may need instruction in the use of text structure patterns to summarize successfully, instruction that is even more systematic than simply asking students to infer the "main point." Taylor and Beach (in press), examining the effects of two different methods for reading and writing instruction on seventh graders' reading and writing skills, found that the group that received specific instruction in hierarchical summarizing scored significantly higher on reading recall and writing quality measures than conventional or control groups. In addition, the reading instruction was more effective in improving writing quality for summaries than was writing instruction apart from the task. Rather than asking students merely to answer "study questions," teachers should provide the necessary instruction for students to learn to respond to a task such as summarizing, instruction that would probably draw their attention to text structure cues.

Obviously, many kinds of recasting call for even more systematic instruction. For example, a "compare and contrast" assignment demands that the writer use "comparing" and "contrasting" organizational structures when analyzing a text that may use an altogether different structure, such as narrative–several cognitive tasks masquerading as one. Using our terms, the writer would have to restate before s/he could recast the information into new structures.

Inventing

With this kind of writing to learn, the student does not have an existing organizing principle to work with, but rather must find a schema to match the information s/he has or one that matches the assigned task. If the task is explicitly defined by the teacher, there may well be an implied schema that the student should use that would also dictate the method s/he would use in gathering information or searching memory. Inventing may also require the student to use writing to develop his/her own insights about experience or ideas. As analyses of students' writing about literature indicate (NAEP, 1981), students have difficulty developing their own insights because they do no more than restate or recast an experience or textbook passage on a literal level, failing to consider the significance, worth, or relevance of an experience or idea according to their own schema; hence, they often adopt a detached, impersonal stance (Britton et al., 1975; Applebee, 1981).

Students could using inventing in writing successfully if they are willing (or are taught how) to engage in what Getzels and Csikszentmihalyi (1976) define as "problem-finding," i.e., determining the inadequacies of their own formulations which leads to further writing and revision. Thus, writing to recast and invent can teach students how to do something with new information they encounter. We will now specifically examine how these kinds of writing tasks can be beneficial for four kinds of learning.

Fostering Problem-solving Through Writing

Recent learning theory in many subject matter areas, particularly the sciences and social sciences, has emphasized the importance of problem-solving approaches to learning. Research on this kind of learning favors the use of highly systematic, well-defined approaches that focus on stages, rather than less precise instruction (Glenn & Ellis, 1982); in many cases, writing was used in this research to help students formulate problems, define reasons for their problems, and pose solutions.

Based on their extensive research on problem solving and writing, Flower and Hayes (1980) have found that effective writers are better able to define the nature of their own problems, relate these problems to goals, and describe the relationships among elements of problems or contradictory goals. Although better problem-solvers are not necessarily better writers, better writers have acquired the skills that researchers find as characteristic of better problem-solvers (see Perkins, 1981, for a review of problem-solving research). Writing can serve as the medium for learning effective problem-solving strategies, but most students need instruction in composing-process options to expand their writing beyond the one-shot draft with little revision (Bridwell, 1981), a pattern of school writing that is not particularly conducive to active learning.

Whatever problem-solving approaches a student uses, a "process" approach can provide a record of the student's method of arriving at answers to problems. As the Applebee report (1981) indicates, teachers generally evaluate only final written products rather than the work the student did to produce that product. Although a final essay may omit, misinterpret, or ignore important bits of information, a teacher can only guess about the range of problems a student might have encountered and attempted to solve along the way. Had the teacher access to the student's earlier drafts or steps in prewriting or self-assessing, s/he could determine what additional instruction the student might need to successfully fulfill the assignment.

Even if they allow students to employ a more process-oriented approach, teachers sometimes assume that students have acquired the heuristic or problem-solving steps necessary to the completion of writing tasks. However, unless they have learned, either through instruction or extensive writing practice, to use heuristic strategies and revision processes, they may have difficulty extending their writing process (Herrington, 1981; Odell, 1980). In some cases, the most concrete kind of instruction a student has had in writing involves systems of "rigid rules" (Rose, 1980) or inert ideas that do not suggest process behaviors, e.g., "always begin your paper with a thesis statement," "a good essay has an introduction, a body, and a conclusion." There is a tendency on the part of teachers simply to discuss and apply definitions of good writing rather than to show students how that writing might be produced through specific inquiry-learning activities.

One such activity is illustrated in a technique called the *cumulative paper* (Klink, 1981). Klink found that in writing lab-project reports in chemistry classes, students often did not have clear perceptions of the problems they encountered or that they drew invalid conclusions from data. To improve their problem-solving processes, he asked students prior to writing their reports to submit abstracts, which he critiqued and returned to them. They also submitted drafts of their methodologies, results, and discussions, which were also critiqued. For the second lab report, having modeled the evaluation process, he had students do the critiques for one another so that they themselves could learn these approaches. Many other established techniques are discussed in more recent writing textbooks (e.g., tagmemic analysis, Burke's pentad), but teachers can develop their own task-specific approaches simply by analyzing the steps they themselves go through in solving problems in their subject areas. Students who do not learn to assess their own writing processes and products may be handicapped in their ability to learn through writing.

LEARNING TO CONSIDER CONTEXT CONVENTIONS AND AUDIENCE

An important developmental task involves learning to vary one's language according to different social and academic contexts. In school, learning to write for teachers of different subjects can help students learn to shift registers and rhetorical strategies to fit the rhetorical demands of varying contexts. In writing for a variety of teacher audiences, students are doing more than simply "writing for the teacher." They are learning to recognize those conventions that constitute writing for a particular purpose for a particular audience. In some cases, a teacher may make explicit certain conventions: "give ample support," "be precise," "avoid jargon"—conventions or maxims that often lack rhetorical validity. Teachers who want to encourage writing to learn should carefully consider the real constraints on a piece of writing, knowing that the characteristics of "good" writing can change with the situation.

More important, from the perspective of speech acts (Cooper, 1982; Grice, 1975; Martin, Ohmann, & Wheatley, 1969), a student must learn to consider the various conventions that constitute successful performance of speech acts such as asserting, requesting, informing, questioning, and inviting. These conventions have to do with both the speaker or writer's knowledge, beliefs, status, sincerity, and abilities and these same characteristics in the listener or reader. For example, in making certain assertions, students must assume that the teacher does not already know the information being conveyed (a convention that is often not adhered to). Moreover, in order to make judgments about the sufficiency, relevancy, or clarity (Grice, 1975) of their assertions, student writers must make inferences about their audience's prior knowledge, needs, or reading ability. In all of this, students are learning to make inferences not only about themselves and their goals, but also about the relationship between writer and audience and the conventions that affect the context.

As was the case when we argued for writing to learn to solve problems, we do not believe students can benefit fully unless a process approach to writing is used. Without frequent feedback about their writing—particularly before they produce a final draft—students may not be aware of errors in their judgments. There is significant research that indicates that older, more cognitively advanced writers are more likely to take audience characteristics into account than younger writers (Rubin & Piche, 1979); however, Beach and Eaton (1983) found that even college freshmen often failed to specify audience considerations that could have helped them revise more successfully.

Writers may actually think about a specific, "actual" audience only in highly structured, conventional genres such as writing a letter of complaint (Park, 1982). In most writing, writers may be considering a hypothetical audience and sometimes considering that audience's possible knowledge, beliefs, needs, etc. While providing background material, for example, a writer may have to consider the audience's prior knowledge, a judgment about the context that can then be used to determine how much background information is necessary. In school writing, the teacher can do more than simply serve as the audience by reminding students of general audience characteristics and related conventions. For example, a reader normally expects a writer to provide examples when an opinion is stated; if the student fails to provide sufficient evidence, s/he needs instruction in the typical expectations a reader might have for logical support. Teachers can also heighten the pragmatic payoff often lacking in school writing by encouraging students to make requests, formulate complaints, propose class activities, prepare for discussion, etc., in writing. With these tasks in particular, it is relatively simple to define the speech-act conventions that operate in successful communication.

There is evidence that providing too much additional information about the context for a writing assignment can work to the disadvantage of the student writer, however. In one study (Metviner, 1980), ninth graders wrote on the same topic twice, once with a specifically defined context and then again for the teacher; the essays written for the teachers were rated significantly higher in quality than those written for the school newspaper. Even this study illustrates our earlier point about "good" writing not being good in all contexts, however. Brosell (1982) also examined the effects of types of information provided about the rhetorical context: (a) the full context: information about topic, organizing principles, purpose, and audience; (b) moderate: information about topic and organizing principles; (c) information about topic only. Students in the moderate group generated writing of the highest quality. The additional information about the hypothetical context, given the time constraints, presented a barrier in that writers often parroted back the information. On the other hand, without some organizing principle, the students in the "topic only" group had difficulty focusing their essays. Of course, these are status studies, i.e., the way student writers cope with context without much training. The results might be significantly different if students had more experiences with writing for legitimate purposes to real audiences.

In a more successful use of contextual information, Florio (1979) developed a hypothetical community in which second graders had to write letters in order to conduct their "community" business. Students who were running a toy store had to write letters to toy manufacturers about their products. Florio's analysis indicated that the students were quite adept at considering audience characteristics in composing their letters, largely because they could define a purpose for writing. "Teacher-student dialogue journals" (Farr, 1982) also appear successful in giving students an immediate sense of audience as they respond to comments and probing questions on specific journal entries. Teachers in a variety of content area classrooms have many opportunities to help students learn more about their relationships to others and their ability to communicate to others if the pragmatic benefits of writing are stressed.

LEARNING TO EVALUATE INFORMATION CRITICALLY THROUGH WRITING

One of the differences between reading and writing is that in reading one's own writing, a writer can alter the meaning of his/her own text, whereas in reading another's text, the reader accepts the fixed nature of that text. While a writer's text may be momentarily fixed, its meaning or "intended meaning" is not. In rereading a text to determine what it says or whether it does what was intended, a writer often alters the "intended meaning" (Wall, 1982). From their experiences in rereading and revising texts, students can learn to recognize that meaning is not a fixed, absolute matter, but subject to continuous reformulation. Once they record thoughts on the page, they can reread them from a slightly different perspective, and a different meaning can emerge.

This kind of writing experience could facilitate cognitive flexibility; however, several factors make this occur rather infrequently in much school writing. Bridwell (1981) discusses the difficulties writers have in shifting from reading others' texts to reading their own; they often treat what is produced as though it were "etched in stone," a fixed text that they do not attempt to revise. She argues that limited experience in "re-seeing" their ideas and limited revising strategies prevent them from thinking critically about their ideas, even when they may experience the dissonance that comes from knowing the writing does not accomplish what they want. Beach (1979) found that a "cognitive style" factor might be involved. Students scoring as more rigid on the Hunt Conceptual Level Sentence Completion Scale revised significantly less than did students scoring as less rigid.

The extent to which students are willing to evaluate their own ideas and, in this case, do this evaluation through revising depends heavily on the nature and quality of the teacher's responses to a student's writing (Beach, 1979). If a teacher is able to specify his/her own reactions or thoughts while reading a draft—what Elbow (1981) calls "telling" responses or "reader-based feedback" (as opposed to strictly text-based feedback)—then students can recognize the teacher-as-reader's difficulties in comprehending the writing or the processes of evaluation the teacher uses. In this process, the teacher is providing the student with insights about his/her *specific* comprehension processes.

For example, the teacher can describe the nature of the text structure as s/he sees it and how that structure creates certain expectations. S/he can then imply that the student has or has not provided enough evidence, not simply because students are supposed to give examples—prescribed advice from the textbook—but because s/he found it easy or difficult to comprehend specific passages. Through this modeling process, the student can learn to switch to a critical reader role by applying similar processes to his/her own writing. Through this active process, the student can learn more about critical thinking than with "inert" textbook advice to question what one reads or writes. With writing, there is also the added advantage that the student writer is the "expert" on the information, particularly if s/he has gone beyond regurgitating to recasting or inventing.

WRITING TO LEARN ABOUT ONESELF

Another basic benefit of writing is that it is related to students' capacities to reflect about personal and intellectual experiences. Certain writing activities encourage students to employ language that Britton et al. (1975) define as language of the "spectator," reflecting about the meaning of experience as distinct from the more pragmatic, "transactional" use of language. Britton cites the example of going to a party and engaging in a number of pragmatic acts—appraising, requesting, asserting, etc.—and then, after leaving the party, reflecting about the nature of that experience. Although these arbitrary distinctions in school writing are imprecise, as are attempts to define literature as a suspension of pragmatic expectations (Pratt, 1977), Britton, Emig, and others find that students often do not use writing to reflect on their personal knowledge, attitudes, or beliefs. Writing in the "poetic mode" is often equated with "creative" writing, as opposed to "expository" writing, and is limited to autobiography, fiction, or poetry writing. Such distinctions assume that expository writing denies personal reflection, a rather circumscribed conception of writing. A more useful perspective for defining the degree of personal reflection is to consider the extent to which students conceive of information or experience in their own terms versus those of another.

Of course, it could be argued that students could develop language in a reflective mode entirely through oral language. However, in writing for an unknown audience, a writer must recognize that, regardless of the unique, personal nature of the experience, an audience needs to be able to share that experience. Thus, in sharing perceptions of an experience, students need to consider whether or not their audience can comprehend the same visual, spatial, psychological, or cultural schemata. As they try to define their ways of knowing the world and responding to it so that another could understand, they may come to know themselves better.

While we know that a writer's perspective or point of view influences the selection of information in writing (Mosenthal & Na, 1981; Pickert & Anderson, 1976), it may also be true that through writing, students acquire and define their own unique perspective or point of view, a process we know little about (Mosenthal, Davidson-Mosenthal, & Krieger, 1981). Developing a particular point of view for younger children is related to the students' verbal interaction patterns or the registers students maintain with their teachers. Mosenthal and Na (1981) have identified three types of students according to their dependency on a teacher's register. Children employing an "imitative response register," who simply repeat or paraphrase the teacher's register, tend to write texts that are more stimulus-bound, reflecting the structure and content of the assignment. In contrast, students with a "noncontingent response register" will introduce new topics without necessarily following the teacher's language; they tend to write texts whose structure and content reflect their own ways of organizing material, independent of the teacher's stimulus. Children with a "contingent response register" are between these two, tending to modify or adapt the teacher's register. Thus, when asked to write a narrative about a picture, fourth graders who employed an imitative response register in the classroom used more descriptive information from the picture to develop their points of view and adopted a more formal expository perspective. Noncontingent-response-register children employed more of their own schemata in selecting information, recasting the description into a narrative form. Whether writing helps students define their sense of self or simply provides a vehicle to allow them to reveal themselves, reflective writing deserves a home beyond language arts or English classrooms.

GENERAL IMPLICATIONS

We have tried to show that writing can be used for a variety of kinds of learning, not just as a "basic skill." However, as experienced writing teachers, we also know how difficult a task we are recommending. Whereas the most energetic and capable teachers always have and always will use every potentially productive approach available to them, we believe writing is so important that its use warrants special support for teachers.

Because much of the current theory regarding writing to learn evolved from relatively recent theory and research, many teachers do not know how writing can be used across the cirriculum. Inservice seminars specifically on ways to use writing for learning offer one kind of support. The research on the effects of such seminars is promising. Carroll (1983), for example, found that students taught by teachers trained in a "process-oriented" method wrote papers of significantly higher quality than students taught by teachers employing more traditional methods. However, Dilworth (1979) found that short, one-time sessions had little effect on changing teacher behavior.

One effective approach to inservice training is the ongoing faculty seminar. Teachers from different subjects meet to discuss such common concerns as designing effective writing assignments and students' writing problems (Herrington, 1981; Raimes, 1980). A common problem that emanates from these discussions is the question of who is responsible for what aspects of writing instruction. Teachers outside of English assume that English teachers will focus their attention on basic mechanics, which others consider to be outside their area of expertise. English teachers accept that responsibility for valid diagnosis of students' errors but also hope that teachers in other subject areas will assume responsibility for helping students by assigning and using writing in creative or challenging ways. One solution to this conflict is the team-teaching approach to writing, whereby students in English classes write papers for other courses, using mutually developed assignments.

For our part, we hope we have offered a positive rationale powerful enough to encourage efforts to use writing for all it is worth. Beyond the personal satisfaction that comes from writing well, students can enjoy the power of writing to learn new information, to solve problems, to understand pragmatic communication, to evaluate critically what they and others present in written language, and to understand themselves.

REFERENCE NOTES

Bransford, J. *The differences between skilled and unskilled learners.* Paper presented at the annual meeting of the American Educational Research Association, New York, 1982.

Brossell, G. *Rhetorical specification in essay examination topics: An experimental study.* Unpublished manuscript, College of Education, Florida State University, 1982.

Clemmons, S. *Identification of writing competencies needed by secondary students to perform assignments in science and social studies classes.* Unpublished doctoral dissertation, Florida State University, 1980.

Farr, M. *Learning to write English: One dialogue journal writer's growth in writing.* Paper presented at the annual meeting of the American Educational Research Association, New York, 1982.

HIDI, S., & KLAIMAN, R. *Inducing expert-like strategies in novice notetakers.* Paper presented at the annual meeting of the American Educational Research Association, New York, 1982.

KLINK, J. *The cumulative paper.* Unpublished manuscript, University of Wisconsin at Eau Claire, 1981.

MAIMON, E., & NODINE, B. *Measuring behavior and attitudes in the teaching of writing among faculties in various disciplines.* Paper presented at the annual meeting of the Modern Language Association, New York, 1978.

METVINER, E. *Rhetorically based and rhetorically deficient writing: The effects of purpose and audience on the quality of ninth grade students' compositions.* University of Connecticut, 1980.

REFERENCES

APPLEBEE, A. *Writing in the secondary school.* Urbana, IL: NCTE, 1981.

ATWELL, M. *The evolution of text: The interrelationship of reading and writing in the composing process.* Unpublished doctoral dissertation, Indiana University, 1980.

ANDERSON, T. Studying strategies and adjunct aids. In R. Spiro, B. Bruce, & W. Brewer (Eds.), *Theoretical issues in reading comprehension.* Hillsdale, NJ: Erlbaum, 1980.

BEACH, R. The effects of between-draft teacher evaluation versus student self-evaluation on high school students' revising of rough drafts. *Research in the Teaching of English,* 1979, *13,* 111–120.

BEACH, R., & EATON, S. Factors influencing college students' self-assessing and revising. In R. Beach & L. Bridwell (Eds.), *New directions in composition research.* New York: Guilford (1983).

BRIDWELL, L. S. Rethinking composing: Implications from research on revision. *English Journal,* 1981, *70,* 96–99.

BRITTON, J., BURGESS, T., MARTIN, N., MCLEOD, A., & ROSEN, H. *The development of writing abilities (11–18).* London: Macmillan Education, 1975.

Carroll, J. Process into product: Teacher awareness of the writing process affects students' written products. In R. Beach & L. Bridwell (Eds.), *New directions in composition research.* New York: Guilford (1983).

COLLINS, A., & GENTNER, D. A framework for a cognitive theory of writing. In L. Gregg & E. Steinberg (Eds.), *Cognitive processes in writing.* Hillsdale, NJ: Erlbaum, 1980.

COOPER, M. The pragmatics of form: How do writers discover what to do when? In R. Beach & L. Bridwell (Eds.), *New directions in composition research.* New York: Guilford (1983).

DILWORTH, C. Locally sponsored staff development for English teachers: A survey of methods and results. *English Education,* 1980, *12,* 98–105.

DONLAN, D. Teaching models, experience, and locus of control: Analysis of a summer inservice program for composition teachers. *Research in the Teaching of English,* 1980, *14,* 319–330.

ELBOW, P. *Writing with power.* New York: Oxford University Press, 1981.

EMIG, J. *The composing processes of twelfth graders.* Urbana, IL: National Council of Teachers of English, 1971.

EMIG, J. Writing as a mode of learning. *College Composition and Communication,* 1977, *28,* 122–128.

FLORIO, S. The problem of dead letters: Social perspectives on the teaching of writing. *The Elementary School Journal,* 1979, *80,* 1–7.

FLOWER, L., & HAYES, J. The dynamics of composing: Making plans and juggling constraints. In L. Gregg & E. Steinberg (Eds.), *Cognitive processes in writing: An interdisciplinary approach.* Hillsdale, NJ: Erlbaum, 1980.

GERE, A., SCHUESSLER, B., & ABBOTT, R. Measuring teacher attitudes toward instruction in writing. In R. Beach and L. Bridwell, *New directions in composition research.* New York: Guilford (1983).

GETZELS, J., & CSIKSZENTMIHALYI, M. *The creative vision: A longitudianl study of problem-finding in art.* New York: Wiley, 1976.

Glenn, A., & Ellis, A. Direct and indirect methods of teaching problem solving to elementary school children. *Social Education,* 1982, *46,* 134–136.

GRICE, H. Logic and conversation. In P. Cole & J. Morgan (Eds.), *Syntax and semantics* (Vol. 3, *Speech Acts*). New York: Academic, 1975.

HERRINGTON, A. Writing to learn: writing across the disciplines. *College English,* 1981, *43,* 379–387.

MARTIN, H., OHMANN, R., & WHEATLEY, J. *The logic and rhetoric of composition.* New York: Holt, 1969.

MEYER, B. J. F. The structure of prose: Effects on learning and memory and implications for educational practice. In R. C. Anderson, R. J. Spiro, & W. E. Montague (Eds.), *Schooling and the Acquisition of Knowledge.* Hillsdale, NJ: Erlbaum, 1977.

MOSENTHAL, P., & NA, T. Classroom competence and children's individual differences in writing. *Journal of Educational Psychology,* 1981, *73,* 106–121.

MOSENTHAL, P., DAVIDSON-MOSENTHAL, R., & KREIGER, V. How fourth graders develop points of view in classroom writing. *Research in the Teaching of English,* 1981, *15,* 197–214.

NATIONAL ASSESSMENT OF EDUCATIONAL PROGRESS. *Reading, thinking and writing.* Denver, CO: Education Commission of the States, 1981.

ODELL, L. Teaching writing by teaching the process of discovery: An interdisciplinary enterprise. In L. Gregg & E. Steinberg (Eds.), *Cognitive processes in writing: An interdisciplinary approach.* Hillsdale, NJ: Erlbaum, 1980.

OLSON, D. From utterance to text: The bias of language in speech and writing. *Harvard Educational Review,* 1977, *47,* 257–281.

PARK, D. The meanings of "audience." *College English,* 1982, *44,* 247–257.

PERKINS, D. *The mind's best work.* Cambridge, MA: Harvard University Press, 1981.

PICKERT, J., & ANDERSON, R. *Taking different perspectives on a story.* (Technical Report No. 14). Urbana, IL: Center for the Study of Reading, 1976.

PRATT, M. *Toward a speech-act theory of literary discourse.* Bloomington, IN: University of Indiana Press, 1977.

RAIMES, A. Writing and learning across the curriculum: The experience of a faculty seminar. *College English,* 1980, *41,* 797–801.

ROSE, M. *The cognitive dimension of writer's block: An examination of university students.* Unpublished doctoral dissertation, University of California at Los Angeles, 1980.

RUBIN, D., & PICHE, G. Development in syntactic and strategic aspects of audience adaptation skills in written persuasive communication. *Research in the Teaching of English,* 1979, *13,* 293–316.

TAYLOR, B., & BEACH, R. The effects of text-structure instruction on 7th graders' comprehension and writing of expository texts. *Reading Research Quarterly,* in press.

WALL, S. In the writer's eye: Learning to teach the rereading/revising process. *English Education,* 1982, *14,* 6–17.

IV SOCIAL CONTEXT AND WRITTEN LANGUAGE

13 The Development of Writing Abilities During the School Years*

James L. Collins
State University of New York at Buffalo

INTRODUCTION

My purpose here is to modify a rather conventional approach to understanding the development of writing abilities. This approach describes writing development in terms of a linear or hierarchical model, as a continuum consisting of identifiable, sequentially ordered stages. I argue that this conception is problematic on two related counts: it appropriately describes only one dimension of writing development, and it neglects societal and instructional influences on writing abilities. It emphasizes cognitive processes and tends to exclude social ones. In place of this conventional approach, I argue for one that includes a functional perspective on writing development during the school years. This latter approach rests on two major theoretical premises. Writing development is viewed as an interaction between cognitive processes involved in writing and educational and cultural contexts that influence these processes (Collins, 1981; Elsasser & John-Steiner, 1977; John-Steiner & Tatter, in press; Kroll, 1980). This influence, furthermore, is accomplished through the functions of writing in particular contexts (Britton, Burgess, Martin, McLeod, & Rosen, 1975; Scribner & Cole, 1978, 1981). In reasoning from these premises, I synthesize findings in research on writing development within what can be called a developmental-functional framework.

---

*The writer wishes to acknowledge Don Rubin for valuable comments on an earlier draft.

COGNITIVE DEVELOPMENT AND WRITING

The key concept in such a framework is that development in writing varies with the functions of writing. Writing development is a hybrid; it combines development in the sense of genetic maturity with development in the sense of learning from instruction and socialization. In the first sense, writing development resembles the learning of oral language or of a second language; the pattern of development shows emphasis on phonology and lexicon at early stages and on syntax and discourse at later ones (Shuy, 1981). In the second sense, writing development is less concerned with form and more with function. Here writers learn to write (or not to write) for socially and educationally determined purposes; the pattern of development becomes dominated particularly by school-sponsored functions of writing. As Bereiter puts the matter, "writing development, in a highly schooled society, is whatever the schools make it to be" (1980, p. 88).

If writing development varies with the functions of writing, we can expect a linear or hierarchical developmental model to most accurately describe an early stage in the growth of writing abilities, a stage where most children have no need for writing or any real sense of its usefulness (Vygotsky, 1934/1962). This does not mean that early writing serves no function; rather, it suggests that writing is functionally associated at first with other symbolic activities. Writing in these early, spontaneous occurrences does show sequential development (King & Rentel, 1979), and a functional association with other activities has been noted (Gundlach, 1981). These activities include gestures (Vygotsky, 1978) and symbolic play (Pellegrini, 1980; Vygotsky, 1978). The association between writing and drawing is particularly strong. Dyson (1982) concluded from her observations of kindergarten writers that writing is at first a form of graphic representation that is made meaningful through talk. Others, as well, have noted that writing by young children often occurs in conjunction with drawing (Graves, 1975; Gundlach and Moses, Note 1). An example of this early writing will illustrate how easily it conforms to a linear developmental model:

> I was wawking thrue the wds,
> Wan I saw a pritty brd. It
> was bringing the babby brds
> a wrm to eat. It was a
> butifl day. The sky was
> blue and clear. I was waring my
> red shrt with the blue trimming
> and my blue geandges.

The paragraph was spontaneously written by a first-grade girl. The writing was done on the back of a piece of paper, and on the front side she had first drawn the scene described in the writing. The writing is personal and concrete, expressive and narrative in form, and shows a high degree of implicit meaning.

The writing leans on graphic representation and on spoken sounds that govern invented spellings in a regularly abstracted way (Chomsky, 1970; Read, 1971). Developmentally, the writing suggests Bruner's (1966) division of representation into three sequential modes (enactive, ikonic, and symbolic), since the writing combines graphic and written modes. The writing also suggests a linear model that places personal writing before social writing, as when Britton (1970, 1975) traces poetic and transactional writing to their roots in expressive writing (see also Emig's, 1971, similar distinctions among reflexive, extensive, and expressive writing). And, of course, the writing also suggests Piaget's (1926/1955) developmental scheme leading from egocentric to socialized speech. Each of these linear or hierarchical models places our writer at the early end of a developmental continuum, and since she is in first grade, such placement in appropriate.

When the same placement is attempted for older writers, however, it becomes problematic. Such an attempt is made when writing problems are attributed to the egocentricity of the apprentice writer (Moffett, 1968; Shaughnessy, 1977). This argument, particularly in its stronger forms—basic writers in college have not attained a concept-forming level of cognitive development (Lunsford, 1979); in matters of coherence, some adult writers are like young children (Brostoff, 1981)—assumes that writing development is a function of cognitive growth. Adult writers, that is, produce writing characterized by egocentric language and thought because they are somehow arrested at an early, egocentric stage of cognitive development. Such reasoning confuses description with explanation (Krauss & Glucksburg, 1977) and is inconsistent with research showing that fourth-grade writers decenter less while writing than while speaking (Kroll, 1978). Curiously, the egocentricity argument is usually supported with reference to Piaget (1926/1955), in spite of his view that particular social environments help children become more sociocentric (Ducksworth, 1979; Inhelder & Piaget, 1959).

LITERACY AND WRITING

An alternative formulation of the linear model of writing development argues that cognitive growth is a function of literacy. In reality this is the same "line of development" just discussed, only now the development of writing abilities proceeds in the reverse direction; writing ability pushes cognitive growth instead of cognition pushing growth in writing abilities. Research supporting this alternative formulation often is based on differences between spoken and written language. Spoken language is concrete and context-dependent; it requires shared reference and an interlocutor. Written language is more abstract and context-independent; reference is textual, thus permitting communication with an absent or unknown reader. Greenfield (1972) argues that these differences distinguish between characteristic modes of thought in oral and literate cultures. Many others (Elsasser & John-Steiner, 1977; Emig, 1978; Goody & Watt, 1976; Hartwell, 1980; Hirsch, 1977; Olson, 1977; Shaughnessy, 1977; see also the essays in Kroll & Vann, 1981) make these differences the basis of a developmental transition from speaking to writing or from dialogue to monologue.

Two parallel concerns characterize recent research investigating this transition. One is the role of instruction in what is perceived as a "natural" cognitive-developmental process. In Bereiter and Scardamalia (1982), for example, a dozen or so experiments reporting the effects of procedural facilitations, i.e., strategies designed to ease the cognitive demands of writing, are reviewed. Generally, they found that teaching that does not involve new knowledge or skills and that does not deal with the content of writing eases the cognitive burdens of writing and the oral-to-written transition for fourth- and sixth-grade writers. The second concern is with the functions of language and writing. In Olson and Torrance (1981), for example, problems in learning to read and write are investigated in respect to the realignment of the primary functions of language that accompanies the speaking-writing transition. These functions, the interpersonal in speech and the ideational in writing, create the demand for explicit and autonomous meaning in written language; thus, mastery of the ideational or logical functions of language results from the development of writing (and reading) abilities.

These concerns for the instructional and functional contexts of writing underscore the problematic nature of an understanding of writing development that is restricted to a linear model. Whether cognitive development promotes or results from literacy is not the real issue. A more meaningful approach to understanding writing development is to admit that cognitive processes and writing abilities develop together in particular educational and social settings. This approach asks that we take a contextualized perspective on writing development, including contexts that are rhetorical (purpose, topic, audience), educational (conditions associated with schooling), and societal (the sociocultural backgrounds of writers and audiences). Consideration of each of these contexts shows that development in writing varies with the functions of writing.

CONTEXTS OF WRITING

The meaning of that variation is illustrated at the rhetorical level by studies of syntactic maturity. These studies analyze student writing in respect to the T-unit (one main clause and other, dependent clauses attached to or embedded in it). Researchers have used mean number of words per T-unit, mean number of clauses per T-unit, and mean number of words per clause as the chief measures of syntactic maturity. The major findings in this research are that written syntactic complexity develops chronologically in the direction of increased complexity (Hunt, 1965, 1970; O'Donnell, Griffin, & Norris, 1967) and that data on syntactic maturity can be regarded as normative (Hunt, 1965; Mellon, 1969; O'Hare, 1973; Stotsky, 1975). Recent research, however, suggests that these findings might be misleading. Studies that show a connection between assigned purpose of discourse and syntactic complexity (Crowhurst & Piché, 1979; Rubin & Piché, 1979; San Jose, 1972; Smith & Swan, 1978) argue against a linear conception of syntactic maturity. Crowhurst and Piché, for example, found a greater difference in mean T-unit length between argument and narration at grade 10 than Hunt (1965) found between grades 8 and 12, suggesting that syntactic complexity varies with the functions of writing more than it varies with chronological age or grade.

Collins and Williamson (1981, in press) found evidence of a similar variation in what can be called *semantic complexity*. They examined a possible developmental transition from implicit spoken dialogue to explicit written monologue at two ability levels (measured by primary trait scoring) in each of three grade levels (4, 8, 12). Measures of dialogic features were personal and demonstrative exophoric references (Halliday & Hasan, 1976) and formulaic expressions (Ong, 1979). In the first study, purpose of writing and audience were held constant, and better writers showed a decrease in the proportion of dialogic features in their writing across grade levels; weaker writers, however, did not. In the second study, better writers adjusted the proportion of dialogic features in their writing appropriately according to assigned variations in purpose and audience. Weaker writers adjusted the same proportion for audience but not for purpose. Taken together, these studies suggest a strong developmental trend toward explicit expression of meaning in writing. That trend, however, varies with grade, ability, and assigned rhetorical contexts, especially purpose.

When we move from consideration of rhetorical context to consideration of the educational contexts of writing, we find that audience and function play an even larger role in the development of writing abilities (Britton et al., 1975). Britton et al.'s report consists of a comprehensive description of factors involved in the development of writing and of how these factors are addressed and neglected in school-sponsored writing in British schools (and a recent report by Applebee, 1981, extends many of the findings to American schools). Britton et al. identified audience and mode, in respect to function or purpose for writing, as the crucial dimensions in writing development. Each of these dimensions was seen as developing through processes of differentiation from the self outward. They described differentiation in the writer's sense of audience in terms of categories ranging from self to unknown general reader. In differentiation of function they described categories that range from expressive, personal, writing outward in two directions, toward the poetic or literary, and toward the transactional or nonliterary. In their analysis of more than 2,000 samples of writing across school disciplines and across ages 11 to 18, Britton and his colleagues found that 92% of school writing is done for a teacher audience, that 49% is done for the teacher in the role of examiner, and that these audiences increase generally with grade level. The results for the function categories are similar: 63% of the writing done in school is transactional, most of which (37%) shows an informative purpose, and this category increases with grade level. Britton et al. concluded that writing experiences in schools seriously neglect the full range of options available to writers. Schooling generally takes a restricted, and possibly restricting, view of writing development. That possibility is illustrated in the following example, written by an eighth-grade girl:

> Propaganda is the spreading of invented
> or real facts to support a particular
> set of beliefs such as a political
> ideology. In *Animal Farm,* George Orwell
> is warning us about the dangers of
> propaganda that is accepted without
> criticism.

This example was written by the same writer whose first-grade writing was quoted earlier. Her writing no longer leans on drawing and experience. Or perhaps she has learned to be a good academic writer, one who writes about recently studied literature in a knowledgeable, abstract, formal, syntactically complex way, since such is a dominant purpose of writing in school. Britton's study suggests that these are one and the same: development in writing is limited to the functions of writing in school.

The Scribner and Cole studies (1978, 1981) of an indigenous writing system used by the Vai of Liberia suggest that the dominance of school-sponsored functions of writing may be culture-specific. This extends our consideration of contexts of writing development to the societal level. Among the Vai, the learning of literacy skills and schooling are separate activities, and the effects of literacy can be studied apart from the effects of schooling. The Scribner and Cole studies of these effects resulted in the conclusions that literacy involves quite particular skills and functions and that schooling develops abilities to generalize intellectual skills across various problem-solving situations. These conclusions contradict the theoretical assumption that writing (and reading) development is tied to cognitive growth either as cause or consequence. Writing development is tied to experiences with literate language. Cole and Scribner make this last point by emphasizing the functions of reading and writing. Functional analysis, that which examines the uses of literate language in and out of school, becomes more promising than developmental analysis by itself. Studying the ways that written language is perceived and used in particular school and social settings can inform our understanding of how and why writing ability develops for some students and not for others. Writing ability is tied to specific uses of writing in the home, school, and larger social settings.

A recent study by Kroll (in press) shows one form that analysis of the developmental influences of language in use can take. Kroll used data from two phases of a major longitudinal study of children's language development in Bristol, England. In the first phase, radio microphones had been used to record samples of spontaneous speech in the homes of 64 children selected to represent Bristol children in terms of gender, age, and social class. The one-half million recorded utterances were transcribed, coded and used to study the relationship among language development, socioeconomic background, and language interaction in the home. In the second phase, a subsample of 20 of the same children at age 7 was studied to determine factors that contribute to the acquisition of reading. (Wells, 1979, 1981).

Kroll used 18 of the 20 children in the reading project at age 9 as the principal subjects in his study, and he included 56 children, identified as typical writers by teachers of the same classes as this project group, as a comparison group. The antecedent factors Kroll examined for influence on writing development were oral language development, preschool knowledge of literacy, parental interest in literacy, socioeconomic background, and level of reading attainment. Kroll devised specific tasks to obtain four writing samples from each child during a 5-week period. The tasks were built around functions of writing: a personal experience (expressive purpose); a story based on a picture (narrative purpose); letters seeking a home for a puppy (persuasive purpose); and instructions to play a new game (explanatory purpose). Kroll analyzed the compositions written in response to these tasks for syntactic complexity measured by mean T-unit length, subordination measured as a mean number of clauses per T-unit, and vocabulary figured by Carroll's (1964) type/token ration. In addition, the overall quality of compositions was determined using holistic scoring (as described by Myers, 1980) for the expressive and narrative tasks, measures of context and appeals for the persuasive task, and a measure of informational adequacy (as in Kroll, 1978; Kroll & Lempers, 1981) for the explanatory task. Kroll's findings identified parental interest in literacy and preschool knowledge of literacy as powerful predictors of writing attainment at age 9. He interpreted these findings in terms of the insight process variables, such as parental interest in literacy, offer in clarifying the meaning of the status variable, socioeconomic background.

Correlational studies of out-of-school language and writing attainment are, of course, not the only way to study writing development from a functional perspective. Ethnographic methods, such as Cazden (in press) used to explore the applicability of Vygotsky's concept of a zone of proximal development, ethnohistorical methods to study the functions of writing in society (Heath, 1981), and sociolinguistic methods to study styles and registers found in school and social contexts (Labov, 1975) are other approaches to a functional understanding of writing development. These examples are not meant to be exhaustive but rather to be representative of diverse methods that can be used to build that understanding.

Functional analysis adds a societal or cultural dimension to our understanding of writing development. The linear, cognitive model does not take into account the ways society distributes and uses literacy skills. We have suspected for some time that writing development is connected to societal contexts: socioeconomic status affects language development (Loban, 1976) and language performance (Bernstein, 1975; Hawkins, 1977); adult basic writers hold membership in residually oral subcultures (Farrell, 1977); writing ability is unevenly distributed along class lines (Hendrix, 1981). These theories can be examined with continued research into functional aspects of writing development.

In addition to implications for further research, the functional perspective has a major implication for the way educators conceive of writing development. The linear model is simply inadequate. Writing development does not have a fixed and uniform pattern; if we want to hold onto the notion of stages, then we have to view these stages as variable (Bereiter, 1980). And it might be better to reject the notion of stages entirely. We are all capable of "egocentric" writing, for example, when the task gets difficult enough (Rubin, 1981; Onore, Note 2). I have often suspected that another example of "regression to an early stage" is available in the charts and lines we use to represent models of writing processes and writing development; perhaps this is the same connection between writing and drawing that was noted in the first-grade sample I provided above. We need a flexible, functional conception of writing development rather than a fixed, linear one. Writing development is negotiated every time written language is used.

REFERENCE NOTES

1. GUNDLACH, R. & MOSES, R. *Developmental issues in the study of children's written language.* Paper presented at the Boston University Conference on Language Development, 1976.
2. ONORE, C. S. *Revision, learning and the myth of improvement.* Paper presented at the Conference on College Composition and Communication, San Francisco, March 1982.

REFERENCES

APPLEBEE, A. N. *Writing in the secondary school.* Urbana, IL: NCTE, 1981.
BEREITER, C. Development in writing. In L. W. Gregg & E. R. Steinberg (Eds.), *Cognitive processes in writing.* Hillsdale, NJ: Erlbaum, 1980.
BEREITER, C., & SCARDAMALIA, M. From conversation to composition: The role of instruction in a developmental process. In R. Glaser (Ed.), *Advances in instructional psychology* (Vol. 2). Hillsdale, NJ: Erlbaum, 1982.
BERNSTEIN, B. *Class, codes and control* (Vol. 1). London: Routledge and Kegan Paul, 1975.
BRITTON, J. *Language and learning.* Baltimore, MD: Penguin, 1970.
BRITTON, J. Teaching writing. In A. Davies (Ed.), *Problems of language and learning.* London: Heinemann, 1975.
BRITTON, J., BURGESS, T., MARTIN, N., MCLEOD, A., & ROSEN, H. *The development of writing abilities, 11–18.* London: Macmillan Education, 1975.

BROSTOFF, A. Coherence: "Next to" is not "connected to." *College Composition and Communication,* 1981, *32,* 278-294.
BRUNER, J., OLVER, R., GREENFIELD, P., HORNSBY, J., KEMEY, H., MACCOBY, M., MODIANO, N., MOSER, F., OLSON, D., POTTER, M., REISCH, L., & SONSTROEM, A. *Studies in cognitive growth.* New York: Wiley, 1966.
CARROLL, J. B. *Language and thought.* Englewood Cliffs, NJ: Prentice-Hall, 1964.
CAZDEN, C. B. Peekaboo as an instructional model: Discourse development at home and at school. In B. Bain (Ed.), *The sociogenesis of language and human conduct.* New York: Plenum, in press.
CHOMSKY, C. Reading, writing, and phonology. *Harvard Educational Review,* 1970, *40,* 287-309.
COLLINS, J. L. *Spoken language and the development of writing abilities.* Paper presented at the Conference on College Composition and Communication, Dallas, 1981. (ERIC Document Reproduction Service No. ED 199 729)
COLLINS, J. L., & WILLIAMSON, M. M. Spoken language and semantic abbreviation in writing. *Research in the Teaching of English,* 1981, *15,* 23-35.
COLLINS, J. L., & WILLIAMSON, M. M. Assigned rhetorical context and semantic abbreviation in writing. In R. Beach & L. Bridwell (Eds.), *New directions in composition research.* New York: Guilford, in press.
CROWHURST, M., & PICHÉ, G. L. Audience and mode of discourse effects on syntactic complexity in writing at two grade levels. *Research in the Teaching of English,* 1979, *13,* 101-109.
DUCKWORTH, E. Either we're too early and they can't learn it or we're too late and they know it already: The dilemma of "applying Piaget." *Harvard Educational Review,* 1979, *49,* 297-312.
DYSON, A. H. The role of oral language in early writing processes. *Research in the Teaching of English,* in press.
ELSASSER, N., & JOHN-STEINER, V.P. An interactionist approach to advancing literacy. *Harvard Educational Review,* 1977, *47,* 355-369.
EMIG, J. *The composing processes of twelfth graders.* Urbana, IL: NCTE, 1971.
EMIG, J. Hand, eye, brain: Some "basics" in the writing process. In C. Cooper & L. Odell (Eds.), *Research on composing: Points of departure,* Urbana, IL: NCTE, 1978.
FARRELL, T. J. Literacy, the basics, and all that jazz. *College English,* 1977, *38,* 443-459.
Goody, J., & Watt, I. The consequences of literacy. In J. Karabel & A. H. Halsey (Eds.), *Power and ideology in education.* New York: Oxford University Press, 1976.
GRAVES, D. An examination of the writing processes of seven year old children. *Research in the Teaching of English,* 1975, *9,* 227-241.
GREENFIELD, P. M. Oral or written language: The consequences for cognitive development in Africa, the United States and England. *Language and Speech,* 1972, *15,* 169-178.
GUNDLACH, R. A. On the nature and development of children's writing. In C. H. Frederiksen and J. F. Dominic (Eds.), *Writing: The nature, development, and teaching of written communication.* (Vol. 2) Hillsdale, NJ: Erlbaum, 1981,
HALLIDAY, M. A. K., & HASAN, R. *Cohesion in English.* London: Longman, 1976.
HARTWELL, P. Dialect interference in writing: A critical view. *Research in the Teaching of English,* 1980, *14,* 101-118.
HAWKINS, P. R. *Social class, the nominal group and verbal strategies.* London: Routledge and Kegan Paul, 1977.
HEATH, S. B. Toward an ethnohistory of writing in American Education. In M. F. Whiteman (Ed.), *Writing: The nature, development, and teaching of written communication* (Vol. 1). Hillsdale, NJ: Erlbaum, 1981.
HENDRIX, R. The status and politics of writing instruction. In M. F. Whiteman (Ed.), *Writing: The nature, development, and teaching of written communication* (Vol. 1). Hillsdale, NJ: Erlbaum, 1981.

HIRSCH, E. D., JR. *The philosophy of composition.* Chicago: The University of Chicago Press, 1977.
HUNT, K. W. *Grammatical structures written at three grade levels.* Research Report No. 3. Urbana, IL: NCTE, 1965.
HUNT, K. W. Syntactic maturity in school children and adults. *Monographs of the Society for Research in Child Development,* 1970, *35,* (1, Serial No. 134).
INHELDER, B., & PIAGET, J. *The growth of logical thinking.* London: Routledge and Kegan Paul, 1959.
JOHN-STEINER, V., & TATTER, P. An interactionist model of language development. In B. Bain (Ed.), *The sociogenesis of language and human conduct.* New York: Plenum, in press.
KING, M. L., & RENTEL, V. Toward a theory of early writing development. *Research in the Teaching of English,* 1979, *13,* 243–253.
KRAUSS, R. M., & GLUCKSBERG, S. Social and nonsocial speech. *Scientific American,* 1977, *236,* 100–105.
KROLL, B. M. Cognitive egocentrism and the problem of audience awareness in written discourse. *Research in the Teaching of English,* 1978, *12,* 269–281.
KROLL, B. M. Developmental perspectives and the teaching of composition. *College English,* 1980, *41,* 741–752.
KROLL, B. M., & LEMPERS, J. D. Effect of mode of communication on the informational adequacy of children's explanations. *The Journal of Genetic Psychology.* 1981, *138,* 27–35.
KROLL, B. M. Antecedents of individual differences in children's writing attainment. In B. M. Kroll & C. G. Wells (Eds.), *Explorations in the development of writing.* Chichester: John Wiley, in press.
KROLL, B. M., & VANN, R. J.(EDS.). Exploring speaking-writing relationships: *Connections and contrasts.* Urbana, IL: NCTE, 1981.
LABOV, W. *The study of nonstandard English.* Urbana, IL: NCTE, 1975.
LOBAN, W. *Language development: Kindergarten through grade twelve.* Research Report No. 18. Urbana, IL: NCTE, 1976.
LUNSFORD, A. Cognitive development and the basic writer. *College English,* 1979, *41,* 39–46.
MELLON, J. C. *Transformational sentence-combining.* Research Report No. 10. Champaign, IL: NCTE, 1969.
MOFFETT, J. *Teaching the universe of discourse.* Boston: Houghton Mifflin, 1968.
MYERS, M. *A procedure for writing assessment and holistic scoring.* Urbana, IL: NCTE, 1980.
O'DONNELL, R. C., GRIFFIN, W. J., & NORRIS, R. C. *Syntax of kindergarten and elementary school children: A transformational analysis.* Research Report No. 8. Urbana, IL: NCTE, 1967.
O'HARE, F. *Sentence combining: Improving student writing without formal grammar instruction.* Research Report No. 15. Urbana, IL: NCTE, 1973.
OLSON, D. R. From utterance to text: The bias of language in speech and writing. *Harvard Educational Review,* 1977, *47,* 257–281.
OLSON, D. R., & TORRANCE, N. Learning to meet the requirements of written text: Language development in the school years. In C. H. Frederiksen & J. F. Dominic (Eds.), *Writing: The nature, development, and teaching of written communication* (Vol. 2). Hillsdale, NJ: Erlbaum, 1981.
ONG, W. J. Literacy and orality in our times. *Profession 79,* New York: Modern Language Association of America, 1979.
PELLEGRINI, A. The relationship between kindergartners' play and achievement in prereading, language, and writing. *Psychology in the Schools,* 1980, *17,* 530–535.
PIAGET, J. [The language and thought of the child] (M. Gabain, trans.). New York: New American Library, 1955. (Originally published, 1926)

READ, C. Pre-school children's knowledge of English phonology. *Harvard Educational Review*, 1971, *41*, 1–34.

RUBIN, D. *Social cognitive dimensions of composing processes*. Durham, NC: Monographs of the Duke University Wiring Project, in press.

RUBIN, D. L., & PICHÉ, G. L. Development in syntactic and strategic aspects of audience adaptation skills in written persuasive communication. *Research in the Teaching of English*, 1979, *13*, 293–316.

SAN JOSE, C. P. M. Grammatical structures in four modes of writing at fourth grade level. (Doctoral dissertation, Syracuse University, 1972). *Dissertation Abstracts International*, 1972, *33*, 5411A. (University Microfilms No. 1, 73–9563)

SHAUGHNESSY, M. P. *Errors and expectations: A guide for the teacher of basic writing*. New York: Oxford University Press, 1977.

SCRIBNER, S., & COLE, M. Literacy without schooling: Testing for intellectual effects. *Harvard Educational Review*, 1978, *48*, 448–461.

SCRIBNER, S., & COLE, M. Unpackaging literacy. In M. F. Whiteman (Ed.), *Writing: The nature, development, and teaching of written communication* (Vol. 1). Hillsdale, NJ: Erlbaum, 1981.

SHUY, R. W. Toward a developmental theory of writing. In C. H. Frederiksen & J. F. Dominic (Eds.), *Writing: The nature, development, and teaching of written communication* (Vol. 2). Hillsdale, NJ: Erlbaum, 1981.

SMITH, W. L., & SWAN, M. B. Adjusting syntactic structures to varied levels of audience. *Journal of Experimental Education*, 1978, *46*, 66–72.

STOTSKY, S. L. Sentence-combining as a curricular activity: Its effect on written language development and reading comprehension. *Research in the Teaching of English*, 1975, *9*, 30–71.

VYGOTSKY, L. S. [*Thought and language*] (E. Hanfmann & G. Vakar, Eds., and trans.). Cambridge, MA: MIT Press, 1962. (Originally published, 1934)

VYGOTSKY, L. S. *Mind in society: The development of higher psychological processes*. (M. Cole, V. John-Steiner, S. Scribner, & E. Souberman, Eds.). Cambridge, MA: Harvard University Press, 1978.

WELLS, C. G. Describing children's linguistic development at home and at school. *British Educational Research Journal*, 1979, *5*, 75–98.

WELLS, C. G. *Learning through interaction: The study of language development*. Cambridge: Cambridge University Press, 1981.

14 The Influence of Communicative Context on Stylistic Variation in Writing

Donald L. Rubin
University of Georgia

INTRODUCTION

An understanding of ordinary language requires comprehension of far more than literal denotation (Weinreich, 1966). Some common utterances—"hello," for example—carry no referential meaning (Searle, 1969). Others, like comments about obvious weather conditions, serve primarily phatic functions (Malinowski, 1935); were they intended as literal reports, they would violate accepted rules of conversation in that they assert the obvious (Grice, 1975). Still other language choices convey an attitude or a sense of relations between interactants, as in one attorney remarking to another, "If you aint got a duly executed instrument of conveyance, you aint got nothin'." An understanding of ordinary language, therefore, represents nonliteral presuppositions, many of which are pragmatic or social in nature (Keenan, 1971).

A study of style takes as its starting point the view that language variation is a constitutive element that contributes to meaning, for it is by means of stylistic variation that pragmatic presuppositions are encoded. Stylistic analysis seeks to describe the manner in which a communicator construes a communicative event such that a message is encoded in one way and not another. Bilingual communities provide the most dramatic instances of code-switching as a vehicle for conveying social meaning (Blom & Gumperz, 1972). But even monolingual and monodialectal speakers control several styles or registers, from which they select as they perceive (or manipulate) the nature of social situations (Halliday, McIntosh, & Strevens, 1965).

As language variation is constitutive of meaning in speech, it is no less so in writing. Though the social contexts of written communication are perhaps more constrained than those of face-to-face interaction, writers nonetheless encode pragmatic meaning through stylistic variation. This chapter outlines the manner in which communicative context affects style in writing. The exposition first develops a rhetorical conception of style and touches upon issues pertaining to intentionality, conventionality, and psycholinguistic processing. The bulk of the chapter then discusses stylistic variation in relation to six components of communicative contexts.

RHETORICAL CONCEPTION OF STYLE

Style can be considered from several distinct perspectives. Students of literature conceive of style as a relatively stable manifestation of an author's personality and aesthetic sense. A stylistic analysis from a literary point of view, then, might seek to demonstrate the linkage between an author's character and his/her idiosyncratic use of the language or might compare features of two different texts to verify common authorship (Enkvist, Spencer, & Gregory, 1965). A related perspective examines textual features that presumably reflect a communicator's mental state at the time a text was generated. Osgood and Walker (1959), by way of illustration, provide a convincing demonstration of the style of suicide notes. Still a third type of stylistic analysis is concerned with the social and diachronic distribution of linguistic variables, with style as a relatively stable indicator of social identity. A researcher operating from this perspective might examine cultural or epochal (Jacobson, 1968) markers in speech or writing.

In contrast with these notions of style as a reflection of individuality (Crystal & Davies, 1969), this chapter adopts a more transactional, rhetorical perspective on style. Individuals are seen to control a number of varieties and devices that they differentially deploy in order to achieve desired effects upon their audiences. For example, a writer might choose to use a sentence fragment or "minor sentence" in order to elicit attention and create emphasis in the mind of a reader (Kline & Memering, 1977).

Note, however, that despite the convenient use of terms like "select" and "choose," this rhetorical paradigm does not require that we attribute to message sources conscious intentionality in style. Although some rhetorical choices do entail deliberation over alternate phrasings and strategies (Millic, 1971), others presume tacit participation in the set of rules for performing a particular speech act within any given speech community (Abrahams, 1969). Thus, a mature writer might worry over the tone conveyed by the verb cluster "doesn't," weighing this option against "fails to." But the same writer intuitively senses that mixing contractions like "doesn't" with low-frequency lexical items like "ingest" violates rules of co-occurrence (Ervin-Tripp, 1972). Although the rhetorical perspective on style does not demand that we attribute conscious choice, it does regard writing and speaking as generally goal-directed activities, in that the model presumes some communicative—or at least mimetic—teleology.

It is likewise interesting to observe that stylistic features may exert effects on audiences either through the force of social convention or through the force of psychological function. Examples of the former include most instances of forms of address ("Sir," "Mr. Thneed," "Jack," or "Poochie") and of genre-specific formulae ("Pursuant to our recent telephone conversation," "And they all lived happily ever after"). Stylistic features that carry meaning by virtue of their discourse-processing functions include topicalization ("It was to the ale house that Tony retreated"), which directs the reader to foreground "new" information (Quirk & Greenbaum, 1973). Broader matters of rhetorical strategy such as degree of explicitness and elaboration are likewise governed by considerations of what is necessary to reduce ambiguity (Hirsch, 1977). Germane to this distinction is the debate over the status of the paragraph. While some researchers contend that paragraphs have psychological reality as ideational units which enable readers to chunk related information, others claim that indenting is merely a matter of arbitrary orthographic convention (Rodgers, 1966).

Style, then, emerges as a communicator encodes pragmatic presuppositions about social situations. Language variables may be selected by deliberate artifice or as a result of tacitly understood conventions. Social meaning inheres in stylistic variation in some cases because of the rules underlying various usages and in other cases because of assumptions about readers' psychological states that are implied by certain text features. A message—written as well as spoken—is situated in a particular context. The communicator adapts to or defines that context stylistically. Thus, style is an outward reflection of the communicator's mental representation of context. As we shall discuss, the course of development in writing is in large part a matter of acquiring two things: a wide repertoire of discourse function and acuity in discerning the contexts of written communication.

CONSTITUENTS OF COMMUNICATIVE SITUATIONS

Drawing upon a number of previous analyses of social context (see Rubin, Note 6), six constituents of communicative situations may be identified: (a) *medium of communication*—e.g., speech, writing, signing; (b) *discourse function*—e.g., persuading, regulating, expressing affect, maintaining channels of communication; (c) *audience-communicator role relations*—e.g., intimacy, power, similarity, expertise; (d) *topic domain*—e.g., familiarity, abstractness, degree and type of value commitment; (e) *setting*—e.g., institutional, self-sponsored, vocational; and (f) *interaction structure*—e.g., genre, inter- and intra-message sequence.

Medium of Communication

The situational variables listed above are readily seen as determinants of spoken style. Their impact on written language is less obvious, perhaps because style in writing is commonly regarded as either wholly individualistic (as in literary theory) or else monolithic and of a single standard (as in prescriptive teaching). Indeed, the very medium of writing does constrain style for reasons relating to time factors in encoding, to physical separation between writer and audience, and to conventional frames or schemata for written discourse.

One of the fundamental differences between speech and writing is the fact that speech is a fast-fading medium, whereas writing retains a physical trace. That trace serves as an adjunct to the writer's short-term memory. As a result, writers, more so than speakers, have grace to attend to the form in which their messages are encoded. Written style, therefore, tends to be less redundant, more densely modified, and marked by more lexical diversity than spoken language (Schafer, 1981, Schallert, Kleiman, & Rubin, 1977). In contrast, time constraints on both oral production and aural reception dictate a particular emphasis on high intelligibility over relatively local stretches of spoken discourse (Cherniss, 1969).

As an adjunct to short-term memory, then, the medium of writing affects linguistic style. Writing, however, also fosters access to more long-term storage, and as such it affects style in more macrocosmic ways as well (Kintsch, 1980). From a historical-cultural point of view, the innovation of writing profoundly influenced the development of civilization by altering the rate at which knowledge could be accumulated and by imposing a more linear and analytic mode of cognition (Goody & Watt, 1963). Oral cultures perceive simultaneity in their worlds; literate cultures are more attuned to sequential cause and effect and attendant styles of reasoning (Scribner & Cole, 1981).

Analogously, the individual's cognitive functioning, and resultant discourse style, becomes more linear and analytic in writing (Olson, 1977). Investigations of composing behavior-in-process reveal reflexive reflection: writers pause at frequent intervals to review what they have already written, to consider it in terms of initial and changing goals, and to engage in recursive "internal revision" (Flower & Hayes, 1980; Murray, 1978). Reflexive reflection points to the capacity of writing for promoting discovery of new insight, new information. By returning to the physical trace of their previous prose, writers can reformulate plans or explore new networks of associations. In this way the cues already embedded in an author's writing act as a springboard to ideas not anticipated initially.

As an illustration of the manner in which writing enables maintenance of linear reasoning over stretches of discourse, Britton and his colleagues (1975) conducted an informal experiment. Writing with an inkless stylus on carbon-backed paper, an author was able to sustain a casual narrative letter to a friend but unable to compose a densely conceptual exposition. Higgins (1978) found a similarly facilitative effect in the referential writing of students in grades 4 through 8. Subjects in all grades encoded more "useful" information concerning a set of portrayed events in writing than in speech. Kroll and Lempers (1981), however, found an opposite effect using a somewhat different task and index of information. Kroll (1978) implies that the stress writing imposes on social cognitive operations (to be discussed in the section on audience relations) militates against the medium's capacity as a general cognitive facilitator, at least for young writers. Nevertheless, it appears that once composing is mastered with reasonable proficiency it can promote cognitive functioning and engender a style of linear analytical reasoning rare in spontaneous spoken discourse (Bruner, 1966).

At the same time that written language is stylistically influenced by factors of real time, it is also affected by factors relating to the physical separation of writers from their audience. The observation is often made that, although speech can be context-dependent, writing must be rendered context-independent (e.g., Collins & Williamson, 1981; Hirsch, 1977). That is, speakers and their listeners share common physical contexts. Therefore, speech appropriately makes use of paralinguistic cues and gestures that modify linguistic meaning. Spoken language can also capitalize on information in the immediate environment and thus utilize ellipsis, deictic pronouns, and other expressions with exophoric reference that in writing would be at best ambiguous.

In short, the physical separation of writer and audience requires that written composition be self-contained and autonomous. It also demands that all information needed to interpret meaning be linguistically packaged in convenient form. This context independence is manifested in explicitness, anaphora or cataphora, and appropriate detail and elaboration. In this sense, written style epitomizes the kind of elaborated code that British researchers associate with flexible, open role systems (Bernstein, 1973).

Beyond time factors and physical separation between encoder and decoder, arbitrary conventions further constrain the range of language appearing in the medium of writing. The kinds of conventions we are referring to at this point are not genre-specific norms, such as the obligatory structure of Italian sonnets. Rather, at issue here are frames, or schemata, for what is to count as written language. At the most atomistic level, these conventions include expectations of more or less standard capitalization, punctuation, and spelling. More interestingly, certain syntactic constructions such as the colloquial passive *got* ("John got hit by the ball") are excluded from writing. Other constructions (e.g., " 'Go to the store', said John") are found only in writing (Burling, 1970). Some conventionalized features stretching over longer units of discourse include more elaborate devices for creating closure at the end of compositions and greater thematic consistency than is commonly found in speech (Cherniss, 1969).

Well before they learn to write on their own, young children assimilate some notion that writing possesses conventions apart from those of speech (Dyson, 1981). Thus, dictated "writing" is often stylistically distinct from oral composition in primary-grade students. Surely the source of these schemata for written style must lie in the materials read to children by caretakers and teachers (King & Rentel, 1981). Indeed, reading continues to be the source of writing schemata for mature authors (Bazerman, 1980). Occasionally, novice writers run into trouble when they stereotype the conventions of written language in an overly rigid fashion. The resulting style is often times stilted, hypercorrect, and prone to malapropisms (Shaughnessy, 1977).

In this section we have discussed stylistic features generic to writing by virtue of both fundamental properties (physical trace, nonpresent audience) and arbitrary conventions. The discussion is guilty of oversimplification, however, in that it treats writing and speech as discontinuous, dichotomous categories of media. In fact, some types of writing have speech-like qualities and, conversely, some types of speech incorporate writing-like elements. For example, the dialogue journals extensively investigated by Staton (1982) would be likely to contain a great deal of speech-like ellipsis and exophora. Similarly, writing meant to be declaimed aloud may intentionally incorporate aspects of oral style (Crystal & Davies, 1969). Indeed, writing is not absolutely context-independent but is more or less independent of context depending on the degree of sociopsychological distance between writer and reader (Rubin & Piché, 1979). A more precise formulation, therefore, would use the term *writing* to designate an extreme pole of a continuous spectrum ranging from interactive, spontaneous, and immediately expressive (oral) to monologic, planned, and reflected (written) language.

Discourse Function

Traditional rhetorical and composition theory has long been concerned with differences among the four major modes of discourse (narration, description, persuasion, and exposition). Indeed, until recently the four modes served as a scheme for organizing instruction. Modes are conceptualized as attributes of texts, but current composition pedagogy has shifted the focus of instruction from product to producer. Hence, the modern trend in teaching writing is to forego "teaching the modes" and instead analyze writers' aims or purposes in composing (Connors, 1981). A third approach to dealing with related aspects of types of writing, an approach more consistent with the rhetorical-sociolinguistic perspective of the present essay, is to direct attention to the functions a piece of discourse plays in writer-reader interaction. In discussing discourse functions, we center neither on formal features of texts, which may or may not have social meaning, nor on writers' intentions, which may or may not be realized in texts, but on the manner in which a text might affect an audience. Nevertheless, it is useful to point out that the terms *mode, purpose,* and *function* are conceptually related and simply place the locus of interest in different components of communication.

It is likewise useful to note that no single piece of discourse is a pure instance of one function, uncontaminated by elements of the others. A writer cannot argue, for example, without presenting some primarily referential material. In fact, the persuasive writing of mature authors is distinguished from that of younger ones by the degree to which it includes descriptive information about the social or historical setting of the issue of persuasion (Rubin & Piché, 1979). Similarly, expert writers often adopt a strategy of personal narration in a work whose primary function is to explain (Flower & Hayes, 1981). Still, it is convenient to analyze writings according to their *dominant* function.

A great many taxonomies of the functions of written discourse have been promulgated (D'Angelo, 1976). One that has obtained a good deal of currency is the tripartite system of expressive, poetic, and transactional language developed by researchers with the British Schools Council (Britton et al., 1975). According to their account, expressive language develops earliest, with the other two functions growing out and depending upon it. Stylistically, expressive writing is close to the form of inner speech, that is, inexplicit and predicate-rich.

Within the category of transactional writing, there appears to be some developmental progress, not yet adequately explained, from narrative and descriptive writing to persuasive. Conventional pedagogical practice has withheld persuasive writing from elementary students despite youngsters' patent abilities to reason and argue in speech (Larson, 1971). The rationale for this curricular sequence presumably rests on Piagetian assumptions that children do better on concrete tasks (e.g., translating sensory experience) than on abstract (e.g., advocating a policy; Moffett, 1968). Indeed, research indicates that young writers produce better narrative and descriptive essays than persuasive (Veal & Tillman, 1971). Researchers have also noted that many young children lapse into narration when asked to produce argumentative writing (Crowhurst & Piché, 1979). Miller (Note 4) found that many typical college students have not attained requisite cognitive abilities to support abstract written argument. Given the fact, however, that writing does not develop by some innate mechanism but rather within the confines of a didactic and institutional environment, the late onset of argumentation may simply be due to a lack of familiarity with persuasive writing.

Other investigators have had little difficulty eliciting persuasive writing from children as young as fourth graders. Bracewell, Scardamalia and Bereiter (Note 2), for example, obtained opinion pieces from young writers and found that their ability to revise those writings in response to the demands of an external editor/audience increased with age. Rubin and Piché (1979) performed content analyses on the persuasive writings of subjects from grades 4, 8, and 12 and a group of expert adults. They found that development in persuasive writing generally paralleled that in persuasive speaking. Older subjects possessed larger repertoires of strategies and were more prone to use strategies based on interpersonal relations and on receiver values. Transition statements that direct readers' attention to particular relationships rarely appeared until grade 12.

A number of studies have investigated development in written referential communication (Higgins, 1978; Kroll & Lempers, 1981; Piché, Rubin & Turner, 1980; Scardamalia, Bereiter, & McDonald, Note 7). One feature of mature style in referential writing is the orienting statement ("I'm going to be telling you about a funny shape that's all angly, and when I'm done you're going to have to draw it;" Scardamalia et al., Note 7). In contrast, orienting statements in persuasive writing ("I'm writing to try to get you to save your glass for recycling") were inversely related to age (Rubin & Piché, 1979).

Despite a fairly extensive literature describing stylistic development in children's oral narratives (Applebee, 1978; Sutton-Smith, Botvin, & Mahoney, 1976), less progress has been made in corresponding studies of written narrative. Growth in early narrative writing (kindergarten and grade 1) manifests increasingly diverse devices for creating cohesion (King & Rentel, 1981). Growth in early narrative writing is also marked by inclusion of more obligatory story elements (background setting, initial event, etc.; King, Rentel, & Cook, Note 3). In slightly older elementary-school children, written narratives progress from loose chronologies to texts that include some backgrounding. By age 14, writers typically can stop the flow of narrative sequence to offer comments and can also include information about characters' motivations (Wilkinson & Hanna, 1980). Curiously, one research team found negative relations between children's explicit knowledge about story structure and their inclusion of those elements in their own written productions (Bereiter, Scardamalia, & Turkish, Note 1).

Studies that examine children's writing styles in one discourse function or another are supplemented by additional investigations that compare styles across different functions. Research in cross-function comparisons, however, has focused on a single stylistic variable: syntactic complexity as reflected in T-unit length, clause length, and degree of subordination (Bortz, 1969; Crowhurst & Piché, 1979; Perron, 1977; Rosen, Note 5; San Jose, 1972; Seegars, 1933). These studies concur on a number of findings. First, discourse function exerts a profound effect on syntactic complexity. Within-age style shifts are of a magnitude equal to or exceeding between-age contrasts. Second, there is a strong tendency for style-shifting in writing to increase with age. That is, more mature writers are sensitive to the differential stylistic demands of the various functions to a greater degree than younger writers.

The nature of those differential demands is also suggested by this body of literature. Those studies that sampled persuasive writing among the functions examined (Crowhurst & Piché, 1979; Perron, 1977; Rosen, 1969; Seegars, 1933) unanimously found that persuasion engendered the highest degree of syntactic complexity. Several alternative explanations have been forwarded. Perron (1977) and Rosen (Note 5) both speculate that the abstract nature of argumentation imposes a developmental "pull" on young writers' cognitive operations and thereby pulls syntactic complexity into ranges higher than age norms. Perelman and Olbrechts-Tyteca (1969) observe, on the other hand, that argumentation naturally calls for subordination and other elements of syntactic complexity that cue readers as to relationships among propositions. This latter explanation is supported by teachers' quality ratings of students' persuasive and narrative writings. Syntactic complexity contributed to judged composition quality in persuasive writing but not in narrative (Crowhurst, 1980).

For adults, the source of syntactic complexity in persuasive writing is rather subtle. Rubin (1982) found a decline with age in certain cohesive conjunctions that signal logical relations. The formalaic use of "so" as a conjunction of conclusion (*"So* if you're smart you'll do what I say") predominated among eighth graders in particular. Adults exhibited the lowest frequency of adverbial clauses of cause and condition. Rather, adult writers achieved syntactic complexity by reducing their logical premises to subclausal units.

We see, then, that function exerts substantial impact on style in writing, both in sentence-level and more global variables. It must be noted, however, that the relation of function to textual realization remains inadequately explained. One promising direction for elucidating the nature of this link lies in emerging work in text linguistics, which might serve to generate a more principled typology of functions than currently exists (Schmidt, 1977).

Audience-Writer Relations

Audience is the central and distinctive concern of all rhetorical models (Wichelns, 1925/1972). As discussed in the section concerning the media of communication, writers must appreciate the consequences of physical separation from their audiences if they are to produce context-independent text. Vygotsky (1962) noted that writing is twice abstracted from immediate social interaction. First, graphemic symbols are abstract (and nonisomorphic) representations of phonological units. Yet more significantly, the writer must construct an abstract representation—"fictionalize" in Ong's (1975) term—of the audience. At the very least, writers must create for themselves a representation of readers engaged in processing the stream of written language (Rubin, in press). If the writer fails to do so, the text will probably be unintelligible to a spatially and temporally remote audience. Social cognitive effort, in short, is necessary to production of autonomous text. Ambiguous or vacuous meaning, poor readability, and a host of other infelicities can be attributed to writers' neglect of their readers' perspectives. Indeed, this type of egocentrism is postulated as a major factor differentiating able adult writers from those requiring remedial assistance (Elsasser & John-Steiner, 1977; Flower, 1979).

Knowledge of the writer as text processor, however, is only one kind of audience awareness that affects writing style. Rubin (in press; Rubin, Piché, Michlin, & Johnson, in press) presents a comprehensive scheme that enumerates five dimensions of social cognition that enter into composing processes: (a) *social cognitive subskills* (perspective differentiation, construct repertoire, sense of instrumentality, cue selection, mental representation, maintenance of role differentiation, sense of applicability); (b) *structure of social cognition* (egocentric, sequential, simultaneous, recursive); (c) *content domain of inferred percepts* (perceptual, cognitive, affective); (d) *content stability of inferred percepts* (dispositional; episodic; processual); (e) *audience determinateness* (ranging from determinate other to generalized other).

Evidence derived from analyses of "thinking aloud" protocols of skilled and unskilled writers in the process of writing illuminates this relation between social cognition and writing. Poor writers are often restricted by rigid and limited notions of reader expectations (Perl, 1980). For superior writers, on the other hand, sense of audience provides a generative, heuristic force throughout the act of writing (Atlas, 1979; Flower & Hayes, 1980). The kinds of ongoing stylistic adaptations that writers reveal in these studies include microstructural features like vocabulary choice, as well as elements of larger structure like overall approach to the subject (personalized, humorous, didactic), major thematic content, use of examples, and degree of elaboration (Berkenkotter, 1981; Flower & Hayes, 1980).

Quantitative methodologies likewise point to effects of audience awareness on written style and begin to provide a more precisely specified set of correspondences between social percepts and stylistic features. In a study of fourth graders' narrative writing (Rubin, *et. al.*, in press), a multivariate battery of measures of social cognitive ability was found to be a strong predictor (canonical $r = .60$) than two well-established textual determinants of writing quality: composition length and rate of errors. A moderate relationship (canonical $r = .43$) held between social cognitive ability and error rate.

As in research on the effects of discourse function, a good deal of inquiry concerning audience adaptation in writing focuses on the variable of syntactic complexity. Smith and Swan (1978) found that subjects rewrote supplied passages with higher syntactic complexity when addressing an older and more sophisticated audience than when addressing children just beginning to read; this effect was more marked for high-school seniors and college freshmen than for younger children. Crowhurst & Piché (1979) elicited student writings directed to teachers and to peers. They found that greater syntactic complexity was addressed to the teacher audience, that this tendency was operating among tenth graders more than among sixth, and that it was most prevalent in persuasive writing as compared to narrative and descriptive. The authors concluded that persuasive writing stimulates audience adaptation most strongly because audience is most salient in conative functions. Rubin (1982; Rubin & Piché, 1979) isolated the audience dimension of intimacy to writer as a potent factor in engendering stylistic adaptation in syntactic complexity. He found, however, differential use of types of syntactic complexity. High intimacy was related to dense subordination, whereas remote audiences received messages marked by relatively longer clauses.

A number of studies have examined more macroscopic strategies in both persuasive and referential writing: Writers must attain considerable maturity before they are able to deploy persuasive appeals differentially in response to varying audience attributes. Those strategies most characteristic of older writers include appeals to readers' internal gratification as well as arguments that anticipate and refute potential reservations (Rubin & Piché, 1979). In referential writing, the informational adequacy of messages is generally found to increase with age (Higgins, 1978; Kroll & Lempers, 1981). It should be noted, however, that informational adequacy by itself is problematical as an index of audience adaptation. A message may be informationally dense and, because of that very economy of communication, may be quite unreadable.

Topic

In oral discourse, topic domain exerts considerable influences on style. In bilingual communities, for example, topic domain (home vs. school) can determine choice of native or second language (Fishman, Cooper, & Ma, 1972). Composition researchers have recognized for some time that failure to control the topic of writing can degrade reliability of writing evaluations (Braddock, Lloyd-Jones, & Shoer, 1963). Of the very few studies that have examined the effects of topic of writing style, Rosen (Note 5) found differences in syntactic complexity due to topic chosen on an exit examination of writing skills. Crowhurst and Piché (1979), on the other hand, detected no significant differences due to topic in this same stylistic variable in repeated writing samples elicited in an experimental task. Crowhurst and Piché's topics, however, were drawn by design from similar domains (activities and experiences relating to nature or animals), whereas the writing examination from which Rosen drew his data provided a wider range of topics (school, world affairs, home life).

The presumption that students will write best about topics that are near to their concrete experiences permeates the teaching of writing. Generally recommended practice moves students gradually from familiar to unfamiliar subjects (Moffett, 1968). Egan's (1979) rather heretical theory of educational development contends quite the opposite, however. Richer understandings of the effects of topic domain on style in writing would be helpful in resolving that issue.

Setting

Under the rubric of setting we may begin to consider the physical and temporal aspects of the context in which writing takes place. Little research has addressed this question. Emig's (1971) case studies do suggest that students' self-sponsored writing produced at leisure is quite distinct from their classroom composition. It would be helpful to determine, from the standpoint of writing-skill evaluation, the degree to which writing samples collected under typical classroom and examination conditions (i.e., limited time and collaboration, physical movement forbidden—conditions most unnatural for most adult writers) are stylistically distinguished from samples produced under less constrained circumstances.

Another aspect of setting, representing perhaps a more fruitful line of inquiry, concerns the effects of institutional settings on style. For example, the style of technical writing used in scientific or engineering settings differs from that of writing expected in commercial settings. Both are distinguished from academic writing, that is, from the freshman composition model that dominates instruction in high schools and college. The most common institutional setting for student writers is, of course, the classroom. It is well worth inquiring into the ways in which the classroom *qua* social institution affects written style.

It is often observed that manuscripts composed for the purpose of fulfilling classroom assignments (i.e., to be evaluated in a standard fashion) are formulaic, seek more to avoid errors than to develop a point of view, and may contain hypercorrect or stereotypically sophisticated phrasing (Macrorie, 1970). A study by Mosenthal and Na (1981) is particularly germane in that it suggests specific elements of style that emerge by virtue of the interaction between classroom context and individual differences in students' modes of response. In a descriptive writing task, students with imitative patterns of teacher-student oral interaction produced purely descriptive compositions. In contrast, students with noncontingent interaction patterns introduced more "schema-creative" propositions. The findings suggest that interaction norms instantiated in particular classroom settings can affect students' writing styles.

Interaction Structure

In explicating relations between reading and writing, Bazerman (1980) introduces the useful notion of writing as a conversation, or transaction, between the writer and a body of previously experienced writing. The analogue to oral interaction is apt. The speaker's style is affected by previous talk in at least three ways. First, speakers gain information by listening in on others' conversation. They not only add to their own store of knowledge from which they can draw in subsequent conversation, but they also discover what information can be presumed, what counts as "old" information, what points need not be elaborated as they enter into the conversation at hand. Second, speakers familiarize themselves with the stylistic conventions (e.g., norms for humor, tempo, turn-taking) of the conversation they wish to join. Speakers in one context must subscribe to the same set of conversational conventions if they are to operate effectively in that context. Finally, to successfully engage in conversation the speaker must be attuned to the stage of interaction into which he is about to plunge. The conversation may be just beginning, searching for focus, or it may be concluding, or perhaps a question was just asked and the speaker's contribution will have to be in the form of a response.

Although writing is most often a solitary activity, the writer's composition, in a manner similar to the conversationalist's comment, enters into a stream of discourse that is already underway and that possesses a particular structure. The first aspect of interaction structure, as it pertains to writing, is *universe of discourse*. The universe of discourse in which a piece of writing is grounded includes the knowledge base that can be presumed among readers of that particular body of literature. Thus, if a writer is operating within the universe of discourse that encompasses scholarly writing about psycholinguistic processes, terms like *mental, sentence,* and even *transformational grammar* can be treated as primitive terms requiring no explanation (unless a point is to be made that illuminates or defines these terms in new ways). The universe of discourse in which much student writing transpires, however, is rather ill-defined. It is possible for a classroom community to create its own universe of discourse—for example, the *Foxfire* books and magazines written by students at Rabun County (Georgia) High School. But when student writings are neither published nor shared, the universe of discourse is amorphous indeed. It should be noted that much of the rationale for using collections of essays as texts for college writing courses is to provide some universe of discourse into which novice academic writers can enter.

The term *genre* denotes types of writing distinguished by stylistic conventions that are, in fact, constitutive of those forms of discourse. For example, the genre of personal narrative is marked by a first-person narrator. When writers participate in a specific genre, they are obliged to use the criterial stylistic features of that genre; otherwise, they have entered into some other form of interaction. School-assigned writing includes several genres that seem to have little currency in other settings: the five-paragraph theme, the senior (or junior or sophomore) library research paper, the book report. Some of the stylistic features associated with each of these genres has a functional basis (e.g., an introductory paragraph serves as an advance organizer for the reader). All genre-specific features, whether or not functional, have a basis in convention. Stotsky (1981), by way of illustration, discusses stylistic and pedagogical issues relating to the genre of essay, discussing the oft-neglected area of lexis. Essay style is conventionally marked by a high density of affixed and suffixed Latinate words. Such vocabulary is particularly suited to this context because it communicates meaning more precisely than Anglo-Saxon derivatives, which tend to communicate more evocatively. According to Stotsky, part of what is learned in mastering essay writing is a repertoire of Latinate terms and a sensitivity to their appropriateness in this context.

Beyond the universe of discourse and genre, the interaction structure of writing contexts is also composed of a *location within a sequence of discourse*. The sequence may be in the nature of "turn-taking" between discrete texts, as when a customer's initial letter of complaint shapes in some way the style of the department manager's response (e.g., "In your letter of 12 October you stated that. . ."). Although a written text is a monologue, writers may similarly enter into dialogic relations with a previous piece of writing by authoring a variety of types of comments, counterstatements, exegeses, or replies. In each case, the style of a subsequent text is affected by the character of the antecedent texts. Staton (1982) has devised and analyzed a technique, called "dialogue journal," that deliberately incorporates interactive turn-taking into writing assignments. In this way, novice writers, especially students for whom English is not a native language, can build upon structure imposed by more experienced writers in preceding turns.

More readily apparent is the sequence of structures internal to a text. Essay introductions are stylistically distinct from conclusions. In letter writing, referential or conative content is often sandwiched between expressive or ritualistic interpersonal sections. Persistent questions about sequence in persuasive writing concern the relative advantages of recency versus immediacy in locating strong or weak arguments. And of course, sequence is a major factor in achieving effect in narrative writing. In short, much of what is discussed under the familiar rubric of "organization" can be construed as a matter of how writers create context for subsequent portions of their texts or conform to antecedent textual context already in place.

CONCLUSION

In presenting this six-part description of contextual factors bearing on style in writing, this chapter extends the position of contemporary composition theory that recognizes effects of function and audience on written language (e.g., Britton et al., 1975). In addition, the conceptual framework here attempts to synthesize perspectives that are sometimes artificially kept distinct. Writers are regarded as encoding pragmatic presuppositions about the way they construe the communicative context of a composition. They select stylistic elements, whether intentionally or tacitly, as part of a goal-oriented process aimed at achieving rhetorical effect. Writers are guided by sociolinguistic norms that associate stylistic variables with contexts by force of convention. They are at the same time controlled by principles of discourse processing. The course of stylistic development in writing ability may be regarded, in sum, as a process of becoming increasingly sensitive to elements of communicative context, as well as increasingly able to control the resources of written language such that those resources are deployed with flexibility in accommodating to medium of discourse, function, audience-writer relations, topic, setting, and interaction structure.

Beyond its usefulness in theory building, this view of style and writing has some immediate applications to research, evaluation, and instructional practice. Research aimed at providing developmental-descriptive accounts of children's writing abilities must tread cautiously in formulating age-norm generalizations that fail to provide for the effects of communicative context. For example, Kroll's (1978; Kroll & Lempers, 1981) findings that children transmit more information through speech than through writing seems diametrically opposed to Higgins' (1978) contrary results. It is possible, however, that the conflict can be resolved by examining the different demands of the writing tasks employed in the two studies.

By the same token, evaluations of children's writing skills or of the quality of their compositions ought not to be premised on arhetorical considerations that simplistically index quality by means of particular discourse variables. Composition length, for example, often predicts judged quality (Page, 1968). But under certain circumstances, the strategy of mature writers is to curtail verbosity (Rubin, 1982). Syntactic complexity has also been used frequently as a reflection of composition quality (Cooper, 1976). Again, however, complex syntax may or may not be appropriate, depending on writing context (Crowhurst, 1980).

Finally, a consideration of communicative context is helpful to teachers in constructing composition assignments. Writing, we have claimed, is purposeful, situated behavior. Yet many typical writing assignments supply students with no purpose other than to submit themselves to evaluation. To be sure, teachers confront a certain dilemma with respect to instantiating context in writing assignments. On the one hand, there is no motivation for writing performance without a context. But at the same time, a context too highly delineated may inhibit some students' abilities to cope with an assignment (e.g., topic: high-energy physics; audience: stockbrokers and financial analysts) and may also preclude crucial experience in allowing students to "find" their purposes for writing. At minimum, however, teachers can adopt roles and attitudes that project to students that a receptive reader who is open to transacting with their texts lies behind each writing assignment.

REFERENCE NOTES

1. Bereiter, C., Scardamalia, M., & Turkish, L. The child as discourse grammarian. Unpublished manuscript, Ontario Institute for Studies in Education, Toronto, n.d.
2. Bracewell, R. J., Scardamalia, M., & Bereiter, C. The development of audience awareness in writing. Unpublished manuscript, York University, Toronto, 1978.
3. King, M., Rentel, V., & Cook, C. A longitudinal study of the influence of story structure on children's oral and written texts. Unpublished manuscript, Ohio University, Columbus, Ohio, n.d.
4. Miller, S. Rhetorical maturity: Definition and development. Unpublished manuscript, University of Wisconsin, Milwaukee, 1979.

5. ROSEN, H. An investigation of the effects of differentiated writing assignments on the performance in English composition of a selected group of 15/16-year-old pupils. Doctoral dissertation, University of London, 1969.
6. RUBIN, D. L. Prologue to a theory of communicative competence. Unpublished master's thesis, University of Minnesota, Minneapolis, 1977.
7. SCARDAMALIA, M., BEREITER, C., & McDONALD, J. D. S. Role taking in written communication investigated by manipulating anticipatory knowledge. Paper presented at the annual meeting of the American Educational Research Association, April 1977.

REFERENCES

ABRAHAMS, R. The complex relations of simple forms. *Genre*, 1969, *2*, 104–128.
APPLEBEE, A. N. *The child's concept of story: Ages 2 to 17*. Chicago: University of Chicago Press, 1978.
ATLAS, M. A. *Addressing an audience: A study of expert-novice differences in writing*. (Report No. 3). Pittsburgh: Carnegie-Mellon Document Design Center, 1979.
BAZERMAN, C. A relationship between reading and writing: The conversational model. *College English*, 1980, *41*, 656–661.
BERKENKOTTER, C. Understanding a writer's awareness of audience. *College Composition and Communication*, 1981, *32*, 388–399.
BERNSTEIN, B. A brief account of the theory of codes. In H. P. Dreitzel (Ed.), *Childhood and socialization*. (Recent Sociology, No. 5). New York: Macmillan, 1973.
BLOM, J., & GUMPERZ, J. J. Social meaning and linguistic structure: Code-switching in Norway. In J. J. Gumperz & D. Hymes (Eds.), *Directions in sociolinguistics*. New York: Holt, 1972.
BORTZ, D. R. The written language patterns of intermediate grade children when writing in three forms: Descriptive, expository and narrative. (Doctoral dissertation, Lehigh University, 1969). *Dissertation Abstracts International*, 1970, *30*, 5332A. (University Microfilms No. 70-10, 586)
BRADDOCK, R., LLOYD-JONES, R., & SCHOER, L. *Research in written composition*. Champaign, IL: NCTE, 1963.
BRITTON, J., BURGESS, T., MARTIN, N., McLEOD, A., & ROSEN, H. *The development of writing ability, 11–18*. London: Macmillan Education, 1975.
BRUNER, J. S. *Toward a theory of instruction*. Cambridge, MA: Harvard University Press, 1966.
BURLING, R. Standard Colloquial and Standard Written English: Some implications for teaching literacy to nonstandard speakers. *Florida FL Reporter*, 1970, *8*, 9–15, 47.
CHERNISS, M. D. Beowulf, oral presentation and the criterion of immediate rhetorical effect. *Genre*, 1969, *2*, 214–228.
COLLINS, J. L., & WILLIAMSON, M. W. Spoken language and semantic abbreviation in writing. *Research in the Teaching of English*, 1981, *15*, 23–36.
CONNORS, R. J. The rise and fall of the modes of discourse. *College Composition and Communication*, 1981, *32*, 444–455.
COOPER, C. R. Tonawanda Middle School's new writing program. *English Journal*, 1976, *65*, 56–61.
CROWHURST, M. Syntactic complexity and teachers' quality ratings of narrations and arguments. *Research in the Teaching of English*, 1980, *14*, 223–232.
CROWHURST, M., & PICHÉ, G. L. Audience and mode of discourse effects on syntactic complexity at two grade levels. *Research in the Teaching of English*, 1979, *13*, 101–109.
CRYSTAL, D., & DAVIES, D. *Investigating English style*. London: Longmans, 1969.
D'ANGELO, F. Modes of discourse. In G. Tate (Ed.), *Teaching composition: 10 bibliographic essays*. Fort Worth: Texas Christian University Press, 1976.

DYSON, A. H. Oral language: The rooting system for learning to write. *Language Arts*, 1981, *58*, 776–784.
EGAN, K. *Educational development*. New York: Oxford University Press, 1979.
ELSASSER, N., & JOHN-STEINER, V. P. An interactionist approach to advancing literacy. *Harvard Educational Review*, 1977, *47*, 355–369.
EMIG, J. *The composing processes of twelfth graders*. (Research Report No. 13). Urbana, IL: National Council of Teachers of English, 1971.
ENKVIST, N.E., SPENCER, J., & GREGORY, M. *Linguistics and style*. London: Oxford University Press, 1965.
ERVIN-TRIPP, S. On sociolinguistic rules: Alternation and co-occurence. In J. J. Gumperz & D. Hymes (Eds.), *Directions in sociolinguistics*. New York: Holt, 1972.
FISHMAN, J. A., COOPER, R. L., & MA, R. *Bilingualism in the barrio*. Bloomington, IN: Indiana University Press, 1972.
FLOWER, L. Writer-based prose: A cognitive basis for problems in writing. *College English*, 1979, *41*, 19–37.
FLOWER, L., & HAYES, J. R. The cognition of discovery: Defining a rhetorical problem. *College Composition and Communication*, 1980, *31*, 21–32.
FLOWER, L., & HAYES, J. R. A cognitive process theory of writing. *College Composition and Communication*, 32, 1981, 365–387.
GOODY, J., & WATT, I. The consequences of literacy. *Comparative Studies in Society and History*, 1963, *5*, 304–345.
GRICE, P. Logic and conversation. In P. Cole & J. Morgan (Eds.), *Syntax and semantics III: Speech acts*. New York: Academic, 1975.
HALLIDAY, M., MCINTOSH, A., & STREVENS, P. *The linguistic sciences and language teaching*. London: Longman, 1965.
HIGGINS, E. T. Written communication as functional literacy: A developmental comparison of oral and written communication. In R. Beach & P. D. Pearson (Eds.), *Perspectives on literacy*. Minneapolis: University of Minnesota College of Education, 1978.
HIRSCH, E. D. *The philosophy of composition*. Chicago: University of Chicago Press, 1977.
JACOBSON, R. The poetry of grammar and grammar of poetry. *Lingua*, 1968, *21*, 597–609.
KEENAN, E. Two kinds of presupposition in natural language. In C. Fillmore & D. Langendon (Eds.), *Studies in linguistic semantics*. New York: Holt, 1971.
KING, M. L., & RENTEL, V. L. Research update: Conveying meaning in written texts. *Language Arts*, 1981, *58*, 721–728.
KINTSCH, W. *Psychological processes in discourse production*. (Technical Report No. 99). Boulder, CO: University of Colorado Institute of Cognitive Science, 1980.
KLINE, C. R., & MEMERING, W. D. Formal fragments: The English minor sentence. *Research in the Teaching of English*, 1977, *11*, 97–111.
KROLL, B. M. Cognitive egocentrism and the problem of audience awareness in writing. *Research in the Teaching of English*, 1978, *12*, 269–281.
KROLL, B. M., & LEMPERS, J. D. Effect of mode of communication on the informational adequacy of children's explanations. *Journal of Genetic Psychology*, 1981, *138*, 27–35.
LARSON, R. L. "Rhetorical writing" in elementary school. *Elementary English*, 1971, *48*, 926–931.
MACRORIE, K. *Telling writing*. New York: Hayden, 1970.
MALINOWSKI, B. *Coral gardens and their magic* (Vol. II). London: George Allen and Unwin, 1935.
MOFFETT, J. *Teaching the universe of discourse*. Boston: Houghton Mifflin, 1968.
MILLIC, L. Rhetorical choice and stylistic option. In S. Chatman (Ed.), *Literary style*. London: Oxford University Press, 1971.
MOSENTHAL, P., & NA, T. J. Classroom competence and children's individual differences in writing. *Journal of Educational Psychology*, 1981, *73*, 106–121.

MURRAY, D. Internal revision: A process of discovery. In C. R. Cooper & L. Odell (Eds.), *Research on composing: Points of departure*. Urbana, IL: NCTE, 1978.

OLSON, D. R. Oral and written language and the cognitive processes of children. *Journal of Communication*, 1977, *27*, 10-26.

ONG, W. The writer's audience is always a fiction. *PMLA*, 1975, *90*, 9-21.

OSGOOD, C. E., & WALKER, E. G. Motivation and language behavior: A content analysis of suicide notes. *Journal of Abnormal and Social Psychology*, 1959, *59*, 58-67.

PAGE, E. The use of the computer in analyzing student essays. *International Review of Education*, 1968, *14*, 253-263.

PERELMAN, C., & OLBRECHTS-TYTECA, L. [*The new rhetoric*] (J. Wilkinsen & P. Weaver, trans.). Notre Dame, IN: University of Notre Dame Press, 1969.

PERL, S. Understanding composing. *College Composition and Communication*, 1980, *31*, 363-369.

PERRON, J. D. *The impact of mode on written syntactic complexity*. (Studies in Language Education, Reports Nos. 24, 25, 27, 30). Athens, GA: University of Georgia Department of Language Education, 1977.

PICHÉ, G. L., RUBIN, D. L., & TURNER, L. J. Training referential communication accuracy in writing. *Research in the Teaching of English*, 1980, *14*, 309-318.

QUIRK, R., & GREENBAUM, S. *A concise grammar of contemporary English*. New York: Harcourt Brace Jovanovich, 1973.

RODGERS, P. C. A discourse-centered rhetoric of the paragraph. *College Composition and Communication*, 1966, *17*, 2-11.

RUBIN, D. L. *Prologue to a theory of communicative competence*. Unpublished masters thesis, University of Minnesota, 1977.

RUBIN, D. L. Adapting syntax in writing to varying audiences as a function of age and social cognitive ability. *Journal of Child Language*, 1982, *9*, 497-510.

RUBIN, D. L. Social cognition and written communication. *Written Communication*, in press.

RUBIN, D. L., & PICHÉ, G. L. Development in syntactic and strategic aspects of audience adaptation skills in written persuasive communication. *Research in the Teaching of English*, 1979, *13*, 293-316.

RUBIN, D. L., PICHÉ, G. L., MICHLIN, M. L., & JOHNSON, F. L. Social cognitive ability as a predictor of the quality of fourth-graders' written narratives. In R. Beach & L. Bridwell (Eds.), *Current trends in composition research*. New York: Guilford, in press.

SAN JOSE, C. P. M. Grammatical structures in four modes of writing at fourth grade level. (Doctoral dissertation, Syracuse University, 1972). *Dissertation Abstracts International*, 1973, *33*, 5411A. (University Microfilms No. 1, 73-9563)

SCHAFER, J. C. The linguistic analysis of spoken and written texts. In B. M. Kroll & R. J. Vann (Eds.), *Exploring speaking-writing relationships: Connections and contrasts*. Urbana, IL: NCTE, 1981.

SCHALLERT, D. L., KLEIMAN, G. M., & RUBIN, A. D. *Analyses of differences between written language and oral language*. (Technical Report No. 29). Urbana, IL: University of Illinois Center for the Study of Reading, 1977.

SCHMIDT, S. J. Some problems of communicative text theories. In W. Dressler (Ed.), *Current trends in text linguistics*. Berlin: de Gruyter, 1977.

SCRIBNER, S., & COLE, M. Unpackaging literacy. In M. F. Whiteman (Ed.), *Writing: The nature, development, and teaching of written communication* (Vol. 1, *Variation in writing: Functional and linguistic-cultural differences*). Hillsdale, NJ: Erlbaum, 1981.

SEARLE, J. *Speech acts*. London: Cambridge University Press, 1969.

SEEGARS, J. C. Form of discourse and sentence structure. *Elementary English Review*, 1933, *10*, 51-54.

SHAUGHNESSY, M. P. *Errors and expectations*. New York: Oxford University Press, 1977.

SMITH, W. L., & SWAN, M. B. Adjusting syntactic structures to varied levels of audience. *Journal of Experimental Education*, 1978, *46*, 29–34.

STATON, J. *Dialogue journal writing as a communicative event* (Vol. 1). (Final Report, NIE-G-80-0122). Washington, DC: Center for Applied Linguistics, 1982.

STOTSKY, S. The vocabulary of essay writing: Can it be taught? *College Composition and Communication*, 1981, *32*, 317–326.

SUTTON-SMITH, B., BOTVIN, G., & MAHONY, D. Developmental structures in fantasy narratives. *Human Development*, 1976, *19*, 1–13.

VEAL, L. R., & TILLMAN, M. Mode of discourse variation in the evaluation of children's writing. *Research in the Teaching of English*, 1971, *5*, 37–45.

VYGOTSKY, L. [*Thought and language*] (E. Haufman & G. Vakar, trans.). Cambridge, MA: MIT Press, 1962.

WEINREICH, U. Explorations in semantic theory. In T. Sebeok (Ed.), *Current trends in linguistics* (Vol. 3). The Hague: Mouton, 1966.

WICHELNS, H. A. The literary criticism of oratory. In R. L. Scott & B. L. Brock (Eds.), *Methods of rhetorical criticism*. New York: Harper and Row, 1972. (Originally published 1925)

WILKINSON, A., & HANNA, P. The development of style in children's writing. *Educational Review*, 1980, *32*, 173–184.

15 Children's Written Dialogues: Intermediary Between Conversation and Written Text?*

Suzanne Hidi and Roslyn Klaiman
The Ontario Institute for Studies in Education

Recent psychological research reflects a dichotomy between the written and oral competence children manifest in their communications. On one hand, children have serious problems producing written discourse, especially expository text. On the other hand, even very young children can express their ideas verbally with some degree of proficiency.

Children's oral competence derives from their early experiences with conversational speech. The language skills developed through conversation include basic turn-taking, maintaining a particular point of view, sustaining coherence over a series of interchanges, elaborations of the topic of the conversation, raising and answering questions, and achieving semantic and syntactic competence (Bereiter & Scardamalia, 1982; Bruner, 1975; Ervin-Tripp, 1977; Keenan & Schiefflein, 1976; Lewis & Freedle, 1973).

Bereiter and Scardamalia (1982) argue that children entering the school system are dependent on conversational interchanges in their discourse production and that in order for them to learn to write compositions they must adapt the complex language system acquired through oral conversation to the requirements of independent discourse production. In writing, the generation of discourse is done without turn-taking (alternation) between two or more persons. Staying on topic and maintaining coherence between different segments of the text are solely the responsibility of the writer; there is no listener present to provide cues whether to proceed or stop, to elaborate or change topic; nor is help forthcoming from the outside to activate semantic memory nodes in search of content. In contrast to the local planning of conversation, written discourse appears to re-

---

*Support for this study has been received from a Sloan Foundation Award to Carl Bereiter.

quire additional planning at the whole text level (overall planning). Thus the additional requirements in writing are extensive and seem to necessitate the development of a new discourse type for composing.

An intermediate stage may exist between conversation and written discourse that allows children to use already existing oral-discourse schemata in producing written text. Bereiter and Scardamalia (1982) suggested that such a stage may occur when the writer can depend on "self-cueing in order to generate extended discourse within a schema that is still structured to depend on conversational inputs" (p. 15). The task of writing a dialogue seems to be singularly suited to serve as this intermediate stage.[1]

Staton (Note 1) and Shuy (Note 2) looked at "dialogue journal" writing where two people (teacher and pupil) participated in the writing process. Although this type of writing is naturalistic and interactive and incorporates many features of oral conversation, such as turn-taking and topic recycling (Staton, Note 1), it does not require generation of extended discourse comparable to prose writing. When a single author writes a dialogue on a given topic, that person generates extended discourse as if two people would be taking turns in a conversation.

The writer has to autonomously compose the speech for both participants from his/her knowledge base, producing each statement on behalf of one "conversant" from the cues provided by the other imaginary speaker. These cues are expected to help generate discourse, since the writer is incorporating the basic turn-taking rules of conversation into the written dialogue. The turn-taking can lead to ideas that are generated to support each speaker or to assertions that are to be refuted by the alternate partner. In each case, the dyadic nature of the dialogue is expected to help the writer generate longer productions. It appears that the information-processing demands of writing this type of dialogue may be less complex than those of writing an expository essay. Another aspect besides turn-taking that makes a single author writing a dialogue similar to conversation is that it permits the writer to develop a clear idea of a specific rather than a general audience.

The main purpose of this study was to examine if indeed an intermediate stage in production could be established. Quantitative and qualitative differences in production were compared between single-author dialogues and opinion essays written on the same topic. It was expected that children would produce longer dialogues than opinion essays since they could use the conversational format for self-cueing in the former but not in the latter genre.

We also predicted that the longer dialogues, although containing increased instances of elaboration, would not feature more topic relevant ideas. These predictions were derived from our notion that interchange in dialogues develops on the basis of cues provided by the conversational partners and that these cues

---

[1] A similar suggestion has been made by Marian Crowhurst in a personal communication (1980).

may take the speakers off on certain tangents that are likely to produce elaborations of the main ideas in the attempt to maintain a particular point of view. Similarly, off-topic points may be generated to support an initial idea instead of a concentrated memory search for additional topic relevant ideas. In opinion essays, on the other hand, cues are not provided by conversational partners. The lack of prompting could be expected to lead to reduced elaborations and to an intensified, goal-directed, semantic memory search for topic-relevant ideas. As a second independent variable, we systematically varied the degree of ego involvement in both discourse types, expecting that more ego-involved tasks would produce more specific and qualitatively different ideas than tasks that were less ego-oriented. Finally, since children's conversational experiences involve a variety of interchanges with various speaker/listeners, we were interested in determining how the use of different roles would affect the content of the dialogues. For example, would a dialogue written between teacher and child differ from a dialogue written between two children? As a result, we compared dialogues written for various subject pairings, in which a child is always included along with either a mother, a teacher, or another child. The productions were compared along several dimensions.[2]

Number of Words Produced

This score was based on the total number of words written by a child, with the exception of terms such as "end," "the end," and the speaker designations, e.g., "mother," in the dialogues. Thus, common objective criteria were used to provide a quantitative measure across the two genres.

Semantic Analysis of Ideas

A primary concern in this study was the number, and the type of the topic-relevant ideas in the two discourse genres. These scores were obtained as follows:

1. The number of topic-relevant ideas was identified by summing each distinct, relevant idea (e.g., TV can teach you bad things) across a child's production. Simplifications (e.g., TV is bad for you), restatements, or elaborations of the same theme were not counted.
2. The topic-relevant ideas were evaluated by two sets of scores: (a) the total principled argument ratings of the topic-relevant ideas per subject and (b) the mean principled argument rating of the topic-relevant ideas per subject. To obtain these ratings, a list was created by noting each distinct topic-relevant idea. The total list consisted of 69 such ideas.

---

[2]We are grateful to Carl Bereiter for his suggestions on the development of the scoring schemes.

Three independent judges ($r = .78$) then rated each of the ideas obtained as 1—naive, simple, ill-considered; 2—minimal evidence of thought, appeal to emotions rather than to principles; 3—some evidence of thought, appeal to principles but reflects insufficient consideration; 4—thoughtful, greater appeal to principles than to emotions; 5—well thought out, rational, principled as opposed to emotional (i.e., the kind of idea that might be raised by a mature, thoughtful person). Scores then were provided for each composition by taking the mean ratings of the respective ideas.

Level of Abstractness of Protocols

Each of the statements included in the production as a whole was rated on a three-point scale by two judges ($r = .70$): 1—personal (i.e., personal incident, experience, or problem); 2—specific (i.e., child-relevant issue excluding personal experience or problem); 3—general (i.e., general issue, specific incident amplifies discussion). The score per subject was the highest score obtained in the composition. Thus, these measures reflected the quality of each production as a whole since the complete protocols, rather than the central ideas, were evaluated.

Type and Quality of Resolutions of Dialogues

The dialogues were rated by type of argument resolution. This rating was obtained by first identifying the type of production written by children in the dialogue condition as follows: 0—exposition; 1—dialogue, agreement at outset; 2—resolved dialogue, starting with two opposing viewpoints; 3—unresolved dialogue, starting with two opposing viewpoints; 4—off-topic dialogue; 5—statement of belief.

Productions rated as 2 or 3 were then rated for resolution (or nonresolution) type, as follows: A—yielding for no apparent reason; B—yielding for reason of cognitive simplicity (e.g., TV is bad for you); C—power-based resolution (e.g., threat, authority, assertiveness); D—compromise, negotiation not based on rational discussion; E—rational negotiation, one opinion changed through principled, rational argument; F—unresolved dilemma, bickering between participants.

METHOD

Subjects

Grade 4 and grade 6 children (3 classes per grade) served as subjects in this study. The children were drawn from two neighboring schools in a lower-middle-class area of North York, a suburb of Toronto.

Materials and Procedures

The same topic sentence—"Should children be allowed to choose their own TV shows?"—was provided for both the dialogue and the opinion essay. Two classes per grade level were asked to write a dialogue between two designated people, and one class per grade level was asked to write an opinion essay.

Children in both the dialogue and opinion essay groups were randomly assigned to one of two conditions: ego-involved task and non-ego-involved task. For the dialogues, the ego involvement was provided by having subjects write a conversation between *themselves* and a parent, teacher, or friend. In the corresponding non-ego-involved task children were asked to write the dialogue between *a child* and a parent, teacher, or friend. For the opinion essays, the ego-involved element could not be manipulated simply by changing the participant, thus the topic statement was altered slightly to provide a comparable ego-involved condition ("Should you be allowed to choose your own TV shows?").

In order to familiarize the children with the requirements of the writing task, two additional topics were selected for classroom discussion and demonstration. In the dialogue group, children helped the experimenter develop written dialogues between two people on two unrelated topics. In the opinion essay group, the experimenter and the children, using the same two topics, developed written opinion essays. Care was taken to ensure that pro and con points were raised in both genres, and the demonstration stopped short of developing a resolution, conclusion, or compromise.

Following the demonstrations, all subjects received a response sheet with the test topic and their specific task typed at the top of the page. Unlimited time was provided, and subjects were asked to write as much as they could.

RESULTS

The means for each variable are shown in Table 1. These data were analyzed by separate analyses of variance for each of the dependent measures.

We first analyzed the results by 2 × 2 × 2 (grade × genre × ego involvement) ANOVAS. Since the analyses revealed no main effect of ego involvement nor a related interaction, the data were collapsed over the two ego-involvement conditions and are so reported here.

The 2 × 2 (grade × genre) ANOVA on the number of words produced showed significant grade ($F(1, 67) = 4.74$, $p < .05$) and genre ($F(1, 167) = 12.82$, $p < .001$) main effects and a significant grade by genre interaction ($F(1, 167) = 8.64, p < .01$). Examination of the data indicated that children in grade 4 produce approximately the same number of words in both genres but that, on the average, sixth graders produce approximately 66% longer dialogues than opinion essays. Thus, it seems that although genre does not affect the number of words

TABLE 1
Means and Standard Deviations[a] for Each Variable of Interest by Discourse Type and Grade

	Discourse Type			
	Dialogues		Opinion Essays	
	Grade		Grade	
Variable	4	6	4	6
Number of Words Produced	64	93	61	56
	(41.59)	(37.29)	(34.86)	(22.21)
Number of Topic-Relevant Ideas	1.20	2.07	1.90	1.76
	(0.84)	(1.05)	(0.82)	(0.78)
Number of Topic-Relevant Ideas/100 Words	2.26	2.39	3.53	3.44
	(1.67)	(1.29)	(1.53)	(1.74)
Sum of Principled Argument Ratings	3.05	6.16	5.39	5.33
	(2.48)	(3.76)	(3.01)	(2.52)
Mean of Principled Argument Ratings	1.96	2.82	2.88	3.02
	(1.77)	(0.73)	(0.76)	(0.64)
Level of Abstractness	2.32	2.73	2.72	2.74
	(0.83)	(0.51)	(0.59)	(0.62)

[a] Standard deviations shown in parentheses.

produced at the fourth-grade level, it does influence the length of production at the sixth-grade level.

The two-way ANOVA on the number of topic-relevant ideas showed a significant main effect for grade ($F(1, 167) = 6.67, p < .01$) and a grade × genre interaction ($F(1, 167) = 12.25, p < .001$). The interaction indicated that Grade 4 children produced more topic-related ideas in the opinion essays than in the dialogues, whereas corresponding genre differences were not found in the sixth-graders' productions. However, these results are difficult to interpret because of the extreme length of the sixth-graders' dialogues; the disproportionate length of these productions may have masked a grade 6 trend to produce significantly more topic-relevant ideas in the opinion essay. In order to test this hypothesis, these data were re-analyzed on the transformed score, number of ideas per 100 words.

Only a significant genre effect ($F(1, 167) = 23.13, p < .0001$) was obtained in this analysis. This result indicates that the density of ideas is significantly greater in the opinion essays than in the dialogues at both grade levels.

Our contention that the length of the sixth-grade dialogues may have biased our results was further substantiated by the analysis on the principled argument ratings of the topic-related ideas. A significant main effect for grade ($F(1, 167) = 8.41, p < .01$) and grade × genre interaction ($F(1, 167) = 11.87, p < .001$) was found on the summed (Total) scores. Corresponding to the earlier analysis on the number of topic-relevant ideas, we found that the grade 4 children produced higher total principled argument ratings in the opinion essays than in the dialogues. In grade 6, on the other hand, no differences were apparent. However, when we examined the mean principled argument (a measure that eliminated the effect of length), we found a significant genre effect ($F(1, 167) = 16.55, p < .001$) in addition to the main effect of grade ($F(1, 167) = 13.26, p < .001$) and a grade × genre interaction ($F(1, 167) = 6.77, p < .01$). Higher ratings were obtained in the arguments than in the dialogues at both grade levels, indicating that the average quality of topic-relevant ideas was judged to be superior in the arguments.

Turning to our analysis of the level of abstractness of the protocols, a significant developmental effect ($F(1, 167) = 4.10, p < .05$) and a strong trend toward genre differences ($F(1, 167) = 3.87, p < .051$) were obtained. The statements in the opinion essays tended to be more abstract than in the dialogues.

Subsequently, we separately examined the data obtained in the dialogue conditions. Two × 3 ANOVAs (grade × speaker) were performed on each of the following: number of words produced; number of topic-relevant ideas; number of ideas per 100 words; the sum and mean of principled arguments; and the level of abstractness. With one exception, only a significant grade effect was obtained on these analyses. Older children received significantly higher scores than younger ones except on the analysis of the number of ideas per 100 words produced. In this analysis, a significant speaker effect was obtained in addition to a grade effect. The means of this analysis are shown in Table 2. Children produced more topic-relevant ideas in teacher-child dialogues than in either of the other two conditions.

Our analysis on the type and quality of resolution of dialogues indicated that 60% of grade 6 subjects wrote dialogues in which the two subjects started out with two opposing views that were eventually reconciled. The reconciliation in half of these dialogues was through rational argument or negotiated compromise. The other half of the protocols were resolved through power, authority, irrational yielding, or cognitively simple arguments. In grade 4 only 36% of the children wrote dialogues with opposing points of view that were eventually reconciled. Frequent responses were dialogues in which agreement was the starting point, off-topic dialogues and unreconciled dialogues in which subjects were bickering without rational argument. This last type of response was nonexistent at the grade 6 level.

TABLE 2
Number of Topic Relevant Ideas Produced per 100 Words in the Written Dialogues

	Grade 4	Grade 6
Mother-child	2.24	2.19
Friend-child	1.62	2.30
Teacher-child	2.87	2.76

DISCUSSION

Our prediction that children would write longer dialogues than opinion essays was upheld for grade 6 subjects. Grade 4 children produced nearly equivalent amounts in both the dialogues and opinion essays (64 vs. 61). We have no clear explanation why the self-cuing of writing a dialogue does not seem to facilitate writing at the grade 4 level, especially since the grade 6 increases were large—the dialogues were 66% longer than the opinion essays. One possible hypothesis is that in grade 4, children can not yet handle the novel combination of an orally acquired conversational schema that has to be produced in a written modality. By grade 6, however, the problems related to having to adopt an orally acquired conversational form to production of written discourse seems to have been overcome. Indeed, the self-cuing underlying the production of written dialogues appears to help generate content.

It is also difficult to understand why the developmental trend was only apparent in the dialogue condition—in the opinion essays grade 4 and grade 6 children produced similar number of words (61 vs. 56). In a previous study (Hidi & Hildyard, in press), in which no demonstration was given during the introductory procedures, significant developmental differences were found between grade 3 and grade 5 productions of opinion essays; third graders' production was extremely low—only 21 words on the average. These children seemed only to answer the question introduced in the task rather than to discuss the issue. Our present results may be related to our procedures, since we demonstrated how one writes an opinion essay prior to introducing the task. It is possible that the younger subjects are more sensitive to these training procedures than was anticipated.

Our analysis on the number of topic-relevant ideas per 100 words produced indicated that in the opinion essays there was a greater density of topic-relevant ideas than in the dialogues at both grade levels. These results seem to suggest that dialogues, which include conversational patterns, lead the writer to produce more elaborations, restatements, and repetitions rather than to produce relevant new ideas on a given topic. The dyadic "dialogue journal" writing studied by Staton (Note 1) resulted in "an unusual kind of discourse," with many of the features of complex oral conversation, such as simultaneous introduction of several topics and topic recycling, that is consistent with the findings in the current investigation. Opinion essays, on the other hand, might discourage these types of extended discourse, resulting in subjects being more precise and relevant.

The arguments produced in both genres provided by grade 6 children were significantly more principled, mature, and sophisticated than those produced by children in grade 4. In addition, the opinion essays included more principled arguments than the dialogues. However, the differences between the opinion essays and dialogues were greater in grade 4 than in grade 6 productions.

It seems that by grade 6, children are able to bring more principled rational arguments to their dialogues as well as to their opinion essays, whereas fourth graders show minimal evidence of principled arguments in their dialogues. Our analysis of the type and quality of dialogue resolutions also seems to support these findings. Similar patterns emerged from our analysis of the level of abstractness. While grade 6 children managed to deal with at least some general issues in both genres, fourth graders seemed to be operating at a more personal, child-relevant level in the dialogues than in the opinion essays.

In summary, the results show that although dialogue may facilitate the production of written text, it does not facilitate the generation of topic-relevant ideas. Thus, it seems that the additional constraints placed on the writer by an expository genre may in fact lead to whole-text planning resulting in more rational and thorough discussions of the topic. Consequently, using dialogue writing as a pedagogical tool should be evaluated in relation to specific educational goals. If the purpose is to improve fluency and expressiveness, then dialogue writing has promise. However, if developing skills to produce coherent, rational arguments on given topics is the goal, then taking children back to a genre that more closely resembles the oral mode may not be effective.

REFERENCE NOTES

1. STATON, F. *"Its just not gonna come down in one little sentence: A Study of Discourse in Dialogue Journal Writing.* Paper presented at the annual meeting of the American Educational Research Association, Los Angeles, April, 1981.
2. SHUY, R. *Relating research on oral language functions to research on written discourse.* Paper presented at the annual meeting of the American Educational Research Association, Los Angeles, April 1981.

REFERENCES

BEREITER, C., & SCARDAMALIA, M. From conversation to composition: The role of instruction in a developmental process. In R. Glaser (Ed.), *Advances in instructional psychology* (Vol. 2). Hillsdale, NJ: Erlbaum, 1982.

BRUNER, J. The ontogenesis of speech acts. *Journal of Child Language,* 1975, 2, 1–20.

ERVIN-TRIPP, S. Wait for me, roller-skate! In S. Ervin-Tripp & C. Mitchell-Kernan (Eds.), *Child discourse.* New York: Academic, 1977.

HIDI, S., & HILDYARD, A. *The comparison of oral and written productions of two discourse types. Discourse Processes,* in press.

KEENAN, E. O., & SCHIEFFELIN, B. B. Topic as a discourse notion: A study of topic in the conversations of children and adults. In C. Li (Ed.), *Subject and topic.* New York: Academic, 1976.

LEWIS, M., & FREEDLE, R. Mother-infant dyad: The cradle of meaning. In P. Pliner, L. Kramer, & T. Alloway (Eds.), *Communication and affect: Language and thought.* New York: Academic, 1973.

16

The Interaction Between Text and Context: A Study of How Adults and Children Use Spoken and Written Language in Four Contexts*

Jane M. Danielewicz
University of California, Berkeley

THE COMMUNICATION CONTINUUM

Spoken and written language are often dichotomized as two distinct forms of language. A more interesting approach to studying differences between spoken and written language is to imagine a continuum of linguistic forms stretching between the extremes of spontaneous speech and expository written prose.

spontaneous spoken language ——————— expository written language

Within this framework, all forms of language fall somewhere on the continuum. For example, classroom lectures are closer to conversation than to written prose, whereas personal letters are somewhere in the middle. Each point along the continuum represents a linguistic form designed to serve a particular communicative function. The range of linguistic outcomes along the continuum is a function of people's goals, message content, and available linguistic structure. Each of these factors influences in subtle ways the forms that language takes. The present research has two major goals. The first concerns the assumption that functions of language affect linguistic form. I would like to discover not

---

*This work is part of a larger project designed to investigate differences between written and spoken language sponsored by Grant NIE-80-0125 from the National Institute of Education. I am extremely grateful to Wallace Chafe for providing the opportunity to collaborate on this project and for his many ideas and suggestions regarding this chapter. I would also like to thank Pamela Downing for her help with the data analysis as well as her insightful criticisms regarding this chapter. The principal, teachers, and children at CVS also deserve special thanks for their enthusiastic participation in the project and for their gracious hospitality.

only what factors contribute to the form of discourse, but also how these factors affect that form. The second goal is to investigate children's development of written language, a new form, in relation to their spoken language, an old form. In particular, I am interested in what strategies children use to acquire written language, and how children change their language in response to the functions which different situations entail.

In general, the continuum represents the possible ways in which literate adults are able to use language. But not every person chooses to use language in all its available forms, or has the knowledge or capabilities to exploit all possibilities. This is particularly the case with elementary school children, who have only limited knowledge and experience with the range of possible forms. Children first acquire a foothold along the continuum with the acquisition of spontaneous spoken language. Although development does not necessarily proceed in a linear fashion along the continuum from left to right, there is a general progression of development from oral to written language; from more basic linguistic forms to more specialized ones; from more concrete uses of language to more abstract ones.

Because children first acquire spontaneous spoken language, it may be considered the most basic linguistic form. Experience with language and the development of new forms is a cumulative process. The acquisition of any one form along the continuum, no matter when it appears in the course of development, will be added to those already in the child's linguistic repertoire. In other words, new forms do not replace old ones, but rather function in conjunction with existing forms. Ochs (1979) supports this view of development, suggesting that strategies for using spoken language continue to function throughout adulthood, even after more complex forms of language have developed. By the time children are about 5 or 6, they have mastered the basic forms of spoken language (Clark & Clark, 1977, p. 337). Once conversational strategies for using spoken language have "matured," they are relied upon throughout adulthood. If this hypothesis is true, children should in certain contexts use spoken language in the same way as adults do. However, differences between children and adults appear in other circumstances, especially when context demands the use of more literate forms of language.

THE DATA

The data reported in this chapter are taken from a larger study designed to investigate differences between spoken and written language used by adults and children in a variety of situations.

Samples of spoken and written language were collected in four conditions in order to study the relationship between the linguistic structures of text and the context in which they were produced. Data were collected from adults, as well as from 8-year-olds (third graders) and 12-year-olds (sixth graders). (Note that although there were 20 subjects in each of these groups, the data presented in this chapter is a preliminary analysis limited to 6 representative subjects, 2 from each group.)

The adult subjects were members of the academic community, and as such they represent the extreme end of the scale in a literate society. The children in this study have middle-class backgrounds and attend an elementary school located in a small town. The children's data were for the most part taken from ongoing classroom activities, and not from contrived assignments or experimental tasks.

Although mode (spoken or written) alone must have an effect on the linguistic elements of text, the effect of another variable on language production should be considered. Ochs (1979) suggests that language that is planned, as opposed to unplanned, has significantly different linguistic structure. Ochs defines unplanned discourse as "discourse that lacks forethought and organizational preparation" and planned discourse as "discourse that has been thought out and organized (designed) prior to its expression" (1979, p. 55). The four conditions in this study result from a combination of the oral/written dichotomy and the unplanned/planned dichotomy.

Data was collected in the following four conditions:

1. *Unplanned spoken language* (US): For adults, dinner table conversations; for children, conversations in the classroom between participant observer and the child.
2. *Planned spoken language* (PS): For adults, class lectures or prepared talks; for children, oral class presentations, sharing time, etc.
3. *Unplanned written language* (UW): For adults, personal letters; for children, journals and personal letters.
4. *Planned written language* (PW): For adults, published articles or academic papers; for children, compositions, essays, or reports.

Although the children's data are not totally analogous with the adult data, care was taken to collect language in situations that placed similar kinds of demands on speakers or writers, regardless of whether they were adults or children. Wherever possible, language samples of comparable size were collected in all conditions from both children and adults.

DATA ANALYSIS

In order to compare language samples collected in such diverse settings, a basic unit of analysis had to be defined. For this purpose, both oral and written texts were divided into "idea units" (following Kroll, 1977). An "idea unit" is defined as the minimal segment of language that is planned and produced by the speaker at any one time. Earlier research in discourse production conducted by Chafe (1980) indicated that spontaneous spoken language is planned and expressed by the speaker in a series of small, coherent units. Other research has supported the notion that language is planned locally, by constituents that are reflected in the intonation, hesitations, and syntax of the speaker (Clark & Clark, 1977; Goldman-Eisler, 1958; Halliday, 1967; Syder & Pawley, in preparation).

Texts of approximately 100 idea units were collected from both speakers and writers in all conditions. Idea units in written text, lacking intonation and hesitations, were identified through syntax as well as the writer's punctuation.

UNPLANNED SPOKEN DISCOURSE

It is useful to begin the analysis with spontaneous (unplanned) spoken discourse because the forms and strategies of conversation serve as the basis for other uses of spoken as well as of written language. The acquisition of speech is primary in relation to other more elaborated uses of language. Spontaneous spoken language can also be considered basic because it is present in all cultures, whereas written language is absent from many. In terms of historical evolution, written language is a recent development compared with oral language (Bloomfield, 1933).

By nature, spoken language is fast and fleeting. Because spoken language is spontaneous, it is a product of the moment, unpolished, immediate (Halliday, 1979). Not only is speech quickly planned and uttered, it quickly disappears. The sounds of language fade or are replaced at a fast rate by succeeding strings of sounds. In some ways the form of spoken language must reflect the juggling act speakers experience as they think of what to say and how to say it while attending to the social demands of discourse.

Chafe has suggested that spoken language has an intermittent quality to it and that it is produced "not in a flowing stream, but in a series of brief spurts" (1980, p. 13). These spurts, or "idea units," can be identified by tracking intonation contours, measuring hesitations or pauses in a speaker's discourse, and examining the syntactic structures set off by pauses and intonation (Chafe, 1980). These spurts of language seem to be the basic productive unit of spontaneous spoken language.

A typical idea unit produced by an adult speaking informally is presented in Example 1. According to our scheme, each numbered item represents a single idea unit, commas and periods represent intonation contours, and a series of dots represents pauses.

Example 1

(1) . . . I haven't heard from her . . . since Christmas.
(2) . . . So . . . I'd better not say anything.

For the adult speakers, one idea unit typically consists of 6 or 7 words ending with a clause final intonation contour. In addition to being relatively short chunks, idea units are "light" in terms of information density. They typically are clauses containing a single predication. Some idea units do contain more than one verb if they include structures such as dependent clauses, but less than 20% of idea units produced by the adult speakers in unplanned spoken discourse contained more than one predication per idea unit. These characteristics of spoken language seem to reflect the fast and fleeting nature of speech. From these data it seems that speakers plan and produce language a little at a time, in chunks that are not too long, nor too "heavy" in terms of information density, and that fall well within the bounds of short-term memory.

Besides attending to factors such as unit length and density of information, speakers also have to package meaning syntactically. Semantic relationships expressed through syntax must be specified at a local level within each idea unit, as well as at the level of discourse between idea units. Adults use fairly simple syntax, both within and across idea units. Approximately 33% of all idea units begin with simple coordinating conjunctions—most often with the word "and." Word order within idea units generally follows the standard English SVO pattern, with little use of passive or cleft constructions; phrases do not usually precede subjects or appear between subject and verb in the same clause. More elaborate syntactic structures, particularly ones that specify relations between clauses are infrequent in spontaneous spoken language. Only 20% of all idea units contain relative clauses or complement clauses.

These characteristics of unplanned spoken language are fairly robust across adult speakers. If we define adult performance as communicatively competent, then children (age 8 and 12) perform in similar ways, given the same context. Several idea units produced by an 8-year-old in spontaneous conversation are shown in Example 2.

Example 2

(1) . . . Um . . . and then there's a lining,
(2) . . . that keeps the duck from f war warm,
(3) . . . and they grow an oil,
(4) . . . inside their body,

The mean number of words per idea unit for adults was between 6 and 7; as a group (both 8- and 12-year-olds) the mean for children's idea units ranged between 5 and 7 words in the unplanned spoken condition. As with adults, children's idea units tended to contain only single predications. Less than 10% of all idea units contained more than one verb. Approximately 42% of all idea units began with simple conjunctions such as "and." In terms of syntactic structures, children tended to keep them simple, but then so did adults under the same conditions. For adults, less than 20% of idea units contained more complex structures; for children, about 10% of all idea units contained more complex structures.

Although there are some differences in frequency between adult and child performance, children use most of the same strategies in unplanned spoken language as the adults. The definition and size of idea units, dependence on coordination as the major strategy of cohesion, and the relative infrequency of more elaborate syntactic structures are characteristics of both adults and children. I would like to suggest that 8- and 12-year-olds have developed spoken conversational forms that change very little with maturity. The children's proficiency in spoken language is all the more striking given that they are being compared with highly literate adult speakers. These data support Ochs' (1979) claim that in unplanned situations adults use morphosyntactic strategies and discourse skills acquired during childhood.

If spontaneous speech is acquired before other forms, it is interesting to speculate about the nature of children's development of other forms. Children's development originates with spontaneous spoken language, the leftmost point along the continuum, and grows toward the acquisition of written language, the rightmost end of the continuum. Still, I do not wish to imply that this "spreading" effect is linear—i.e., that children acquire new linguistic forms in a stepwise fashion. Many factors influence the range of linguistic forms children acquire and the order in which they develop.

Thus far we have discussed very general qualities of spoken language in terms of a limited range of possible linguistic variables. Given the scope of the question—differences between oral and written language in four conditions and developmental differences between children and adults—the analysis must necessarily be limited. Since it is impossible to trace all directions at once, I will focus on the use of a small set of dependent structures (subordinate, relative, and complement clauses) in relation to the context in which they are found (unplanned spoken, planned spoken, unplanned written, and planned written).

Example 3

subordinate
(1) The speaker's treatment of an item as given should cease *when he has reason to believe that the item has left his addressee's consciousness.*
relative
(2) There is nothing in the world *which corresponds to the objects named in the poem,*
complement
(3) The visionary realism of the later word reflects the earlier novel's inability *to match adequately word to thing,*

Previous research (Kroll, 1977; Loban, 1976) has indicated that these kinds of structures have different distributions in spoken and written language, suggesting

TABLE 1
Summary of Adults and Children—Use of Features in Four Conditions (US, PS, UW, PW)

Features	Eight Year Olds US	Eight Year Olds PS	Eight Year Olds UW	Eight Year Olds PW
Words per idea unit	6.44	5.50	6.89	5.96
Dependent Clauses				
subordinate	9.00	20.00	31.00	28.00
relative	7.00	7.00	13.00	15.00
complement	10.00	35.00	35.00	17.00
Total Dependent	26.00	62.00	79.00	60.00
Coordinate Clauses	147.00	177.00	54.00	42.00
Nominalization	1.60	4.00	0.00	13.00
Attributive Adjective	54.00	36.00	60.00	64.00
Participles	4.00	9.00	16.00	20.00

Features	Twelve Year Olds US	Twelve Year Olds PS	Twelve Year Olds UW	Twelve Year Olds PW
Words per idea unit	5.62	5.99	7.10	6.44
Dependent Clauses				
subordinate	17.00	1.00	15.00	17.00
relative	8.70	26.70	20.00	6.60
complement	4.80	54.00	30.00	19.00
Total Dependent	30.50	81.70	65.00	42.60
Coordinate Clauses	137.00	79.00	50.00	71.00
Nominalization	0.00	0.00	0.00	0.00
Attributive Adjective	80.00	74.00	102.00	120.00
Participles	11.00	62.00	20.00	9.60

Features	Adult US	Adult PS	Adult UW	Adult PW
Words per idea unit	7.09	7.42	9.49	14.46
Dependent Clauses				
subordinate	19.00	31.00	30.00	16.00
relative	20.00	30.00	9.00	21.00
complement	18.00	57.00	36.00	28.00
Total Dependent	57.00	118.00	75.00	65.00
Coordinate Clauses	89.00	81.00	58.00	22.00
Nominalization	1.60	22.00	6.00	62.00
Attributive Adjective	49.00	74.00	67.00	140.00
Participles	18.00	14.00	37.00	28.00

Note: Figures represent raw occurrences that have been standardized to represent number of occurrences per 1,000 words.

that they play different roles in different contexts. An examination of these features will provide some interesting information about how context interacts with form, as well as providing some insights into children's acquisition of new linguistic forms. An analysis of the children's language in the remaining three conditions (UW, PS, and PW), as well as developmental comparisons with adult performance, will follow the adult analysis. (Refer to Table 1 for a summary of data collected from all three groups in the four conditions.)

PLANNED WRITTEN LANGUAGE

Following the example of earlier research, we will begin by contrasting unplanned spoken language with planned written language. Several studies of both adult and child language have reported that written language contains more dependent structures than does spoken language (Harrell, 1957; Kroll, 1977; Loban, 1976; O'Donnell, 1974). In particular, Kroll reports the use of more dependent structures in written language (35%) as compared with spoken language (14%), whereas coordination (36%) was the major strategy for linking ideas in spoken language. As a way of explaining these differences, Kroll proposes that the amount of planning time available in writing allows writers to build more explicit dependent relationships into text. Although this hypothesis may be correct, it is difficult to judge from her data (collected in unplanned spoken and planned written conditions) whether differences in mode (spoken or written), differences in context (planned or unplanned), or the interaction between these factors affected the production of dependent structures.

The size and structure of idea units in discourse can be quite revealing with regard to the process of producing oral versus written language. In the planned written condition, writers use approximately twice as many words per idea unit as in the unplanned spoken condition. One hypothesis is that writers are packing more information (words) into each idea unit. Chafe (1982) suggests that integration is an important feature of written language: "In writing we have time to mold a succession of ideas into a more complex, coherent, integrated whole . . ." (1982, p. 5). Because of the higher density of information, it is also possible that writers arrange or package information differently. A dependent structure, such as a subordinate clause within an idea unit, increases the number of words per idea unit and also explicitly marks a relationship between elements in the text. The use of subordinating clauses, relative clauses, and complement clauses all have the potential to function this way in written language.

Surprisingly, for these data there is very little variation in the number of these particular dependent structures used by adults in the unplanned spoken and planned written condition. Planned written language does have more dependent structures, but judging from past research a greater difference would have been expected. For instance, Kroll (1977) reported approximately 2.5 times more of these structures in planned written language than in unplanned spoken language. However, the variation between the studies may be the result of sample differences, genre differences, differences in method of analysis, or differences in sample size. On the other hand, perhaps the raw number of occurrences of dependent clauses in spoken or written language doesn't really tell the whole story. It may also be important to consider both how these structures are constructed in spoken versus written discourse and the textual environments in which they occur.

Dependent structures are not present in isolation in written discourse but tend to appear in conjunction with other syntactic elements that add to the richness of written language. If we consider the idea unit in spoken language as a basic structure, our data suggest that writers fill out or expand the basic idea unit by adding features such as attributive adjectives (e.g., *salient* items), nominalizations (e.g., such an *investigation,*) and participles (e.g., referents *mentioned* by a speaker). Features such as nominalizations and participles incorporate additional verbal elements into the main clause of an idea unit (Chafe, 1982), whereas features such as attribute adjectives add more descriptive content. Loose connections, such as those provided by coordinating conjunctions in spoken language, largely disappear in this type of discourse. Thus, writers rely more on the use of dependent structures embedded within a rich textual environment, whereas speakers join together fairly lean segments of discourse.

Adding information is only one strategy for altering the form of the basic unit as it appears in spoken discourse. Because of more flexible time constraints, writers can manipulate the normal word order most often found in spoken language. The addition of new elements, such as participles, into the discourse allows for the possibility of new arrangements, especially to establish clear reltionships among the elements. In unplanned spoken language, standard English word order (SVO) without extraneous clauses or phrases is most common; but in planned written language, standard word order is often embellished. Writers punctuate simple clauses by placing elements before the subject, between the subject and the verb, and between the verb and the object, as shown in Examples 4, 5, and 6.

Example 4: Before subject

(PW 1) *Applying his distinction to poetry,*
    (2) Frege concludes that literature is that kind of language which has only sense,

Example 5: Between subject and verb

(PW 1) For Knoepflmacher,
  (2a) realism,
    (3) *defined as a writer's presentation of the actual and commonplace,*
  (2b) is still a possible undertaking;

Example 6: Between verb and object

(PW 1) From the speaker's point of view,
   (2a) he knows,
      (3) *before making reference to any particular character,*
   (2b) whom he has in mind.

It is also important to consider how dependent structures are used by speakers and writers in different conditions. In unplanned spoken language, dependent structures such as relative clauses appear to be constrained both in length and location. They are usually either added at the end of the idea unit or attached to the object (as opposed to the subject) in the utterance. This location of the dependent structure suggests that the clauses are planned one at a time. If two clauses appear in the same idea unit, one tends to be short and simple. Therefore, the number of words per idea unit, while larger for two-clause idea units, is still fairly small in spoken language. In planned written language, dependent structures are inserted at any position within a clause and are often added one on top of another.

In this study, we do not view the presence of dependent structures alone in discourse as the definitive difference between the unplanned spoken and planned written forms of language. Although there are more subordinate, relative, and complement clauses in planned written language than in unplanned spoken language, the numerical difference in not overwhelming. Other factors—the density of information within clauses, the co-occurrence of other linguistic variables with dependent clauses, and the arrangement of clauses—more clearly distinguish unplanned spoken from planned written language.

PLANNED SPOKEN LANGUAGE

The amount of time a writer has to plan certainly has an effect on what is said (how much information is added to the discourse) and how the writer chooses to say it (choice of syntax and semantics). Because two variables (speaking vs. writing; unplanned vs. planned) have been traditionally confounded, the effect of planning time has not been separated from the effect of mode on the written product. Based on the analysis we have performed thus far, we can say that the combination of planning and writing, as a single condition, generates language that is denser and more integrated. It also promotes the arrangement of information in ways that are more varied than in spoken language.

So far we have described differences between spontaneous conversations and formal academic prose in terms of the number of dependent structures they contain and the textual environment in which they occur. How is language affected when speakers are addressing an expectant audience, given that they have planned ahead of time what to say? As the features presented in this analysis are extremely limited, it is premature to conclude that planning time has only the restricted role in discourse production that the use of dependent clauses reflects. A glance at the data in the planned spoken condition reveals that planning affects discourse schemas at the global rather than at the local level of utterance. For instance, planned spoken texts are generally organized around a central theme or argument. Therefore, planning time seems to influence the amount and type of evidence that a speaker uses to build an argument and affects the ways in which meaning is threaded throughout the discourse.

Across the conditions, there is considerable variation in the use of dependent clauses. In terms of the total number of dependent clauses, there are nearly twice as many in the planned spoken condition as in the unplanned spoken or the planned written condition. Although these results are only tentative, variation in the use of dependent clauses suggests that speakers and writers are sensitive to contexts and use particular strategies in response to particular demands. If we examine the three types of clauses included in this general category, the increase is primarily due to the use of complement clauses. Some typical complement clauses found in planned spoken language are shown in Example 7.

Example 7:

(1) . . . You remember *he says,*
(2) . . . Well you never knew *she was sick.*
(3) But we say that . . . *"paying the price" is a metaphor.*

The complement clauses in these examples expand verbs, not nouns. There is some evidence that verbal expansion, as opposed to nominal expansion may be a strategy more common in spoken than in written language (Michaels & Collins, in press). In particular, the verbs used in these clauses, such as "remember," "know," "want," etc., seem to fall into a class of members that describe some mental state or cognitive process, of either the audience, the speaker, or some general "other." It may be that the speaker is attempting to communicate "knowledge" or "facts" to the audience, or to give the audience a sense of what the speaker thinks about the subject under discussion.

Aside from the large number of complement clauses, planned spoken language is more similar to unplanned spoken than to planned written language. For instance, the number of words per idea unit varies little from unplanned spoken to planned spoken. This may result from the fact that spoken language, no matter how planned (aside from that memorized), is always spontaneous because it is produced simultaneously with the stream of thought. The data in both spoken conditions support this hypothesis. Structures in spoken language are planned locally and in a linear fashion. Therefore, prior planning does not seem to affect the actual size or arrangement of the planning unit. For the limited set of variables presented, planning had an effect on:

1. *Content words.* An increase in the number of nominalizations and attributive adjectives from unplanned spoken to planned spoken indicates that the choice of individual lexical items may be affected by planning. However, use of these structures did not seem to affect the number of words per idea unit. The size and shape of idea units vary little from unplanned spoken to planned spoken, suggesting that speakers in a planned context replace individual items rather than adding to or rearranging the basic unit used in unplanned spoken language.
2. *Structure.* An increase in the number of complement clauses (there were two times as many in PS as in US) may be due to the fact that speakers were responding to the presence of an audience. Complement clauses are present in all spoken conditions, suggesting that they are fairly easy structures to plan and produce locally. It is possible that the use of these structures in planned spoken language may be related to the speaker's communicative intentions.

UNPLANNED WRITTEN DISCOURSE

The data from the unplanned written condition complete the description of adult performance in all four conditions. The unplanned written condition, in contrast with the unplanned spoken condition, can provide information about the process of speaking versus writing without the confounding factor of planning. In writing there is more variability in the actual pace at which words are produced because the speed of production is not as essential as it is in speaking. Writing as a physical process is much slower than speaking; even very fast typing is about three times slower than the normal rate of speaking (Chafe, 1982). In comparison with speaking, writing has the built-in advantage of "more time." In addition, writers can choose to spend more than the minimum amount of time required to move the pen across paper or hit the keys of the typewriter. But in the unplanned written condition, writers are producing text at a fairly fast rate (first-draft writing), without the benefit of time for revision.

In general, the change from speaking (US) to writing (UW) results in a change in the size of the idea unit. In the unplanned written condition, idea units are about 25% larger than in the unplanned spoken condition. The slower pace of writing seems to result in an increase in the number of words used by writers in their basic units. Considering the use of dependent clauses in the two unplanned conditions (US and UW) we see that writers do use more of these types of constructions than speakers. However, if we examine the rest of the features, we see that with the increase in dependent clauses there is a corresponding decrease in the use of coordinating conjunctions (a strategy of speaking), as well as an increase in the use of other integrating devices (a strategy of writing). In this sense, unplanned written language is more like planned written language than spoken.

The major differences between the unplanned and planned written conditions may have to do with writers taking the "more time" option that is possible in writing. In the planned condition, writers have taken the time to produce successive drafts, each time incorporating more and more dependent structures or integrating devices. The idea units in planned written are about 33% larger than those in unplanned written and about 50% larger than those in either of the spoken conditions. Besides packing in more information, writers in the planned written condition have taken time to weave the elements of their sentences into a more varied and complex structure. The extra time afforded the writer in the planned written condition also has an effect on the larger level of discourse schemas, the same effect that planning seems to have in the planned spoken condition.

CHILDREN'S SPOKEN AND WRITTEN LANGUAGE

In terms of considering adult performance, we have found that speakers and writers are sensitive to different contextual constraints. But the adults in this sample have control over a wide range of linguistic forms. It may seem as if there is very little basis for comparison between the language of 8-year-olds, who are just learning to write, and academic veterans. In the unplanned spoken condition, however, children's language exhibited many of the same linguistic features as adults'. The number of words per idea unit for the 8-year-olds, 12-year-olds, and adults differed only slightly, varying from 5 to 7 words. In terms of discourse strategies, both children and adults relied heavily on the use of coordinating conjunctions to chain one unit to the next.

On the other hand, a comparison of the total number of dependent clauses used in conversation reveals that adults use approximately twice as many as children (8- and 12-year-olds as a group). There is very little developmental difference between 8- and 12-year-olds in the use of dependent structures, although the 12-year-olds use slightly more than the 8-year-olds. Instead, children use about 40% more coordinating devices than adults in this condition. Although simple coordination between relatively short idea units is the major strategy for all speakers in the unplanned spoken condition, children depend on this strategy to an even greater extent than adults. In the planned written condition, adults increased the size of their idea units by packing more information into them and by rearranging or ordering them in different ways. Children do not use either of these strategies in this condition. In fact, they maintain approximately the same number of words per idea unit, regardless of condition.

The basic unit of spoken language, which is modified by the adults in written language, is preserved intact by the children. The restricted size of idea units in children's writing also suggests that structures within these units are limited as well.

It is important to notice that as writers in the planned condition, all three groups use more dependent structures than they did as speakers in the unplanned condition. Nevertheless, children's planned written language is thin compared with the density of adult language, and the arrangement of words, phrases, and clauses is simple, resembling unplanned spoken language. The following examples contrast the simple planned written prose of children with the heavy prose of adults:

Example 8: 8-year-old

(PW 1) One day it was vaery rainny.
(2) Then thait night it was evan more raniy.
(3) It was thunder and lightning.

Example 9: 12-year-old

(PW 1) There is a lot of different countrys
(2) and a lot of nice schools
(3) and pretty ones to.
(4) It doesn't snow very much
(5) it snows like every two years.

Example 10: Adult

(PW 1) If it becomes difficult to decipher the identity of the referents mentioned by a speaker,
(2) as in cases of ambiguity which occurred in these narratives
(3a) we can view the speaker as having failed,
(4) to some small degree at least,
(3b) in performing the listener-oriented task of reference successfully.

These examples illustrate clearly that children do not write the way adults do. Children retain the basic structure of spoken language, whereas adults extend their basic structure with dependent clauses, prepositional phrases, adjectives, and other modifiers. As writers, children carry over the basic idea unit used by both adults and children in unplanned spoken discourse.

But it is also important to realize that although children's written language resembles their spoken language, even 8-year-olds write differently than the way they speak. Children are aware of differences between spoken and written language, though they may not be able to explain consciously what these differences are. Yet in spite of their recognition of differences, they have little control over the production processes.

The differences that exist between children's spoken and written language are subtle. Instead of conjoined strings, children use relatively short, independent sentences in their writing, and they have begun to shift away from using coordination as a major strategy of coherence. Two idea units that might be strung together in spoken language with an "and" become independent sentences in written discourse. In contrast with their spontaneous spoken language, children use a slightly greater number of dependent clauses in their planned writing, paralleling adult performance. Twelve-year-olds have made more progress in this regard and use a more balanced combination of coordinate and independent clauses, along with dependent constructions.

In the planned spoken condition, adults maintain the same number of words per idea unit as in the unplanned condition, and they use approximately the same amount of coordination to hold the discourse together. Planning seems to influence the number of dependent clauses adults use, particularly complement constructions attached to the verb. Both 8- and 12-year-olds, like the adults, have increased dramatically their use of complement clauses in this condition. Yet they do not change idea-unit length from the unplanned to the planned spoken conditions. This was true for adults as well.

In terms of developmental differences in the planned spoken condition, children use more coordinating conjunctions (37%) than do adults, but both children and adults use a combination of coordinating strategies and dependent structures. Again, although the pattern of using a combination strategy is shared by all groups, there is a developmental difference between groups in the composition of this strategy. For example, adults use approximately 30% fewer coordinating conjunctions than dependent structures; 12-year-olds use a 50% mixture of both structures, and 8-year-olds use 30% more coordinating structures than dependent structures (the reverse of adult performance).

The final comparisons concern children's performance in the unplanned written condition. For adults, the number of words per idea unit in the unplanned written condition (9.49) was found to lie halfway between those in the unplanned spoken (7.09) and planned written conditions (14.46). For both the 8- and 12-year-olds, the length of idea units in the unplanned written condition (7.00) does not vary substantially from those in unplanned spoken (6.03) and planned written (6.2). In the unplanned written condition, adults produce slightly longer idea units, perhaps due to the slower physical process of writing. Children, on the other hand, are not proficient writers and perhaps the slowness of the writing process interferes with the production process and preserves the basic size of their idea units. In other respects, however, performance by adults and children in this condition is very similar. There is little variation across the age groups in the use of dependent clauses or coordinating strategies.

For adults and children, unplanned writing is more sketchy and streamlined than planned writing. Adults do not restructure their text in the elaborate ways used in the planned written condition, and their idea units are not as heavily laden with information. In this condition, adult writers seem to be producing language as fast as they can without revision. The children's bare, unelaborated style of writing, as well as the difficulty they experience with the writing process, matches adults' first-draft writing.

CONCLUSIONS

We have seen that the form that language takes results from the interaction of context, mode, and individual ability to write or speak. In this study I examined the ways in which both differences in condition (unplanned vs. planned) and in mode (spoken vs. written) affect the form of language people produce.

The process of producing spoken language as compared with written language does have an impact on linguistic structure. Because of the quick nature of spoken language, adult speakers plan and produce short, coherent, chunks of language that are limited in terms of information density as well as size. The slower rate of writing seems to allow writers to increase the size and complexity of the basic production unit.

In addition to mode differences, contextual differences also influence linguistic form. Changing the amount of time speakers or writers have for the planning of discourse results in linguistic changes. Given the opportunity to plan a lecture, speakers manipulate lexical choices and dependent structures in ways that differ from those used in spontaneous conversation. Writers, on the other hand, use extra planning time to add more information to idea units and to arrange this information in different ways.

Although adult language uses a greater range of linguistic resources than child language, there are times when adults and children perform in similar ways. Because of their limited linguistic experience, children are most proficient with spontaneous spoken language. As this is the most basic form of language, adult and child language most closely resemble one another in conversational contexts. Outside of the realm of conversation, even in contexts which have different demands related to audience or purpose, children tend to rely on conversational strategies even when they may not be appropriate.

Although children do not have the same breadth of structures as adults, or the ability to manipulate structures as fluently as adults do, children's spoken language can still be clearly distinguished from their written language. The acquisition of writing is a slow process in which children learn about the nature of written language and practice using these new structures. Children rely as much as possible on their spoken language knowledge and skill as they are learning to write. For instance, the data from this study suggest that in their writing children retain the basic size and structure of idea units found in speaking. This does not mean, however, that children are insensitive to differences between spoken and written language. Even the youngest children in this study made some attempt to transform the familiar forms of spoken language into forms resembling written language. Initially, this transformation is limited, but is reflected in third and sixth grade writing by a reduction of certain oral language features such as coordinating conjunctions and an increase in the number of independent clauses. The large number of independent clauses in children's writing signals an intermediate step in writing development. This stage, during which children use short strings of independent sentences, will eventually be replaced by those strategies found in adult writing. Developing written language is part of a gradual process in which children differentiate speaking and writing by stripping out some features of oral language and slowly, over the course of development, adding features often associated with written language.

In speaking, children's major strategy for maintaining coherence is the use of coordinating conjunctions. In writing, children, especially at the sixth grade level, begin to use a strategy which mixes coordinating conjunctions and independent sentences. Although this strategy is different from that which children use in conversational settings, they do not use either of the two strategies adults use most often in writing, particularly in the planned written condition. Adults vary the size and content of their idea units depending on whether they are writing or speaking, or on whether their discourse was planned or unplanned. In written texts, adults usually add more content words to each idea unit, a procedure which contributes to the density of adult's written language in contrast to the sparsity of children's written language. In writing, adults vary the arrangement of elements both within and between idea units in writing, whereas children arrange their written idea units as they do in speaking.

This study has demonstrated that there is a direct relationship between language form and language function. Adults have more control over various forms of language and therefore can make more dramatic changes to reflect the processing constraints or goals of speakers and listeners, writers and readers. Because children are still in the process of acquiring new forms, they don't have as much control over language as do adults. Changes in children's linguistic forms are not as obvious, but they are present, and can be studied from a developmental perspective.

REFERENCES

BLOOMFIELD, L. *Language.* New York: Holt, Rinehart & Winston, 1933.
CHAFE, W. L. The deployment of consciousness in the production of a narrative. In W. L. Chafe (Ed.), *The pear stories.* Norwood, NJ: Ablex, 1980.
CHAFE, W. L. Integration and involvement in speaking, writing, and oral literature. In D. Tannen (Ed.), *Oral and written language.* Norwood, NJ: Ablex, 1982.
CLARK, H. H. & CLARK, E. V. *Psychology and Language.* New York, NY: Harcourt Brace Jovanovich, 1977.
GOLDMAN-EISLER, F. Speech production and the predictability of words in context. *Quarterly Journal of Experimental Psychology,* 1958, *10,* 96–106.

HALLIDAY, M. A. K. Notes on transitivity and theme in English, Part 2. *Journal of Linguistics*, 1967, *3*, 199–244.
HALLIDAY, M. A. K. Differences between spoken and written language: Some implications for literacy teaching. In G. Page, J. Elkins & B. O'Conner (Eds.), *Communication through reading*. Proceedings of the Fourth Australian Reading Conference. Adelaide, South Australia: Australian Reading Association, 1979, *2*, 37–52.
HARRELL, L. E., JR. A comparison of the development of oral and written language in school age children. *Monograph of the Society for Research in Child Development*, 1957, *22*, (3, Serial no. 66)
KROLL, B. Combining ideas in written and spoken English: A look at subordination and coordination. In E. O. Keenan & T. L. Bennett (Eds.), *Discourse across time and space*. Southern California Occasional Papers in Linguistics, No. 5. Department of Linguistics, University of Southern California, Los Angeles, 1977.
LOBAN, W. *Language development: Kindergarten through grade twelve*. Urbana, IL: NCTE, 1976.
MICHAELS, S. & COLLINS, J. Children's discourse styles: Classroom interaction and the acquisition of literacy. In D. Tannen (Ed.), *Coherence in spoken and written discourse*. Norwood, NJ: Ablex, in press.
OCHS, E. Planned and unplanned discourse. In T. Givon (Ed.), *Syntax and semantics: Discourse and syntax*. New York: Academic, 1979.
O'DONNELL, R. C. Syntactic differences between speech and writing. *American Speech*, 1974, *49*, 182–110.
SYDER, F., & PAWLEY, A. *English conversational structures*. (Manuscript in preparation)

AUTHOR INDEX

A

Abbot, R., 186, *197*
Abrahams, R., 214, *228*
Anderson, E. S., 124, *127*, 148, *152*
Anderson, R., 184, 195, *198*
Anderson, T., 188, *197*
Applebee, A. N., 108, 109, 110, 113, 114, 115, 186, 189, 190, *197*, *208*, 220, *228*
Aronsson, K., 49, *53*
Atlas, M. A., 222, *228*
Atwell, M., 184, *197*
Ayers-Lopez, S., 149, *152*

B

Bakeman, R., 4, *28*
Baker, N., 45, 50, 51, 52, *53*
Baker, W., 159, *165*
Barker, R. G., 72, *90*
Barnes, S., 45, *56*
Bartlett, E., 130, *140*
Bates, E., 48, *53*, 96, *103*
Bateson, G., 97, *103*, 108, *115*
Bazerman, C. A., 218, 224, *228*
Beach, R., 189, 192, 193, 194, *197*, *198*
Beebe, B., 4, *29*
Bell, Q., 71, *90*
Bellugi, U., 37, *54*
Benigni, L., 96, *103*
Bennett, S. L., 4, *29*

Bereiter, C., 202, 204, 208, *208*, 219, 220, *227*, *228*, 233, 234, 235n *241*, *228*
Berkenkotter, C., 222, *228*
Berndt, R., 120, *127*
Berney, T. D., 108, *116*
Bernstein, B., 130, 139, *140*, 167, *181*, 208, *208*, 217, *228*
Bijou, S. W., 73, *90*
Bloom, L., 50, 51, *53*, 89, 90, *91*
Bloomfield, L., 246, *259*
Blom, J., 213, *228*
Blount, B. D., 49, *54*
Blount, B. G., 4, 5, 13, 16, 24n, 26, *28*, 49, *54*, 58
Bonvillian, J. D., 32, 36, 37, 41, 47, 48, 49, 50, 51, *53*, *54*, 55
Borman, K., 130, *140*
Bortz, D. R., 220, *228*
Botvin, G. J., 114, *115*, 220, *231*
Bracewell, R. J., 219, *227*
Braddock, R., 223, *228*
Bradley, R. H., 73, *91*
Brainerd, C. J., 114, *115*
Bransford, J., 184, *196*
Brantley, J. C., 111, *115*
Brazelton, T. B., 4, *28*
Bretherton, I., 48, *53*, 96, *103*
Bridwell, L. S., 190, 193, *197*
Britton, J. B., 115, 185, 189, 194, *197*, 201, 203, 205, *208*, 216, 226, *228*
Bronfenbrenner, U., 72, *91*

261

Brossell, G., 192, *196*
Brostoff, A., 203, *209*
Brown, A. L., 113, *115*
Brown, J., 4, *28*
Brown, R., 37, 39, 49, *54*, 71, *91*, 147, *152*, 176, *181*
Bruner, J. S., 4, *28*, 58, *68*, 97, 98, 99, *103*, 139, *141*, 203, *209*, 217, *228*, 233, *241*
Bullowa, M., 3, *28*
Burgess, T., 185, 194, *197*, 201, 205, *208*, 216, 219, 226, *228*
Burling, R., 217, *228*
Butterworth, G., 4, *28*

C

Caldwell, B. M., 73, *91*
Camaioni, L., 96, *103*
Cambourne, D., 64, *68*
Carroll, J. B., 196, *197*, 207, *209*
Carskaddon, G., 47, *55*
Casagrande, J. B., 5, *28*
Cazden, C., 34, *54*, 155, 156, *165*, 207, *209*
Chafe, W. L., xii, *xv*, 246, 250, 251, 254, *259*
Chaillé, C., 97, 98, *102*, 123, *127*
Chandler, M. J., 74, *91*
Chappell, P. F., 4, *28*
Charney, R., 176, *181*
Cherniss, M. D., 216, 217, *228*
Cherry, L., 150, *153*
Chiang, C., 150, *153*
Chomsky, C., 203, *209*
Chomsky, N., 95, *103*
Chuprikova, N., 61, *68*
Cicourel, A., 157, *165*
Clark, E. V., 244, 246, *259*
Clark, H. H., 244, 246, *259*
Clark, R., 51, *54*
Clay, M. M., 164, *165*
Clemmons, S., 186, *196*
Coates, D. L., 4, *29*
Cochran, E., 4, *28*
Cole, M., 201, 206, *211*, 216, *230*
Coles, L., 155, 156, *165*
Collins, A., 187, *197*
Collins, J., 253, *260*
Collins, J. L., 201, 205, *209*, 217, *228*
Collis, G. M., 4, *28*
Connolly, K., 25, *29*, 148, *153*
Connors, R. J., 218, *228*

Cook, C., 220, *227*
Cook-Gumperz, J., 109, 110, 114, *115*, 130, *140*, 157, *165*
Cooper, C., 149, *152*
Cooper, C. R., 223, *228*
Cooper, M., 148, *152*, 191, *197*
Cooper, R. L., 223, *229*
Corsaro, W., 130, *140*, 148, *152*
Coulthard, R. M., 158, 159, *165*
Crowhurst, M., 205, *209*, 219, 220, 221, 222, 223, 227, *228*, 234n
Cross, T. G., 45, 46, 47, 48, *53*, *54*
Crystal, D., 214, 218, *228*
Csikszentmihalyi, M., 189, *198*
Curtis, S., 48, *54*

D

daCosta, A. Nicolai, 50, *53*
Dale, P. S., 25, *29*
D'Angelo, F., 219, *228*
Dansky, J. L., 111, 112, 113, *115*
Davidson-Mosenthal, R., 195, *198*
Davies, D., 214, 218, *228*
Denninger, M., 36, 37, 50, 51, 53, *53*
DePaulo, B. M., 47, 49, *54*
DeStefano, J., 66, *69*, 155, 156, 157, 158, 159, *165*
Devin, J., 100, 101, *103*, 148, *153*
Dilworth, C., 196, *197*
DiPaolo, M., 149, *152*
Dixon, D., 106, 111, 112, 113, *117*
Donlan, D., 186, *197*
Dore, J., 176, *181*
Duckworth, E., 203, *209*
Dyson, A. H., 202, *209*, 218, *229*

E

Eaton, S., 192, *197*
Eckland, B. K., 72, *91*
Edelsky, C., 9, *28*, 148, *152*
Eifermann, R. R., 112, *115*
Egan, K., 223, *229*
Eilers, R. E., 4, *28*
Eichorn, D. H., 96, *103*
Elardo, R., 73, *91*
Elbow, P., 194, *197*
El'Konin, D., 105, *115*
Ellis, A., 190, *198*
Elsasser, N., 201, 204, *209*, 221, *229*

AUTHOR INDEX 263

Emig, J., 183, *197*, 203, 204, *209*, 223, *229*
Enkvist, N. E., 214, *229*
Ervin Tripp, S., 8, *28*, 74, *91*, 150, *152*, 214, *229*, 233, *241*

F

Farr, M., 193, *196*
Farran, D. C., 4, *28*
Farrell, T. J., 208, *209*
Fein, G. G., 96, *103*, 106, 107, 109, 114, *115*, *116*, 120, *128*, 136, 139, *141*
Feitelson, D., 111, *115*
Ferguson, C. A., 11, *28*, 37, 50, *54*, *56*, 147, *152*
Firth, J., xii, *xv*
Fisher, K. W., 73, *91*
Fisher, S., 155, 156, *165*
Fishman, J. A., 223, *229*
Flavell, J. H., 64, 65, 66, *68*
Florio, S., 193, *197*
Flower, L., 190, *197*, 216, 219, 221, 222, *229*
Fogel, A., 4, *28*
Freedle, R., 4, *28*, 233, *241*
Fuson, K. C., 57, *68*, 136, *140*

G

Galda, L., 111, 112, 113, 114, *115*, 138, *140*
Gardner, H. E., 107, 108, 110, 114, *115*, *116*, *117*
Gardner, J., 110, 114, *115*
Garvey, C., 4, *28*, 96, 97, 98, 100, *103*, 108, 109, *115*, 120, *127*
Gearhart, M., 120, *127*
Gelman, R., 50, *56*, 148, *153*
Genishi, C., 149, *152*
Gentner, D., 188, *197*
Gere, A., 186, *197*
Getzels, J., 189, *198*
Gilman, A., 147, *152*
Gleason, J. B., 31, 37, 49, *54*, 72, *91*
Gleitman, H., 31, 50, *55*
Gleitman, L. R., 31, *56*, *55*
Glenn, A., 190, *198*
Glenn, C. G., 110, *117*
Glucksberg, S., 99, *103*, 203, *210*
Goelman, H., 173, *181*
Goffman, E., 147, *152*
Goldin-Meadow, S., 51, *54*
Goldman, J., 97, 98, *102*, 123, *127*

Goldman-Eisler, F., 246, *259*
Goodwin, C., 9, *28*
Goody, J., 204, *209*, 216, *229*
Graves, D., 202, *209*
Green, J. A., 4, *28*
Greene, H., 68, *69*, 111, *116*
Greenbaum, S., 169, *181*, 215, *230*
Greenfield, P. M., 51, *56*, 203, *209*
Gregory, M., 214, *229*
Grice, H., 191, *198*, 213, *229*
Griffin, W. J., 204, *210*
Gumperz, J., 157, *165*, 213, *228*
Gundlach, R., 202, *208*, *209*
Gustafson, G. E., 4, *28*
Gutfreund, M., 45, *56*

H

Halliday, M. A. K., xiii, *xv*, 130, 131, 132, 137, *140*, 157, 159, 160, 161, 163, *165*, 205, *209*, 213, *229*, 246, *260*
Hanlon, C., 49, *54*
Hanna, P., 220, *231*
Hartshorn, E., 111, *115*
Hartwell, P., 204, *209*
Harrell, L. E., Jr., 250, *260*
Hasan, R., 157, 159, 160, 161, 163, *165*, 205, *209*
Havstad, L. F., 51, *56*
Hawkins, P. R., 208, *209*
Hayes, J. R., 190, *197*, 216, 219, 222, *229*
Heath, S. B., 207, *209*
Hendrix, R., 208, *209*
Herrington, A., 183, 188, 190, 196, *198*
Hess, R. D., 74, 75, *91*
Hidi, S., 188, *197*, 240, *241*
Higgins, E. T., 217, 220, 223, 227, *229*
Hildyard, A., 240, *241*
Hirsch, E. D., 204, *210*, 215, 217, *229*
Hirschbiel, P., 4, *28*
Hjertholm, E., 58, *68*
Hoff-Ginsberg, E., 75, *91*
Hogan, R., 100, *103*
Hogarty, P. S., 96, *103*
Hood, L., 50, 51, *53*, 89, *91*
Horan, E. A., 50, *54*
Horgan, D., 52, *54*
Horner, V. M., 108, *116*
Hornsby, J., 203, *209*
Hunt, K. W., 204, 205, *210*
Hymes, D., xiii, *xv*, 130, *140*, 155, *165*

I

Inhelder, B., 203, *210*
Ives, W., 110, 114, *116*

J

Jacobs, D., 148, *152*
Jacobson, R., 214, *229*
Jaffe, J., 4, *29*
Jambor, T., 112, *116*
James, S., 148, *153*
Jay, S., 4, *28*
Jennings, K., 157, *165*
Jennings, S., 157, *165*
Jensen, A. R., 65, *68*
John, V. P., 108, *116*
Johnson, F. L., 222, *230*
Johnson, G., 48, *53*
Johnson, J. E., 80, *92*, 106, 111, 112, 113, *117*, 122, *128*
Johnson, M. L., 48, *55*
Johnson, N. S., 110, *116*
Johnson-Laird, P., 169, *181*
John-Steiner, V. P., 201, *209*, 203, *210*, 221, *229*
Joynt, D., 64, *68*
Juchnowski, M., 48, *53*

K

Kaplan, B., 96, *103*
Kaplan, B. J., 36, 37, 50, 51, *53*
Kaye, K., 3, 4, *28*, 176, *181*
Keenan, E. O., *229*, 233, *241*
Kelly, H., 110, 114, *116*
Kemey, H., 203, *209*
Kempton, W., 24n, *28*
Kendler, H., 65, 66, *68*
Kendler, T., 65, 66, *68*
Kernan, K., 149, *153*
King, M. L., 202, *210*, 218, 220, *229*
Kirkman, M., 47, *54*
Kintsch, W., 169, *181*, 216, *229*
Klaiman, R., 188, *197*
Kleiman, G. M., 216, *230*
Kline, C. R., 214, *229*
Klink, J., 191, *197*
Kohlberg, L., 58, *68*
Krauss, R. M., 99, *103*, 203, *210*
Kreiger, V., 195, *198*
Kroll, B. M., 201, 203, 204, 206, 207, *210*, 217, 220, 223, 227, *229*, 245, 248, 250, *260*
Kuczaj, S. A., 51, *54*

L

Labov, W., 108, 114, *116*, 156, *165*, 207, *210*
Lakoff, R., 147, *153*
Larson, R. L., 219, *229*
Learnerd, B., 65, 66, *68*
Lee, K., 107, *115*, 124, *127*
Leech, G., 169, *181*
Lehiste, I., 14, *28*
Leiter, K., 157, *165*
Lempers, J. D., 148, *153*, 207, *210*, 217, 220, 223, 227, *229*
Levin, H., 107, *115*, 124, *127*
Levina, R., 68, *68*
Lewin, K., 72, *91*
Lewis, M., 3, 4, *28, 29*, 233, *230*
Lieberman, M. J., 97, *103*
Lightbrown, P., 50, 51, *53*
Lindholm, K. J., 49, *54*
Liublinskaya, A. A., 62, *68*
Lloyd-Jones, R., 223, *228*
Loban, W., 208, *210*, 248, 250, *260*
Luria, A., 61, 62, 63, 64, 67, *68, 69*
Lunsford, A., 203, *210*

M

Ma, R., 223, *229*
Maccoby, M., 203, *209*
Macrorie, K., 224, *229*
MacKay, R., 157, *165*
Maimon, E., 187, *197*
Mahony, D., 220, *231*
Majoribanks, K., 72, 73, *91*
Malinowski, B., xiii, *xv*, 213, *229*
Mandler, J. M., 110, *116*
Markus, G. B., 72, *92*
Maroules, N., 155, 156, *165*
Marquis, A., 149, *152*
Martin H., 191, *198*
Martin, N., 194, *197*, 201, 205, 208, 216, 219, 226, *228*
Martlew, M., 148, *153*
Masur, E. F., 72, *91*
Matalon, R., 159, *165*
Matthews, W. S., 112, *116*
May, G., 159, *165*

McCall, R. B., 96, *103*
McCleod, C., 148, *153*
McCune-Nicolich, L., 107, *116*
McDonald, J. D. S., 220, *228*
McGillicuddy-Delisi, A. V., 80, *92*
McGrew, W., 138, *140*
McIntosh, A., 213, *229*
McLeod, A., 185, 194, *197*, 201, 205, *208*, 216, 219, 226, *228*
McLoyd, V. C., 112, *116*
McNamee, G. D., 109, 110, 114, *116*
McNeil, D., 95, *103*
McNew, S., 48, *53*
Meara, N. M., 159, *165*
Mehan, H., 146, *153*, 155, 156, 157, 159, *165*
Mellon, J. C., 205, *210*
Memering, W. D., 214, *229*
Menyuk, P., 31, *55*
Merritt, M., 149, *153*
Metviner, E., 192, *197*
Meyer, B. J. F., 184, *198*
Michaels, S., 109, 110, 114, *115*, 253, *260*
Michlin, M. L., 222, *230*
Miller, G. A., 169, *181*
Miller, J. F., 39, *55*
Miller, S., 64, 65, *69*
Miller, S., 219, 227
Miller, W., 74, *91*
Millic, L., 214, *229*
Mitchell-Kernan, C., 149, *153*
Modiano, N., 203, *209*
Moerk, E., 31, 37, *55*, 71, 89, *91*
Moffett, J., 203, *210*, 219, 223, *229*
Montessori, M., 129, *140*
Morse, P. A., 25, *29*
Mosenthal, P., 195, *198*, 224, *229*
Moser, N., 203, *209*
Moses, R., 202, *208*
Mueller, E., 99, 100, *103*
Murray, D., 216, *230*
Musatti, T., *127*
Myers, M., *210*

N

Na, T., 195, *198*, 224, *229*
Neisworth, J. R., 96, *103*
Nelson, K., 32, 48, 50, 51, *55*, 99, *103*
Nelson, K. E., 36, 37, 45, 47, 48, 49, 50, 51, 52, *53*, *54*, *55*
Newport, E. L., 31, 45, *55*

Newsome, J., 4, *29*
Nicolich, L., 96, 101, *103*
Nienhuys, T. G., 47, *54*
Nodine, B., 187, *197*
Norris, R. C., 204, *210*

O

Ochs, E., 244, 245, 248, *260*
Odell, L., 188, 190, *198*
O'Donnell, R. C., 204, *210*, *260*
O'Hare, F., 205, *210*
Ohmann, R., 191, *198*
Olbrechts-Tyteca, L., 221, *230*
Olmsted, P., 75, *92*
Olson, D. R., 173, 174, *181*, 184, *198*, 203, 204, *209*, *210*, 216, *230*
Olver, R., 203, *209*
Ong, W. J., 205, *210*, 221, *230*
Onore, C. S., 208, *208*
Osgood, C. E., 214, *230*
Oviatt, S. L., 48, *53*

P

Padgug, E., 13, 16, *28*, 49, *55*
Page, E., 227, *230*
Park, D., 192, *198*
Parmenter, J., 48, *53*
Parten, M., 130, *140*
Patton, M. J., 159, *165*
Pawley, A., 246, *260*
Pellegrini, A. D., 59, 66, 68, *69*, 88, *91*, 107, 111, 112, 113, *116*, 120, *127*, 128, *140*, 202, *210*
Pepinsky, H., 156, 158, 159, *165*
Perelman, C., 221, *230*
Perl, S., 222, *230*
Perkins, D., 190, *198*
Perron, J. D., 220, *230*
Peters, D., 96, *103*
Phillips, S., 130, *141*
Phyfe-Perkins, E., 129, *141*
Piaget, J., 57, 58, 59, 60, *69*, 101, *103*, 106, *116*, 203, *210*
Piche, G., 192, *198*, 205, *209*, *211*, 218, 219, 220, 222, 223, *228*, *230*
Pickert, J., 184, 195, *198*
Pinnell, G., 130, *141*
Pitcher, E. G., 108, *116*
Potter, M., 203, *209*
Pratt, M., 194, *198*

Prelinger, E., 108, *116*
Prorok, E. M. S., 50, *55*

Q

Quiltich, H., 129, *141*
Quirk, R., 169, *181*, 215, *230*

R

Raeburn, V. P., 50, *54*
Raimes, A., 196, *198*
Ratner, M., 97, *103*
Read, B., 150, *153*
Read, C., 203, *211*
Reisch, L., 203, *209*
Reilly, J., 51, *56*
Rentel, V., 202, *210*, 218, *229*
Risley, T., 129, *141*
Robinett, F. M., 4, *29*
Rocissano, L., 89, *91*
Robins, C., 156, *165*
Robinson, E., 173, *181*
Rodgers, P. C., 215, *230*
Rose, M., 190, *198*
Rosen, C. E., 111, *116*, 220, *228*
Rosen, H., 185, 194, *197*, 201, 205, *208*, 216, 219, 223, 226, *228*
Rosenblatt, D., 96, 101, *103*
Rosenblum, L. A., 3, 4, *29*
Rosner, F. C., 88, *91*
Ross, G., 111, *115*, 139, *141*
Roth, D., 157, *165*
Rubin, A. D., 216, *230*
Rubin, D. L., 192, *198*, 205, 208, *211*, 215, 218, 219, 220, 221, 222, 223, 227, *228*, *230*
Rubin, K. H., 59, 66, 67, *69*, 106, 107, 111, 112, 114, *116*, 120, *128*, 129, 136, 137, 139, *140*, *141*
Rubin, S., 116
Rutter, M., 50, *55*

S

Sachs, J., 48, 51, *55*, 97, 98, 101, *102*, *103*, 107, 109, 112, 114, *117*, 120, 123, *127*, *128*, 148, *153*
Saltz, E., 106, 111, 112, 113, *117*, 122, *128*
Sameroff, A. J., 74, *91*
Sander, L. W., 3, 4, *28*, *29*
Sanders, T., 156, 158, 159, *165*
San Jose, C. P. M., 205, *211*, 220, *230*

Satferly, D., 45, *56*
Scardamalia, M., 204, *208*, 219, 220, *227*, 233, 234, *241*
Schafer, J. C., 216, *230*
Schaffer, H. R., 3, *29*
Schallert, D. L., 216, *230*
Schieffelin, B. B., 47, 50, *56*, 233, *241*
Schiff, N., 48, *56*
Schluessler, B., 186, *197*
Schmidt, S. J., 221, *230*
Schoer, L., 223, *228*
Schwam, F., 50, *56*
Schwartzman, H. B., 121, *128*
Scollon, R., 109, *117*
Scollon, S. B. K., 109, *117*
Scribner, S., 201, 206, *211*, 216, *230*
Searle, J. R., 66, *69*, 175, *181*, 213, *230*
Seegars, J. C., 220, *230*
Seibel, C., 129, 137, 138, *140*
Shantz, C. U., 96, *103*
Shatz, M., 31, 50, *56*, 75, *91*, 147, 148, *153*
Shaughnessy, M. P., 203, 204, *211*, 218, *230*
Shelton, J., 64, 65, *69*
Shipley, E. S., 50, *56*
Shipman, V. C., 74, 75, *91*
Shonkoff, F., 107, *115*, 124, *127*
Shore, C., 48, *53*
Shotwell, J. M., 108, *117*
Shuy, R. W., 202, *211*, 234, *241*
Sigel, I. E., 68, *69*, 73, 74, 75, 80, 85, 90, *91*, *92*
Silverman, J., 110, 111, 114, *116*
Simons, H., 157, *165*
Sinclair, J. McH., 158, 159, *165*
Skinner, B. F., 95, *103*
Slobin, D. I., 60, 61, *69*
Smilansky, S., 106, 112, *117*, 131, *141*
Smith, C. S., 50, *56*
Smith, W. L., 205, *211*, 222, *231*
Snow, C. E., 31, 37, 49, *56*, 107, *115*, *127*
Sokolov, A. N., 60, 61, *69*
Sonstroem, A., 203, *209*
Spencer, J., 214, *229*
Spinelli, F., 150, *153*
Spring, D. R., 25, *29*
Stabus, A., 159, *165*
Stark, R. E., 26, *29*
Staton, F., 234, 240, *241*
Staton, J., 218, 226, *231*
Stein, N. L., 110, *117*
Stern, D. N., 4, *29*

Stotsky, S. L., 205, *211*, 225, *231*
Stratton, P., 25, *29*
Strevens, P., 213, *229*
Sutton-Smith, B., 111, 114, *115, 117,* 121, *128,* 220, *231*
Swann, M. B., 205, *211,* 222, *231*
Swann, W., 50, *56*
Svartik, J. A., 169, *181*
Syder, F., 246, *260*

T

Tatter, P., 201, *210*
Taylor, B., 189, *197*
Tikhomirov, I. K., *69*
Tillman, M., 219, *231*
Torrence, N., 204, *210*
Trevarthen, C., 4, *29*
Turkish, L., 220, *227*
Turner, L. J., 220, *230*

V

Vachek, J., xiii, *xv*
Vandenberg, B., 107, 109, 114, *116,* 120, *128,* 136, 139, *141*
Vann, R. J., 204, *210*
Veal, L. R., 219, *231*
Vendler, Z., 175, *181*
Voegelin, C. F., 5, *29*
Volterra, V., 96, *103*
Vygotsky, L. S., 57, 58, 59, 60, 62, 67, *69,* 108, *117,* 136, *141,* 202, *211, 231*

W

Wall, S., 193, *198*
Waletzky, J., 114, *116*
Walker, W. G., 214, *230*
Watson, K., 112, *116*

Watt, I., 204, *209,* 216, *229*
Weintraub, S., 31, 37, 49, *54*
Weinrich, U., 213, *231*
Wellman, H., 148, *153*
Wells, C. G., 207, *211*
Wells, D., 65, *68*
Wells, G., 45, 51, *56, 164, 165,* 167, 169, 178, *181*
Werner, H., 96, *103*
Wertsch, J., 68, *69*
West, M. J., 4, *28*
Westerman, M. A., 51, *56*
Wheatley, J., 191, *198*
Wheldall, K., 50, *56*
Whitaker, H. A., 25, *29*
Wichelns, H. A., 221, *231*
Wilder, L., 61, *69*
Wilkinson, A., 150, *153,* 220, *230*
Wilkinson, L. Cherry, 145, 146, 150, *153*
Williamson, M. M., 205, *209*
Williamson, M. W., 217, *228*
Wills, D. D., 4, *29*
Wilson, B., 48, *56*
Wilson, M., 48, *56*
Winer, B., 133, *141*
Wolf, D., 108, *116, 117,* 121, 122n, *127*
Wood, D., 139, *141*
Wozniak, R. H., 63, 64, *69*

Y

Yaeger, J., 58, *68*
Yawkey, T. D., 96, *103*
Yudovich, F., 62, *69*

Z

Zajonc, R. B., 72, *92*
Zankov, L. V., 61, *69*
Zukow, P. G., 51, *56*

SUBJECT INDEX

A

Age and language functions, 134–137, 139–140
Analyses, discourse, 176, *also see,* Dialogue writing, scoring
  oral languages, *see* structural features of children's language
  semantic, 235–236
  structural, 170–176
Auxiliaries in input, 32–33

C

Children's spoken and written language, 255–258
  compared to adults, 256–258
Cognitive development and writing, 201–203
  function, for social and educational purposes, 202
  hierarchical developmental model, 202–203
    association with drawing, 202
    problematic for older writers, 203
Cohesion analysis, 159–164
  density, 159
  devices used by teacher, 162–163
  ellipsis, 161, 163
  endophoric, 161–162
  exophora, 161–162
  lexical cohesion, 161–163
  reference, 161–162
  student-dominated ties, 160
  student's devices, 162–164
  teacher-dominated ties, 160
  ties, 159–160
  types of textual cohesion, 160–161
Communication continuum, 243–244
  spontaneous spoken language to expository written language, 243
Communicative competence, 130, 155–157
Communicative situations, constituents, 215–226
  audience–communicator role relations, 215, 221–223
  discourse function, 215, 218–221
    developmental course, 219–220
    persuasive writing, 218–221
    taxonomies, 218–219
  interaction structure, 215, 224–226
    genre, 225
    location within a sequence of discourse, 226
    universe of discourse, 225
  medium of communication, 215–218
  setting, 215, 223–224
  topic domain, 215, 223
Computer-assisted language analysis system (CALAS), 159

269

SUBJECT INDEX

Context conventions and audience, 191–193
   contextual information, 192–193
   inferences about audience, 191
   process approach, 192
Contingent maternal replies, 36–45
   complex recasts, 37–41
   continuations, 38–45
   cultural differences, 46–47
   imitations, 38, 41–43
   outcomes for composite variables, 39–41
   maternal predictors, 38–39
   simple recasts, 37–46
      expansions, 37
   topic changes, 38–41, 43–44
Conversational competence, see Conversational skill
Conversational skill, 177–180
   interpersonal, 178, 180
   logical or ideational, 178, 180
Critical evaluation through writing, 193–194
   cognitive flexibility, 193
   "reader-based feedback," 194
Culturally different children, 156–158
   appalachian, 157–158
   black inner-city, 157–158
   communicative competence, 157

D

Data collection procedures, 6–12, 78, 113, 120, 132, 158–159, 168–169, 236–237, 244–245
Daycare and language acquisition, 48
Dependent structures, 248–258
   complement clauses, 248–249, 252
   relative clauses, 248–249, 252
   subordinate clauses, 248–249, 252
Developmental-functional framework, 201
Dialogue writing, 234–241
   grades 4 and 6, 236–241
   principled rational arguments, 236, 238–241
   scoring, 235–236
      level of abstractness, 236, 239
      number of words, 235, 239
      topic-relevant ideas, 235, 238–239
      type and quality of resolutions of dialogues, 236
Discourse features, 169–170, 176–180
   cohesive, 176–177
   conjunctions, 177, 179–180
   turnabout, 176–180
   maintenance of topics, 170
   number of remote or abstract topics introduced, 177–179
   turn-taking, 170
Discourse production, 233
Disturbed or unusual language, 47–48, 50–51
Dramatic play, 105–115, 119–127
   abilities necessary for successful play, 125–126
   action utterances, 122–125
   and age, 112
   causal factors, 112
   coding, 121
   context, 121
   decontextualization, 120
   definitions, 106
   developmental changes, 2–3½, 4–5-year-olds, 122–125
   developmental trends, 107
   effects on narrative competence by grade, 113
   enactment or planning, 121–124
   five-year-olds, 123–125
   and language, 106–107
   linguistic transformations, 112
   modes of symbolization, patterners, and dramatists, 108
   narrative structure, 107–108
   object transformations, 122–123
   resolving conflict, 122–126
   role taking, 122–127
   and SES, 112
   signifiers and signified, 106
   theme or plot, 102–127
   three-and-a-half-year-olds, 122–123
   training studies, 11–114
      comparing dramatic play, discussion or drawing, 112–113
      thematic fantasy play, 111
   two-year-olds, 122
Dramatic play and story telling, 108
   divergent development in primary school, 109
   parallels, 108–109

E

Ecology, classroom, 129–130, 134–140
   learning centers, 129–130, 134–138
   number of adults present, 138–140
   time elapsed between observation sessions, 138

Environment, 72–75
  interaction with organism, 73–74
  physical or biological, cultural, and social structural variables, 72–73
  verbal distancing behaviors as, 75–78
  views of, 72–73

G

Gender effects on language functions, 133–134, 136–137
Genre, 192, 225, 237–239, 241
  dialogue, 237, 240–241
  opinion essay, 237, 240–241
  stylistic conventions, 225

H

"Hidden curriculum," 156

I

Idea units, 245–259
Imperatives, 150

L

Language adaptations to environmental demands, 100–101
  early emergence of social understanding, 100–101
  sensitivity to listeners' states, 101
Language, children's written and oral, 233–235
Language, functions of, 99–100, 130–131, 134
  heuristic, 130–131
  imaginative, 130–131, 134
  instrumental, 130–131, 134
  interactional, 130–131, 134
  joint attention and joint activity, 99–100
  maintenance of verbal exchanges, 99
  personal, 130–131
  regulatory, 130–131
  representational, 130–131, 134
Language in school, 155–156
Language in the classroom, 145–146, 149–152, 155–164, 167–168
  assumptions of a sociolinguistic approach, 145–146
  classroom as unique communicative context, 146
  communicative or interactional competence, 145–146
  contrasted with language of the home, 167
  kindergarten to second grade, 168
  rules for using language, 150–152
Language scoring procedure, 132–133
Language, uses in play, 107
Learning centers, 129–130, 134, 136–138
Linguistic forms continuum, 243–244
Literacy, 155–159, 162–164, 173, 203–204
Literacy and writing, 203–204

M

Mainstream culture and schooling, 158
Maternal non-adjustment in mean length of utterance, 32
Maternal speech, *see* Parental speech
Mean length of utterance, 32, 34–37, 39
Memory and writing, 216
Metapragmatic knowledge of request function of language in school-age children, 150–152
Mother–infant interaction, 3–5
  coordinated activity, 4
  methodology, 4
  process, 4

N

Narrative competence, 105–115
  definition, 105
  development in early school years, 110–111
  development of story telling, 108
  origins, 105–106
  teacher–child interaction, 109–110
Noncontingent maternal syntax, 33–36
  adjustment between children and mothers, 35–36
  children's measures, 33–34
  follow-up measures, 35

O

Oral language competence, 167–168, 173–174, 180
  related to learning to read, 173–174, 180

P

Parental distancing behaviors, 75–86
  assessment of, 78
  communication handicapped versus normally developing children, 80–81
  form, telling versus inquiry, 76–77, 87

higher level distancing, 76–78
low-intermediate and high-level distancing, 76
mother's versus father's use, 80
task differences, 79
Parent distancing verbalizations and child ability, 81–86
   children's representational abilities, 85–87
   tests of intellectual ability, 81–84
Parental input and child's language acquisition, 51–52
Parental speech, early studies, 5–6
Parnetal speech, English and Spanish, 6–24
   baby talk of parental speech register, 10–12, 27
   inventory of features, 12–16
      interpretation, 16
      modelling role, 15
      paralinguistics, 13–14
      prosody, 13–14
      structural interactional feature attentionals, 15
      tag questions, 15
   methodology, 6–12
      observer absence, 7–8
      transcription-terminology problem, 8–9
   usage patterns, 16–21
      coder realiability, 16
      parental accommodation overtime, 16–17, 24
      profile rate scores, 18–19, 22
Parental speech, English and Spanish comparisons, 21–24
   summary, 23–24
Parental speech, functions, 25–26
   attention, 25–27
   interaction, 25–27
Parent–child interactions, 74–76, 89
   direction of causality, 89
Planned spoken language, 252–254
   complement clauses, 253–254
   content words, 254
   dependent clauses and structures, 252–253
Planned written language, 250–252
   adding information, 251
   compared to unplanned spoken language, 250
   dependent structures, 250, 251
   size and structure of idea units, 250
   word order, 251–252
Play definitions, 106
Pretend play and complex language use, 96

Pretend play, *see* Dramatic play
Private speech, cognitive functions, 60, 63–68
   age-specific characteristics, 63–64
   empirical studies, 63–68
   self-regulating function, 63–65, 67
   spontaneous private speech in different contexts, 66–67
   verbal mediation, 65–66
Private speech, social origins of, 58–60
   development during preschool period, 59
   dyadic dialogue, 58–59
   egocentric speech, Piaget, 58–59
   research evidence, 58–60
   social context, 59
   social dialogue view, Vygotsky, 58–59

R

Rare events, 42, 48–49, 52
Red Cap, 113–114
Representational abilities, 75
   definition, 75

S

Scaffolding by adults, 139
Semiotic function, 106
Social context, 147
Social play and language development, 97–99
   play as framework for syntactic development, 98
   role reversals between mother and child, 98
Social play as context, 97–98
   mother–child social play, 98
   play versus nonplay, 97
Sociodramatic play, *see* Dramatic play
Soviet views of language and thought, 60–63
   behavior change through verbal interaction, 60–61
   first and second signals, 61–62
   Marxist influence, 60–61
   verbal stimulation, 62
Status, 145–150, 152
   black children, role playing tasks, 149
   children's arguments, 149
   cultural differences, 147
   definition, 146–147
   relationship between social status and linguistic behavior, 147
   school age children, 149
   social control acts, 150

young children's linguistic adjustments, 148
Status, a sociolinguist view, 146–147
Storytelling by children, *see also* Narrative competence
Storytelling by children, 109–110
   adult scaffolding, 109
   competence, 110
Storytelling competence, *see* Narrative competence
Structural features of children's language, 169–175, 179–180
   pronominal analysis, 169
   propositional analysis, 169
   psychological verbs, 170–172, 175, 179–180
      affective, 172, 179
      cognitive verbs, 172–175, 179
      linguistic, 172–179
      perceptual, 172–179
Style, 213–215
   as communicator, 215
   definitions of, 214
   social convention or psychological function, 215

T

Teachers manual, 159
Tests and tasks, 78, 89–90, 113, 168–170, 237
   block description task, 168
   dialogue writing, 237
   Durrell analysis of reading difficulty, 168–170
   free speech, 168, 170
   lego task, 168, 170
   origami (paper-folding) task, 78, 90
   story comprehension, 113
   story-retelling task, 113, 168
   story-telling tasks, 78, 89
   WISC, vocabulary and block design, 168, 170
   WPPSI, vocabulary and block design, 168, 170
Thematic fantasy play, 106

U

Unplanned spoken discourse, 246–250
   adults and children compared, 247, 249
   density of information, 247
   syntax, 247
   typical idea unit, length, 246–247
   "more time" option, 255
   size of idea unit, 254

V

Verbal reconstruction, 112

W

Writing, 183–196, 201–208, 213–227
   changing teacher behavior, 196
   cognitive functioning, linear reasoning, 216–217
   context-independent, nonpresent audience, 217–218
   conventions, 218
   culture-specific, 206
   fostering problem solving, 190–191
      cumulative paper, 191
   functional analysis or perspectives, 207–208
   functions of, 183–184
   and heuristic strategies, 184, 190
   studies of, across the curriculum, 185–187
   versus oral language, 184
   versus reading, 184
Writing, contexts of, 204–208
   antecedents of writing development, 207
   audience and function, 205
   cross-cultural, Vai of Liberia, 206
   semantic complexity, 205
   syntactic maturity, 204–205
Writing development, 201–208
   developmental functional framework, 201
   similarity to learning oral language, 202–203
Writing to learn about self, 194–195
   acquiring a unique perspective, 195
   response registers, imitative or noncontingent, 195
Writing tasks, 187–189
   inventing, 187, 189
   recasting, 187–189
   restating, 187

Z

Zone of proximal development, 207